The World Bank and Governance

This timely book offers the first critical retrospective of World Bank policy reforms and initiatives during the past decade.

The World Bank Group is viewed as one of the most powerful international organizations of our time. The authors critically analyse the influence of World Bank policy and engagement during the past decade in a variety of issue areas, including human rights, domestic reform, and the environment.

This book delves into the bowels of the World Bank, by exploring its organizational structure, professional culture and bureaucratic procedures, and illustrates how these shape its engagement with an increasingly complex, diverse and challenging operational environment. The book includes chapters on two under-researched divisions of the World Bank Group – the International Finance Corporation (IFC) and the Multilateral Investment Guarantee Agency (MIGA). Several illuminating country studies are also included, analysing the World Bank's activities in Argentina, Bolivia, Lebanon, Hungary and Vietnam.

The collected authors seek to widen our understanding of the changing role and influence of the World Bank in the age of globalisation. Students and scholars of International Relations, Development, Politics and Economics will find this volume to be of strong interest.

Diane Stone is Marie Curie Chair in the Center for Policy Studies at the Central European University in Budapest, and Reader in Politics and International Studies at the University of Warwick, UK.

Christopher Wright is a PhD candidate in the International Relations Department at the London School of Economics (LSE), UK.

Routledge/Warwick Studies in Globalisation
Edited by Richard Higgott and published in association with the Centre for the Study of Globalisation and Regionalisation, University of Warwick.

What is globalisation and does it matter? How can we measure it? What are its policy implications? The Centre for the Study of Globalisation and Regionalisation at the University of Warwick is an international site for the study of key questions such as these in the theory and practice of globalisation and regionalisation. Its agenda is avowedly interdisciplinary. The work of the Centre will be showcased in this new series.

This series comprises two strands:

Warwick Studies in Globalisation addresses the needs of students and teachers, and the titles will be published in hardback and paperback. Titles include:

Globalisation and the Asia-Pacific
Contested Territories
Edited by Kris Olds, Peter Dicken, Philip F. Kelly, Lily Kong and Henry Wai-chung Yeung

Regulating the Global Information Society
Edited by Christopher Marsden

Banking on Knowledge
The Genesis of the Global Development Network
Edited by Diane Stone

Historical Materialism and Globalisation
Edited by Hazel Smith and Mark Rupert

Civil Society and Global Finance
Edited by Jan Aart Scholte with Albrecht Schnabel

Towards a Global Polity
Edited by Morten Ougaard and Richard Higgott

New Regionalisms in the Global Political Economy
Theories and Cases
Edited by Shaun Breslin, Christopher W. Hughes, Nicola Phillips and Ben Rosamond

Globalizing Democracy
Political Parties in Emerging Democracies
Edited by Peter Burnell

Routledge/Warwick Studies in Globalisation is a forum for innovative new research intended for a high-level specialist readership, and the titles will be available in hardback only. Titles include:

1. **Non-State Actors and Authority in the Global System**
   Edited by Richard Higgott, Geoffrey Underhill and Andreas Bieler

2. **Globalisation and Enlargement of the European Union**
   Austrian and Swedish Social Forces in the Struggle over Membership
   Andreas Bieler

3. **Rethinking Empowerment**
   Gender and Development in a Global/Local World
   Edited by Jane L. Parpart, Shirin M. Rai and Kathleen Staudt

4. **Globalising Intellectual Property Rights**
   The TRIPs Agreement
   Duncan Matthews

5. **Globalisation, Domestic Politics and Regionalism**
   The ASEAN Free Trade Area
   Helen E. S. Nesadurai

6. **Microregionalism and Governance in East Asia**
   Katsuhiro Sasuga

7. **Global Knowledge Networks and International Development**
   Edited by Diane Stone and Simon Maxwell

8. **Globalisation and Economic Security in East Asia**
   Governance and Institutions
   Edited by Helen E. S. Nesadurai

9. **Regional Integration in East Asia and Europe**
   Convergence or Divergence?
   Edited by Bertrand Fort and Douglas Webber

The World Bank and Governance

A Decade of Reform and Reaction

Edited by Diane Stone and Christopher Wright

MARIE CURIE **ACTIONS**

Routledge
Taylor & Francis Group

LONDON AND NEW YORK

CENTER FOR POLICY STUDIES

First published 2007
by Routledge
2 Park Square, Milton Park, Abingdon, Oxon OX14 4RN

Simultaneously published in the USA and Canada
by Routledge
270 Madison Ave, New York, NY 10016

Routledge is an imprint of the Taylor & Francis Group, an informa business

Transferred to Digital Printing 2006

Typeset in Times New Roman by
Taylor & Francis Books

British Library Cataloguing in Publication Data
A catalogue record for this book is available from the British Library

Library of Congress Cataloging in Publication Data
A catalog record for this book has been requested

ISBN10: 0-415-41282-X (hbk)
ISBN10: 0-415-41650-7 (pbk)

ISBN13: 978-0-415-41282-7 (hbk)
ISBN13: 978-0-415-41650-4 (pbk)

Contents

Tables

Contributors

Lauren Flejzor is a Projects Manager at the International Tropical Timber Organization, a UN Conference on Trade and Development-affiliated organisation in Japan. She has previously worked on foreign policy issues related to international organisations, environment and security at the US Department of State. Her Ph.D., undertaken at the London School of Economics and Political Science, focused on comparative strategic change outcomes in international organisations. Her future research interests include democratic governance and change in the UN system, with respect to environment, development, security and management issues. She would like to acknowledge the financial support of the University of London Central Research Fund, which facilitated her travel to the World Bank during 2004, and the helpful assistance provided to her by Bank staff throughout the course of her research.

Nisrine el Ghaziri is a doctoral student at the Institute of Social Studies. This chapter is based on an ongoing Ph.D. research titled 'Administrative Reform in Lebanon: Dynamics of Government/Donor Interactions in a Post-war Context'. I am grateful to my supervisors, Professor Dr James Warner Björkman and Dr Des Gasper, for their guidance. I am also thankful to the Institute of Social Studies and the Netherlands Organization for Scientific Research in The Hague, the Netherlands, for providing academic and financial support. Comments about this chapter are welcome and can be addressed to my e-mail address, ghaziri@iss.nl.

Ian Goldin, Vice President, External Affairs, Communications, and United Nations Affairs, The World Bank, assumed his current position in May 2003. Dr Goldin provides leadership in the relationship between the Bank and the global community. This includes questions of global governance and the development and communication of ideas to enhance development effectiveness. In this position, Dr Goldin is responsible for managing the World Bank's contact with key constituencies – government officials, parliamentarians, NGOs, businesses and academics – and for overseeing relations with the United Nations and the global affairs agenda. Previously, Ian was the Director of Development Policy at the World Bank. Prior to joining the World Bank in 2001, Dr Goldin was Chief Executive of the Development Bank of Southern Africa and previously served as Principal Economist at the OECD and European Bank for Reconstruction and Development.

Nilima Gulrajani is a Visiting Research Associate at the Global Economic Governance Programme, University College, Oxford University. Her research interests include organisational reforms within international development organisations, the application of new public management systems within the development field, and the study of the development sector as a business industry. Her chapter is a product of a larger doctoral study that was generously supported with academic grants from the Bill Gates Foundation, the Fonds de recherche sur la société et la culture, the Overseas Research Studentship, and Trinity College, Cambridge. Valuable suggestions for improvement of her chapter were received from Sandra Dawson, Diane Stone, Michael Tierney and Ngaire Woods, and generous research assistance granted by many helpful Bank staff. She can be reached at N.Gulrajani@cantab.net

Pascale Hatcher is a doctoral student at the Institute of Social Studies in The Hague, the Netherlands, and a researcher for the Groupe de Recherche sur les Activités Minières en Afrique (GRAMA) at the University of Quebec at Montreal, Canada. The following contribution is based on her thesis proposal. The thesis thus expands on the chapter's main themes such as ownership and the redefinition of political space between the state and civil society. She would like to thank thesis supervisors Richard Robison and Kees Biekart, for their comments. She would also like to thank Christopher Wright for his valuable comments and patient revision of the chapter. Comments are welcome at hatcher@iss.nl

Desmond McNeill has a B.A. in economics from the University of Cambridge, and a Ph.D. in economics from University College, London. He is a Research Professor, and former Director, at SUM (Centre for Development and the Environment), University of Oslo, Norway. He has worked as adviser or consultant in more than fifteen developing countries, mostly in Africa and Asia, for various aid agencies. He is Vice-President of EADI (European Association of Development Research and Training Institutes). His books include: *Development Issues in Global Governance: Public–Private Partnerships and Market Multilateralism* (with B. Bull), Routledge (2006); *Global Institutions and Development: Framing the World?* (ed. with M. Bøås), Routledge, 2004; *Multilateral Institutions: A Critical Introduction* (with M. Bøås), Pluto Press, 2003.

Susan Park is a Lecturer in International Relations in the School of International and Political Studies, Deakin University. Her research interests include environmental change within international organisations, including the World Bank Group and the United Nations, as well as the role of environmental non-government organisations. She would like to thank staff at IFC and MIGA for their insights, and the assistance of activists who provided valuable information. Many thanks to those who have made comments on previous versions of this chapter: Christina Davis, Matt McDonald, Marc Williams, Chris Wright and Diane Stone. She can be reached at susan.park@deakin.edu.au

M. Ramesh is Associate Professor at the LKY School of Public Policy at the National University of Singapore. He has held regular or visiting appointments in Australia, Canada, Hong Kong, New Zealand, Norway, and the USA. He is the author or co-author of *Social Policies in East and Southeast Asia, Welfare Capitalism in Southeast Asia, Studying Public Policy*, and *Canadian Political Economy*. He has also published widely in senior refereed journals and is Editor of the journal *Policy and Society.* He currently teaches business and government, globalisation and public policy, and social policy. He is the current Co-President of the Asian Political and International Studies Association. He may be contacted at: sppmr@nus.edu.sg

Maria Pía Riggirozzi (Ph.D. Warwick) is Research Associate in the Department of Politics, University of Sheffield (M. P.Riggirozzi@Sheffield.ac.uk). Her principal research areas are in the field of international and Latin American political economy. Pía's current research is a project on the political economy of pro-poor adjustment, with a particular focus on Argentina and Bolivia. She is grateful to Diane Stone and Chris Wright for their comments on this chapter; and also to Jan Aart Scholte, Fernanda Tuozzo and the participants of the World Bank Research Group. She would also like to thank in particular the interviewees for sharing their knowledge and time. This chapter is based on her doctoral research.

Asunción Lera St Clair is Associate Professor at the section on Gender and Development, Department of Education and Health Promotion, University of Bergen, and Senior Research Fellow at the Centre for Development and the Environment, University of Oslo, Norway. St Clair is Secretary of the International Development Ethics Association (IDEA). Recent publications include 'The World Bank as a Transnational Expertised Institution', *Journal of Global Governance* 12 (1); 'Global Poverty: The Co-production of Knowledge and Politics', *Journal of Global Social Policy* 6 (1); 'How Can Human Rights Work for Poverty Reduction?: An Assessment of the Human Development Report 2000', in Lucy Williams (ed.) *International Poverty Law: An Emerging Discourse*, London: Zed Books, 2006.

Diane Stone is Marie Curie Chair in the Center for Policy Studies at the Central European University in Budapest, and Reader in Politics and International Studies at the University of Warwick. Current research addresses global networks and global governance. Specific interests include the influence of ideas and expertise on policy, the political economy of higher education; the role of non-state actors in domestic, regional and global affairs; conceptual developments in the study of policy networks; and the political process of lesson-drawing and policy transfer. Her most recent book is *Global Knowledge Networks and International Development: Bridges Across Boundaries* (Routledge, 2005) co-edited with Simon Maxwell. Other books have addressed the role of think tanks in contemporary politics.

Celine Tan is writing her doctoral thesis at the School of Law, University of Warwick. This chapter is drawn from the thesis analysing the Poverty Reduction Strategy Paper (PRSP) framework as part of a larger shift in the regulatory framework of global economic governance. Celine is also Production Editor of the *Law, Social Justice and Global Development* electronic journal (http://go.warwick.ac.uk/lgd) based at the Warwick Law School. Prior to Warwick, Celine was a researcher and policy officer with the Third World Network (TWN). She wishes to thank Christopher Wright and Diane Stone for strengthening the theoretical and empirical content of this chapter and for organising this collection. Thanks also to the organisers and sponsors of the Budapest 'Workshop on the World Bank' for the opportunity to present the original draft of this chapter; and to Martin Khor and Goh Chien Yen of TWN, without whom the chapter would be wanting in many ways. And her gratitude always to her supervisors, Abdul Paliwala and Upendra Baxi, for their unfailing support and encouragement. Email: Celine.Tan@warwick.ac.uk

Krisztina Tóth is a research assistant and Ph.D. candidate under the direction of Prof. Dr Bernard Dafflon at the University of Fribourg, Switzerland. Mailing address: Department of Economics, Chair for Public Finance, University of Fribourg, Bd. de Pérolles 90, Bureau F512, CH-1700 Fribourg, Switzerland; krisztina.toth@unifr.ch; http://www.u-nifr.ch/finpub. The author thanks the participants of the 'Research Bank on the World Bank' (Budapest, 1–2 April 2005), for their precious feedback on the first version. Special thanks to Diane Stone and Bernard Dafflon for their valuable suggestions and continuous support.

Antje Vetterlein is Departmental Lecturer in Social Policy at the University of Oxford. Her research areas are political sociology in combination with international relations, with particular interests in the politics of social policy, and the role of ideas within political discourses. Prior to coming to Oxford, she finished her Ph.D. at the European University Institute in Florence, Italy; this being a comparative study of the World Bank and the IMF regarding the development of their social (development) policies over the last thirty years.

Christopher Wright is a Ph.D. candidate in the International Relations Department at the London School of Economics (LSE). His research interests include the role of international financial institutions in global environmental governance, the integration of environmental and social concerns into public and private financial institutions, and the merits of voluntary codes of conduct in encouraging sustainable finance and investment. He would like to thank those current and former International Finance Corporation staff who kindly shared their views and gave their time in support of this research. In addition, he would like to thank Diane Stone, Susan Park and Glen Armstrong for comments on preliminary drafts.

Preface

I am pleased to present to the reader this unique volume of papers produced by researchers whose principal area of study is the World Bank.

The World Bank has evolved substantially over the past decade. We have been learning from both the successes and the failures of the past as we work to fulfill our important contribution to global development. We aim to be able to respond quickly to new challenges and to keep pace with the rapidly changing world. This process is far from complete – we will always be confronted with challenges and the need to learn from them. One of the most valuable achievements of the World Bank in the last ten years, which is pointed out in the chapters of this volume, is its growing openness to engage in dialogue with a variety of key constituencies: academics, youth, non-governmental organizations, parliamentarians, private sector. The World Bank has recognized the importance of learning from new ideas as well as critical thinking about what works and what does not work in development.

Part of the World Bank's mission is to act as a knowledge-producer and knowledge-broker on development issues. The Bank has been generating and disseminating in-house research since it was established, and it has reached out to the academic community, linking World Bank and external research, to increase the flow of fresh and innovative ideas on development. The World Bank has, for example, initiated a series of activities engaging the research community worldwide and linking them to World Bank staff and other players on the development arena. This book is a product of our collaboration in recent years with the Researchers Alliance for Development (RAD) – an open, action-oriented academic network coordinated from the World Bank Paris Office. Under the RAD umbrella, the Bank, together with the Central European University in Budapest, organized a workshop of young researchers in spring 2005 in Budapest to present and exchange research work about the World Bank. This volume of papers is a compilation of the work presented there and marks the beginning of a broader joint initiative.

Following the successful Budapest seminar, we want to reach out to other graduate students and researchers working on the World Bank and offer them the opportunity to share their research on a web platform (http://www.worldbank.org/sup) and to work together with us on a regular basis – through, for example, participating in our Annual Bank Conference on Development Economics (ABCDE), a dynamic forum for dialogue on diverse topics in development, or in other projects sponsored by the RAD and other academic groups and individuals in collaboration with the Bank. We have also decided to encourage our colleagues in Bank offices all over the world to suggest possible research topics to researchers willing to take up the World Bank as the subject of their study. The Bank welcomes the input of academics at universities, research centers and think tanks, even if critical. We also believe that the research community can benefit considerably from closer collaboration with the World Bank.

This book is unique for several reasons. It is a collection of chapters each one of which applies a different lens to the intricate and complex organization that is the World Bank. One common feature of all of the texts, diverse as they are, is that they provide an invaluable outsider's perspective on the structure, functioning, policies and programs of the World Bank. These authors' papers also demonstrate that development is not limited to the discipline of economics – within the development debate, there is room for the voices of sociologists, political scientists, anthropologists, engineers, medical doctors and others.

I would like to acknowledge the intellectual and organizational efforts of all of the many persons who contributed to the creation of this volume. I would like to give special thanks to Diane Stone and Christopher Wright, the editors, and to all of the authors of the individual chapters, as well as to others who have provided constructive comments along the way. The World Bank is glad that so many academics are willing to study its policies and programs and work together on joint projects. We hope that this volume will help convince others, within the World Bank and outside, that it is worthwhile to continue this dynamic dialogue on development ideas.

Ian Goldin,
Vice President, External Affairs,
Communications, and United Nations Affairs,
The World Bank

Acknowledgements

The editors would like to thank four organisations for the financial and scholarly support. The European Commission (through its Marie Curie Chair grant), the Centre for the Study of Globalisation and Regionalisation at the University of Warwick, and the External Affairs Presidency of the World Bank, via its Paris Office, provided the funding for a workshop in Budapest. The Center for Policy Studies at the Central European University organised and hosted the workshop in April 2005 that subsequently led to the publication of this volume.

We would like to express particular thanks to a number of individuals. In Budapest, Viola Zentai, Ivona Malbasic, Agnes Batory, Zsuzsa Gabor, George Guess and especially Heni Griecs provided an excellent working environment and professional support for the Budapest workshop. From the World Bank, Jean-Christophe Bas, Jean-Jacques Dethier, Ingrid Johansen, Nina Maqami and Anna Kuznicka provided encouragement and logistical support. As Chair of the Researcher's Alliance for Development steering committee, Odd-Helge Fjeldstad has been a strong supporter all along. And our final note of thanks to all of the participants who came to Budapest and made it such a lively and noisy meeting.

Abbreviations

ABCDE	Annual Bank Conference on Development Economics
ARLA	Assistance for the Re-establishment of the Lebanese Administration
CANDID	Creation, Adoption, Negation, and Distortion of Ideas in Development
CAO	The IFC's Office of the Compliance Advisor/Ombudsman
CDF	Comprehensive Development Framework
CEE	Central and Eastern Europe
CES	The IFC's Environmental and Social Development Department
CEU	Central European University
CIEL	Center for International Environmental Law
COS	The IFC's Operational Strategy Group
CPIA	Country Policy and Institutional Assessments
CSO	Civil Society Organisation
DAC	Development Aid Committee (OECD)
DECRG	Development Economics Research Group
DfID	Department for International Development
DPL	Development Policy Lending
EDF	Environmental Defense
ESAF	Enhanced Structural Adjustment Facility
ESSD	Environment and Socially Sustainable Development
ESW	Economic and Sector Work
EU	European Union
FOCAL	Canadian Foundation for the Americas
FOCJ	Functional, overlapping and competing jurisdictions
FOEI	Friends of the Earth International
FPSI	Finance and Private Sector Infrastructure
GABB	Grupo de Accion por el Bibio
GDN	Global Development Network
GEF	Global Environment Facility
GOL	Government of Lebanon
GPGs	Global Public Goods
HD	Human Development

HDR	Human Development Report
HIPC	Heavily Indebted Poor Countries Initiative
IBRD	International Bank for Reconstruction and Development
IDA	International Development Association
IDF	Institutional Development Facility
IDM	Integrated Development Model
IEO	Independent Evaluation Office (IMF)
IFC	International Finance Corporation
IFI	International Financial Institutions
IFIAC	International Financial Institutions Advisory Commission
ILO	International Labor Organization
IMF	International Monetary Fund
IO	International Organisation
IR	International Relations
IUCN	The World Conservation Union
LDCs	Less Developed Countries
LIC	Low Income Country
MDBs	Multinational Development Banks
MDGs	Millennium Development Goals
MIGA	Multilateral Investment Guarantee Agency
NARP	National Administrative Rehabilitation Programme
NESS	Non-Economist Social Scientist
NGOs	Non-Governmental Organisations
NIE	New Institutional Economics
NIEO	New International Economic Order
NPE	New Political Economy
NROC	Natural Resources Defence Council
OED	Operations Evaluation Department
OEG	The IFC's Operations Evaluations Group
OEU	Operations Evaluation Unit
ONEP	Oficina Nacional de Etica Pública (National Office of Ethics)
OPIC	Overseas Private Investment Corporation
PAYG	Pay As You Go
PFP	Policy Framework Paper
PREM	Poverty Reduction and Economic Management
PRGF	Poverty Reduction and Growth Facility
PROJUM	Proyecto Juzgado Modelo (Model Court Project)
PRS	Poverty Reduction Strategies
PRSC	Poverty Reduction Strategy Credit
PRSP	Poverty Reduction Strategy Paper
RAD	Researchers Alliance for Development
SAF	Structural Adjustment Facility
SAL	Structural Adjustment Lending
SALs	Structural Adjustment Loans
SAP	Structural Adjustment Programme

SAPRIN	Structural Adjustment Participatory Review International Network
SPs	Safeguard Policies
TAG	Technical Advisory Group
TI	Transparency International
UNDAF	United Nations Development Assistance Framework
UNDP	United Nations Development Programme
UNRISD	United Nation Research Institute for Social Development
US	United States
USAID	United States Agency for International Development
USD	United States Dollar
US-ED	US Executive Director
WBB	World Bank-Bolivia
WBCSD	World Business Council on Sustainable Development
WBG	World Bank Group
WBI	World Bank Institute
WBV	World Bank-Vietnam
WDR	World Development Report
WSSD	World Summit on Sustainable Development

1 Introduction

The currency of change: World Bank lending and learning in the Wolfensohn era

Diane Stone and Christopher Wright

The World Bank Group is at a critical juncture in its history. The departure of James Wolfensohn as president in mid-2005 and the appointment of Paul Wolfowitz marked a milestone in the Group's history. This transition represents an ideal opportunity to reflect on the legacy of the initiatives and reforms undertaken during the previous decade that continue to direct many existing trajectories in development policy.

James Wolfensohn's ten-year tenure as president of the World Bank was a period where the organization was under the increasingly intense scrutiny of the international community. The decade saw 'radical changes' in thinking about development policy, in which the ideas and policy prescriptions from the 1980s were being increasingly questioned (Gilbert and Vines 2000). This was not only due to greater pressures from dominant shareholders and a growing array of stakeholders, it was also a time of internal institutional soul searching with the reforms and evaluations that responded to and reflected the implacable problems of ameliorating poverty and generating growth and development.

As an organization, the World Bank met with some dramatic changes and has become a more open actor (Miller-Adams 1999). This has meant that the Bank is increasingly becoming a forum for conflicting ideas and sources of knowledge to confront each other, which has increased scrutiny of the Bank's own development policy prescriptions. The challenge is to understand how, if at all, this has affected the nature of policy change at the Bank, in terms of introducing new factors that drive or hinder organizational change.

The contributors to this volume reveal a variety of explanations for policy reform or continuity in different areas of the Bank's work. For example, the continuity of certain policy prescriptions and types of interventions is explained by some as a function of the Bank's professional culture and persistent ideological bias. Meanwhile, the emergence of new policies or amendments to existing ones is attributed by others to organizational learning or the work of internal policy entrepreneurs, or as a strategic desire within the Bank's management to enhance its organizational legitimacy with dominant shareholders, civil society groups and clients.

This introduction is structured into three parts. In the first section, we consider the aspects of the Bank's mandate, mission and activities that have arguably made it the most influential development organization in the world. In doing so, we address the sources of its financial and discursive power, and consider how new policy frameworks introduced in the last decade have augmented, yet transformed, the Bank's influence in developing countries. In the second section, we describe the knowledge-production and knowledge-sharing practices of the Bank, one of the most significant aspects of the Bank's emerging policy agenda. In the third section, we address the nature of conducting research on the World Bank, and discuss the advantages of getting inside the 'black box' of the Bank, while outlining the themes and structure of the book.

A decade of changing fortunes

Established in 1945 after the Bretton Woods meeting (along with its 'sister institution' the International Monetary Fund – IMF), the World Bank Group is an intergovernmental organization whose primary function is to provide financial assistance to developing countries. Since its inception, it has gradually grown into a multi-pronged development institution comprised of four organizations that collectively provide financial assistance, risk guarantees, technical assistance and policy advice to both governments and the private sector in developing countries. The International Bank for Reconstruction and Development (IBRD) provides medium-term loans at a marked-up rate that ensures profitability. In contrast, the International Development Association (IDA), established in 1960, provides long-term loans at concessional rates meant to cater to poorer countries with very limited access to private capital. The International Finance Corporation (IFC), created in 1956, provides financing to the private sector without government guarantees, whereas the Multilateral Investment Guarantee Agency (MIGA) offers political and non-financial risk guarantees to private investors.

Today, the World Bank Group represents an organization with over 10,000 employees, managing significant resources as a financial and knowledge intermediary between powerful shareholders and both public and private sector recipients in developing countries. Consequently, it has become one of the most powerful institutions in the global political economy. It is powerful for reasons that are now well documented.

First, its lending power far exceeds that of other financial institutions and cannot be deduced from the volume of paid-in capital alone. While its lending to developing countries is less than that of commercial banks, the Bank enjoys greater leverage and influence by virtue of its superior credit rating and close relationship with governments. Additionally, and in contrast to commercial banks, its financing is deeply embedded in an economic development agenda driven in part by the Bank's own research department. This means its role as a financial intermediary between powerful shareholder governments and both public and private sector recipients in developing countries has a significant discursive dimension (see Barnett and Finnemore 1999; Bøås and McNeill 2004).

Second, mission creep has long been a feature of the Bank, and has continued during the Wolfensohn era (see Einhorn 2001; Ascher 1983). Its original purpose – to aid the reconstruction of post-war Europe – soon shifted in the advent of decolonization to fostering economic development in developing countries. During this stage, Bank funds were often channelled through public development agencies in support of large-scale physical infrastructure projects, reflecting a development model that placed the state at the centre of economic growth. With the rise of neo-liberalism in the 1970s, the Bank came to increasingly favour a private-sector-driven development model that sought to avoid the corruption and political favouritism that had mired much of its previous lending through public development agencies. In addition, it attributed soaring sovereign debt in some of its borrower countries to overextended government that limited private enterprise and capital. The structural adjustment policies that were imposed to roll back the state in the 1980s were driven by an understanding of development that regarded public ownership and regulation as an impediment to economic growth.

Popularized as the Washington Consensus policies, this development agenda was in turmoil as Wolfensohn assumed his presidency. The 'Consensus' was increasingly criticized for its unwavering faith in free market principles and its reliance on financing conditionalities for pushing through economic and political reform programmes that proved to inflict adverse consequences on the poor and the environment. In its place, a more holistic development model emerged, in part driven by the Bank's own research on the role of institutions in economic development, that increasingly recognized the human, social and environmental dimensions of economic growth. Accordingly, its current mission and expertise go well beyond the narrow confines of economic development, as it has evolved into 'the institution of choice for working with developing countries on global commons issues such as the environment and health' (Einhorn 2006: 19).

Third, during the course of its history, its power to persuade has, of course, not been unrelated to its ability to impose conditions on the use of its funds. During the 1970s, the introduction of policy-based lending was meant to create a favourable policy environment for economic growth. This financing modality expanded its influence by the use of policy conditionalities, in which financing depended on the implementation of particular economic reform programmes. The use of this tool broadened with structural adjustment lending in the 1980s, when Bank and IMF interventions converged around the Washington Consensus policies and pushed for deregulation, privatization and the liberalization of capital markets in developing countries.

The effectiveness and legitimacy of policy conditionality was increasingly being questioned, and has been the source of considerable interest to the Bank and external observers alike (see Gilbert and Vines 2000: 24–9; World

Bank 1998). Since then, while legally binding conditions have been gradually declining in Bank lending, the Bank's influence and agenda-setting capabilities have arguably expanded, primarily by the emergence of various development assistance mechanisms that have reinforced its position as the world's foremost development institution.

Fourth, with recent advances in information technology and communication, the volume of knowledge that is of and about the World Bank, and the public access to this, has significantly increased. Indeed, the production and diffusion of knowledge has become an explicit objective of the World Bank Group in the last decade, and has been promoted by various external sources as the Bank's real comparative advantage (see Gilbert and Vines 2000; IFIAC 2000).

Fifth, the power of the World Bank has frequently been attributed to its governance structure, and, in particular, the dominant position of the United States. To understand its institutional behaviour, this literature focuses on the Bank's formal governance model: the Bank's president is commonly a US citizen and directly appointed by its government. The voting power of shareholder governments is proportionate to their paid-in capital, providing the USA with an effective veto.

Analysis of the implications of this governance structure varies. Some see it as evidence that the Bank functions as a tool of US imperialism (see Kapur 2003: 6; Wade 1990, 2002). These studies point to the propensity of the Bank to favour strategic priorities, policy interventions and financing practices that conform to US geopolitical and economic interests in developing countries. In these cases, the neo-liberal policy framework promoted by the Bank, in particular its policy or regulatory reform programmes, is seen as a manifestation of US hegemonic power.

Others have suggested this governance structure simply explains changes in the Bank's institutional behaviour. In particular, Nielson and Tierney (2003, 2005) drew on the principal-agent theory of institutional change. They argued that the timing and scale of environmental reforms at the Bank can be explained by principal control over an agent, where the USA had threatened to withhold replenishment funds from the Bank unless its demands for environmental reforms were met. In turn, they analysed the environmental dimension of the Bank's lending activities and argued that, generally, its environmental projects portfolio expanded following periods of environmental reform. However, these conclusions, and those of similar agency-centred studies analysing institutional change in international organizations, have been contested by others (see Barnett and Finnemore 1999; Gutner 2005; Park, this volume, Chapter 9).

The legitimacy deficit

As with many of his predecessors, Wolfensohn sought to put his mark on the Bank's activities early on. Shrugging off internal scepticism, he called for development planning to be transparent and accountable, void of corruption, and driven by the needs of borrower countries (Mallaby 2005). His ideas would be encapsulated in the Comprehensive Development Framework (CDF), the major new policy initiative during his tenure (see Gulrajani, this volume, Chapter 3). Subsequently, the framework would provide the foundation for the poverty reduction strategy papers (PRSPs) which the Bank produced in collaboration with low-income countries (see Tan, this volume, Chapter 8). Meant to break with the heavy-handedness of the Bank's interventions in the past, the PRSPs were introduced as a means to ensure country ownership and put borrowers in the position of deciding upon a policy mix that best meets their own economic and political objectives (see Hatcher, this volume, Chapter 10). In many cases, these have become guiding documents for multilateral and bilateral aid programmes and projects, multiplying the effect of the Bank's policy prescriptions. Notwithstanding these new policy initiatives, unsurprisingly, the Bank has faced a welter of criticism from the sources outlined below.

US influence

The United States, its principal shareholder, continued to put pressure on the Bank to reform itself. While previous calls for reform focused on changes to operational policies that could enhance the Bank's accountability, the development outcome of its programmes and projects and its relationship with civil society, policy recommendations emanating from the legislature of its most powerful shareholder considered much more draconian measures. Specifically, in the aftermath of the Asian financial crisis, the US Congress established a commission to review the role and effectiveness of international financial institutions as part of authorizing legislation to grant additional funding to the International Monetary Fund. Released in March 2000, the *Meltzer Report*, named after its principal author, called for broad changes to multilateral development assistance and made damning remarks regarding the Bank's effectiveness at reducing poverty in developing countries (IFIAC 2000). Among its most radical suggestions, and one that has since been repeated by critics on both the left and the right, was a recommendation to phase out lending to middle-income countries in favour of concessional financing to the poorest countries (see also Einhorn 2006; Rich 2002). In these countries, development needs are most dire and access to private capital is particularly limited As for the IFC and other development banks targeting the private sector, it was recommended that they abolish their financing practices altogether, and instead focus their complete attention on providing technical assistance and disseminating best practices.

While these policy positions were not entirely shared by the US Treasury, they nevertheless underscored the major reservations towards the need for multilateral financing in developing countries that national legislators were developing as a result of the major transformations in the global economic and financial system in the 1990s. While the IFC and the IBRD survived the political assault, this experience made them increasingly aware of the need to demonstrate their relevance and achievements to shareholders and stakeholders alike.

Less developed country influence

The influence of developing country governments on the Bank, as both shareholders and loan recipients, has also been transformed in recent years. A particularly noticeable trend is the growing gap among developing countries in the power and influence they can exert over the Bank's programmes and projects. The highly uneven growth of transnational private capital flows in the early 1990s significantly strengthened the bargaining position of a few large middle-income countries relative to the Bank, as they became less dependent on Bank funds for undertaking major development projects. This posed a problem for the Bank, as lending large volumes to these countries is critical to the Bank's profitability.

Increasing the attractiveness of Bank loans in more competitive markets where borrowers have access to multiple sources of long-term financing has therefore become an important imperative for the Bank. For example, the reforms associated with the Strategic Compact in 1996 gave country directors more decision-making autonomy and control of the Bank's budget, and were part of an overall trend to tailor development assistance to country-specific circumstances.

For developing countries that have yet to benefit significantly from financial globalization, the Bank and other multilateral lenders still represent the only source of long-term financing. In these cases, the Bank exerts more influence on economic development by being able to make funds available only for specific purposes under certain conditions. In recent years, the Bank has looked for commitments to 'good governance' as criteria for deciding the volume of aid allocations between countries. It is a strategy driven by findings by its own research department which suggest that policy conditionality can increase aid effectiveness in cases where borrower governments are committed and able to implement reforms supported by the Bank (Burnside and Dollar 1997).

Yet, the legitimacy and effectiveness of this heavy-handedness has been central to the debates surrounding the persistence of poverty in many low-income countries. Recent Bank policies and strategies have emphasized the importance of customizing lending programmes according to the expressed needs of borrowers, and giving them a sense of 'ownership' in preparing and carrying out programmes and projects. This is driven by a recognition that its influence and development effectiveness in low-income countries is still significantly dependent on the commitment and implementation capacity of borrowers. It can be dramatically compromised in cases where financing conditions are breached, as seen in the Chadian parliament's amendment to a Bank-supported oil revenue law in 2005. But the extent to which newly introduced financing frameworks, notably the poverty-reduction strategies under the Comprehensive Development Framework (CDF), delegate significant and meaningful decision-making authority to low-income countries is still hotly disputed.

NGO pressures

In addition, the Bank is continuously pressured by a variety of external stakeholders, either directly or through shareholder governments. These are often conceptualized in the context of the anti-globalization and the alter-globalization social movements that came to prominence in the late 1990s and early twenty-first century. The demands for accountability are voluble, and denouncements of the Washington Consensus palpable. 'Fifty Years Is Enough' was one coalition of voices that directly focused upon the international financial institutions (Danaher 1994). NGOs and think tanks have pumped out critiques of the World Bank and other international financial and trade organizations (see, for instance, EDF 2005; Rich 2002; Buira 2003; Goldman 2005).

Critiques have come from longstanding programmes within established environmental organizations in the United States and Europe, such as Environmental Defense, Friends of the Earth, and the World Wildlife Fund. More permanent associations are dedicated to the monitoring of and the reporting on international financial institutions (IFIs), such as the Bank Information Center, the Bretton Woods Project and CEE BankWatch. In addition, advances in information and communications technologies have increased and strengthened connections between them and civil society groups in developing countries, which has increased the legitimacy of the former and amplified the voices of the latter. These connections have also augmented and accelerated the flow of project-specific information from remote areas in developing countries to major centres of power and influence in Western capitals. Significantly, it has reduced the transaction costs associated with producing petitions and engaging with the Bank, and enabled the rapid mobilization of political coalitions around emerging issues. As a result, more so than ever, advocacy campaigns against the IFIs are organized in and through networks of geographically dispersed civil society groups that share information, coordinate advocacy, and, ultimately, aggregate their political leverage (see Keck and Sikkink 1999).

Critiques from Academia

With mounting evidence of the intractable nature of poverty, the travails of transition and the poor record of economic development in many parts of the world, devastating critiques of the role of international agencies have also emerged from within the development studies community. (For a discussion of some of the debates see Buira 2003; Gilbert and Vines 2000; Kapur 2003; Pincus and Winters 2002; Ritzen 2005; Woods 2006.) Considerable criticism has focused on the Bank's economistic and technocratic approach to development problems that 'elided any discussion of the political economy of development' (Bebbington *et al.* 2004: 34). Other studies have reflected on the relationship between aid legitimacy and effectiveness, and the ideological biases and staff incentives that exist within its organizational culture. For example, the fact that task managers operate within an internal incentive structure common to lending institutions in which they are often rewarded, either financially, socially or both, for disbursing large volumes of funds quickly. This has been recognized as severely undermining many of the Bank's operational objectives and the development impact of its funds (see Rich 2002).

Academic attention has always been devoted to the Bretton Woods institutions, given their place in history and their prominence in national and international affairs. Monographs and learned papers on the development challenges faced by sub-Saharan nations, the 'good governance' reforms in Latin American economies or the financial crises of East Asia (amongst a multitude of other issues) have addressed the integral role of the World Bank as one of the key institutional actors. Undergraduate and graduate courses in development studies, as well as in economics and international relations, invariably devote lectures and seminars to this international organization. A Bank 'survey of development courses in leading universities found that fully one-sixth of the references on reading lists came from the Bank' (Dethier 2005: 4). And as is manifested by this volume, a burgeoning number of doctoral students are directing their dissertation research and analysis at the topic of the Bank.

Within the Bank

The relative autonomy the Bank enjoys in certain areas of its activities allows for new ideas and policy initiatives to emerge from within its ranks. The organizational structure, professional culture and a gradual expansion of its engagement with external stakeholders are all factors that may encourage individuals or groups of staff to lobby for policy reforms. Indeed, a number of chapters in this volume highlight how policy change would not have occurred without the deliberate actions of individual staff. That is, staff who were strategically positioned and politically motivated to promote and diffuse particular policy ideas internally, and who were successful in building alliances and persuading the right people to join their cause.

As some of our contributors argue, factors such as the creativity of staff, the involvement of new actors in development debates, the support from key leaders and significant analytical work have prompted both radical change and gradual reform within the Bank. This is perhaps most explicitly manifested in the power and influence that the president of the Bank enjoys compared to heads of other international organizations. But it also extends to senior executives and departmental managers, and its increasingly influential country offices.

The knowledge bank

A former vice president describes the Bank as 'comparable to an American or Anglo-Saxon university in its organisational culture' (Ritzen 2005: 110). Part of the mission of the World Bank is to conduct research and produce new ideas to inform policy, as well as to spread knowledge about best practices and persuade client countries and other stakeholders of the validity of such knowledge. More generally, the 'knowledge agenda' has become a central part of the discourse of both developing societies and advanced economies, as well as a tool of management within organizations. According to the Bank, 'knowledge for development' 'aims to turn Bank lending activities and policy engagement into an active, research-based springboard for improving development activities ... as an integral part of the Learning Lending Knowledge circle' (Dethier 2005: 16).

Taking into consideration the research engagements, products and communications of the Bank is important to understanding how different units, networks and groups within the Bank conceive of development and justify their priorities. This is more than agenda-setting, as it becomes a source of institutional legitimacy for chosen development paths. Furthermore, the World Bank has devoted considerable financial resources to both in-house and contracted research that is reflective of the generation, re-generation and evolution of discursive realities. A focus on World Bank 'knowledge production' and 'knowledge sharing' also provides insight into which disciplines are deemed relevant to development, whose knowledge is recognized as credible or superior, and those groups and interests that are recognized as having the authority to 'speak' in development debates.

World Bank knowledge creation

There is an extensive amount of written material about the World Bank that is produced within the World Bank by its staff. The World Bank is probably the largest single organizational producer of research on development. Its analytical capacity is extensive, having broadened somewhat from a reliance on economists – predominantly trained in the leading economics departments of North American universities, and to a lesser extent Europe – to incorporate social scientists, social development practitioners and natural scientists. Through its research capacity, and products such as the annual *World Development Report*, its two in-house journals, and as a major provider of statistical data, the Bank has been able to shape the analytical terms of research within the policy community.

In-house, the Development Economics Research Group (DECRG) and Vice Presidency are described as the 'theoretical core' of the institution and often associated with the 'more orthodox and institutionally sanctioned positions on development, albeit with notable exceptions' (Bebbington *et al.* 2004: 45, 41; exceptions such as Ellerman 2005; Kanbur 2003). The research – conducted by around eighty-five full-time researchers – 'is not theoretical; it is intended to offer practical advice to Bank clients' (Dethier 2005: 1). Other sources of in-house research include the World Bank Institute (WBI) which is noted for its work on governance, especially corruption and transparency. Similarly, the Operations Evaluation Department (OED) has become increasingly important for its evaluation reports, such as that of the Bank's global programmes through which it finances even more research (OED 2004).

There is some tension played out between analytical staff and operational staff about the utility of research. This is not to suggest that operational staff ignore or disdain the results of research. However, time constraints, mounting workloads and consultations with stakeholders, contribute to a bifurcation of development debates among operational and research staff. Moreover, once on the ground, the application of concepts confronts a multiplicity of implementation interests.

The utilization of concepts, research and data by task managers in their daily work is not something that happens spontaneously due to the innate persuasiveness of such analytical work. Instead, there is a slow diffusion of ideas between organizational units, that are backed up by networking within the Bank, and networking of ideas with professional and scholarly counterparts outside the Bank. These strategic networks 'are also manoeuvred by developing strategic external alliances, with groups to whom information is deliberately channelled, and with funding agencies with interests in the strategic financing of work that might contribute to paradigmatic change' (Bebbington *et al.* 2004: 57).

The strategic interplay of both ideas and actors in these networks reveals the extent to which the Bank is increasingly permeable. However, it also raises the question 'who speaks?' and to whom or what groups is the Bank permeable? Permeability and the prospects for interaction on an equal footing are often under-pinned by prior assumptions of professional expertise in development, scholarly credentials and mastery of technical codes among participants in dialogues. Those without a Western doctoral degree or institutional affiliation with a leading think tank or university institute can avail themselves of the Bank-sponsored training networks and capacity-building programmes (see Ellerman 2005: ch. 6).

One critique of Bank research production is that there has been too little analysis of 'the quantum of resources devoted to research, the distribution of those resources among different research activities or the optimal institutional mechanisms to generate the research' (Kapur 2003: 22). For instance, in the period to the end of the last century, researchers based in less developed countries accounted for barely 4 per cent of authors at the

Annual Bank Conference on Development Economics (ABCDE). While representation has improved at ABCDE, the example is indicative of more general processes of global knowledge production. And as Kapur notes, 'if knowledge is power, it underlies the powerlessness of LDCs' (Kapur 2003: 22).

Notwithstanding the resources devoted to research partnerships, capacity building and scholarships, there are strong individual and institutional imperatives leading to perverse outcomes where the bulk of economic and sector work (ESW) continues to be conducted inside the IFIs and other elite development agencies (Ritzen 2005: 111; Toye and Toye 2005: 8). The frequently stated rationale for extensive in-house research is to maintain high standards. However, resistance to out-sourcing research and to research competition also serves to preserve positions (Ellerman 2005: 135–7). The consequence is difficulty for researchers to breach the edifice of Bank professional consensus alongside complaints of gate-keeping and a 'neo-liberal economic orthodoxy'.

Knowledge sharing

The World Bank itself has become a popular subject of research. This interest contributes to increased demand for the Bank's research product and access to its conferences and consultations.

A multiplicity of products, services and engagements are available for the researcher. In this regard, WBI is notable in its role of capacity building for researchers. 'Through courses, seminars, knowledge networks, communities of practice, and expert advice, WBI and its partners reach people all over the world, promoting the exchange of global and local knowledge' (for a critique see Ellerman 2005).[1] The WBI's 'knowledge sharing' function is complemented by other initiatives, such as the beleaguered Development Gateway (King and McGrath 2004) as well as the Global Development Network (GDN, Stone 2000) which promotes research collaborations between think tanks and policy institutes worldwide.

Notwithstanding evident interest among researchers on the World Bank, the social sciences are all too often divided by their disciplines. Economists usually do not 'speak' to sociologists; political scientists are often unfamiliar with the work of geographers and anthropologists. And so on. As a consequence, those examining the Bretton Woods institutions from different disciplinary perspectives might encounter few opportunities to interact. This assumption formed the basis of organizing a small conference for doctoral researchers and post-doctoral scholars. All the contributors to this volume were involved as paper presenters at the April 2005 'Research Bank on the World Bank' conference at the Central European University (CEU) in Budapest.[2] However, the idea for the conference originated at a steering committee meeting of the Researchers Alliance for Development (RAD) in June 2004. As detailed below, the genesis of this volume is entwined with the Bank's interaction with the research community, which forms part of its wider ambitions both for engagement with civil society, and in its incarnation as a 'knowledge bank'.

In mid-2003, the Researchers Alliance for Development began as a dialogue with the World Bank External Affairs Office in Paris. It is a loose association composed of representatives from academic institutions, research centres – including those research units based inside NGOs, bilateral agencies, trade unions and corporations – that have an active interest in development issues. As a network, it is weakly institutionalized. Given its present state of development, it is important not to overstate the influence or impact of this body. Nevertheless, it is an interesting experiment in dialogue designed to help propel academics into the orbit of the Bank. In March 2005, space for a web page for RAD was created on the World Bank's website. It states that:

> The RAD is an informal, action oriented and multidisciplinary network of researchers. Recognizing the engagement of academia in the global intellectual debate on development cooperation, the RAD aims to strengthen the interaction between the World Bank and the research community worldwide.
>
> (http://www.worldbank.org/rad)

The Secretariat is located at the World Bank's Vice Presidency for Europe, in Paris, and is coordinated by the Development Policy Dialogue Team. As is apparent, there is a close affinity between RAD and the Dialogue Team. This is most marked in relation to its input to ABCDE and the potential RAD may have in achieving better representation of development policy researchers from less developed countries and/or outside the mainstream of development research.

Its nascence has confounded some external observers who regard the exercise as evidence of Bank duplication. RAD competes with (or complements) similar initiatives supported by other units of the Bank. A question often asked of RAD is to what extent is it different from the Global Development Network (GDN). It is a crucial question for members of the RAD steering committee in order for RAD to raise funds and to carve out a distinctive identity and lay claim to 'added value' in its activities. With its genesis as a joint venture of WBI and DECRG, the GDN has also maintained close connections with the Bank when it became a NGO and in its recent reincarnation as an international organization (Angelescu and Squire 2006).

RAD and GDN operate on the same terrain. They speak to similar constituencies. But RAD seeks to do it differently. One objective of RAD – in common with GDN – is to facilitate the communication and utilization of research and analysis. Where the GDN is focused on research activities, RAD has taken a wider ambit within the educational terrain, seeking engagement with undergraduate and postgraduate teaching, and, to a lesser extent, high school students.

An early criticism of the RAD has been from members of the development community who view the relationship of RAD with the World Bank as being too close. For instance, at ABCDE 2005, one representative from a Nordic foreign ministry said RAD 'looks as if it is a "fan club" of the World Bank'.[3] The nature of the RAD–World Bank relationship and the related issues of independence and autonomy have presented a challenge for the steering committee. It has meant trying to direct observers' attention not to the formal ties between the network and the Bank, but to the content of activities, the nature of the dialogues where RAD 'can agree or disagree with the Bank's approaches and policies' and the space for critical thinking.[4]

Nevertheless, in some degree, this mode of research/policy interaction does entail a mutual implication in development discourse. Knowledge production and political economy are mutually constitutive and co-dependent. The policy priorities and reform initiatives of the past decade did not emerge perfectly formed from the boardroom of the executive directors or spontaneously combust in Wolfensohn's office. Instead, the policy rationales were hammered out through the many engagements of professionals working in government, NGOs, firms and Academe. They debated and disagreed at public events such as ABCDE and the Annual Meetings, as well as in closed expert consultations and private meetings.

'The battlefield of ideas'?

The ideas and policy proposals contained in development knowledge do not compete on a level playing field. It is not always the case that the most rigorous and scientifically compelling analysis will be selected on sound scholarly criteria to inform and shape policy. Another study known as CANDID – the creation, adoption, negation and distortion of ideas in development – noted that it is equally the case that political and other interests come into play to shape how ideas are instrumentalized into policy tools (Bøås and McNeill 2004). In other words, different kinds of knowledge are in constant contest.

> The World Bank might be viewed as a battlefield of knowledge with different arenas in which the contests are waged: internally among its staff ... externally with non Bank actors and those encountered in the course of implementing projects; and ... cross-border battles in which different sub-communities in the Bank are linked to different communities outside the Bank, and where the battles engage larger communities whose memberships transcend institutional boundaries.
>
> (Bebbington *et al.* 2004: 38)

Key to these battles and truces among coalitions are debates over the content of knowledge. That is, how knowledge is conceptualized or what constitutes knowledge. For example, several authors suggest that technocratic understandings of policy problems have often obfuscated the introduction of new operational objectives or decision-making processes that aim to diversify the Bank's knowledge base beyond economics and finance. In a more critical vein, one UNRISD report argues that international bureaucracies in general impose particular constraints on research agendas that result in subtle forms of self-censorship in tune with management objectives and operational necessities (Toye and Toye 2005). Or as has been said of the Bank: 'It is owned by the rich countries and it has operational policies that need to be defended' (Kanbur 2003: 263). Without impugning the professional standards of research staff, there are some well-publicized instances where the intellectual product of staff has generated official opprobrium within the Bank.

It is not only the content of knowledge – the theory, the questions, and the results – that are determinant in shaping development agendas and discourses. It is also *how* that knowledge is deployed, through *what* social and professional mechanisms knowledge is disseminated, *when* and with *whom* such knowledge is persuasive, and *why* certain interests align themselves with specific artefacts (such as a report) and development discourses.

The approach by which Bank knowledge and development ideas are diffused, communicated, or imposed has changed. Long gone are the 'one-size-fits-all, silver-bullet policy packages regularly prescribed for all countries' in favour of context-specific and more cross-disciplinary approaches to development (Wolfensohn and Bourguignon 2004: 4). From the late 1990s, the direction of debates inside the Bank has been to put developing countries in the 'driving seat' (Stiglitz 2000), which in practice meant tailoring policy prescriptions to the stated needs and demonstrated capacity of the borrower government.

Nevertheless, the Bank still acts as a disseminator of development knowledge and policy lessons as well as an arbiter of 'best practices' and 'international standards'. In doing so, the World Bank casts itself as a 'global public good' (GPG) provider. Knowledge has the properties of a public good but so does the dissemination of that knowledge. Diffusing knowledge about successful (and failed) policy experiments and innovations of one country can be of benefit to other countries. Such was the theme of the 1999 *World Development Report* (World Bank 1999). However, private interests in knowledge production can also be pursued under the guise of GPGs and can have the negative externality of promoting 'crony intellectualism' (Kapur 2003: 18, 23). That is, an in-breeding tendency within intellectual networks to contact, consult and invite to conferences those who speak the same technocratic language or come from similar academic backgrounds. There is also scepticism that IFI research can be considered a global public good 'when there is widespread perception that the research is in service of a particular line or policy stance to the exclusion of others' (Kanbur 2003: 260). In short, an increasingly perceptible complaint is that the 'theoretical core' of the Bank is not exposed to the same market forces and competitive pressures so frequently prescribed for their clients. Such exposure may enable LDC policy elites and intellectuals to better mediate the one-way diffusion of development knowledge and 'best practices' from the Bank.

Needless to say, the diffusion of development knowledge has been facilitated by advances in telecommunications. The World Bank has been a forerunner in maximizing the uses of the technology for knowledge sharing, as a tool of transparency as well as internal knowledge management (Laporte 2004). Research is also spread internationally through professional associations, think tanks, development consultants, research institutes and universities. In theory, governments are 'in the driving seat' and policy professionals adapt or synthesize 'global forms' of knowledge to suit their local circumstances where hybrid results or policy innovations possibly emerge. Potentially, there is also a promising reverse effect in the extent to which these organizations are able to feed 'grass-roots knowledge' back into international organizations and donor agencies. However, much criticism has been of the extent to which powerful institutional actors promote particular worldviews or normative frameworks and act as advocates of specific policy patterns. This is a line of critique with a couple of contributors to this volume who address the 'norm brokerage' or 'norm diffusion' activities of the Bank.

Nevertheless, national contexts do shape the success, or otherwise, of Bank projects. The contingent nature of diffusion and adoption of policy ideas 'on the ground' is taken up by Pía Riggirozzi in her analysis of World Bank advocacy of good governance reforms in Argentina. She argues that judicial reforms could only be accepted and adopted with local policy elite support. In Chapter 12 on Lebanon, Nisrine el Ghaziri also argues that the national context is important but that lack of capacity meant that the state was not able to effectively negotiate and take ownership of development projects. Rather than the uptake of policy ideas being mediated by local elites, she highlights how the Bank's normative advocacy of 'country ownership' has been undermined due to the lack of country policy capacity along with the competitive interests of international organizations and resulting battle of ideas between them.

The contest of knowledge does not of necessity lead to policy failure or the mire of institutional conflict. A number of chapters in this volume bring to the fore the prospects of both organizational learning as well as policy learning. Here, the emphasis is on cognition and the redefinition of collective interests on the basis of new knowledge and/or policy experience that affects the fundamental beliefs and ideas behind policy approaches. This has led to the kinds of policy shifts identified with the adoption of the CDF (see Gulrajani, this volume, Chapter 3), in approaches to fiscal decentralization (Tóth, this volume, Chapter 13) and pension policy (Ramesh, this volume, Chapter 6). Instead of a monolithic and unchanging organization, these contributions highlight how various parts of the World Bank Group are evolving, absorbing, resisting or adjusting in different ways.

The World Bank 'black box': methodologies and a map of the book

The objective of this book is to engage in a ten-year retrospective of some World Bank policy initiatives and departures. The novelty of this collection is that it focuses on the World Bank as an organization energized by its staff. In this regard, the book is able to address some of the legacies of the Wolfensohn era, and the changing role of the Bank in global governance as well as the domestic affairs of borrowing countries. As such, the contributors are able to make some observations about the Bank that Wolfowitz inherited in mid-2005 as the new president and the challenges his team have had to face.

The contributors highlight the origins, influence and implications of a variety of policy developments during the last decade. They demonstrate how the Bank's autonomy and involvement in an ever-widening array of development concerns have expanded and deepened its interactions with external actors. In doing so, they each illustrate the extent to which the Bank's walls are increasingly permeable, allowing ideas and interests to flow between external interest groups and internal departments. This means it is becoming difficult to identify the original source of particular policy initiatives within the Bank, as a new initiative can originate from a multitude of both internal and external sources.

However, the Bank is by no means a melting pot of development thinking, in which ideas and policy solutions brought to the Bank's attention are given equal salience. Rather, the legitimacy and influence that they acquire within the Bank are mediated by its organizational structure, the professional culture that shapes the behaviour of staff and interactions between them, and the ease by which they can be operationalized in the Bank's bureaucratic decision-making procedures in the context of its programmes and projects. Therefore, even in an ideal scenario, and perhaps an unlikely one, in which the borrower has diagnosed a particular development problem through a multi-stakeholder dialogue and approached the Bank for funding to implement a corrective programme to which it is fully committed, the internal dynamics within the Bank still play a very influential role in determining the parameters of the Bank's intervention and the ultimate use of its funds.

To identify the origins and impacts of policy change, it is necessary to understand the complexity of these internal dynamics, the interface between them and the myriad of external actors that seek to influence it. In many cases this requires 'getting inside' the Bank and understanding policy changes through the eyes of those shaping them or directly affected by them (Xu and Weller 2004). Such perspectives help us better understand the influence or relative significance of broader development debates on internal policy discussions, which may be misrepresented in the Bank's external communications. Regarding the development discourses on social capital, Bebbington *et al.* argue that the wealth of analytical publications has potentially contributed to a problem of 'selection bias' with a neglect of operational positions that are less effectively documented and captured as codified knowledge (Bebbington *et al.* 2004: 45). As a result, there has been a tendency among outside researchers who have 'overstated the operational significance of these debates, understated the political significance of actual programmatic changes stemming from them, and miss-specified the causal relationships in their production' (2004: 34).

Focusing on what happens inside the organization brings greater attention to human agency and intentionality, as well as the manner in which new practices and knowledge emerge inside the Bank (Xu and Weller 2004). An actor-oriented focus on the role of task managers, interpersonal networks, leadership appointments and professional promotions, is extremely useful in bringing into sharp relief a much neglected feature of development discourses: the social practices and institutional politics involved in the production and dissemination of such discourses. As noted, participant observation is difficult to achieve. There are also potential pitfalls if internal access and participation in Bank activities is acquired. That is, there are tendencies towards self-legitimation or self-censorship, selective readings of institutional debates or over-inflation of the role and relevance of certain Bank projects or personalities. Such tendencies might occur, for instance, in the case of our discussion of RAD earlier in this introduction.

Outside researchers are often reliant upon the texts – reports, websites, speeches, etc. – produced by the Bank. While these remain important texts for deciphering official policy positions and understanding the institution's public responsibilities, they are not useful in uncovering the more informal operational debates that regularly take place within the Bank. However, 'getting inside' the World Bank is not easy for the researcher. It requires more of an anthropological approach – and often times, a considerable investment of time and resources – of engagement at the 'coal face'. That is, acquiring data that may be gleaned from interviews, participation in conferences, correspondence or periods resident in Washington DC or country offices.

With that said, the 'methodological position of the observer' is an important consideration to take into account, whether the researcher is commenting from inside or outside the Bank. It must be noted that many within the Bank are very adept at 'auto critique' of themselves and the institution that employs them. However, it is equally the case that those engaging in external critiques 'see' dynamics that those inside cannot due to their sheer proximity to the details of these debates.

By including both internal and external perspectives, this book is a valuable contribution to our understanding of the World Bank as an organization, as it provides insights into why some ideas or policy initiatives emerge and rise to prominence, while others are cast aside or fail in their implementation. Looking at its internal features opens up the 'black box' of the Bank and distinguishes this volume from others that look at the World Bank as a cohesive organization projecting a unified set of ideas. These are often too simplistic, and overestimate the extent to which the ideas originate within the Bank, and not outside it (see also Toye and Toye 2005: 6).

The book is organized into two parts, each of which addresses one piece of the larger puzzle of how a particular understanding of development becomes institutionalized in the Bank's operations, informs policy change and produces identifiable change on the ground. Part I contains a set of chapters written by authors who have sought to uncover how policy ideas or initiatives, even those that are products of external pressures, are shaped by the Bank's organizational structure, the professional norms that guide staff behaviour, and the social structure and bureaucratic procedures that mediate interactions between them. The research which sheds light on how the Bank functions as a complex organization is based on extensive contextual analysis of Bank publications and other external communications, and in many cases in-depth interviews with Bank staff who shaped or were affected by the policy changes in question.

'Inside' the black box

As with most large bureaucracies, the World Bank does have inertia present in its ranks that affects the extent and pace of organizational change, as entrenched interests rally around preserving the status quo to defend their political influence (Weaver and Leiteritz 2005). However, compared to other international organizations, the Bank can be quite dynamic, as illustrated by Vetterlein in her comparison of the Bank and the International Monetary Fund (this volume, Chapter 7). Drawing on interviews with staff on the nature of policy innovation inside their respective organizations, she provides a description of the organizational personality of the Bank and identifies how it functions as a filter through which new knowledge enters the organization. She finds that the Bank's organizational personality is much more receptive to taking on a broader development agenda, and illustrates how its organizational structure depends less on hierarchically organized decision-making, which provides more opportunities for policy initiatives to emerge from within.

Vetterlein also observes that its structure and professional culture are more conducive to engaging deeply with policy problems, by producing research, disseminating knowledge and framing policy discussions. As such, it is a powerful diffuser of norms. But what determines the success or failure of particular norms in gaining acceptance within the Bank? In this regard, McNeill and St Clair (Chapter 2) provide an insightful explanation of the relative marginalization of 'human rights-based approaches' to understanding poverty and the role of development agencies within the Bank. Drawing on a careful analysis of its flagship publications and the limited influence of those promoting human rights internally, they argue that the distinctly technocratic and economistic conception of development that characterizes the Bank's understanding of poverty creates moral distance between the Bank and those who should benefit from its funds, and prevents it from reflecting on the ethical dimension of its own activities and the responsibilities for development problems it may itself bear.

The pervasiveness of the Bank's organizational culture, which is derived from the professional expertise of its staff and the procedural focus of its interventions, is a theme that surfaces in many chapters. For example, Gulrajani (Chapter 3) takes the reader inside two of the Bank's country offices and observes that the institutionalization of the CDF process can be read as the outcome of a discursive clash between technocratic and socio-political logics. Drawing on in-depth interviews with Bank staff, she finds that the CDF proved difficult to implement in the case of Bolivia, because it overtly challenged centralized accountability structures and the strong adherence to disbursement indicators in its country office. In contrast, the process was far smoother in the case of its country office in Vietnam, because the socio-political logic embedded in the CDF did not directly threaten the integrity of its sectoral activities and interests, antagonize the government over political reform, or brandish the Bank's powers of coercion.

Gulrajani's illustrative discussion identifies how the relative influence of certain policy ideas or initiatives is not necessarily driven by the extent to which they respond more effectively to particular development challenges, but rather, whether they happen to conform with the normative and political predispositions of staff or borrowers. Reaching a similar conclusion, Wright (Chapter 4) identifies the impetus of a strategic initiative at the IFC that responded to and sought to rectify the problematic introduction of the environmental and social safeguard policies in its investment practices. Based on interviews with the senior executives that put it together and oversaw its implementation, he argues that the Sustainability Initiative, and the associated push for a more commercial understanding of environmental and social issues, was primarily driven by a need to gain greater acceptance for the IFC's new-found environmental and social mission among internal investment staff and its private sector clients.

Very often, research reveals how the need for legitimacy and credibility shapes many policy processes. This is particularly the case for policy areas that attract the critical attention of NGOs, who often look to the Bank's policy revision processes as a litmus test for its commitment to accountability, transparency, and inclusive decision-making. However, more inclusive and transparent decision-making inevitably means the Bank cedes some control of the decision-making processes in return for enhanced legitimacy. In some cases, this trade-off seems to be carefully and deliberately managed. In Chapter 5, Flejzor analyses the internal dynamics that shaped the creation of a new forest strategy and the revision of the Bank's forestry policy in the 1990s. She finds that the regional stakeholder consultations conducted as part of the former not only enhanced the legitimacy of the new strategy, they also led to significantly new outputs in both the strategy and policy documents. She also uncovered how the revision of the operational policy was conducted with much more centralized control than the formation of the strategy, in part because it would have greater implications for the Bank's forest sector work.

In an interesting parallel to Flejzor, Ramesh (Chapter 6) also considers the factors that drove policy innovation in a particular area of the Bank's work. In his analysis of the evolution of the Bank's views on pension reform, Ramesh attributes changes in policy recommendations to an internal learning process in which new economic realities in developing countries undermined the legitimacy and appropriateness of previous policy prescriptions and caused the Bank to reconsider its policy positions. By reviewing the main Bank publications on pension reform, Ramesh argues that for the Bank to retain its lead position relative to other international organizations, it was forced to respond to the flaws detected in its proposals and revise its views accordingly.

Confronting the 'outside'

The first part of the book contains chapters that analyse the Bank's organizational structure, professional culture and leadership to understand how various parts of the World Bank interpret, absorb and engage with external pressures or events. In turn, the second set of chapters considers the impact of the Bank's financial resources, technical expertise and policy prescriptions on particular development contexts or geographic regions. This includes various critical assessments of new policy initiatives introduced during the Wolfensohn presidency, in some cases by him personally.

The authors who reflect on these developments have sought to place the ideas, norms and rationales behind them in a historical perspective, considering the extent to which they extend or break with previous practice. In addition, some of these analyse the interface between the Bank's professionalized development expertise and local sources of knowledge, thereby going beyond the a-contextual nature of much of the research that discusses the impact of the Bank's operational policies and broader initiatives. Collectively, they therefore provide an overall assessment of the extent to which the recent decade was truly transformative, or whether the normative and ideological aspects of previous policy initiatives have been retained and simply been given another name.

In cases where the Bank's activities in a particular policy area indeed underwent a transformation, it was often due to extensive, concerted pressure from external actors who possessed some kind of leverage over the Bank. Apart from powerful shareholders, the professionalized NGOs that routinely descend on the Bank's headquarters for consultation meetings and staged protests are perhaps the most influential of its external stakeholders. In her chapter on the IFC, Park (Chapter 9) illustrates they were able to push through extensive environmental and social reforms by processes of direct and indirect socialization. In a comparison with MIGA, she notes that the IFC proved much more susceptible to integrating sustainable development into its activities.

In contrast, authors covering other thematic areas found that despite the numerous new policy initiatives launched by the Bank in the last decade, the normative and ideological foundation of its development assistance has not changed dramatically. For example, Tan (Chapter 8) provides an insightful contextual analysis of the poverty reduction strategies (PRS), perhaps the most influential and heralded policy initiative during the past decade. By placing the policy initiative in a historical perspective, she argues that instead of reflecting a clean break with the underlying notions of structural adjustment programmes, the poverty reduction strategy papers (PRSPs) could in fact only be operationalized as a result of the regulatory precedents set by them. By reflecting on its impact on state construction in developing countries, she finds that the new architecture of aid, of which the PRSPs are an integral part, extends rather than redresses the asymmetric power relationship between donors and beneficiaries of their funds.

In a similar vein, Hatcher (Chapter 10) reflects on the underlying normative perspectives of the Bank's new development paradigm, which is meant to embrace holistic, participatory and country-driven development. By offering a critical perspective on the Bank's interventions in developing countries, she finds that since the Bank still furthers a distinctly technocratic approach to governance, its growing enthusiasm for civil society has in fact had the perverse effect of restrictively redefining social and economic rights and depoliticizing the notion of citizenship in countries undergoing political and economic reform.

Some of these observations and arguments are vindicated in the chapters that discuss the Bank's interventions into country contexts. For example, in her analysis of donor-supported public administrative reforms in Lebanon in the 1990s, el Ghaziri (Chapter 12) illustrates how the Bank's enthusiasm for rolling back the state, and its desire to push through these reforms, was not diminished by the fact that the Lebanese public sector was in considerable disarray after more than a decade of civil war. Furthermore, she finds that while the broad set of public sector reforms aimed at reducing the cost of central government were first presented by the government in a Statement on Administrative Reform, they were in fact drafted by World Bank officials.

The Lebanese case revealed the extent to which the Bank often seeks out and comes to rely on the support of loyal domestic allies in influential political positions to attain and retain domestic consent for its reform agendas. In an interesting parallel, Riggirozzi (Chapter 11) explores the role of the World Bank in two governance reforms carried out in Argentina since the mid-1990s seeking to enact judicial reform and establish anti-corruption policies. On the basis of these two cases, she concludes that despite its financial and knowledge leverage, the World Bank could not implement its programmes on its own. Rather, she argues, policy change emerged out of the relations between certain actors and World Bank staff, and the integration of contesting impulses into a broader consensus.

In other cases, the implementation of the Bank's reform prescriptions was adjusted over time to local political contexts. Tóth (Chapter 13) provides an analysis of the intellectual forces that influenced the Bank's fiscal decentralization agenda in transitional economies in Central and Eastern Europe during the 1990s. She argues that, upon discovering the constraints imposed on its reform programme by local political realities, the Bank's policy on fiscal decentralization underwent a 'maturation process' in which, increasingly, its policy experts realized the political sensitivity of intergovernmental fiscal regimes and the need to adapt them to changing local circumstances. Such implementation difficulties suggest that policy recommendations that do not find any adherents for several years are not necessarily doomed to failure. What does not work today may work well tomorrow.

Politics as the coin of development

'Politics is the art of the possible', von Bismarck famously remarked. The same can be said about the Bank's difficult engagement with development. Collectively, these chapters reinforce the notion that increasingly, development thinking is collectively produced. New norms of public consultation dictate that major policy revisions are considered illegitimate unless stakeholders have been given opportunities to voice their concerns and comment on preliminary drafts. This has put pressure on development experts to consider and address the environmental and social costs of their economic policy prescriptions.

In practice, the increasingly complex policy process means development assistance is not apolitical, and the implementation of individual programmes and projects is often a product of an intensely political process in which the policy prescriptions and intervention targets set by the Bank are negotiated and transformed to fit local realities. Apart from building alliances with local political forces, the Bank may also have to fend off competition from other donors as well in order to continue exercising influence over institutional reforms. Finally, the widening and deepening of engagements with the scientific community, and the inter-discursive struggles that result, will see the Bank's policy prescriptions and knowledge increasingly contested and challenged. It will be a matter for future reflection whether or not research from outside the reaches of the Bank promotes critical dialogue and policy engagement or whether it valorizes the Bank's intellectual currency.

Notes

1 WBI at a glance: http://web.worldbank.org/WBSITE/EXTERNAL/WBI/0,content
   MDK:20097853~menuPK:204763~pagePK:209023~piPK:207535~theSitePK:213799
   9,00.html

2 This conference was organized by the Centre for Policy Studies at CEU with support from the European Commission (through its Marie Curie Actions), the Centre for the Study of Globalisation and Regionalisation at the University of Warwick, and the External Affairs Department of the World Bank.
3 Statement made in confidence at the Annual Bank Conference on Development Economics in Amsterdam, Monday 23 May 2005.
4 Email correspondence to RAD steering committee, 25 May 2005.

References

Angelescu, R. and Squire, L. (2006) 'Local Research, Global Governance: A Challenge for Institutional Design', *Global Governance* 12(1), pp. 21–30 forthcoming.

Ascher, W. (1983) 'New Development Approaches and the Adaptability of International Agencies: The Case of the World Bank', *International Organisation* 37(3), 415–39.

Barnett, M. N. and Finnemore, M. (1999) 'The Politics, Power and Pathologies of International Organizations', *International Organization* 53(4), 699–732.

Bebbington, A., Guggenheim, S., Olsen, E. and Woolcock, M. (2004) 'Exploring Social Capital Debates at the World Bank', *Journal of Development Studies* 40(5), 33–64.

Bøås, M. and McNeill, D. (2004) 'Introduction', in Bøås, M. and McNeill, D. (eds) *Global Institutions and Development: Framing the World*, London: Routledge.

Buira, A. (ed.) (2003) *Challenges to the World Bank and IMF*, London: Anthem Press.

Burnside, C. and Dollar, D. (1997) 'Aid, Policies and Growth', Policy Research Working Paper 1777, Washington DC: World Bank.

Danaher, K. (ed.) (1994) *50 Years is Enough: The Case Against the World Bank and the International Monetary Fund*, USA: Global Exchange.

Davis, G. (2004) 'A History of the Social Development Network in the World Bank 1973–2002', *Social Development Paper* 56, Washington DC: World Bank.

Dethier, J-J. (2005) 'Sustainable Growth and Equity in Developing Countries: An Overview of Research at the World Bank', presentation to the conference, 'Research Bank on the World Bank', Center for Policy Studies, Central European University, Hungary, 1–2 April.

EDF (2005) *Retreat from the Safeguard Policies – Recent Trends Undermining Social and Environmental Accountability at the World Bank*, prepared by Shannon Lawrence (Environmental Defense), in collaboration with Peter Bosshard (International Rivers Network), Bruce Jenkins (Bank Information Center), Jen Kalafut (Bank Information Center), Anne Perrault (Center for International Environmental Law), Andrea Durbin (Environmental Defense), and Suzanne Hunt (Environmental Defense), January 2005.

Einhorn, J. (2001) 'The World Bank's Mission Creep', *Foreign Affairs* 80(5), 22–35.

——(2006) 'Reforming the World Bank', *Foreign Affairs* 85(1), 17–22.

Ellerman, D. (2005) *Helping People Help Themselves: From the World Bank to an Alternative Philosophy of Development Assistance*, Ann Arbor MI: University of Michigan Press.

Gilbert, C. L. and Vines, D. (eds) (2000) *The World Bank: Structure and Policies*, Cambridge: Cambridge University Press.

Goldman, M. (2005) *Imperial Nature: the World Bank and Struggles for Social Justice in the Age of Globalization*, New Haven CT and London: Yale University Press.

Gutner, T. (2005) 'World Bank Environmental Reform: Revisiting Lessons from Agency Theory', *International Organization* 59, 773–83.

Harrison, G. (2004) *The World Bank and Africa: the Construction of Governance States*, London and New York: Routledge.

IFIAC (International Financial Institutions Advisory Commission or Meltzer Commission Report) (2000) 'Final Report and Transcripts of Meetings and Hearings', Washington DC: http://phantom-x.gsia.cmu.edu/IFIAC

Kanbur, R. (2003) 'International Financial Institutions and International Public Goods: Operational Implications for the World Bank', in A. Buira (ed.) *Challenges to the World Bank and IMF*, London: Anthem Press.

Kapur, D. (2003) 'Do As I Say Not As I Do: A Critique of the G-7 Proposals on "Reforming" the World Bank', unpublished paper prepared for the G-24.

Keck, M. E. and Sikkink, K. (1999) 'Transnational Advocacy Networks in International and Regional Politics', *International Social Science Journal* 51, 89–101.

King, K. and McGrath, S. (2004) *Knowledge for Development: Comparing British, Japanese, Swedish and World Bank Aid*, London: Zed Books.

Laporte, B. (2004) 'Knowledge Sharing at the World Bank: The Fad That Would Not Go Aaway', reproduced from *Knowledge Management Magazine* (Dec./Jan.) at: http://siteresources.worldbank.org/WBI/Resources/TheFadthatWouldNotGoAway.pdf

Mallaby, S. (2005) *The World's Banker*, New Haven CT: Yale University Press.

Miller-Adams, M. (1999) *The World Bank: New Agendas in a Changing World*, London: Routledge.

Nielson, D. J. and Tierney, M. L. (2003) 'Delegation to International Organizations: Agency Theory and World Bank Environmental Reform', *International Organization* 57, 241–76.

——(2005) 'Theory, Data, and Hypothesis Testing: World Bank Environmental Reform Redux', *International Organization* 59, 785–800.

OED (World Bank Operations Evaluation Department) (2004) *Addressing the Challenges of Globalization: An Independent Evaluation of the World Bank's Approach to Global Programs*, Washington DC: International Bank for Reconstruction and Development.

Pincus, J. R. and Winters, J. A. (eds) (2002) *Reinventing the World Bank*, Ithaca NY: Cornell University Press.

Rich, B. (2002) 'The World Bank Under James Wolfensohn', in Pincus, J. R. and Winters, J. A. (eds) *Reinventing the World Bank*, Ithaca NY: Cornell University Press.

Ritzen, J. (2005) *A Chance for the World Bank*, London: Anthem Press.

Stiglitz, J. (2000) 'Scan Globally, Reinvent Locally: Knowledge Infrastructure and the Localization of Knowledge', in Stone, D. (ed.) *Banking on Knowledge: The Genesis of the Global Development Network*, London: Routledge.

Stone, D. (ed.) (2000) *Banking on Knowledge: The Genesis of the Global Development Network*, London: Routledge.

Toye, J. and Toye, R. (2005) *The World Bank as a Knowledge Agency*, Programme Paper no. 11, November, UNRISD.

Wade, R. (1990) *Governing the Market*, Princeton NJ: Princeton University Press.

——(2002) 'US Hegemony and the World Bank: The Fight over People and Ideas', *Review of International Political Economy* 9(2), 215–43.

Weaver, C. E. and Leiteritz, R. J. (2005) 'Our Poverty is a World Full of Dreams: Reforming the World Bank', *Global Governance* 11(3), 369–88.

Wolfensohn, J. and Bourguignon, F. (2004) *Development and Poverty Reduction: Looking Back, Looking Ahead*, Washington DC: World Bank.

Woods, N. (2006) *The Globalizers: The IMF, the World Bank and Their Borrowers*, Ithaca NY and London: Cornell University Press.

World Bank (1998) *Assessing Aid: What Works, What Doesn't, And Why?*, Washington DC: World Bank.

——(1999) *Knowledge for Development: World Development Report 1998/99*, New York: Oxford University Press.

Xu Yi-Chong and Weller, Patrick (2004) *The Governance of World Trade: International Civil Servants and the GATT/WTO*, Cheltenham: Edward Elgar.

Part I

Policy change inside 'the black box'

2 Development ethics and human rights as the basis for global poverty reduction

The case of the World Bank

Desmond McNeill and
Asunción Lera St Clair[1]

Introduction

> It is justice, not charity, that is wanting in the world.
>
> (Mary Wollstonecraft)

Reducing poverty is the overarching goal of the main development agencies, as reflected in the Millennium Development Goals (MDGs). Yet progress has so far been slow and there are indications that the MDGs are far from being accomplished in the next decade (Vandemoortele 2003; UNDP 2003). No matter how poverty is defined and measured, the statistics indicate an appalling situation: millions of people live in subhuman conditions and many die of easily preventable causes. A focus on poverty represents a welcome return to the central objective of development. In parallel with this there has been, in recent years, a return to fundamental ethical issues: asking not only 'how' but also 'why' development must be provided. In the past, the motives for giving aid have tended to be a mixture of charity and self-interest; and the procedures for aid allocation have been based mainly on technical and economic considerations. An ethics-based approach may challenge both the 'why' and the 'how' of development assistance, and indeed the appropriateness of many approaches underpinning aid to the South.

In recent years, it has been increasingly argued that severe poverty is a violation of human rights. This may come to be accepted by the international community; but many hundreds of millions will continue to live in life-threatening poverty. To attack severe poverty effectively, this idea must be complemented by another: that there are specific agents who are violating other persons' specific human right not to be poor. While ethical language is taking root among development aid actors, and increasingly becoming part of proposals for global governance, debate about responsibilities for poverty is minimal (but see Held 2004; Pogge 2006; Pogge and Føllesdal 2005; and the Ethical Globalization initiative at http://www.eginitiative.org/). The recent report by the International Council on Human Rights Policy (2003), *Duties Sans Frontières: Human Rights and Global Social Justice*, is a welcome exception to much academic and policy work.

Rather than taking a specific moral theory of responsibility as the basis for formulating a normative distribution of responsibilities, our aim is to examine empirically what practices of responsibility are occurring in development agencies and among their staff. We are concerned to investigate actual 'practices of responsibility', for it is through these, rather than stated moral claims, that moral agency, blame for harms, and ascriptions of obligations, are ascribed or avoided.

Ascribing responsibility is a highly complex and controversial issue that entails not only the application of ethical values to practical life but also requires addressing the distribution of power, authority and social positions (Smiley 1992). Moral responsibility is, as Bauman argues, a sphere of culture (Bauman 1973), arguably a sphere of organizational culture also. In addition, practices of responsibility produce and reproduce moral behaviour; practices of responsibility are then not only expressions of morality, but prescriptions of what ought to be the distribution of moral labour (Walker 1998). Identifying actual practices of responsibility may be a first step to initiate an open dialogue on a fair and appropriate distribution of responsibilities for the eradication of poverty in expert institutions and people working for the reduction of poverty.

In brief, therefore, this chapter is concerned with which notions of responsibility for the eradication of poverty are to be found among global institutions; and more particularly (in this instance) the World Bank. The Bank may be described as an expert institution – indeed the most influential in the world in matters of development and poverty reduction. This is because of its research capacities, its power to formulate what are or are not the proper ways to understand poverty reduction and development, to disseminate ideas and policy recommendations, and to create communities of experts (St Clair 2006b).

Linking the why and how of aid through practices of responsibility

Over a thirty-year period, the policy debate concerning poverty and human rights among development actors moved from a concern with basic needs (ILO 1976; Streeten *et al.* 1981; ul Haq 1976), to the notion of human development, much influenced by the work of Amartya Sen (1999). The process by which the earlier ideas became successively adopted and refined by development ethicists is analysed by Alkire (2002); Crocker (forthcoming); Doyal and Gough (1991) and Gasper (2004). To accept the notion of human development implies defining the 'essentials' without which people cannot exercise free agency, that is, freedom to choose to lead the lives they wish or have reason to value (various Human Development Reports – HDRs; World Bank 2001; Sen 1999). Under this interpretation, poverty refers to the lack of a core of human needs that are necessary conditions for the exercise of free agency. But the question remains, who has responsibility when the basic core needs of people are not satisfied?

A radical claim, addressing poverty as a human rights violation, is found in the work of Thomas Pogge (2002, 2004, 2006). According to this view, a focus on needs or basic social services is insufficient. Their provision addresses the symptoms of poverty but often not the forces that produce and aggravate severe poverty in the first place. Human rights add a political force to the protection of needs while calling for an adequate ascription of responsibilities for their protection and fulfilment. With few exceptions (Crocker forthcoming; Pogge 2006; Pogge and Føllesdal 2005), there is at present little research addressing responsibilities for the economic, social, and political processes that cause poverty – internationally as well as nationally. Yet development agencies are amongst the most important actors in these processes. They are 'agents' whose actions have substantial consequences for other groups. They are organizations whose policy recommendations and development programmes shape the socio-economic structures of most developing countries and thus affect the life chances of millions of people. In their attempts to mainstream concerns for rights, however, development agents generally avoid discussing the structural causes and social processes of impoverishment that cause human rights violations to occur. And they rarely engage in self-reflection as to how they themselves may be related to such outcomes, or how ethical reflection may help in clarifying their role. We regard this as not only logically flawed but – as a practice of responsibility that may be characterized as avoidance – perhaps also morally flawed.

Development ethics

The field of development ethics leads us to go beyond economics, and focus on human beings and human well-being. It focuses our attention towards 'the types, distribution and significance of the costs and gains from major socio-economic change, and at value-conscious ways of thinking about and choosing between alternative paths' (Gasper 2004: xi). Most ethical theories consider extreme poverty as dispossessing human beings of their dignity. Rights provide one of the best ways to 'recognise and respect human dignity and to counteract pure power, whether physical, market or other power' (Gasper 2004: 226). An ethics-based understanding of the 'why' of development aid reinforces common moral intuitions regarding duties to help those in need, especially the most vulnerable. And it leads us to focus on the moral and political agency of both givers and recipients of aid, whether this agency is personal or institutional. We favour the view that much severe poverty today may be viewed as a violation of human rights, traceable to national and global schemes of social institutions which the non-poor both support and benefit from (Farmer 2003; Pogge 2002).

Attributions of harm, however, and ascriptions of past and forward-looking responsibility to particular global institutions, tend to be dismissed, whether because of the lack of clear causal connections, the difficulties in identifying actors, or the complexity of the moral analysis. Even though the incidence and depth of poverty in the world today violates the moral intuitions of most people, a social construction of moral distance is created; a distance that hinders moral awareness and ethical reflection. The creating of such distance should not be seen as an explicit choice, which implies that the people concerned are morally 'bad' (although they may be). It is a more implicit, unquestioned phenomenon, which is supported by technocratic and economistic views of development. In recent 'human rights-based approaches' favoured by development agencies, lawyers are also becoming involved. It may transpire that legalistic views of development also encourage moral distance.

In earlier research, we have investigated the ways in which ideas are taken, used and transformed by multilateral organizations (Bøås and McNeill 2004; St Clair 2004, 2006a, 2006b). We have argued that ideas are often drained of their analytical and political potency. For example, in the World Bank the concept of social capital becomes an expression of the cognitive values of the dominant discipline – economics. Ideas are thus often transformed into notions that do not challenge dominant knowledge and ideologies. The same may occur with responsibilities and ascription of blame for harms and obligations. These may end up distorted or transformed in ways that produce and reproduce moral distance and avoidance of responsibility. Blame for harms and forward-looking obligations to help, may thus be displaced outside their moral agency (in the case of individuals), outside their field of work (in the case of institutions) and outside the scope of knowledge. In our past work we also argued that multilateral agencies are partly social constructions (Bøås and McNeill 2003), and that their ideas co-produce both global knowledge and global politics (St Clair 2006a). We argue now that practices of responsibility within these organizations are also partially socially constructed and partly related to the political and economic power of both individuals and the institutions themselves. They are embedded in social institutions; embedded in the processes of formulating knowledge for development and poverty reduction. There is a risk that human rights mainstreaming by development agents will remain a cosmetic change rather than a recasting of the why and how of aid. A rather different risk is that the morally underpinned language of rights – already seen by some as a new moral imperialism – may be captured by powerful individuals and institutions to promote their own interests.

The ascription of responsibilities: values and contexts

Judgements of responsibility are not only expressions of values being held by people or defended by institutions, but also practices. For some, morality itself is a human practice embodied in social forms of life where power, authority and positions in society matter as much as values (Walker 1998). This does not imply a moral relativist position, merely that contexts matter; the specification of human rights will vary according to time and space. It is important to pay attention to what is the domain of ethical consideration in assessing personal, collective and institutional responsibility. As Onora O'Neill argues, the domain of ethical consideration pertinent for a given context can be fixed by considering the assumptions people make about the agency of others, whose lives they take to be connected to their own (1996). We add that such an argument applies to institutions as well. Iris Young's (2004) treatment of political responsibility points in a similar direction. Assigning responsibilities for structural injustice entails questioning the background conditions that common ascriptions of blame and future obligations assume as normal. Our task is to examine what leads the staff of a complex organization dealing with poverty reduction (such as the World Bank) to form opinions about the moral agency of others, and to relate this to their role as experts and as staff of the institution in question.

Practices of responsibility are not only ascriptions of moral agency, but may also be denials of moral agency. Such denial may be institutional or collective as well as individual. Ascription or denial of responsibility is a highly difficult matter that often has to do with 'negotiating' diverse interpretations of facts and events more than with disagreements about values. Ascribing responsibility is partly a negotiation about harms, obligations, blame and credit related to the actions of both individuals and institutions, and often related to positions and tasks individuals hold or perform within institutions (French 1992; Goodin 1985). To ascribe interpersonal responsibility is for

> some person to identify another person as the cause of a harmful or untoward event, because of some action that was performed by that other person, and in light of the fact that the person that was identified occupied a certain type of position or role or station and cannot support an acceptable defence, justification, or excuse for the action.
>
> (French 1991)

Actions could also refer to acts of omission, when people fail to do something that could have avoided harm. But this is a far more complicated case to make. Institutional responsibility is a hybrid case where both individuals and collectives are held responsible. Ascribing political responsibilities is related to *different ways to reason about actions in relation to injustices*, for instance reasoning derived or related to the actual power or privilege agents may have, or related to the connections they may hold with the injustice (Young 2004).

Most theories of responsibility agree that the tasks or roles one may perform are among the most important determinants of responsibilities for one's actions. The same argument holds for organizations. In fact, most ethical codes, common in business organizations but also others, relate to tasks and roles: what it is that people are expected to do, or to refrain from doing. However, such a 'responsibility logic' tends to be ignored in the case of global institutions. Here sources of accountability are more related to (formal and informal) mechanisms and rules of action; or even resolved by reference to legal articles of agreement, no matter how little relevant these may be in relation to the tasks and roles actually performed.

Thus, we view individual and institutional practices of responsibility also as discursive – manifested in the ideas and concepts used by these actors, and their capacity to refer or deny moral agency in their accounts of what is relevant knowledge for reducing poverty. Our earlier work tells us that development agents like the World Bank or UNDP have accepted many of the values enshrined in the Universal Declaration of Human Rights, and view their work – as organizations – as protecting and promoting rights. Our sense is that, personally, many of the individuals working for these organizations would feel uneasy to work for an institution that violates or ignores human rights. What seems to happen is not a denial of the values promoted by human rights, but a denial or distancing of the institutional roles and personal roles (as experts and practitioners) in relation to the forces producing and perpetuating poverty. The result is moral distance and not an environment conducive to awareness, one that would acknowledge and thus abide by obligations or responsibilities.

Yet moral distance is socially created. Social distance allows for a 'diffusion of responsibility'; for a de-legitimization of moral motives (Bauman 1973). Such a view is not a theoretical construct one takes lightly, but a very basic issue with far-reaching consequences. This is the same argument made by Jonathan Glover in his attempt to explain the moral distance that permitted the biggest moral atrocities of the twentieth century (Glover 2001). An understanding of the complex ways in which moral principles interact with everyday life is, Glover reminds us, precisely *the way* to understand a 'side of human nature often left in darkness'.

Ascription of responsibility is then not only about a straightforward application of moral values, but something that society manipulates, exploits or redirects (Bauman 1973; Glover 2001).[2] And we must understand society here in broad terms, including social institutions such as multilateral development agencies. Bauman's analysis of moral responsibility refers to an extreme case, the ways in which the Nazis were able to create the social distance that allowed them to perform the most heinous crimes without compromising their moral values. But the point is a general one. By looking only at ethical principles as abstract forms of theorizing about human nature, societies and institutions, we are left in the dark, as Glover argues, as to why some practices that most cultures and peoples deem unethical and unacceptable, are repeatedly occurring across history. This argument applies, we argue, to the pervasive poverty that millions of human beings suffer across the globe, including the poverty of citizens in advanced economies.

What is important is not explicit ethical language, but how ethical values are imbued in ideas and embedded in institutions in ways that frame the choices they make. Some development actors seek to bridge their moral distance from the poor through explicit value analysis and the use of ideas with imbued moral values that have eventually become embedded in the organizational culture: for example the UNDP's notion of human development (St Clair 2004). Often the ethical language or stated ethical principles defended by development agencies are disconnected from their discourse and practice. In the same way that we found that potentially path-breaking ideas are often drained of their political impact, largely because multilateral development agencies have interpreted their task as mostly technical and apolitical, we may see that responsibilities are avoided and social distance constructed by interpreting tasks, social positions or descriptions of events and roles, in technocratic and apolitical ways. If left unchallenged, such practices perpetuate the questionable belief that development actors are already performing their obligations, that they are not the cause of poverty nor do they harm the poor or support institutions and individuals that do harm them; a picture of *the facts* that requires further investigation and that prevents open debate about responsibility ascription.

Bringing in ethics not only introduces a new intellectual inspiration, it also introduces the normative dimension in a far more explicit form than in our earlier CANDID[3] analysis of how institutions incorporate new impulses. Here, it was important to take account of *inter* and *intra* institutional competition and collaboration, and to examine how institutions and divisions within institutions maintain their different 'identities'. The dilemma for the individual in such circumstances is seen to be how to relate to two, contrasted peer groups: of academics and practitioners. When ethics is explicitly included, the dilemma for the individual becomes still further complicated – since he or she may feel it not only appropriate but even necessary that policy also reflect their own personal ethical convictions.

It is important, we argue, to investigate what mechanisms allow staff of these agencies and the institutions themselves to approach or to distance themselves from obligations towards poverty. What allows them to be both morally engaged but also detached in the face of widespread, de-humanizing poverty? What types of moral, political and technocratic substitutions permit such detachment and how do these translate into interpreting or accounting for facts in particular ways? What determines the actual responsibility practices of staff in the multilateral organizations who work on poverty? How does the institutional framework in which people work make a difference?

Answers to these questions may help clarify how to mainstream human rights with development knowledge and policy in ways that avoid instrumentalizing the essential intrinsic value of human rights: as the expression of the moral worth of all human beings. This may help linking the 'why' of aid with the 'how': how aid policies are thought through and implemented. This in turn may lead to new ways of thinking about evaluation, and the meanings of development effectiveness. In the remainder of this chapter, we take the World Bank as an example; presenting a preliminary examination of some of the issues just discussed in relation to a specific case.

Responsibilities for the eradication of poverty: the case of the World Bank

The issue of human rights may be taken up at two different, but related, levels within the Bank. One is at the overall, strategic level; the other is at the operational level. We will discuss each in turn. In formal, organizational terms, the World Bank's concerns for ethics were first explicitly addressed in a small department created after the World Development Report (WDR) 2000/1, *Attacking Poverty*. This department is in charge of coordinating a project on interfaith dialogue, recently extended to include ethical values more generally. So far it has had a marginal role in the Bank. (Nevertheless, the Bank has for many years had an informal gathering called the 'Friday morning group' where a few staff members meet to discuss some of the moral aspects of their work.) More recently, former President Wolfensohn appointed Alfredo Sfeir-Younis as the World Bank's Senior Advisor on Human Rights. Although he left his position in summer 2005, this appointment may be interpreted as another sign of the Bank's commitment to engage with human rights issues and more generally to include concerns for basic moral responsibilities. This, however, in fact depends on the amount of influence that the Advisor is allowed to exert, not least over operational policy.

The two initiatives just mentioned may be taken as strategic 'signals' emanating from the highest echelons of the Bank concerning the issue of moral responsibility; but in formal terms it is the Board of the Bank that has executive power. It appears from its documents that the Bank's notion of rights is thin and somewhat incoherent, often expressed in legalistic more than ethical terms. We find declarative statements such as 'the mainstreaming of human rights into everything we do' (World Bank 2002). However, according to a recent summary of a meeting addressing human rights in the Bank, staff members tend to ask: 'Should an economic development institution embrace the fundamental values, elements, and instruments of a human rights approach to sustainable development?' (World Bank 2002). There appears to be a reluctance to address rights directly, perhaps derived from the legal constraints of the Bank's mandate, which says that the institution should avoid engaging in political matters. The Legal Department has always played an important part in interpreting the Bank's mandate and status, and its role is discussed below.

The World Bank's Senior Advisor on Human Rights, Sfeir-Younis, has given a number of talks, and also written speeches for President Wolfensohn.

His style seems to be more theoretical-philosophical than that of Wolfensohn. Perhaps the most clear statement of his position is in his essay 'Human rights and economic development: can they be reconciled? A view from the World Bank' (Sfeir-Younis 2003). (It is important to note that the text expresses Sfeir-Younis' own opinions, and not those of the Bank as an institution.)

First, Sfeir-Younis argues that it is crucial to address the role that economics, and in particular economic values, play in restraining the Bank from engaging more openly with human rights issues. Economics can be characterized, he argues, as a collection of values – albeit changing with context and over time; it is impossible to view economic issues, rights and the operationalization of policies as separate matters. What weave them together are precisely underlying values; and a focus on values is the most important way to mainstream human rights into economic development (Sfeir-Younis 2003: 3). Some values are dominant (thus consumerism and individualism dominate economics), but it is not clear that this should continue; and different countries and contexts have their own values as well. Today we are in a situation in which economic thinking dominates values related to common issues or to the value of inclusion. It is crucial then to see the role played by institutions, Sfeir-Younis claims, in changing the course of humanity, in enabling change. The reconciliation between economic and human rights issues needs to occur at an institutional level, Sfeir-Younis argues, as much as at an ideological level. He then moves on to address matters of governance at the country level, the roles of non-state organizations like NGOs and some reflection on the ways in which the Bank itself may be transformed as an agent of change. Sfeir-Younis focuses his attention on the strengthening of the UN system in general, and the added value to which linkages on human rights across the system's diverse institutions may lead. He then addresses the ways in which new approaches in the Bank related to poverty reduction have put the Bank closer to human rights principles, such as for example the recent emphasis on empowerment or lack of 'voice'.

A second important area of emphasis in Sfeir-Younis' article is the relation between rights-based development and socio-economic rights. He argues that this leads us to investigate processes of wealth creation and wealth accumulation. Unless wealth creation is linked to socio-economic rights, human rights may remain disassociated from economic planning and economic decision-making. Human rights, Sfeir-Younis argues, may learn from the intellectual journey of sustainable development, which led to a re-linking of environmental matters with wealth creation.

In summary, Sfeir-Younis raises some very basic and challenging issues. Given the preliminary nature of our research, it is not clear to what extent – if any – these have been followed up within the Bank. But this depends not simply on the Bank's mandate, but also on the 'culture' of the Bank: the many formal and informal rules, norms and practices of different departments and the power some of those may have above others.

In the operational departments a powerful imperative is to lend money, and the attitude taken to human rights issues is predominantly instrumental, that is, 'will such an approach make for more and better lending?' Among economists, whose views tend to dominate, there is some scepticism. Among other social scientists such as anthropologists or sociologists there appears to be more openness – but even here a degree of caution. While they are generally convinced (as argued in the recent Social Development Strategy) that, for example, accountability is a very important element, this does not necessarily mean that this can or should be operationalized through explicit reference to human rights. Among those who emphasize the importance of human rights, there is still some discussion as to whether a human rights dimension is qualitatively different in some sense, or whether it can best be integrated with concepts that have already been advanced in recent years; that is, empowerment and participation or a more expansive use of Sen's capability approach. However, human rights still play a quite limited role in the intellectual work the Bank produces. Perhaps the best insight into the core values and ideas of the Bank is the annual World Development Report (WDR). Two recent reports are of particular significance and deserve extended discussion.

WDR 2000/1 was on the topic of poverty, and the debates concerning its content were unusually transparent since drafts were posted on the Bank's website, and comments invited. The process was quite turbulent, and the lead editor of the report, Ravi Kanbur, quit in protest claiming undue influence from the US Treasury Department (Kanbur 2001). Much of the debate regarding this incident can best be seen as value frameworks clashing with one another, rather than cognitive differences.

The WDR 2000/1 report claims to offer a new view of poverty that recognizes the now widely accepted idea that poverty eradication is about the human beings behind the statistics. The report claims to draw its conception from two main sources: (1) the voices of the poor themselves; and (2) the philosophical arguments by Amartya Sen and others for viewing poverty as a deprivation of basic capabilities rather than merely low incomes (WDR 2001: 1.2, 1.3). Even though these references may lead to a more explicit role of ethical values in the WDR, in the end the report elaborates on poverty through instrumental argumentation. That is, the report 'still bases poverty alleviation policies on economic growth and consumption thereby blurring the important distinction between a people oriented approach to poverty and a people oriented conception of economy' (Skirbekk and St Clair 2001: 11).

In short, the report states that Sen's capability approach helps to explain that poverty is more than lack of income, and offers arguments to include deprivations in health and education. But 'the text does not provide further explicit claims regarding Sen's approach to poverty. ... The report is blind as to how Sen's approach may be incompatible with other theses stated in the report or with long-held beliefs inside the World Bank bureaucracy'

(Skirbekk and St Clair 2001: 14). In brief, this may be seen as a missed opportunity to address the connections between basic capabilities, the linkages between liberty and socio-economic rights, and even the linkages with human rights that Sen's work directly provides.

The forthcoming WDR 2005/6 is on Equity and Development.[4] The report makes use of Sen's notion of capability but, as with WDR 2000/1, in a largely rhetorical way, disconnected from the rest of the logic of the report. The first draft risks collapsing intrinsic and instrumental values in a fallacious way. It is unclear as to whether equity is a fundamental and non-tradable value (referring to justice, and ultimately based on the intrinsic moral worth of all human beings); or an instrumental economic value (more equitable distribution leads to more economic growth). If the case for equity is made primarily on instrumental rather than intrinsic grounds, this implies a modest place for human rights, if any. The final draft has the merit of clarifying the distinction between the intrinsic and instrumental case for equity, but chooses to focus primarily on the latter. Thus the main argument in Part II, entitled 'Why Does Equity Matter',[5] is instrumental. Human rights, as such, receive very modest attention: human rights legislation is referred to as one of five types of evidence that 'fairness matters'.

The human rights obligations of the World Bank: legal positions

The Articles of Agreement of the Bank state that 'The Bank and its officers shall not interfere in the political affairs of any member country. ... Only economic considerations shall be relevant to their decisions.' The Legal Department, which has responsibility for advising on the interpretation of these articles, was long seen as a conservative element in the World Bank. In the early 1990s, when issues of governance entered more explicitly onto the agenda (whether broadly defined, or more narrowly focusing on corruption and 'good management'), there was much discussion, in which the Senior Vice-President (General Counsel) played an important part. This led to what may be described as cautious change. The question now arises whether further change is desirable and possible; and there is some evidence that this is so.

There has been discussion both within and outside the Bank as to its possible legal obligations, as an institution, and in particular as an expert body offering knowledge and policy for poverty. According to Van Genugten (2003), for example, what is important is that new approaches and directions in the Bank – such as governance, social safety nets, or efforts to enhance countries to meet health and education targets – be expanded and evaluated according to both socio-economic and cultural rights, national regulations and international human rights laws. Even though a focus on poverty issues is important, it is *per se* not sufficient to guarantee protection of basic rights nor necessarily consistent, procedurally, with rights broadly understood (Van Genugten 2003).

An important debate among legal scholars is the extent to which the Bank is bound to respect and/or promote international law. One of those who have made detailed investigations of the possible legal obligations of the Bank argues that the institution was established according to international law, 'through the adoption, ratification and entry into force of their Articles of Agreement as treaties among states' (Skogly 2001: 46). Flowing from the Articles of Agreement, it follows that the Bank is a legal person with duties and responsibilities, arguably in the same way as business corporations are treated as legal persons. This means, according to Skogly, that the Bank has a responsibility to carry its mandate 'within the framework of international law' (Skogly 2001: 47). From this, it follows that the Bank is also obliged to respect human rights as articulated by the UN Charter, as well as by customary international law and 'general principles' of law (Darrow 2003). This obligation entails that Bank programmes and policies ought not to violate human rights. Skogly adds, furthermore, that such obligation is not only negative, but also positive.

Even though the Bank has recognized its positive role in the promotion of economic, cultural and social rights, there is no indication as to how this is ensured or monitored (Skogly 2001: 55). Regarding positive obligations to protect and to fulfil people's rights, it may be argued, from a legal perspective, that although the Bank itself does not hold full (perfect) human rights obligations (as it is not a ratifying party to human rights treaties), it has implicit obligations to the degree that its member states are committed by ratification. According to the principle of extraterritorial obligations, it can be argued that member states are bound by the conventions they have ratified with regard to their behaviour through the Bank's operations (Andreassen and McNeill 2005).

In short, some scholars agree that the Bank is legally bound to comply and even to promote human rights. Perhaps, the most detailed attempt to provide guiding principles is found in the 'Tilburg Guiding Principles of World Bank, IMF and Human Rights' (Van Genugten *et al.* 2003; see also Van Genugten and Perez-Bustillo 2001).

Moral responsibility: roles and capacities

The legal arguments just stated have their counterparts, still more broadly expressed, in the moral arena. It is important to recall that moral responsibility embraces broader aspects than any legislation, and that it is desirable that this be the case. A central issue in both cases is the responsibility of an institution as opposed to an individual. Literature on responsibility ethics has determined, from many different perspectives and through diverse lines of argumentation, the ways in which collectivities and institutions, such as business corporations, may be considered moral persons as well as legal persons (French 1992; more recently, on institutions, Erskine 2003). Broadly, both the legal and the moral arguments are ultimately based on the particular capacities and roles that an institution – such as the Bank – has and performs. From a moral perspective, the shift from an economic to a human rights- and ethics-based perspective with regard to poverty aims to appeal to the same sense of moral concern, and even outrage, that extreme human rights violations such as genocide or torture give rise to. But it is a challenging task to link this to the everyday practices, including discursive practices, of actors and institutions engaged in poverty reduction, their knowledge and their policies.

As we have outlined above, responsibility ascription requires tracing actions (or omissions) and their consequences. Clearly, the causal relations between actions or omissions and the severe poverty of a particular individual or group are highly difficult to establish. Yet, this is no reason to refrain from investigating those linkages. In fact, many violations of civil or liberty rights are also highly complex to trace; yet many incentives are put in place simply to prevent these violations from occurring, often at an extremely high cost. Moral responsibility is in itself much broader than causal responsibility, although ideally the presence of both leads to more transparent ascriptions of responsibility. It is reasonable to expect that global institutions entrusted with gaining and applying expertise in poverty reduction should follow the precautionary principle: to protect people from severe poverty. The argument for a forward-looking responsibility to protect can be made both at a legal and at a moral level. However, in keeping with the theoretical framework outlined in the former section, our aim in this study is to make an empirical investigation of actual responsibility practices, including discursive practices.

What follows are some preliminary suggestions regarding the World Bank, outlining a number of responsibilities that apply to this global institution, (a) in relation to its capacities; and, linked to those, (b) in relation to its roles. Response-ability, that is, the ability or capacity to respond either by solving a problem or preventing harm, is one of the most fundamental grounds for ascribing responsibility. Thus, investigating responsibilities of the Bank requires a very detailed account of its capacities. In addition, the scope of moral agency, as outlined above, depends very often on the context. It is here that it is important to look at the roles played by the Bank as an organization, and at the roles and audiences of the experts as they work and represent the Bank.

At a general level, it may be argued that if – as most ethical theorists agree – there are duties and responsibilities to create institutions that protect the rights of people, then surely development aid agencies are precisely such institutions. The tax revenue from donor country citizens is appropriated precisely under such rationale: to aid poor countries and their people in achieving what is considered a better quality of life. However, such responsibilities, even at the broad level, need to be qualified. We agree with Henry Shue 'that one wants institutions that function effectively to honour rights while imposing only duties that make fair demands on those who bear them' (1996: 166). For citizens of advanced economies, which are mostly those donating funds for development, the least that democratic citizenship allows us to demand is a transparent debate as to what mechanisms allow, hinder or diffuse moral proximity needed for the ascription of responsibilities for poverty in development aid agents.

Responsibility and roles: thinking about expertise and responsibility

There is little research addressing the issue, but we agree with Martin Hollis that 'expertise carries special ethical responsibilities' (Hollis 1991: 205). Our earlier work suggests that the way in which knowledge is applied in making and advising on policy may diffuse or avoid rather than promote acknowledgment of either human rights or ethical concerns related to poverty and the poor.

Regarding the content of recommended policies, one may refer to both the global and the national/local level. To promote market openness in its various manifestations on the grounds that this leads to increased economic growth and thus the reduction of poverty begs the question of what alternative global systems one could envision that would primarily avoid severe poverty. The extent to which the economic restructuring occurring worldwide is producing or reducing poverty is one of the most debated issues in globalization studies; and critics often identify the Bank as one of the main actors in such restructuring. However, the discussions tend to take place within a very limited scope; begging the actual question of how poverty is produced. As Thomas Pogge rightly argues, one of the most fundamental matters for the moral assessment of an economic order is 'whether there is a feasible institutional alternative under which starvations would not occur. It does not matter, or does not matter much, in what causal relations the relevant order stands to the starvation in question' (Pogge 2002: 13). A similar argument is made by Amartya Sen in evaluating more generally current globalization processes.

> The criticism that a distributional arrangement from cooperation is unfair cannot be rebutted by just noting that all the parties are better off than would be the case in the absence of cooperation: there are many of such arrangements and the real exercise is the choice between these various alternatives (Sen 2002).

It is here that the roles and capacities of the Bank, with regard to knowledge and policies addressing poverty, are fundamentally inter-linked. The Bank's economic advice to client countries, and its 'global ideas' (e.g. related to social policy, safety nets, the provision of people's basic needs), cannot be separated from the overarching system of rules and regulations that constitute the global economic system. The Bank has both the capacity (in terms of power and in terms of knowledge) to challenge the global architecture, and the responsibility to address the manifold problems related to the scientific uncertainty surrounding economic knowledge and economic policy prescriptions. Not only are economic advisors, including the Bank and its experts, responsible for the consequences of their recommendations (for example structural adjustment programmes) on people's lives; they are also responsible, as Stiglitz claims, for disclosing the limits of the knowledge they provide (Stiglitz 2001).

The forthcoming WDR 2006 indicates both the potential of and the likely limits to World Bank action in this respect. The report is quite critical of international laws and agreements. For example:

> The laws that govern the functionings of global markets, like all international laws, are the result of complex negotiations ... questions about the legitimacy of negotiating processes and enforcement mechanisms risk undermining the applications of laws ... greater participation and voice in rule setting bodies would help ensure that outcomes are more favourable to developing countries.
>
> (World Bank 2005: 10.67)

The World Bank is a very important organization concerning poverty-reduction policies, and such passages indicate how it might actively engage in trying to redress such imbalances of power. This can be promoted both through advocacy (as implied in some sections of this WDR 2006), and, for example, by providing technical assistance to developing countries in negotiating international agreements more beneficial to their needs. Yet, the report is in other respects quite cautious. There is no attempt to take on the arguments of Sfeir-Younis, summarized above. Moreover, the report is, like its predecessors, written in economic language for economists, thus leaving it constrained within a technocratic frame which sets the domain for ethical consideration with regard to poverty in a very narrow and limited way. To change this it would be necessary to address the most fundamental sources of legitimacy and credibility of the Bank's knowledge, and to challenge the circularity between the knowledge produced and promoted by the Bank and the ways in which it is legitimized (St Clair 2006b). However, this is not to deny the numerous, and sometimes vociferous, critical voices in the organization – although these are seldom heard outside – and high profile examples of staff leaving the Bank.

To conclude, the Bank is certainly not the only agent endowed with the task of eliminating poverty; many other institutions and individuals share that responsibility, including poor countries' citizens, politicians and bureaucrats. Nevertheless, the roles and capacities of the Bank as a particularly powerful actor in global politics and in global knowledge call for an in-depth investigation into its role as an expert body; including the question of how moral distance is created and perpetuated. The legitimacy of the World Bank may be seriously damaged if it is not able to respond to the increasing calls for democratic accountability. And these may legitimately include a 'responsibility to protect', to *protect people's freedom from poverty*. Such a forward looking notion of responsibility would require a deep analysis of the roles and capacities of the Bank, an assessment of the manifold areas of uncertainty of economic science, and a transparent treatment of the entanglement between ethics, knowledge and politics. The audience of a legitimate World Bank, we suggest, is not, or at least not only, mainstream economists and powerful global elites, but all the citizens of all the countries that make up this global organization.

Notes

1 We thank Dan Banik, Benedicte Bull, David Crocker, Andreas Føllesdal, Des Gasper, and Thomas Pogge, for useful revisions and suggestions during the preparation of the first draft of this chapter. We also thank the participants of the Workshop Research Bank on the World Bank, in particular Dick Robinson and the editors of this volume Diane Stone and Chris Wright, for useful and improving comments and suggestions.
2 Interestingly, Glover does not refer to Bauman's earlier work, one of the landmark studies of the role of morality in society. A possible explanation is the gap that exists also between the social sciences and the humanities. In our opinion, both are needed for a proper elaboration of moral responsibilities for the eradication of poverty. The conceptual work resulting from this project aims to establish a dialogue between philosophers and social scientists. Neither Bauman's landmark study, nor Glover's work, has, to our knowledge, been applied to study poverty.
3 CANDID is the acronym of our former research project investigating the Creation, Adoption, Negation and Distortion of Ideas in Development. See http://www.sum.uio.no/research/global_governance/candid/index.html
4 At the time of writing this chapter, only the final draft of the report has been available. The comments that follow are based on the written drafts, and public presentations in Oslo, Washington DC and Dakar, Senegal.
5 A significant change from the earlier draft in which it was 'Does Equity Matter?'

References

Alkire, S. (2002) *Valuing Freedoms: Sen's Capability Approach and Poverty Reduction*, Oxford: Oxford University Press.
Andreassen, B. Å. and D. McNeill (1991) *Modernity and the Holocaust*, London: Polity Press.
——(2005) 'A note on the World Bank and the human rights agenda', unpublished.
——(2004) *Global Institutions and Development: Framing the World?*, London: Routledge.
Bøås, M. and D. McNeill (2003) *Multilateral Institutions: A Critical Introduction*, London: Pluto Press.
Bauman, Z. (1973) *Culture as Praxis*, London: Routledge.
Crocker, D. (forthcoming) 'Development ethics, globalization, and Stiglitz', in D. Chatterjee and M. Krausz (eds) *Globalization, Democracy, and Development: Philosophical Perspectives*, Lanham MD: Rowman and Littlefield.

Darrow, M. (2003) *Between Light and Shadow: The World Bank, the International Monetary Fund and International Human Rights Law*, Oxford and Portland OR: Hart Publishing.

Doyal, L. and I. Gough (1991) *A Theory of Need*, London: Macmillan.

Erskine, T. (ed.) (2003) *Can Institutions Have Responsibilities? Collective Moral Agency and International Relations*, London: Palgrave.

Farmer, P. (2003) *Pathologies of Power: Health, Human Rights, and the New War on the Poor*, Berkeley CA: University of California Press.

French, P. (1991) *The Spectrum of Responsibility*, New York: St Martin's Press.

——(1992) *Responsibility Matters*, Lawrence KS: University Press of Kansas.

——(1995) *Corporate Ethics*, Fort Worth TX: Harcourt Brace College Publishers.

Gasper, D. (2004) *The Ethics of Development: From Economism to Human Development*, Edinburgh: Edinburgh University Press.

Glover, J. (2001) *Humanity: A Moral History of the Twentieth Century*, New Haven CT: Yale University Press.

Goodin, R. (1985) *Protecting the Vulnerable*, Chicago: Chicago University Press.

Held, D. (2004) *Global Covenant: The Social Democracy Alternative to the Washington Consensus*, London: Polity.

Hollis, M. (1991) *The Philosophy of Social Science: An Introduction*, Cambridge: Cambridge University Press.

Ignatieff, M. (2001) *Human Rights as Politics and Idolatry*, ed. A. Gutmann, Princeton NJ: Princeton University Press.

International Council on Human Rights Policy (2003) *Duties Sans Frontières: Human Rights and Global Social Justice*, Geneva: ICHRP.

ILO (International Labour Organization) (1976) *Employment, Growth, and Basic Needs: A One World Problem*, Geneva: ILO.

Kanbur, R. (2001) 'Economic policy, distribution and poverty: The nature of disagreements', *World Development* 29, 1083–94.

O'Neill, O. (1996) *Towards Justice and Virtue: A Constructive Account of Practical Reasoning*, Cambridge: Cambridge University Press.

——(2000) *Bounds of Justice*, Cambridge: Cambridge University Press.

Pogge, T. (2002) *World Poverty and Human Rights: Cosmopolitan Responsibilities and Reforms*, Cambridge: Polity Press.

——(2004) '"Assisting" the global poor', in Deen Chatterjee (ed.) *The Ethics of Assistance: Morality and the Distant Needy*, Cambridge: Cambridge University Press, 260–88.

——(2006) 'Severe poverty as a human rights violation', in T. Pogge (ed.) *Freedom from Poverty as a Human Right: Who Owes What to the Very Poor*, Oxford: Oxford University Press.

Pogge, T. and A. Føllesdal (eds) (2005) *Real World Justice*, New York: Springer.

Rawls, J. (1993) *Political Liberalism*, New York: Columbia University Press.

Sen, A. (1999) *Development as Freedom*, New York: Knopf.

——(2002) 'Global inequality and human security', Lecture 2, Ishizaka Lectures, Tokyo, 18 February, http://www.ksg.harvard.edu/gei (accessed 2 September 2003).

Sfeir-Younis, A. (2003) 'Human rights and economic development: can they be reconciled? A view from the World Bank', in W. Van Genugten, P. Hunt and S. Matthews (eds) *World Bank, IMF and Human Rights*, Nijmegen, Netherlands: Wolf Legal Publishers.

Shue, H. (1996) *Basic Rights: Subsistence, Affluence and U.S. Foreign Policy*, Princeton NJ: Princeton University Press.

Skirbekk, G. and A. L. St Clair (2001) 'A philosophical analysis of the World Bank's conception of poverty', in *A Critical Review of the World Bank Report: WDR 2000/1, Attacking Poverty*, CROP, http://www.crop.org (accessed 1 September 2005).

Skogly, S. (2001) *The Human Rights Obligations of the World Bank and the International Monetary Fund*, London: Cavendish Publishing.

Smiley, M. (1992) *Moral Responsibility and the Boundaries of Community: Power and Accountability from aPragmatic Point of View*, Chicago: University of Chicago Press.

St Clair, A. L. (2004) 'The role of ideas in the United Nations Development Programme', in M. Bøås and D. McNeill (eds) *Global Institutions and Development: Framing the World?*, London: Routledge.

——(2006a) 'Global poverty: The co-production of knowledge and politics', *Global Social Policy*, 6:1.

——(2006b) 'The World Bank as a transnational expertised institution', *Global Governance*, 12:1.

Stiglitz, J. (2001) 'Ethics, economic advice, and economic policy', Inter-American Development Bank (IDB) Electronic Library, available at http://www.iadb.org/etica/sp4321-i/DocMain-i.cfm

——(2002a) 'Ethics, economic advice, and economic policy', http://www.iadb.org/etica/documentos/dc_sti_ethic-i.htm (accessed 1 September 2005).

——(2002b) *Globalisation and its Discontents*, London: Penguin Press.

Streeten, P. S., J. Burki, Mahbub ul-Haq, Norman Hicks and Frances Stewart (1981) *First Things First: Meeting Basic Human Needs in the Developing Countries*, Oxford: Oxford University Press for the World Bank.

Turner, S. (2005) 'Expertise and political responsibility: The Columbia shuttle catastrophe', *Democratization of Expertise? Exploring Novel Forms of Scientific Advice in Political Decision-Making*, Dordrecht: Springer.

ul Haq, M. (1976) *The Poverty Curtain: Choices for the Third World*, New York: Columbia University Press.

UNDP (United Nations Development Programme) (2003) *Human Development Report*, New York: Oxford University Press.

Vandemoortele, J. (2003) 'Are the MDGS feasible?', *UNDP Development Policy Journal* 3, April 2003.

Van Genugten, W. (2003) 'Introduction', in W. Van Genugten, P. Hunt and S. Matthews (eds) *World Bank, the IMF and Human Rights*, Nijmegen: Wolf Legal Publishers.

Van Genugten, W., P. Hunt and S. Matthews (eds) (2003) *World Bank, the IMF and Human Rights*, Nijmegen: Wolf Legal Publishers.

Van Genugten, W. and C. Perez-Bustillo (eds) (2001) *The Poverty of Rights: Human Rights and the Eradication of Poverty*, CROP International Studies in Poverty Research, London: Zed Books.

Vaux, T. (2002) *The Selfish Altruist: Relief Work in Famine and War*, London: Earthscan.

Walker, M. (1998) *Moral Understandings: A Feminist Study on Ethics*, London: Routledge.

World Bank (2001) *World Development Report 2000/2001: Attacking Poverty*, Oxford: Oxford University Press.

——(2002) 'Human rights and sustainable development: What role for the Bank?', summary of proceedings, meeting of 2 May 2002.

——(2004) 'Human rights and development: toward mutual reinforcement', remarks at a Dialogue on Human Rights and Development organized by the Ethical Globalization Initiative and New York University Law School, by James D. Wolfensohn, President, The World Bank Group, New York City, 1 March.

——(forthcoming) *World Development Report 2006*.

Young, Iris (2004) 'Responsibility and global labor justice', *Journal of Political Philosophy* 12(4), 365–88.

3 The art of fine balances

The challenge of institutionalizing the Comprehensive Development Framework inside the World Bank

Nilima Gulrajani

Introduction

Christmas 1998. Jackson Hole, Wyoming. A multi-millionaire ex-investment banker sits by the fireplace in his ranch, tucked away from the hustle of Washington DC and the misery of the developing world's poor. He writes on yellow legal pad in an indecipherable longhand about the need for a radical re-thinking about the processes and contents of international development assistance. Drafted as a memo to the Board of Governors of the World Bank and its management and staff in January 1999, the Comprehensive Development Framework (CDF) became an ambitious and elaborate endeavour by World Bank President James D. Wolfensohn to 'change the way the Bank works'. It had important repercussions for the wider development field.

Despite the significance of the CDF, studies of its process and outcomes remain limited to a Bank-sponsored evaluation (Operations Evaluation Department 2003) or a discussion in an unofficial biography of Wolfensohn (Mallaby 2005). With Wolfensohn's departure, an assessment of the legacy of his CDF by scholars of the World Bank is surely merited. This paper takes a step in this direction, from the perspective of sociological institutionalism, by engaging in an analysis of the CDF initiative within two World Bank country offices. It explores the ways the CDF heightened institutional tensions and seeks to understand its consequences for the employee experience of dislocation, for organizational politics and power, for the trajectory of the CDF itself and finally, for future prospects of organizational reform under Wolfensohn's successor, Paul Wolfowitz.

In order to do this, the chapter is divided into four sections. The first section presents the theoretical framework adopted and methods used in order to engage in a study of dynamics within the Bank. This proceeds to a discussion of the institutional logics of development and a review of the CDF. The third section then investigates the implications of the CDF experiment for intra-organizational politics and external power relations by examining the employee experience of institutional tension. The concluding discussion suggests that this examination of the trajectories taken by the

CDF can shed light on the sources of leverage and limitation in future reforms of the World Bank.

Theoretical framework and methods

In order to engage in a finely grained and methodologically robust analysis of the dynamics inside the Bank, the theoretical perspective of organizational sociology frames this study. Sociological institutional theory directs attention to organizational responses to social norms or institutions governing society (DiMaggio and Powell 1983; Meyer and Rowan 1977; Scott 1987). Institutions exercise normative, coercive and mimetic pressures such that conformity to them endows organizations with legitimacy that increases survival prospects, power and resource flows. Once institutional conformity is achieved through processes of institutionalization, the result is enhanced social stability for organizations.

In recent years, institutional theory's focus on the legitimacy and stability acquired through institutional adaptation has been criticized for downplaying the tensions and contradictions characteristic of pluralistic societies (Clemens and Cook 1999; Friedland and Alford 1991; Seo and Creed 2002; Whittington 1992). These theorists point to the multiplicity and conflicting institutional logics that defy assimilation and conformance to a singular, homogeneous institution. Institutional logics are defined as the symbolic systems and organizing principles that furnish guidelines for actor behaviours and meanings, supplying a sense of self and vocabularies of motive (Friedland and Alford 1991: 248). Logic plurality provides a basis for institutional contradiction, conflicts and uneven adaptive trajectories (Sewell 1992: 16–19). Political action in these overlapping and fragmented institutional contexts is expected to be oblique and subtle, possibly cloaked within acceptable models or deploying familiar models of organization in unfamiliar ways (Clemens and Cook 1999: 459).

Two stages characterized the analysis adopted to investigate the institutional logics and trace institutionalization processes within the World Bank. In the first stage, awareness of contradictory institutional logics embedded in the CDF emerged inductively after thirty exploratory interviews with World Bank bureaucrats in Washington DC in November 2002. A literature review of critical development theory further supported the results of this inductive analysis. In the second stage, the CDF process was traced in a comparative *post hoc* analysis of the experience in the Bank's Bolivia and Vietnam country offices. Narrative process analysis is the basis for exploring perceptions and consequences of the CDF within the World Bank (Langley 1999; Pentland 1998). Overall, the goal was to become 'intimately familiar with each case as a stand-alone entity' so as to write a narrative that employees themselves could recognize in focus group discussions after completing fieldwork in each office and, which could then be iteratively compared against one another (Eisenhardt 1989: 540). The analysis centred on identifying institutional tensions deriving from the CDF experience, as identified by country-office Bank employees. Through a comparative processual narrative analysis, the direction of the institutional tension experienced through the CDF is assessed, as well as the consequences for organizational power and politics and future possibilities of reform.

In total, twenty-nine interviews (13 in Bolivia, 16 in Vietnam) lasting between 45 and 90 minutes were conducted, taped and transcribed. Interviews were semi-structured and sought to treat three main themes, but otherwise ceded control of the interview to the interviewee; the main themes being (1) perceptions of the new 'poverty' paradigm in the wider development field; (2) the process and consequences of the CDF in the country office; (3) and the personal lived experience of the employee within the CDF. Analysis proceeded by thematically coding narrative interview data according to major events or consequences of the CDF process using the qualitative data software package Atlas.ti. Each coded text segment was reviewed in an iterative manner and instances of 'lived institutional tension' within these identified. These instances of 'institutional tension' were further reviewed and the generic category refined into two observed trends, a tendency to *downplay*, excuse or reconcile a self-described tension deriving from the clash between institutional logics, or a *problematic* institutional tension that generated anger, resentment, or questioning by informants. Other codes included 'power', and 'political' consequences, and these were repeatedly examined to narrow them into sub-classifications, identify trends and draft analytical chronologies of the CDF process.

Access was negotiated through the CDF Secretariat in Washington DC, with country offices in Bolivia and Vietnam inviting the researcher for a visit lasting approximately three weeks in each case. Organizational embeddedness allowed for ethnographic observations that complemented the formal interview process. The public identification of country offices as 'Bolivia' and 'Vietnam' was accepted when the request for research access was made. Interviews with employees were tape-recorded with their agreement that they might be quoted in any published results, albeit anonymously. Preliminary interpretations and impressions were presented in focus groups to employees at the end of in-country visits and provided an early form of validating findings. For further validation, a draft copy of this paper was circulated to World Bank staff who granted permission for this project.

Technocratic and socio-political logics in development: the case of the CDF

In his book *The Anti-Politics Machine*, James Ferguson classifies literature on the development industry into two streams (1994: 9–11). In the first, the focus is on managing development to make it more effective. This school is essentially a branch of policy science that sees the development apparatus as a tool at the disposal of the planner. Development is a neutral 'technical' instrument that can generate desired poverty outcomes if the right combination of goals, processes and conditions are selected. In the second strand of essentially post-modern research, development is a political project of subjugation and domination of the Third World. These two academic approaches to the study of development are identified as contradictory and irreconcilable. This dichotomy is a useful characterization not only of the development literature, but also broadly of the institutional logics that govern the practice of development. On the one hand, technocratic logics in the interactive realm privilege professional expertise and management, economic science and stability and hierarchical bureaucracies that produce measurable results quickly and efficiently. On the other hand, socio-political logics champion social and economic justice for the poor, welcome evolutionary locally embedded participative change and shun externally imposed, top-down bureaucratic interventions. While these logics are antithetical, they are also both interdependent and integral to all development engagement.

If legitimacy in the development field currently derives from conforming to both technocratic and socio-political logics, as the history of development in fact points to (Amrith 2004; Pieterse 2001; Rist 2002), the contradictions and conflicts that can result should become immediately apparent. To remain open to plurality and accept competing values and evolutionary concepts of change is difficult when planning decisions and priorities must be made, often based on scanty and incomplete knowledge. Although technical logics value single-mindedness and rapid, global progress, socio-political logics champion debate and slow, embedded change. While technical logics typically exist as resources of the powerful, socio-political ones challenge their rights to this authority. While technocratic approaches favour economic modernization and industrialization, socio-political logics espouse the broader cause of social and democratic justice. Thus, the challenge for development organizations is how to maintain their accountabilities and legitimacy in an institutional context where such a duality of social beliefs pervades. This challenge can extend to the individual bureaucrat in the World Bank who is obliged to operate across the competing norms and identities of an intellectual-activist and specialized professional expert (Ascher 1983).

The recent emphasis in the development field on poverty alleviation achieved through partnership and participation (Craig and Porter 2003; Maxwell 2003; Stubbs 2004) provides an opportune moment for studying these contradictory, if fundamental, institutional logics in the development sector. This new development paradigm appears to be internally torn between technocratic and socio-political logics in three overlapping ways:

1 uncertainty over the balance between the values and methods of science and the social world;
2 tensions between professional norms and the desire for empowerment and justice;
3 conflicts over the balance between complex hierarchical managerial systems and local definitions of progress.

In the first dimension, there is concern that the poverty alleviation agenda has adopted a naively 'scientific' and 'economistic' approach in analysing and acting upon local political realities in the developing world. Buzzwords like poverty, participation and ownership are acutely political concepts that are *de-politicized* of their structural political-economy contexts to the detriment of local autonomy and democracy but the advantage of state and/or local elite power (Chhotray 2004; Crawford 2003; de Herdt and Bastiaensen 2004; Ferguson 1994).

In the second dimension, the new agenda's emphasis on empowerment and social justice challenges professional values that privilege specialized expertise and quick results. There is a widespread belief that professional pragmatism imposes limits on genuine empowerment, if only because the latter 'results in complete inertia' (de Herdt and Bastiaensen 2004: 877). Maintaining professional standards of 'excellence' and preserving monopolies of power may lie in tense relation to demands for local political engagement and involvement (Cooke 2003; Craig and Porter 1997).

Finally, managerial systems associated with new public management orthodoxy abstract from the morass of local culture and community, knowledge of which is often uncertain (Craig and Porter 1997: 53–4; Townley 1997). Strategic performance management systems like results-based management tools and monitoring and evaluation mechanisms strive to achieve operational results through time-bound, target-oriented planning frameworks. These management techniques embrace a 'Christmas tree of aims' (Easterly 2002: 25) packaged as 'technically necessary actions' and 'assembled into compelling comprehensive frameworks' (Porter 1995: 83). Nonetheless, these managerial systems can be impractical and untenable given the nature of local dynamics, or they may also control and usurp local development goals.

The Comprehensive Development Framework

The Comprehensive Development Framework emerged in 1999 against the backdrop of an emerging normative consensus in development that privileged poverty reduction achieved through partnership and participation, the term 'CDF' gradually becoming eponymous with this new paradigm. As such, the CDF lends itself to an examination through the analytical lenses of the technocratic and socio-political logics introduced above. While the CDF is widely recognized as the philosophical basis underpinning the Poverty Reduction Strategy Papers (PRSPs) as well as the brainchild of James Wolfensohn, its role as an impetus for internal organizational change for mid-level staff inside the Bank is less widely known.

In the wake of this new moniker, a new department – the CDF Secretariat – was created with the support of many bilateral agencies and presidential sponsorship. The secretariat was expected to monitor ten countries (and Bank country offices) that volunteered to 'pilot' the new framework, including Bolivia, Côte d'Ivoire, the Dominican Republic, Eritrea, Ethiopia, Ghana, Jordan, Kyrygz Republic, Morocco, Romania, Uganda and Vietnam. Piloting the CDF inside Bank country offices was supposed to display the 'willingness of key development agencies ... to change their culture and practice' (Wolfensohn 2000: 3). The CDF involved the creation of a 'management matrix' that would visually set out 'who was doing or planning what' in order to create 'real chances of achieving longer term targets in a more effective and accountable manner' (Wolfensohn 1999: 27). The need for comparative monitoring and evaluation of these pilots marked the codification of the CDF into four 'measurable' principles. These were: equal treatment between social and 'structural' concerns and macroeconomic and financial issues, country ownership of the policy agenda, partnership with all stakeholders, and a long-term holistic vision of development built through national consultations and focused on results (CDF Secretariat 1999).

While the CDF has already been criticized for believing that 'largely intangible benefits can be programmed, produced, and measured much like any other project output' (Pincus 2002: 78), it makes sense to examine the micro-consequences within the CDF pilot offices to assess this claim. The rest of this chapter explores the institutional contradictions arising from these antithetical logics as experienced by World Bank staff situated within CDF pilot country offices.

Experiencing the CDF inside the World Bank

The CDF may have been a set of four lofty principles but what did it actually entail in local offices? What were its achievements? What, if any, obstacles did it encounter, and what can this tell us about the way organizational reform happens inside the World Bank? This section begins to address some of these questions based on an understanding of the CDF process inside two World Bank offices – Bolivia and Vietnam – that agreed to pilot the framework.

In a relatively propitious political context, Country Directors of World Bank offices in Bolivia and Vietnam capitalized on the plurality and ambiguity embedded within the CDF to engage in experiments of organization.

> And then when the CDF came, it was great. [It] provides a sort of institutional backing in which you can do anything. ... The people working in Bolivia said, 'Great, the CDF provides the institutional cover to do things in the name of CDF things that you wanted to do in the Bolivian pilot which you wouldn't have had the cover to do. ... This is a wagon to hitch to'.
>
> (WBB P1: 0277–0232)[1]

Notably, the CDF was largely perceived to have had a far smoother and more successful trajectory in Vietnam than in Bolivia. The following section argues that this derived from the CDF's apparent incompatibility with the Bank's existing technocratic practices and norms in Bolivia. The ambitiousness of the Bolivian pilot to challenge internal disbursement pressures and centralized lines of accountability, that is, to actively pursue some of the norms and practices of the socio-political logic, generated problematic, intense and explicit institutional tensions for employees. In contrast, in Vietnam institutional tensions were downplayed, subtler and less vivid. The following section presents these findings by referring to employee narratives to explore, in the first instance, the intra-organizational political consequences of the CDF; and second, the power implications for Bank-government relations. The discussion between the political and power repercussions for the Bank arising from the CDF is separated for the sake of clarity rather than from a rejection of a reciprocal relationship between the Bank's internal political relations and its external power resources.

Decentralization and the CDF: the politics of partnerships and pillars

In Bolivia, the World Bank office piloted the CDF by organizing itself into a 'pillar structure' mirroring the government's 1997 *Plan General de Desarrollo Economico y Social* to demonstrate their support for Bolivia's national development strategy. Three expatriates were decentralized to the local office to staff units that had become known as the Institutionality, Equality and Opportunity pillars. These pillars crosscut traditional operational sectoral divisions at the Bank – Environmentally and Socially Sustainable Development, Human Development, Poverty Reduction and Economic Management (PREM), Private Sector Development and Infrastructure, Financial Sector – leading to confusion over accountabilities. Meanwhile, decentralizing power to local offices entitled country staff to draft contracts and appoint consultants without headquarters' approval. Procurement reform also launched as part of the CDF challenged centralized and universal procurement practices. The Bolivia office recruited a financial manager and procurement specialist to facilitate the work of decentralized pillar leaders, while a national professional filled the position of 'Civil Society Coordinator'. Equality among pillar leaders was accepted and each rotated as the Bank's Resident Representative, with this representative accountable to the Country Director in Washington DC. The Country Director for Bolivia decentralized to La Paz during the summer of 1999 as part of the CDF pilot.

This decentralized pillar structure proved problematic for the Bank's bureaucracy because it interfered with its traditional centralized and hierarchical structures. In the Bank's matrix management structure, sector staff are directly accountable to their Sector Coordinators (traditionally located at headquarters), although they are also seen to have responsibilities towards the geographic units in which they are located. The pillar structure challenged this accountability relation as the Bolivian office used the CDF to publicly throw its weight behind a short-lived domestic government strategy. National professional staff within the Bank sensed that decentralization was still resisted in Washington, although they too shared scepticism of the appropriateness of modelling their internal organization on the Government's pillar strategy.

> In Bolivia, an experiment was also made with decentralizing the Bank's decision-making process. Which ended up being kind of a sham. ... [I]t never really worked because in reality the process really wasn't decentralized. Ultimate decision-making was in Washington, not only at the Board but also with Washington managers. And also, the way it was internally organized here was incoherent in managerial terms. Three pillars and they were all equal and nobody came with a final decision. Nobody was in charge of saying 'the buck stops here' ...
>
> [T]he most stupid decision was made that the Bank's processes would not only be decentralized in Bolivia, be concentrated is the right word actually, but that the office itself would model, would model itself in terms of the Government's plan. And that was like, ridiculous! I mean, how can you do such stupidity! (laughter). I mean the Government itself is not organizing itself according to its own plan: how can the Bank organize itself according to the Government's plan! And that stupidity became evident when the plan was revised and the Government destroyed its own pillars! And the Bank was like, 'Now what do we do with our pillars?' I mean that was something. I mean that was really stupid.
>
> (WBB P9: 0313–0358)

The pillar structure pushed the norms of localism forward by challenging sectors on the need for top-down bureaucracy with neatly defined lines of accountability and responsibility. While the CDF justified this desire for increased autonomy from centralized managers and the greater importance attached to the 'local' collective interest, it also resulted in 'managerial incoherence' that generated an explicit and intense experience of institutional tension for staff.

Vietnam represents an entirely different scenario. Prior to the launch of the CDF, the Vietnam office had exercised decentralization opportunities first offered through the 1997 Strategic Compact that aimed to improve the Bank's business activities with a one-time injection of US$250 million. With the arrival of the CDF, decentralization accelerated as six Sector Coordinators moved from Washington DC to the local office and national professional staff numbers dramatically increased. Demand for 'greater partnership' by the Vietnamese prime minister resulted in the Bank actively championing 'Partnership Groups' across all sectors of donor activity. These groups met regularly and sought to improve information sharing and coordination (World Bank 2000). The twenty-six Partnership Groups set great importance on who chaired and coordinated donor activities. While the donor agencies chairing these groups varied by sector, the Bank assumed leadership in areas dealing with economic and financial policy as well as the highest profile group of all, the Poverty Working Group. The stated aim of all groups was to eventually yield the position of chair to government, a powerful symbol of enhanced 'country ownership'. The Bank also hired a 'Partnership Specialist' who, among other responsibilities, oversaw the production of Partnership Reports. These reports eventually became a biannual monitoring tool of the Partnership Groups.

Unlike in Bolivia, in Vietnam the CDF pilot did not antagonize central managers in Washington as it respected the Bank's operational sector divisions. This being said, the CDF did generate conflicts as operational sector staff were now expected to engage in 'innovative' activities (e.g. community development projects, participatory forums, etc.) that placed high demands on their time with little measurable benefit for either speed or quality of project implementation. Nonetheless, senior management and economists in the PREM sector continued to push these new poverty alleviation activities.

> Q. *You talked about the sectoral partnership groups. What was that and were you involved?*
> Again it is a very good idea. I mean you have, in this country, hundreds, literally hundreds and hundreds of different people participating in development, external agencies participating in development. All going in various directions and often contradicting each other in policy advice, the requirements they impose on government. Obviously it makes sense to try to bring people together. ... But it takes a lot of time. But we do have a partnership in [my] sector and it is fairly effective. But again, I can't spend much time on it. It is not as perfect as it could be. There are various competing ... I see my number one priority is to ensure that all the projects that I am responsible for are prepared on time and are implemented properly. And anything else for me is less important. Now, as we said right at the beginning, I am not sure that Senior Management would have seen it that way. They probably wouldn't have disagreed but certainly during [the last Director's] time that would have been seen as a sore point. It would have been more important to go to the Partnership Meeting than to supervise the project.
>
> (WBV P10: 0370–0392)

Political tensions between operational sectors and PREM in Vietnam arose from the way the CDF challenged the meaning of development professionalism itself. What did respect for professional norms entail – project management or 'partnerships' and policy dialogue? Who was a professional poverty alleviator – sector managers or PREM policy analysts? In Vietnam, narratives by operational staff identified such tensions but underlined their commitment to handling both 'project and partnership'. Nonetheless, they often mentioned 'lack of time' as an important obstacle to reconciling both logics, and thus generally were able to justify their continued allegiance to traditional technocratic practices. Unlike in Bolivia, however, the underlying rationality of the socio-political logic embedded in the CDF was never doubted, mainly because the CDF did not pose an imminent threat to existing configurations of professional autonomy and authority. The CDF conformed to existing norms of professionalism within the Bank, which can explain why there was less resistance to its institutionalization than in Bolivia where the location and definition of professionalism was explicitly challenged.

Focusing on development results: the fight for power

In Bolivia, the CDF provided a rationale for initiating a costly offensive against corrosive corruption that threatened the managerial integrity of Bank projects. This intrusion into domestic matters was resisted not only by the Bolivian government, but also by senior Bank management fearful of the implications of this political action on their portfolio. Portfolio success in a country office is an important internal proxy for the Bank's performance, acting as a strong symbol of its technocratic competence. Four factors measure overall portfolio success: (i) size and value of loans; (ii) rates of fund disbursement or disbursement ratios; (iii) quality of lending in terms of development results; (iv) project supervision costs. Many studies of the Bank have suggested it possesses an over-riding concern with quick disbursement that has resulted in poorly implemented projects that fail to meet development objectives (Miller-Adams 1999; Payer 1982). Ironically, in such situations portfolio performance will appear to be better. While there are additional indicators of project quality within the Bank that seek to measure poverty impact and 'results', the difficulty of tracing causality has translated into portfolio success remaining an important internal proxy of Bank effectiveness.

Frustration with government corruption in Bolivia resulted in the Bank using the pretext of the CDF to suspend disbursements across all projects in fiscal year 2000. This spurred a conflict between the Bolivian Bank office and the government over the limits and possibilities of the socio-political logic represented by the CDF Local office received little support or sympathy from Bank management at headquarters, who feared short-run negative portfolio consequences. The government defended itself against the Bank's attack on corruption by drafting an alternative version of the CDF, the *Nuevo Marco de Relacioniamento*, which underlined the importance of respecting 'local' ownership norms. For its part, the local office countered this argument by underlining the importance of preserving the integrity of management practices, including auditing and disbursement regulations, despite the impulse of localism. They also justified their political intrusion into the arena of corruption in the short run as a means of securing long-run improvements in disbursement ratios and project effectiveness.

> We had here a very difficult project [that] was suspended for almost two years because we found corruption in the implementing agency. . . . For instance in that case, the Bank had some requirements. And the Bank said okay, we cannot go ahead with disbursement if the audit is not ready. An acceptable audit saying that at least the funds that were not involved in those corrupted processes were used for intended purposes. And we were two people from the Bank in a meeting with twenty people from the government. . . . Telling them these are the rules, we need this, this and this because of this. And suddenly a government official stood up and said, 'I don't care. We as a government have the right to decide because the CDF gives us the right to decide.' And the CDF says, 'You have to be flexible with the government because of this and this and this.' And he simply said, 'I am going to talk to the Country Director.' . . .
>
> That speech was made many times by different project officials, 'No, the CDF says this.' So that was difficult to use because I couldn't go to the disbursement [unit] and say, 'You know the Government says they are not going to do this because the CDF gives them the right to do it.' So that was when disbursement at some point said, 'I don't understand that CDF. But the Bank rule says this. And this is the rule that governs my work. And I am going to require this.'
>
> (WBB P7: 0659–0693)

The CDF became a medium through which the contestation of power between the Bank and the government occurred. But without higher-level management support for such an offensive, the local office quickly lost both internal and external credibility as a 'partner' of government. This resulted in accounts of dislocations and tension for staff disappointed that the CDF could not generate internal consensus and courage to champion socio-political logics. The Bolivian office rapidly recovered their previous disbursement ratios, accelerated in part due to the emergence of a financial crisis in 2003 that legitimated pumping in greater aid resources to avert economic collapse.

In direct contrast to the Bank's experience with the CDF in Bolivia, in Vietnam the office successfully obtained consensus with government on the relative balance to be maintained between technocratic and socio-political logics. Here, it is important to recognize that the relation of power between the Bank and the Vietnamese government favours the latter to the extent that Vietnam is a reluctant and slow Bank borrower. This is despite being assessed as having an extremely high capacity to absorb development funds (approximately US$800 million annually in concessional loans) and remaining the Bank's second largest concessional borrower in the world with its cumulative portfolio valued at over US$2 billion (World Bank 2004). The need to convince a potentially huge client of the merits of greater and faster borrowing for development requires donors to tread softly and subtly (Eyben 2003: 9).

Thus, the Bank was left to tactfully persuade the Vietnamese government of the merits of their financing. This was achieved by emphasizing that Vietnam's expected growth rates would soon make it ineligible for concessional Bank financing.

> In other words, if they don't lift their game over there in Government and if we don't lift our game in portfolio issues, the country loses anywhere between three to four billion concessional money that at some stage has to be borrowed from the financial markets at much higher rates.
>
> (WBV P12: 0375–0379)

Given this reversal of traditional donor–recipient power relations, the Bank moved cautiously in addressing the controversial issue of corruption in an opaque communist state for fear of jeopardizing an under-performing portfolio. Instead, the Bank sought to foster the government's trust through the CDF and informally lobby for faster project implementation.

The Bank's measured lobbying of government did not generate sought-after improvements in the portfolio, however. Portfolio performance stagnated as basic bureaucratic inefficiencies to disbursal within the Vietnamese government lay outside the negotiated consensus over the socio-political logic parameters of the CDF. Nonetheless, through CDF-inspired displays of confidence and good faith (e.g. partnership groups, consultations with other stakeholders, etc.), the Bank acquired credibility in relation to the wider development community and government. The CDF also enhanced the office's internal profile within the Bank, with Wolfensohn visiting in 2000 and staff receiving a Presidential Award for Excellence for their involvement with the CDF. These added internal legitimacy benefits may offer one explanation as to why the Vietnam office could deflect organizational pressures over its poorly performing portfolio for as long as it did (in sharp contrast to the Bolivian case), and why the CDF continued two years past the official end of the pilot phase.

> [The Country Director] was spending all his time on this partnership stuff and people were saying, 'Our portfolio is going down the spout.' Which it was, true to say, because he was spending all his time on donor relations and relations with government and being on TV, and all the rest of it. But people recognize that it has raised our profile

enormously and on the whole went along with it. Vietnam has been
the biggest feather in [senior management's] cap because of everything
on the CDF, and piloting everything. Because Wolfensohn came here
and absolutely loved it, and still talks about it three years later. And
because of everything else we do. That more than compensates for the
difficulties in the lending program. And, because other countries also
have difficulties. We are not a worse case scenario by any means.

(WBV P1 0747: 0754, 0838–0854)

Nevertheless, the arrival of a new Country Director to Vietnam in December
2002 did seem to be directing attention towards the more conventional
managerial concerns of project implementation and disbursement indicators.
Operational staff in particular welcomed this shift in priorities away from
partnerships and dialogue. In this new era, they described the previous
Country Director as a visionary leader who had failed to achieve an
appropriate balance between 'portfolio' and 'partnership' – the countervailing
practices of the technocratic and socio-political logics of development.

Implications of CDF trajectories for Bank reform

The legacy of the CDF is certainly a mixed one. While Wolfensohn
successfully generated field-wide support for his framework and bequeathed
it a lasting legacy in the PRSP, his ability to translate its socio-political
norms into concrete and lasting organizational practices within Bank offices
proved more challenging. In the Bolivia office, strained relationships with
government and headquarters resulted in a recentralization of sector staff,
the elimination of pillar groupings and the CDF's termination in September
2000 at the official end of the eighteen-month pilot stage. Meanwhile,
'partnership practices' and decentralization continued for at least an additional two years in Vietnam, even if disbursement ratios continued to stagnate.
Understanding this divergence in the ways the CDF unfolded inside the
Bank can shed important light on the possibilities and limitations of future
reform efforts.

It would seem there remains great difficulty challenging entrenched technocratic norms and practices of development inside the World Bank. While
technocratic logics have been institutionalized in the development field since
the post-war era and continue to be a characteristic feature of all bureaucracies, the strength of socio-political logics has ebbed and flowed in the
history of development (Amrith 2004; Pieterse 2001). Practices that enact
socio-political logics are typically framed as political resistance and social
movements (Escobar 1995a, 1995b; Ferguson 1994) that do not square
easily with the existence of large bureaucracies like the Bank. The CDF
experience points to the fact that the Bank is still confronted with the
dilemma of enacting socio-political logics through the application of technocratic practices (Cooke 2003; Crawford 2003). It must face the difficult

question of how to bureaucratically organize for the championship of socio-political norms associated with practices of empowerment, social justice and cultural embeddedness. Platitudes like partnership largely remained decoupled from core project work in Vietnam, while more radical efforts in Bolivia seem to generate considerable resistance from higher levels of Bank management. These tensions and conflicts ultimately result from the antithetical nature of the constitutive institutional logics of development.

Second, the difficulty in challenging the entrenched technocratic logic of development to advance the socio-political logic points to their intrinsic interdependence in the practice of development. It is this fundamental interdependence that must be acknowledged, and then exploited, if the Bank is truly committed to the advancement of the socio-political logic. One way this can occur is if organizational reform processes inside the Bank at least give the appearance of conforming to the scientific, professional and managerial norms of development. In our account, the Bolivian pilot experienced far greater difficulty institutionalizing the CDF because it overtly challenged technocratic practices like centralized accountability structures and disbursement indicators. In contrast, in Vietnam the CDF did not threaten the integrity of sectoral activities and interests directly, nor did it antagonize government over political reform or brandish the Bank's powers of coercion. As might be expected, this subtler and more tactful approach in Vietnam provided a stronger platform of legitimacy that, in turn, could be used to deflect internal disbursement pressures and justify decentralization beyond the CDF pilot phase.

The technocratic veneer of the CDF camouflaged an inherently political project of organizational reform that could challenge key ingredients of the Bank's organizational culture – including the principles of a centralized bureaucracy where preoccupations with disbursement reigned supreme. This finding supports those who suggest development organizations do strategically resort to technocratic languages and practices in order to launch challenges against them (Arce and Long 2000: 40). While more empirical and ethnographic attention within the Bank would be needed to determine whether Bank staff routinely exploit technocratic practices to camouflage engagement and advancement of socio-political goals, this chapter marks an early attempt to highlight that room for manoeuvre does remain within the Bank (see also Bebbington *et al.* 2004). It gives reason for some optimism about the prospects of institutionalizing socio-political logics at the World Bank, even under James Wolfensohn's controversial successor, Paul Wolfowitz. In fact, this paper highlights that widespread preoccupation with the appointment process of Bank presidents may be misplaced, as it ignores the significant ways Bank bureaucrats can and do manipulate executive directives.

In addition to conforming to technocratic logics, reform within the Bank will proceed with greater ease if it can secure legitimacy from external sources. For example, organizational tolerance of portfolio deterioration during the CDF pilot in Vietnam can also be explained by compensatory enhancements to the office's bargaining position and reputation with the external development community. This points to the fact that within the Bank, legitimacy may be an alternative standard of excellence to 'development results' and 'disbursement ratios'. In contrast, in Bolivia where the CDF nakedly challenged technocratic practices both within and outside the Bank, limited external legitimacy could not compensate for lack of internal legitimacy, with the result that even the slightest transgression of technocratic practices was met with hostility. These divergent trajectories of the CDF may explain why in Vietnam, the experience of institutional tension was of lower magnitude and intensity than in Bolivia, with employee narratives taking pains to downplay the severity of institutional conflicts.

Finally, the type of institutional dislocation experienced in the CDF process may be an important indicator of possibilities for future reform. This finding supports theoretical claims that unsettling, emergent contexts heighten self-consciousness and improve future possibilities for acts of agency (Emirbayer and Mische 1998: 1006–7). In Bolivia, the legacy of problematic institutional contradiction and the emergence of a growing and seemingly acute political crisis at the time of fieldwork in September 2003 combined to expand capacities for imaginative and/or deliberative responses to this uncertain context. This instability prompted a distinct imperative to disburse funds to provide the Bolivian government with the liquidity to prevent political and financial collapse. Nonetheless, the CDF had generated knowledge of opportunities for manoeuvre by the Bolivian office that could be brought to bear even in the present moment of crisis.

> Before we were working for CDF, in the name of the CDF. Now I don't think it has any power. Now the new name of the game is harmonization. Now, before everybody was scrambling internally, institutionally to show progress on the CDF. Now they don't give a damn. Now they want to show progress on harmonization. Or doing the same sort of thing they were trying to do under CDF but now calling it harmonization instead of CDF. Now we are cooking something to bring out champions of harmonization. Saying it is okay to do this. It is okay to do this alignment. ... Now the buzzword is harmonization. The task is to say, 'Well, if this works, I'll use it.'
>
> *Q. So the CDF isn't over?*
> It is a change of names, emphasis and actors. That's all.
>
> (WBB P1: 0501–0514)

Narrative accounts of problematic institutional tension in Bolivia also demonstrate the excitement of unfolding possibilities for agency, largely missing in accounts from Vietnam (with the possible exception of those working in the PREM sector who stood the most to gain from the CDF). Meanwhile, a relatively unproblematic experience of institutionalization in

Vietnam generated less need for considering alternatives to the CDF that had served the office reasonably well, with the result that ideas for future reform were considerably less ambitious.

Conclusion

This chapter has highlighted the ways the CDF, both conceptually and practically, suffered from contradictions deriving from a fundamental conundrum arising from multiple and conflicting institutional logics operating in the field of development. Traditionally governed by technocratic logics that have privileged professional expertise and management skills, economic knowledge and apolitical and hierarchical bureaucratic interventions, development organizations realize that institutional legitimacy also requires adaptation to a logic demanding greater social justice for the poor and embedded change processes driven by local participation and devolved control of the development apparatus. This institutional contradiction is highly apparent in country offices where employees are located on the threshold of clashing logics, as in the case of Bank country offices trying to institutionalize the new poverty agenda by experimenting with the CDF.

The divergent trajectories of the CDF experiment derived in no small part from the ways the CDF was exploited to alter the balance between technocratic and socio-political logics within the specific intra-organizational and national contexts of each office. In Bolivia, the CDF was more visibly antagonistic to traditional constituencies as it explicitly sought to challenge entrenched technocratic practices to advance reform; hence the greater intensity and prevalence of problematic institutional contradiction. In contrast, the less ambitious political project in Vietnam framed itself as conforming to the Bank's technocratic norms and practices, which may explain why employees could and did reconcile institutional tensions in their accounts of the CDF. As the office gained legitimacy and power through the CDF, even underperformance of the traditional standard of technocratic excellence – the portfolio – could be tolerated. These divergent processes and experiences of institutional tension provide some tentative indication of the direction that future reforms within each office might take.

In his critique of the CDF, Devesh Kapur writes that it 'paper[ed] over the inevitable conflicts between competing objectives by a mindless win-win argot that substitutes saccharine for substance and avoids the reality of trade-offs' (Kapur 2002: 74). Although the CDF proposal was certainly an ambitious project of organizational reform that did present itself as a way to reconcile conflicts between technocratic and socio-political logics, this chapter should also demonstrate that its institutionalization was always going to be a fine balancing act between the institutional logics embedded in the new poverty alleviation paradigm. By paying lip service to the 'reality of trade-offs', the CDF permitted strategic actors to challenge entrenched bureaucratic interests and practices and discover the relative costs and benefits of trade-offs themselves as they pushed the boundaries of acceptable organizational reform. While the CDF failed to transform technocracy in any sustainable or systematic way, that a strategic challenge could, and indeed was, temporarily mounted against technocracy in both offices bodes well for future efforts to take socio-political logics forward within the World Bank.

Note

1 The codes included after quotations refer to the country office (WBV for the Bank's Vietnam office and WBB for the Bolivian office), the primary document (a coded reference to the informant in question), and the actual lines of the transcribed text.

References

Amrith, S. S. (2004) 'The United Nations and Public Health in Asia, c. 1940–1960', unpublished Ph.D. thesis, History Faculty, Cambridge University.

Arce, A. and Long, N. (2000) 'Reconfiguring modernity and development from an anthropological perspective', in Arce, A. and Long, N. (eds) *Anthropology, Development and Modernities: Exploring Discourses, Counter-tendencies and Violence*, London: Routledge.

Ascher, W. (1983) 'New development approaches and the adaptability of international agencies: the case of the World Bank', *International Organisation* 37(3), 415–39.

Bebbington, A. J., Guggenheim, S., Olson, E. and Woolcock, M. (2004) 'Exploring social capital debates at the World Bank', *Journal of Development Studies* 40(5), 33–64.

CDF Secretariat (1999) *Comprehensive Development Framework Progress Report*, Washington DC: World Bank.

Chhotray, V. (2004) 'The negation of politics in participatory development projects, Kurnool, Andhra Pradesh', *Development and Change* 35(2), 327–52.

Clemens, E. S. and Cook, J. M. (1999) 'Politics and institutionalism: Explaining durability and change', *Annual Review of Sociology* 25, 441–66.

Cooke, B. (2003) 'A new continuity with colonial administration: participation in development management', *Third World Quarterly* 47.

Craig, D. and Porter, D. (1997) 'Framing participation: Development projects, professionals and organizations', in Tegegn, M. (ed.) *Development and Patronage: A Development in Practice Reader*, London: Oxfam.

——(2003) 'Poverty reduction strategy papers: A new convergence', *World Development* 31(1), 53–69.

Crawford, G. (2003) 'Partnership or power? Deconstructing the "Partnership for Governance Reform" in Indonesia', *Third World Quarterly* 24(1), 139–59.

de Herdt, T. and Bastiaensen, J. (2004) 'Aid as an encounter at the interface: The complexity of the global fight against poverty', *Third World Quarterly* 25(5), 871–85.

DiMaggio, P. J. and Powell, W. W. (1983) 'The iron cage revisited: Institutional isomorphism and collective rationality in organizational fields', *American Sociological Review* 48(2), 147–60.

Easterly, W. (2002) *The Cartel of Good Intentions: Bureaucracy versus Markets in Foreign Aid*, Washington DC: Centre for Global Development.

Eisenhardt, K. M. (1989) 'Building Theories from Case Study Research', *Academy of Management Review* 14(4), 552–50.

Emirbayer, M. and Mische, A. (1998) 'What is agency?', *American Journal of Sociology* 103(4), 962–1023.

Escobar, A. (1995a) *Encountering Development: The Making and Unmaking of the Third World*, Princeton NJ: Princeton University Press.

——(1995b) 'Imagining a post-development era', in Crush, J. (ed.) *Power of Development*, London: Routledge.

Eyben, R. (2003) 'Donors as political actors: Fighting the Thirty Years War in Bolivia', IDS Working Paper no. 183, 1–32.

Ferguson, J. (1994) *The Anti-Politics Machine*, Minneapolis MN: University of Minnesota Press.

Friedland, R. and Alford, R. R. (1991) 'Bringing society back in: Symbols, practice, and institutional contradiction', in Powell, W. W. and DiMaggio, P. J. (eds) *The New Institutionalism in Organizational Analysis*, Chicago: University of Chicago Press.

Kapur, D. (2002) 'The changing anatomy of governance of the World Bank', in Pincus, J. and Winters, J. A. (eds) *Reinventing the World Bank*, Ithaca NY: Cornell University Press.

Langley, A. (1999) 'Strategies for theorizing from process data', *Academy of Management Review* 24(4), 691–710.

Mallaby, S. (2005) *The World's Banker: A Story of Failed States, Financial Crises and the Wealth and Poverty of Nations*, New Haven CT: Yale University Press.

Maxwell, S. (2003) 'Heaven or hubris: reflections on the new "New Poverty Agenda"', *Development Policy Review* 21, 15–25.

Meyer, J. W. and Rowan, B. (1977) 'Institutionalized organizations: formal structure as myth and ceremony', *American Journal of Sociology* 83(2), 340–63.

Miller-Adams, M. (1999) *The World Bank: New Agendas for a Changing World*, London: Routledge.

Operations Evaluation Department (2003) *Toward Country-led Development: A Multi-Partners Evaluation of the CDF*: Synthesis Report, Washington DC: World Bank.

Payer, C. (1982) *The World Bank: A Critical Analysis*, New York: Monthly Review Press.

Pentland, B. T. (1998) 'Building process theory with narrative: From description to explanation', *Academy of Management Review* 24(4), 711–24.

Pieterse, J. N. (2001) *Development Theory: Deconstructions/Reconstructions*, London: Sage.

Pincus, J. (2002) 'State simplification and institution building in a World Bank-financed development project', in Pincus, J. R. and Winters, J. A. (eds) *Reinventing the World Bank*, Ithaca NY: Cornell University Press.

Porter, D. (1995) 'Scenes from childhood: The homesickness of development discourses', in Crush, J. (ed.) *Power of Development*, London: Routledge.

Rist, G. (2002) *The History of Development: From Western Origins to Global Faith*, 2nd edn, trans. P. Camiller, London: Zed Books.

Scott, W. R. (1987) 'The adolescence of institutional theory', *Administrative Science Quarterly* 32, 493–511.

Seo, M-G. and Creed, W. E. D. (2002) 'Institutional contradictions, praxis, and institutional change: A dialectical perspective', *Academy of Management Review* 27(2), 222–47.

Sewell, W. H. (1992) 'A theory of structure: Duality, agency and transformation', *American Journal of Sociology* 98(1), 1–29.

Stubbs, P. (2004) 'International non-state actors and social development policy (Policy Brief no. 4), Globalism and Social Policy Programme, 2003' (cited 31 August 2004). Available at http://www.stakes.fi/gaspp

Townley, B. (1997) 'The institutional logic of performance appraisal', *Organization Studies* 18(2), 261–85.

Whittington, R. (1992) 'Putting Giddens into action: Social systems and managerial agency', *Journal of Management Studies* 29(6), 693–712.

Wolfensohn, J. D. (1999) *A Proposal for a Comprehensive Development Framework (A Discussion Draft)*, Washington DC: World Bank.

——(2000) Note from the President of the World Bank to the Development Committee, Prague.

World Bank (2000) *Vietnam 2010: Entering the 21st Century, Partnerships for Development*, Hanoi: World Bank.

——(2004) 'IDA in action (1999–2002): Partnership for Poverty Reduction: A retrospective overview 2002' (cited 27 September 2004). Available at http://siteresources.worldbank.org/IDA/Resources/IDA_Retro_Publication.pdf

4   From 'safeguards' to 'sustainability'

The evolution of environmental discourse inside the International Finance Corporation

Christopher Wright[1]

Introduction

As an intermediary between powerful shareholder governments and both public and private borrowers, the World Bank is influential in defining what is considered the legitimate balance between public and private interests in economic development, and how these are integrated into particular development projects. Since the late 1980s, relations between the World Bank and project-affected stakeholders on particular projects have been mediated by a due diligence framework that centers on an environmental review process and a set of thematic operational policies. In 1997, this framework was formalized as the World Bank's *Environmental and Social Safeguard Policies*, and the following year, a subset of these were formally adopted by the International Finance Corporation (IFC), the World Bank Group's private sector lending arm.

The process of integrating the *Safeguard Policies* into the operations of the World Bank and the IFC has been contentious and divisive. Yet, while they continue to define the World Bank's environmental and social mission, the IFC has recently replaced them with a new Policy on Social and Environmental Sustainability and a set of Performance Standards that reflect a more private sector-driven understanding of environmental and social issues (see IFC 2005). The chapter will explore the evolution of environmental discourse in the IFC's operations and argue that the institutional role ascribed to it by civil society groups in the mid-1990s increasingly conflicted with its organizational identity as a commercial bank. This incoherence led to the Sustainability Initiative, a strategic agenda that sought to redefine how the IFC understood and promoted its environmental and social mission to clients and stakeholders. In short, this new understanding refuted the notion that environmental, social, and financial objectives were inherently separate operational concerns best achieved by dividing responsibilities between banking and support departments. Instead, it was based on a belief that its public mandate was best fulfilled by aligning its environmental and social expertise with its commercial imperatives as a lender to the private sector.

This chapter argues that the evolution of the strategies, policies and procedures that govern the IFC's engagement with environmental and social issues have been principally informed by two competing environmental discourses. While not direct opposites, they are based on norms and values that attribute a different identity and social purpose to multilateral development banks (MDBs) as publicly mandated organizations charged with financing private sector development in developing countries. The first, referred to as the 'safeguards' discourse, is primarily produced and reproduced in the advocacy campaigns and policy literature of civil society groups targeting the environmental and social practices of large banks. The understandings, linguistic formulations and perspectives in this discourse reinforce the view that the IFC, as a publicly mandated organization, should effectively act as a facilitator and regulator of private sector development that explicitly promote the public interest in countries where government capacity or commitment to do so is often lacking. As such, it calls for an assertive and aggressive institutional role in which investments are supply-driven and selected on the basis of their direct benefits to the poor and the environment.

The second, referred to as the 'sustainability' discourse, is mediated within the institutional relationship between the IFC and its private sector clients, and focuses on the constraints and opportunities that private companies face for undertaking environmentally and socially beneficial investments in emerging market economies. Within this policy discourse, interventions that benefit public interests are cushioned in business language and principally justified for their commercial rationale. In this client-driven perspective, the IFC projects its environmental and social standards as a competitive advantage in the marketplace in relation to achieving its commercial goals and those of its clients. As such, its environmental and social mission is aligned with its commercial objectives as an investment bank, rather than being conceptualized as a different and often conflicting set of operational objectives that need to be reconciled in individual projects.

The 'sustainability' discourse, manifested in the rationale behind the Sustainability Initiative introduced in 2001, has become increasingly influential in shaping the IFC's operational strategies, policies and procedures. While the strategic behaviour of key executives explains the timing and rapid diffusion of 'sustainability' within the organization in the late 1990s, the chapter argues that its acceptance within the IFC can be attributed to the fact that the concept of 'sustainability' conformed to the financial-technocratic policy discourse that is embedded in its organizational structure and professional culture. Furthermore, by depoliticizing environmental and social issues and legitimizing a commercial orientation of its public mandate, it is argued that the emergence of 'sustainability' discourse within its operational strategies may over time redefine the terms upon which multilateral financing to the private sector engages with environmental and social issues.

The analysis aims to provide an insight into the internal dynamics that preceded this shift in the environmental and social mission of the IFC, by providing an analysis of organizational change through the eyes of a small group of key individuals. It draws primarily on semi-structured interviews with some of the IFC staff who played a central role in devising and implementing the Sustainability Initiative. It is arguably biased, as it seeks to produce an account that documents the observations and exposes the motivations of those directly engaged in its implementation, rather than those of staff affected by these changes or external observers on the outside. It will identify the ideas and perspectives of some of the executives that championed and brought about these internal organizational changes, and will only consider external events or the behaviour of external actors in so far as these significantly affected dynamics within the IFC. As such, the analysis is limited to analysing organizational change rather than critically assessing its legitimacy, effectiveness or impact (see EDF 2005).

A discursive approach to examining policy change

The analysis will examine policy development at the IFC in the context of discourses, or 'sets of linguistic practices and rhetorical strategies embedded in a network of social relations' (Litfin 1994: 3). Such an approach recognizes that conflicts over the environmental and social practices of MDBs in many cases reflect fundamental disagreements over the ideas, norms and values that should inform decision-making, rather than the actual decisions. Thus, organizing the analysis around the concept of 'discourse' is meant to emphasize that conflicting policy preferences are not simply grounded in material disagreements over particular decisions, but are often embedded in deeper discursive differences over how particular policy problems should be defined and interpreted and the roles and responsibilities of different actors.

Understanding the discursive dimension of policy changes within MDBs is valuable for several reasons. First, prevailing understandings of power and authority in international relations are primarily focused on specific forms of behaviour and sources of influence, rather than their content and social purpose (Ruggie 1983). In turn, the power and influence of MDBs is not only derived from their legal standing, formal powers, financial assets and expertise, but also the norms and values that they promote in their activities. Therefore, analysing ongoing behaviour requires an appreciation of MDBs as 'social systems ... anchored in some sort of perception about the kind of collective good one would like to achieve, and more broadly in a "shared" set of ideas' (Bøås and McNeill 2004: 206–7). This collective idea of progress can be identified by analysing the policy discourses within which decision-making takes place. MDBs influence and promote particular policy discourses by conducting research and issuing publications that define, analyse and recommend specific solutions to problems, building strategic alliances with particular research institutes, business associations and civil society groups, and more recently, actively participating in and promoting knowledge networks (Stone 2005). But equally significant, as MDBs through these activities reaffirm the legitimacy and moral authority of particular norm structures, they implicitly delegitimize counter-discourses that promote conflicting norms and values.

Second, since material perspectives assume that the behaviour of international organizations is principally governed by their original mandates or the material interests of formal shareholders, they have paid less attention to how international organizations behave after they have been created (Barnett and Finnemore 1999; Miller-Adams 1999). Over time, as their development interventions have broadened and deepened and staff diversity has expanded beyond economists and financial professionals, MDBs have become intensely contested social spaces where competing norms confront each other (Bøås and McNeill 2004; Hajer 1995). In this context, sets of norms 'govern relations of authority and the values promoted define and regulate activities in a particular issue area' (Bernstein 2001: 6). In the multilateral system, these discursive struggles have most prominently manifested themselves in the debates over the development impact of globalization.

Third, when organizational change is primarily understood as instrumental responses to demands coming through the formal governance structure of the organization, the extent to which amendments to operational strategies are products of internal policy innovation is often overlooked. A focus on policy discourses may prove useful in understanding how the organizational structure and professional culture of MDBs influence the rate, scope and direction of policy change. For example, major policy initiatives at the World Bank can sometimes be attributed to individuals or groups of staff who have managed to build internal alliances around particular norms, values and interests (Fox 1998; also see chapters by Gulrajani, and Vetterlein in this volume, Chapters 3 and 7). In many cases, these proved successful because the norms and values they advocated conformed to existing dominant discourses within the organization, which enabled them to be introduced as statements of fact rather than subjects of debate.

The IFC and sustainable development

For over three decades, the IFC gained its legitimacy as a development bank from realizing positive financial returns on investments, similar to commercial banks. Its project finance loans to private sector clients by and large operated in the shadow of the World Bank's much larger, more complex development projects, and it showed little interest, either rhetorically or in operational terms, for systematically considering environmental and social issues in its investments (IFC 2002a). Until 1989, the IFC regarded its policy to only lend to projects with a 'satisfactory ex-ante economic rate of return' to be its most fundamental development contribution, and considered the financial profitability of the projects it supported as the 'sine qua non' of their development impact (IFC 1989). At this stage, it had no separate environmental and social policies and procedures designed to address the diverse, and often unique, operational contexts of private sector projects. Nor did it have environmental staff that would conduct environmental reviews of project proposals under consideration. Instead, it claimed the World Bank's environmental staff handled the environmental assessment of its projects, but by most accounts, this was under-resourced and largely ineffective at evaluating the Bank's own projects, let alone those of the IFC (Le Prestre 1989; Rich 1993; Wade 1997).

In the early 1990s, greater public scrutiny of development projects forced the IFC to more systematically address the environmental and social impacts of its investments.

Between 1989 and 1997, the IFC undertook a series of incremental reforms and multiplied its environmental staff, expanded the scope of its due diligence practices, and increased its environmental projects portfolio. It took place largely in response to the demands of civil society groups who scrutinized individual projects for their adverse environmental and social impacts, and forced the IFC to place environmental and social conditions on the use of its funds, and confront clients who failed to comply with these (see Park, this volume, Chapter 9). In 1998, the IFC formally adopted most of World Bank's *Safeguard Policies*, thus institutionalizing environmental review and assessment as a formal aspect of project preparation, as well as thematic policies covering impacts in a variety of areas, such as natural habitat, international waterways, and involuntary settlements (see IFC 1998). Combined, these produced a policy framework that would become the 'foundation for IFC's work in the environmental and social areas and for assessments of IFC's compliance and accountability' until its revision in 2006 (IFC 2002a: 33).

The turn to 'sustainability' and beyond

The formal adoption of the due diligence framework was part of a broader internal reassessment and reorganization of IFC's operations to better systematize and manage its portfolio. In 1998, it also completed its first comprehensive client survey, which found that while clients valued its membership in the World Bank Group, the expertise of its staff, and the environmental and social guidance it provided, they also felt that the IFC was 'too slow to respond, shunned risk, and had a culture which had become bureaucratic and inward looking' (IFC 1998: 2). In response to these findings and in an attempt to clarify its mission, the IFC's senior management became increasingly focused on understanding the financial and technical needs of its clients, and finding ways to improve its development impact. This was in part motivated by the growth in private capital flows and the expansion of bilateral and other sources of multilateral financing in some regions, which had forced the IFC to more forcefully consider and assert its market competitiveness as a financial institution.

In 1997, Glen Armstrong had joined the IFC's Technical and Environment Department under its director Andreas Raczynski, as a manager of its

Environmental and Social Review Unit. In his position, Armstrong led the group of environmental specialists charged with conducting environmental reviews of IFC's direct-lending projects worldwide. In this role, he soon came to the conclusion that the *Safeguard Policies* had to become more integrated into the IFC's investment practices for the environmental review process to be effective. In addition, he found the scope of environmental and social risks commonly used in project analysis to be too narrow to ensure a positive development impact, particularly in large infrastructure projects. In relation to these, he thought the IFC as a public development institution should exploit the leverage it enjoyed to push for change beyond the narrow confines of a given project. In his words, 'the IFC was punching below its weight' (Armstrong, personal communication, 11 January 2006).

In 1999, Peter Woicke, a career investment banker, succeeded Jannik Lindbaek as the IFC's Executive Vice President, and soon found himself in charge of an organization under considerable pressure. In March 2000, the US Congress-appointed International Financial Institutions Advisory Commission (IFIAC) had released a report that argued that in light of the growth in private capital flows to developing countries, multilateral engagement with the private sector should no longer include investments or guarantees, and should be limited to the provision of technical assistance and the dissemination of best practice (Meltzer 2000). Meanwhile, civil society groups continued to question its commitment to fostering sustainable private sector development by alluding to the large share of its portfolio invested in sectors typically associated with significant adverse environmental and social impacts, and the lack of attention given to maximizing and measuring real benefits for the poor and the environment (FOEI 2002; Wilks 2000). Responding to critics, Woicke countered that a unique opportunity existed for the IFC to extend benefits to the millions of poor who had yet to benefit from globalization, and contribute to resolving environmental problems (IFC 2000).

At about the same time, the IFC had in partnership with the World Bank become engaged in financing the highly contentious Chad-Cameroon oil pipeline, the single largest foreign investment project in Africa. Civil society groups opposed multilateral involvement in the project by arguing, amongst other things, that it would threaten biodiversity, undermine the livelihoods of indigenous people, and only marginally benefit the poor (EDF 1999; FOEI 2001). In contrast, Armstrong felt the IFC could use the complex project to demonstrate its commitment to a broader development agenda. By then, and with the consent of Raczynski, he had presented Woicke with his concerns about the narrow scope of the environmental review process, the need to increase its credibility with investment staff, and the value of embedding the IFC's environmental and social mission in the context of 'sustainability'. According to Armstrong, Woicke 'engaged with the concept of sustainability very quickly', and after attending an environmental leadership programme, he 'came back completely inspired' (Armstrong, personal communication, 11 January 2006).

The Sustainability Initiative

The IFC's *Annual Report* in 2000 signalled the growing significance of competitive pressures in particular regional markets (IFC 2000). While the retreat of private capital flows since the Asian crisis had caused many private financial institutions to scale back their emerging market investments, the presence of both bilateral and multilateral development institutions in some markets had grown. The report reflected its strategic desire to more proactively identify its competitive advantage over other financial institutions in servicing the private sector in developing countries, and identified its environmental and social expertise as an area of positive differentiation.

With the Chad-Cameroon project as a backdrop, Woicke expressed a desire to introduce an initiative that would 'change the face of the organization by placing sustainable development central to its organization, management and values' (Armstrong, personal communication, 11 January 2006). In 2001, as an element of this strategic reorientation, the IFC launched the Sustainability Initiative, which was presented by Woicke as a 'redefinition of the [IFC's] basic philosophy'. Its purpose was to move the IFC beyond the compliance-driven approach in order for its accumulated expertise in managing environmental and social issues to fully benefit clients and enhance its market competitiveness as a financial institution (IFC 2001). Significantly, while it sought to expand the IFC's environmental and social mission, it was forcefully launched as a business-driven initiative aimed at improving relationships with clients and enhancing their competitiveness.

Until that point, the promotion of the sustainability agenda within the IFC had largely been driven by the Technical and Environment Department, later renamed the Environmental and Social Development Department (CES). But perhaps a victim of its own success, it soon migrated to the Operational Strategy Group (COS) under its Director and chief strategist, Bernie Sheahan. At first, he was a bit sceptical of the sustainability agenda which, according to Armstrong, was not unreasonable given the plethora of new initiatives he was expected to manage in his role as Director of Operational Strategy. But once convinced, Armstrong recalls, Sheahan 'became highly effective at selling it internally because he was very operationally focused and respected by the investment staff' (Armstrong, personal communication, 11 January 2006). According to Shawn Miller, a former NGO liaison officer and environmental specialist at the IFC, the fact that the initiative became managed by COS gave it much needed legitimacy within the organization (Miller, personal communication, 20 December 2005).

In March 2001, Gavin Murray succeeded Andreas Raczynski as Director of CES. Murray would focus on the mainstreaming agenda, or the implementation of a new business model that sought to make environmental and social issues organization-wide concerns by decentralizing environmental and social expertise and responsibilities. By 2004, over 60 per cent of the IFC's environmental and social specialists were partially based within investment departments and regional offices (IFC 2004a). Meanwhile, having decided against an offer to become Director of CES, Armstrong stayed on as a Senior Environmental Advisor for another two years, collaborating with Sheahan to diffuse the sustainability concept internally, and developing new metrics for measuring project performance.

The Sustainability Initiative redefined the IFC's environmental and social mission around the concept of sustainability. Within this discursive context, the IFC's new institutional role was to supplement its due diligence framework with a focus on identifying, enhancing and realizing the 'business case' for its clients to voluntarily adopt environmental and social practices (IFC 2002). The premise was that 'many opportunities exist for businesses in emerging markets to benefit from actions which advance sustainable development', and it became the role of the IFC to convince private clients of the financial benefits of considering environmental and social issues (IFC 2002: 6). In doing so, it sought to assert itself as 'a partner of choice', by claiming to possess 'an expertise in sustainability that is second to none among financial institutions and MDBs' (IFC 2003: 2).

To foster a more constructive dialogue with clients, an internal outreach effort was launched to debunk myths and reshape attitudes amongst investment staff whose experience with environmental and social issues was limited at best. Sheahan, together with Armstrong, was central to spreading awareness of the new approach and conducted hundreds of meetings with staff at various levels to build alliances and advocate the commercial merits of the sustainability agenda. And even though 'sustainability' as a concept in principle allowed environmental and social issues to be legitimately discussed in the context of maximizing profit, he recalled that 'when speaking about sustainability in the beginning, some looked at me like I was from the moon' (Sheahan, personal communication, 3 June 2005).

The outreach effort to convert doubters creatively included a cartoon series distributed regularly by email to all internal staff that depicted various informal conversations between two fictional characters, Joe Skeptic and Sustainability Sam.[2] In one exchange, Joe Skeptic reflects the cynicism that needed to be overcome.

JOE SKEPTIC: All the people preaching sustainability are leftover flower children of the 60s who have no clue about running a business, right?
SUSTAINABILITY SAM: Joe, Joe, Joe. Spending a little too much time in the old cubicle? Where have you been? You can't mean people like the chief executives of companies such as Levi Strauss, BP, Shell, Dupont, Nike, ABB, Storebrand, and IFC, do you?

The emails also directed readers to a database on the IFC's intranet that identified companies that had realized commercial benefits from addressing 'sustainability' issues. This database provided the basis for a report co-authored by key IFC executives, including Armstrong, Sheahan and Woicke, which was launched in 2002 with the World Business Council on Sustainable Development (WBCSD) at a co-hosted side event to the World Summit on Sustainable Development (WSSD) in Johannesburg. The report, *Developing Value*, effectively marked the transition to its new perspective by aiming to be a resource for 'business people in emerging markets who are struggling to find the right balance between financial pressures on the one hand, and sustainability challenges on the other' (IFC 2002: 7). It presented a series of carefully chosen case studies identifying ways in which companies had benefited from implementing a 'sustainability action', grouped in seven categories: governance and engagement, stakeholder engagement, environmental process improvement, environmental products and services, local economic growth, community development and human resource management.

In 2003, it instituted an internal training programme aimed at making investment staff more comfortable with presenting the 'business case' for sustainability during their early consultations with clients. The focus on 'sustainability' also had implications for the way project performance was evaluated. While previous ex-post evaluations of environmental performance tended to focus on compliance rates with covenanted environmental and social requirements, the new 'sustainability framework' proposed to also measure whether 'expected [*sic*] project performance goes significantly beyond compliance with IFC's safeguard policies, associated guidelines, and economic and governance expectations to create benefits' (IFC 2004: 16). It introduced a graduated scale in which compliance with standards represented the minimum level of acceptable performance, and creating additional environmental and social benefits beyond those produced by complying with standards would earn a 'high impact' mark. Annually, the percentage of new projects expected to have a 'high impact' would constitute the IFC's contribution to sustainable development (IFC 2003).

During the same year, IFC's Office of the Compliance Advisor/Ombudsman (CAO) released a report that reviewed the implementation and impact of the IFC's *Safeguard Policies* since their formal adoption in 1998. It observed that many clients found them difficult to interpret and implement, and many of its own staff did not even regard them as part of the IFC's core business (IFC 2003a). In cases where potential clients lacked the capacity or commitment to address environmental and social concerns and had access to multiple sources of finance on reasonable terms, there was some concern among internal staff that the IFC was losing business because other banks were more 'pragmatic' in addressing environmental and social issues (IFC 2003a). This could potentially mean that placing environmental and social requirements on clients that regarded these as administrative or political burdens would induce them to pursue other sources of finance.

The recommendations made in the *CAO Report* informed a comprehensive revision of three policy frameworks: the *Safeguard Policies*, the *Policy on Disclosure of Information*, and the *Environment, Health and Safety Guidelines.* Launched in October 2004, the stated objective of the policy revision process was to produce a due diligence framework better suited for the private sector context and its new strategic focus on 'sustainability'. And wanting to break with the past, it was perhaps no coincidence that the language of 'safeguards' was not retained. After a tumultuous and delayed policy revision process, in which both civil society groups and a selection of multinational commercial banks voiced their dissatisfaction with the consultation process, the IFC concluded the consultation period of the new *Policy and Performance Standards on Social and Environmental Sustainability* in November 2005 (IFC 2005).

Environmental discourses in the multilateral system

In 2000, Woicke approached Armstrong and asked him to present the basic tenets of the sustainability concept at an IFC senior management retreat in November that year. According to Armstrong, the reception that the presentation would receive from departmental directors and managers would 'either make or break the adoption of sustainability agenda within the IFC' (Armstrong, personal communication, 11 January 2006).

The IFC was at a crossroads. During the late 1990s, it had increasingly found itself straddled between two forms of environmental discourse that each offered a different interpretation of the IFC's environmental and social mission. The 'safeguards' discourse centred on a perceived necessity for placing requirements on clients, extending rights and entitlements to vulnerable people, and protecting sensitive environmental areas from development, as a way to ensure that IFC investments did not have negative environmental and social impacts. This viewpoint gained its legitimacy from reports that indicated a failure on the part of the IFC to adequately assess and mitigate adverse environmental and social impacts in some of its large projects (Hair *et al.* 1997). In contrast, the 'sustainability' discourse embedded the environmental and social agenda into a broader private sector development context that rationalized the application of minimum standards and broader business-centred interventions as an element of profitability. The centrality of developing a 'business case' underscored the notion that the private sector, and profit-seeking companies, would be the agents of positive social change, not multilateral financial institutions.

The next section will outline and contrast the norms, values and understandings that underpinned these two discourses.

The 'safeguards' discourse

It is argued that, in particular, the early evolution of the IFC's environmental and social policies and procedures primarily took place within a 'safeguards' discourse, which rests upon the notion that development finance is inherently political, involving difficult trade-offs between financial, environmental and social objectives. In turn, clear normative distinctions are made between public and private interests, which force a public institution that services the private sector, such as the IFC, to undertake a particularly delicate balancing act. Crucially, within this discursive context, it is assumed that unless legal conditions and restrictions are placed on investment projects, environmental due diligence would in most cases be rushed and incomplete. While this depiction conflicted with the official pronouncements of the IFC during this period, the public exposure of investment projects with significant adverse environmental and social impacts forced it to engage with civil society groups on these terms. Indeed, the impetus for initially adopting the World Bank's environmental and social policy framework was to respond to public demands for greater accountability and transparency.

As environmental and social issues are expressed in terms of placing restrictions on development in environmentally-sensitive areas, and extending more rights to local communities for project-related information and compensation, policy deliberations inevitably focus on whether project-based operations should be subjected to additional environmental conditions, consultation and disclosure requirements. By conceptualizing the management of environmental and social issues as a compliance requirement, the discourse reinforces the impression that private sector development without appropriate safeguards would be inherently unsustainable in environmental and social terms. As such, the discourse has a uniquely normative logic, in that technocratic policies and procedures are assessed against their conformance with broadly recognized norms, values and principles of human rights, social justice and environmental conservation.

With regards to the IFC, the 'safeguards' discourse understands its institutional relationship with clients on environmental and social issues as analogous to that between the public regulator and the private regulated firm at the domestic level. In this context, the IFC would be judged as a public institution in the democratic institutional sense, as a guardian of public interests against the excesses of private markets, and accountable to the citizens of its shareholder governments and project-affected communities. Indeed, more generally, acknowledging the validity of these 'public' concerns is precisely what grants MDBs legitimacy as public development institutions in this discourse. Over time, the extent to which they adequately responded to the demands of civil society groups for more thorough environmental and social review procedures, more extensive public consultation, and more systematic information disclosure, became increasingly critical to mitigating the 'crisis of legitimacy' that they found themselves in (Rich 1993; Wade 1997). In relation to the IFC, the environmental reform process, and the demonstration that the legal framework was applied consistently across individual projects, was significantly driven by a need to instill-public confidence in the development contribution of private sector investment projects (IFC 2003a).

The 'safeguards' discourse was produced and reproduced by the institutional relationship between the IFC and civil society groups. In terms of the latter, the 'safeguards' discourse positions them as the *de facto* representatives of local communities and sensitive ecosystems in the multilateral system. Transnational networks of civil society groups often transmit the concerns of local communities to the centres of decision-making in major capitals, and blend these project-specific messages with broader demands for greater accountability and transparency. Indeed, the leverage of civil society groups in policy discussion stems precisely from this notion of representativeness. Their legitimacy is enhanced further through media coverage that depicts confrontations between them and the IFC as conflicts between guardians of the poor and the environment on the one side, and promoters of unconstrained economic development on the other. In this social context, the IFC is forced either to succumb to the demands from civil society for greater accountability and transparency, and by doing so, enjoy temporary praise, or rebuff critics and have its legitimacy as a development institution questioned.

This confrontational policy dynamic is a legacy of the controversy over World Bank projects in the 1980s. It produced a deep sense of mutual mistrust and suspicion between civil society groups and multilateral institutions that significantly shaped their respective policy positions and interactions (Wade 1997). Among the former, there was a deep-rooted sense that environmental and social reforms were largely ineffective in delivering substantive change in how projects were prepared and implemented. In fact, among some there was a suspicion that they were not motivated by a genuine commitment to integrate environmental and social issues into investment decisions, but rather, to give an impression that the demands of civil society groups had been heeded (Rich 1993). In the case of the IFC, these suspicions were substantiated by independent reports that had observed inconsistent application of the *Safeguard Policies* across investment projects, and varying levels of commitment to environmental and social issues among IFC staff and its clients (IFC 2003a; Hair *et al.* 1997). These revelations and others legitimized the demands of civil society groups for an expansion of binding minimum standards, and a requirement for the IFC to publicly disclose the basis and rationale for its investment decisions.

The 'sustainability' discourse

While the 'safeguards' discourse largely evolved in the context of the IFC's institutional relationship with civil society groups, the 'sustainability' discourse is primarily driven by the IFC's interactions with clients and is firmly embedded in the norms and understandings that govern business management practices. Central to this framing is an assumption that the relationships between private sector development, environmental protection and poverty alleviation can be complementary and mutually reinforcing. By emphasizing synergies rather than trade-offs, it does not conceptualize the environment-development nexus in adversarial terms, nor does it frame environmental and social issues as sources of costly mitigation measures for clients. Instead, the concept of sustainability presents its environmental and social mission as a component of business profit, and by implication, it 'offers a positive agenda for businesses' which is not primarily about 'bowing to NGO demands' (IFC 2002: 32).

In addition, while the 'safeguards' discourse focuses on the instances where environmental and social concerns are adversely affected by market-driven decision-making, the scope of societal concerns and business responses that fall under the rubric of 'sustainability' is considerably broader. By mixing typically contentious, costly and time-demanding activities, such as stakeholder engagement and environmental impact mitigation and prevention, with more intuitive strategies that have clear short- or long-term financial benefits, 'sustainability' discourse produces an agenda that allows the IFC to engage its clients in more positive and constructive terms. For example, the case studies in the *Developing Value* report highlighting sustainability approaches also included business practices that private companies would conceivably consider in the absence of external pressures, such as integrating the local economy into their supply-chains and improving human resource management. As is noted, 'in many cases the owners were not explicitly addressing sustainable development, but were simply implementing what they saw as good management practices and sound business decisions' (IFC 2002: 7).

In this context, the institutional role of the IFC is more closely associated with identifying and demonstrating the existence of a 'business case' for undertaking interventions that are normally understood as public interest concerns. While the 'safeguards' discourse largely externalizes environmental and social issues from financial profitability, sustainability integrates all of these under the assumption that they are complementary, rather than conflicting. In this context, the act of imposing standards on borrowers in order to manage the environmental and social aspects of projects is reconceptualized as 'disseminating best practice and understanding of evolving risks and opportunities related to sustainability' (IFC 2002: 49). As such, the focus is on the creation and diffusion of knowledge and information in support of collective learning towards the common objective of marrying financial profit-motives with public interest concerns. Within this agenda, the IFC projects itself as the primary resource for 'sustainability' expertise and advice for private companies, and a leader among financial institutions in applying these concepts to project finance operations.

While the practice that arose out of the compliance-based approach sought to maximize economic benefits but merely satisfy environmental and social requirements, the Sustainability Initiative purports to go 'beyond compliance' by focusing on increasing the environmental and social benefits of investments. In this context, the act of extending rights to project-affected communities and placing legal conditions on development in sensitive eco-systems is valued not primarily because it is morally and ethically called for, but because private clients may derive some future financial benefit from doing so. As such, it differs from the 'safeguards' discourse by primarily viewing environmental and social concerns from the commercial vantage point of profit-driven clients in emerging markets, rather than project-affected communities or the local environment. In the context of individual project finance transactions, the approach encourages investment officers to identify opportunities for making profitable investments that address environmental and social issues beyond what is required by IFC's minimum standards or host country laws and regulations. This differentiated approach conforms to the 'client-driven' agenda that increasingly influences policies and strategies at the World Bank Group more broadly.

By more strategically taking on an advisory role, the IFC pretends to 'move beyond a predominantly compliance-oriented approach to one that systematically focuses on adding value' (IFC 2001: 14). Achieving the latter places less emphasis on broadening and enforcing rules and requirements, and more on understanding and, in its own words, appealing 'to firms' self-interest as a means of enhancing the sustainability of economic activity' (IFC 2003: 20). In turn, it encourages an engagement strategy whereby environmental and social issues are mixed in with general financing advice. To enable this, its project-related environmental work under 'sustainability' would migrate from a defensive 'do no harm' strategy that predominantly focuses on mitigating or preventing adverse impacts associated with its projects, to a more proactive strategy that seeks to 'add value' to invest-ments. This positions the IFC more directly on the side of its clients, by aligning its engagement with environmental and social issues with the norms, values and principles that are advocated by private companies and markets.

The internal diffusion of the 'sustainability' discourse

This section will identify the ideas and perceptions that contributed to the emergence of the Sustainability Initiative. It argues that while the com-pliance-driven understanding of its environmental and social mission was driven by external demands to increase the accountability and legitimacy of its investments and align its due diligence processes with those of the World Bank, the ideas behind the Sustainability Initiative were much more a pro-duct of social learning and norm diffusion inside the organization. Specifi-cally, while the initial reforms in the early 1990s added an entirely new mission to the IFC's role as a promoter of private sector development in developing countries, the internal management initiatives that later drove the sustainability agenda drew on past experiences and sought to rid preconceptions and introduce new norms and values that would allow a better integration of its environmental and social mission into its commercially driven private sector projects.

Initially, this required confronting the internal scepticism towards the environmental and social agenda that had peaked with the politically contentious disclosure of the Hair Report in 1997, and its strong criticism of the IFC's lack of systematic environmental and social review in the context of the Pangue project (Hair *et al.* 1997). This process largely depended on internal email campaigns, hundreds of meetings with internal sceptics, and networking with sympathetic external organizations who could lend credibility to the cause. As such, the discursive shift that took place went beyond simple procedural changes to bureaucratic decision-making, as it introduced new terms and concepts for defining and rationalizing the IFC's environmental and social mission. The objective was to trigger a 'significant culture change' that would see investment officers being comfortable with raising environmental and social issues with clients and identifying opportunities to add value to projects (IFC 2001).

Depoliticizing its environmental and social mission

The roll-out of this organizational change initiative was prompted by two underlying motivations, both related to improving relations with clients. First and foremost, the growing competition from multilateral, bilateral and commercial lenders in emerging markets had prompted the IFC to differentiate itself and seek ways to increase its attractiveness as a source of long-term finance. In many regions, this meant the IFC was pressured to offer clients a valuable benefit beyond simply providing affordable long-term financing. This implicated its environmental and social mission and the Safeguard Policies framework, because there was a real concern among some investment staff that the IFC was losing business because other banks were more 'pragmatic' in addressing environmental and social issues (IFC 2003a).

And to the proponents of the sustainability concept, the implementation of the IFC's environmental and social mission was impeded by internal divisions and a failure to go beyond minimum standards to maximize its development impact. According to Armstrong, the environmental review process could fail at many levels. In most cases, the environmental and social standards were deemed completely acceptable by clients as long as they were informed early on in the project preparation phase. When clients resisted the standards, it was either because they lacked a commitment, or because the requirement to fulfil them was communicated very late in the project preparation process. CES staff were commonly not engaged in these early discussions and investment officers sometimes failed to mention them 'in the mistaken belief that they might scare away the client, which very rarely if ever happened' (Armstrong, personal communication, 11 January 2006).

It was thought that making its environmental and social practices conform to those favoured by many multinational corporations, some of whom were clients of the IFC, would enhance its legitimacy in the private sector. According to Rachel Kyte, who became Director of CES in 2004, migrating away from viewing environmental and social issues as 'burdens' in the IFC's operations, to 'value added activities' that provide direct financial benefits to clients, would entail an approach to due diligence that more accurately reflected what the market was increasingly looking for, namely the 'consideration of environmental and social issues in the context of a risk and opportunity framework' (Kyte, personal communication, 3 June 2005). In Sheahan's view, moving beyond the narrow conception of environmental and social issues as risks to the *status quo* was instrumental in making its environmental and social mission consistent with its mandate to foster social change in developing countries in the form of private sector development (Sheahan, personal communication, 3 June 2005).

The *CAO Report* observed that the IFC's institutional relationship with civil society groups over time had produced a 'vicious circle of process compliance' in which compliance with the *Safeguard Policies* was perceived by stakeholders as a 'yardstick of accountability' (IFC 2003a: 43). According to Gavin Murray, Director of CES between 2001 and 2004, 'intransigence on both sides in terms of willingness to sit down and think through the role and implementation of the *Safeguard Policies* had produced a high degree of indifference between civil society groups and the IFC' (Murray, personal communication, 20 December 2005). The impetus to reassess its engagement with environmental and social issues was in part aimed at identifying 'a way out of [this] box' (Sheahan, personal communication, 3 June 2005).

Overcoming internal scepticism

The compartmentalization of environmental and social expertise in one support department was perceived to be an impediment to promoting its potential business value for clients. Within this organizational structure, according to Murray, 'there was a view that not everyone was aligned and working in the same direction – to the degree that the business units considered themselves impeded by support functions' (Murray, personal communication, 20 December 2005). This was in large part because CES was almost exclusively in charge of implementing the IFC's environmental and social agenda, which meant that environmental specialists came to act as 'an internal police force ensuring that project proposals and the decisions made by investment staff were in compliance with the *Safeguard Policies*' (Sheahan, personal communication, 3 June 2005). In addition, since these interventions often occurred late in the project cycle, many investment staff regarded them as obstructive to their work, and by extension, to the IFC's commercial mandate as a development institution (IFC 2003a).

According to Stuart Turnbull, an organizational change specialist at the IFC who undertook an informal surrey of investment officers and managers in the late 1990s, some investment officers perceived that the *Safeguard Policies* framework 'gave clients more things to do, added cost, and slowed things down'. This meant that the commercial benefits of the framework became difficult for them to justify, which increased the importance of describing it well to clients, a task for which they often lacked experience or evidence (Turnbull, personal communication, 1 June 2005). The mainstreaming agenda, managed by Murray, was introduced to overcome this problem, and proponents hoped this would reduce the perception that environmental and social issues were 'burdens' in the IFC's operations, and instead convince sceptics among investment staff that these were 'value added activities' that could provide direct financial benefits to clients. This was perceived as central to enabling the IFC to promote environmental and social expertise and discuss its value to clients, and overcome the problem of 'unwilling compliance', in which clients 'followed rules only if they had to, or if they could not find a way around them' (Turnbull, personal communication, 1 June 2005).

Mainstreaming meant eradicating the 'compliance mentality' and introducing a 'team-based approach' to the IFC's project work (IFC 2002a). One of its central aspects was the co-location of some CES staff within investment departments, and the transfer of some environmental and social responsibilities to investment staff, a management change that got mixed reviews from those directly affected. Murray recalled that 'while some CES staff felt comfortable in a business unit working alongside investment officers, others felt as if they would be leaving the mother's breast and were vulnerable to potential capture and loss of independence'. Likewise, 'whereas some investment staff were easily convinced, others considered the new responsibilities a distraction that would do little to enhance their career prospects in investment banking around the world' (Murray, personal communication, 20 December 2005).

This analysis suggests that the reform of its professional culture was central to implementing 'sustainability', and indeed critical for it to succeed. But while not being able to draw any substantive conclusions on whether the envisioned 'significant cultural change' has occurred since the launch of the Sustainability Initiative, these observations suggest that it remains a momentous, yet critical task.

Summary

Two key observations in relation to policy change at the IFC can be extracted from this brief overview of the emergence and diffusion of 'sustainability' discourse within the IFC, as manifest in its influence on operational strategies and the IFC's organizational purpose.

First, while the IFC, as other MDBs, may indeed be experiencing mission creep as a result of external demands from shareholders and stakeholders, the nature in which new organizational priorities or objectives become institutionalized is significantly shaped by its organizational culture and the ideological affiliations of staff. This analysis suggests that, once external shareholders and stakeholders had been successful at adding a new mission to the IFC's operations, in this case the assurance that private sector financing contributes to sustainable development, the organizational response was significantly driven by factors internal to the organization. In this particular case, executive management sought to integrate its new mission with its core *modus operandi*, namely its commercial objectives as an investment bank, and by extension, the financial interests of its clients in developing countries. This essentially involved translating normative claims and moral prerogatives into operational terms, by embedding these in economic and technocratic language that legitimized them in the eyes of internal investment staff and external private clients. As such, its environmental and social mission came to reflect a 'liberal environmentalism', in which the liberalization of finance was seen as consistent and a prerequisite for international environmental protection (Bernstein 2001).

Second, the analysis demonstrates that in order to succeed, policy change that challenges the ideological predispositions of staff requires the active support of senior managers and executives in positions of power. In this case, the ideas and norms that define the concept of sustainability emerged, were diffused, and eventually informed changes to operational strategies because of the actions of key executives, and despite the scepticism of other staff. These executives had realized that once the environmental and social agenda had been added to the organization's mission, the external legitimacy of the organization rested on ensuring and demonstrating that IFC projects had a positive development impact. At the same time, increasing competition between multilateral, bilateral and private financial institutions in some regions and sectors meant the IFC was increasingly pressured to demonstrate its credentials for being a 'partner of choice' in the market place. For the IFC, the two realities produced by 'the push of reformers and critics ... and the pull of businesses in the marketplace' had to be reconciled (IFC 2000: 2). It meant that the addition of an environmental and social review process, which included comprehensive environmental assessments and extensive public consultation in some cases, had to be legitimized and promoted as a business value for clients. This was attempted by reframing and re-rationalizing its environmental and social mission within the context of sustainability, so that it no longer would stand in opposition to the core ideas and objectives of the organization. In turn, this policy initiative represented a discursive shift in the IFC's environmental and social mission, and would provide the normative framework within which subsequent decision-making would take place.

Conclusion

This chapter has suggested that in general terms, the social purpose of MDBs is subject to evolving interpretations of their organizational mandate, which is mediated within particular policy discourses. It has argued that the evolution of the IFC's own understanding of its environmental and social mission can be usefully analysed in the context of two policy discourses. It has identified the 'sustainability' discourse as the normative context that increasingly defines the IFC's engagement with environmental and social issues and its relationships with external stakeholders. It has argued that the alignment of the IFC's environmental and social mission with the concept of 'sustainability' can be explained by a strategic desire to increase its legitimacy and appeal with private clients, which was seen as critical to increasing the effectiveness of its environmental due diligence framework. But significantly, the diffusion of 'sustainability' discourse within the IFC would not have occurred had it not conformed to the existing financial-technocratic discourse embedded in its organizational structure and professional culture.

As social institutions, MDBs are filters through which normative claims and moral prerogatives are translated into terms that enable them to be integrated into investment decision-making. In turn, these are promoted through their operations and partnerships, and gain legitimacy and influence by virtue of being associated with the financial resources and expertise of MDBs. In terms of the IFC, the reconceptualization of its environmental and social mission in line with 'sustainability' was conducive to an attempt at reconciling the conflict between its various operational objectives, and increasing its legitimacy and influence with private clients. Its growing influence has most recently manifested itself in the Equator Principles, a set of environmental and social investment standards adopted by dozens of financial institutions, and based on the IFC's own policies and procedures (see Wright and Rwabizambuga 2006). And as evidence suggests that multilateral and corporate environmental discourses are gradually converging around the concept of 'sustainability', the influence of MDBs in shaping global and local environmental governance arrangements is likely to increase.

Notes

1 I am deeply indebted to Glen Armstrong, Rachel Kyte, Suellen Lazarus, Shawn Miller, Gavin Murray, Bernie Sheahan, Stuart Turnbull and two anonymous IFC staff members for kindly offering their valuable time in support of this research. In addition, I want to thank Glen Armstrong, Susan Park and Diane Stone for providing comments on preliminary drafts.
2 Reproduced with the kind consent of Bernie Sheahan, the IFC's Director of Financial Advisory Services, and Joseph O'Keefe, IFC's Corporate Relations Manager.

References

Barnett, M. and Finnemore, M. (1999) 'The Politics, Power and Pathologies of International Organizations', *International Organization* 53(4), 699–732.

Bernstein, S. (2001) *The Compromise of Liberal Environmentalism*, New York: Columbia University Press.

Bøås, M. and McNeill, D. (2004) 'Introduction', in Bøås, M. and McNeill, D. (eds) *Global Institutions and Development: Framing the World?*, London: Routledge.

EDF (2005) *Retreat from the Safeguard Policies – Recent Trends Undermining Social and Environmental Accountability at the World Bank*, prepared by Shannon Lawrence (Environmental Defense), in collaboration with Peter Bosshard, (International Rivers Network), Bruce Jenkins (Bank Information Center), Jen Kalafut (Bank Information Center), Anne Perrault, (Center for International Environmental Law), Andrea Durbin (Environmental Defense), and Suzanne Hunt (Environmental Defense), January 2005.

——(1999) *The Chad Cameroon Oil and Pipeline Project: Putting People and the Environment at Risk*, September 1999, written by Korinna Horta (Environmental Defense Fund), Samuel Nguiffo (Center for Environment and Development, Cameroon), and Delphine Djiraibe (Association Tchadienne pour la Promotion et la Défense des Droits de l'Homme), September 1999.

FOEI (2002) *Dubious Development: How the World Bank's Private Arm Is Failing the Poor and the Environment*, Amsterdam: Friends of the Earth International (FOEI).

——(2001) *Broken Promises – The Chad Cameroon Oil and Pipeline Project: Profit at Any Cost?*, written by Samuel Nguiffo (Center for Environment and Development/ Friends of the Earth Cameroon) and Susanne Breitkopf (Urgewald), June 2001. Amsterdam: Friends of the Earth International (FOEI).

Fox, J. A. (1998) 'When Does Reform Policy Influence Practice? Lessons From the Bankwide Resettlement Review', in Fox, J. A. and Brown, L. D. (eds) *The Struggle for Accountability. The World Bank, NGOs, and Grassroots Movements*, Cambridge MA and London: MIT Press.

Hair, J., Dysart, B., Danielson, L. J. and Rubaleava, A. O. (1997) *Pangue Hydroelectric Project (Chile): An Independent Review of the International Finance Corporation's Compliance with Applicable World Bank Group Environment and Social Requirements*, IFC Internal Document, 4 April, World Bank, Santiago, Chile.

Hajer, M. (1995) *The Politics of Environmental Discourse: Ecological Modernization and the Policy Process*, Oxford: Clarendon Press.

IFC (2005) *International Finance Corporation's Policy and Performance Standards on Social and Environmental Sustainability*, Washington DC: International Finance Corporation (IFC), Public Release Draft, 22 September 2005.

——(2004) *Annual Report 2004*, Washington DC: International Finance Corporation.

——(2004a) *Sustainability Review 2004*, Washington DC: International Finance Corporation.

——(2003) *Sustainability Review 2003*, Washington DC: International Finance Corporation.

——(2003a) *A Review of IFC's Safeguard Policies – Core Business: Achieving Consistent and Excellent Environmental and Social Outcomes*, Washington DC: International Finance Corporation's Compliance Advisor/Ombudsman (CAO), January 2003.

——(2002) *Developing Value – The Business Case for Sustainability in Emerging Markets*, Washington DC: International Finance Corporation, SustainAbility and the Ethos Institute.

——(2002a) *The Environmental and Social Challenges of Private Sector Projects: The IFC's Experience*, Washington DC: International Finance Corporation.

——(2001) *Annual Report 2001*, Washington DC: International Finance Corporation.

——(2000) *Annual Report 2000*, Washington DC: International Finance Corporation.

——(1998) *Environmental and Social Review Procedures*, Washington DC: International Finance Corporation, December.

——(1989) *The Development Contribution of IFC Operations*, Washington DC: Economics Department, International Finance Corporation, Discussion Paper no. 5.

Le Prestre, P. (1989) *The World Bank and the Environmental Challenge*, Selinsgrove PA: Susquehanna University Press.

Litfin, K. (1994) *Ozone Discourses: Science and Politics in Global Environment Cooperation*, New York: Columbia University Press.

Meltzer, A. (2000) *Report of the International Financial Institutions Advisory Commission (IFIAC)*, Washington DC: IFIAC.

Miller-Adams, M. (1999) *The World Bank: New Agendas in a Changing World*, London: Routledge.

Payne, R. A. (2001) 'Persuasion, Frames and Norm Construction', *European Journal of International Relations* 7(1), 37–61.

Rich, B. (1993) *Mortgaging the Earth: Environmental Impoverishment and the Crisis of Development*, Boston MA: Beacon Press.

Ruggie, J. (1983) 'International Regimes, Transactions, and Change: Embedded Liberalism in the Post-war Economic Order', in Krasner, S. (ed.) *International Regimes*, Ithaca NY: Cornell University Press.

Stone, D. (2005) 'Global Knowledge Networks and Global Policy', in Stone, D. and Maxwell, S. (eds) *Global Knowledge Networks and International Development: Bridges Across Boundaries*, London: Routledge.

Wade, R. (1997) 'Greening the Bank: The Struggle over the Environment, 1970–1995', in Kapur, D., Lewis, J. and Webb, R. (eds) *The World Bank: Its First Half Century*, vol. 2, Washington DC: Brookings Institution Press, 611–734.

Wilks, A. (2000) 'An Analysis of the IFC's Role and Impact', Bretton Woods Project, September.

Wright, C. and Rwabizambuga, A. (2006) 'Institutional Pressures, Corporate Reputation and Voluntary Codes of Conduct: An Examination of the Equator Principles', *Business and Society Review* 111(1), 89–117.

5 Explaining change in the World Bank's forest strategy and operational policy

Lauren Flejzor

Introduction

Change initiatives in large, complex organizations can occur in rapid bursts, in incremental steps or on a continuous basis. The focus of this book, changes to policies and initiatives in the World Bank during the Wolfensohn presidency, has shed light on a variety of changes in the Bank's internal and external organizational environments. This chapter analyses how the combination of executive leadership, strategy entrepreneurs and process innovation led to a punctuated, or transformational, change episode within the Bank. Specifically, it explains how President Wolfensohn, by delegating and relying on a small team of departmental staff, initiated and supported major changes to the World Bank's 1991 Forest Strategy and the 1993 Forest Operational Policy.

Leadership can help stimulate innovations and change in relatively inert organizations that rely on norms and routines to perform day-to-day work. 'Leadership plays a critical function in defining the boundaries of search behaviour as it makes investment decisions to continue the cycle of divergent and convergent innovation development' (Van de Ven *et al.* 1999: 204). However, the presence of a strong leader is not, on its own, a way to enact major change in international organizations. Leaders can set the pace for innovations and strategic processes within organizations, but must have the strong support of organizational actors in order to succeed.

Departmental staff played a key role in acting as strategy entrepreneurs during the World Bank's forest strategy and policy change process. A small team of departmental staff, in receiving support from corporate leadership, designed new strategy processes that required significant outreach to the Bank's regional stakeholders. This new process established informal governance structures and generated important feedback necessary to reorient the Bank's 1991 Forest Strategy and 1993 Operational Policy. Although the transaction costs were high, Bank staff increased the process legitimacy of the strategic exercise by conducting extensive stakeholder consultations. Process legitimacy is about how 'decisions are made rather than what decisions ultimately result' (Hult and Walcott 1990: 66).

To understand the Bank's punctuated change outcome, the internal and external environments of the Bank's Environment and Socially Sustainable Development (ESSD) Network were analysed. The approach used to analyse the change outcome is process-oriented; that is, it examines a range of factors within and outside the ESSD Network to explain why and how transformative changes resulted in the 2002 Revised World Bank Forest Strategy and Operational Policy. The empirical work is based on the revision process of the Bank's 1991 Forest Strategy and 1993 Forest Operational Policy, and illustrates how the Bank's poor performance in the forest sector was a primary motivation for new strategic outputs.

This chapter first examines the linkage between punctuated change and corporate leadership. Second, it will explain why information feedback on the Bank's poor performance in the forest sector prompted a new approach to the Bank's forest work, and how an innovative strategic process design resulted. The chapter then analyses the consultative process used to form the revised strategy and policy. The fourth section of the chapter explains the influence of Bank norms and powerful governance structures in forming the revised forest policy and implementation plan. The fifth part discusses a critical element of the new strategy and policy's acceptance: the formation of a business plan. The final part of this chapter discusses the success as well as the constraints of the Bank's strategic change process in the forest sector.

Punctuated change and the influence of leadership

Theories of punctuated change have been used to explain policy outcomes in the early 1990s and and the new millennium. Evolutionary biology turned a corner when Eldredge and Gould (1972) suggested that biological evolution was not continuous, but in fact happened in short bursts or 'punctuated' changes. Punctuated change also describes how the accumulation of processes can drive 'occasional discontinuous reorientations in part or all of a social system, while evolution characterizes the period of continuous convergence and metamorphosis' (Van de Ven 1987: 338). Transformation is largely captured in the idea of adaptation, which is how an organization changes to better fit its environment.

Political scientists and management scholars have since used the concept of punctuated change to explain various outcomes in policies and strategies. Political science suggests that such transformational shifts can occur when policy windows or entrepreneurs appear in a system (Kingdon 1995; Barzelay and Campbell 2003). Baumgartner and Jones (2002) provide empirical evidence of how transformational shifts occur in policy outcomes due to responses to events and political attention shifting.

Management scholars have also explained punctuated change in large organizations. Tushman and Anderson (1987) explained how organizations experience slow periods of change alongside rapid bursts of change. Sastry (1997) bases her theory of punctuated organizational change on strategic reorientation and the appropriateness of a strategy's fit in its internal and external organizational environments. Drawing on Sastry, an organization's strategy can be revised and a transformational change can result if the original strategic orientation is a poor fit with its environment.

Poor performance and inertia are two key indicators of an organization's ability to undergo transformational change. As Sastry notes,

> as inertia builds up ... signals of poor performance must be stronger for the organization to react, as organizational members are slower to perceive discrepant signals of poor performance after a long period of convergence, and new ideas are more difficult to assimilate into an organization that has not changed in a long while.
>
> (1997: 244)

Thus, routines in the form of rules and norms are created and build over time, thus limiting the organization's ability to change.

Particularly in international organizations, inertia is created within powerful governance structures. Norms and routines are generated in structures – usually governing bodies or institutions – that are responsible for decision-making and initiating organizational activities. McNeill (2005) draws on Gramsci to categorize such structures as consistent with hegemonic and dominant forms of power. These structures act as powerful control mechanisms for decision-making within organizations. While such institutionalization of decision-making and power may help manage uncertain internal and external organizational environments, they also build inertial forces in organizations. Powerful governance structures can take the form of centralized institutions that slow the pace of change and act as control mechanisms in organizations.

For punctuated change to occur in international organizations, old norms and routines must be broken and radically new processes and outcomes must emerge. Pettigrew *et al.* (1992) suggest that crises help mobilize such change, which can be perceived as both opportunities and threats. However, such threats and opportunities can only create major change where 'the processes of bargaining and negotiation can accrue support and legitimacy for the new order of things' (Pettigrew *et al.* 1992: 271). The accumulation of evidence, time and support to change the direction of a strategy can help induce successful change outcomes. 'Accumulation appears to be the basic process underlying discontinuous punctuations because the resulting transformation represents a metamorphic or radical change which no longer includes representations of the earlier organization' (Van de Ven 1987: 338).

At the same time, however, it takes the support of key leaders to move forward the new strategy process. Tushman and Romanelli (1994) note that transformational change within an organization cannot occur unless there is also support from senior leadership. If the change process begins at the departmental level, the process is more likely to succeed and gain legitimacy if it has the support of departmental- as well as corporate-level leadership. In addition to corporate leadership, however, external organizational consultation with community leaders and non-governmental organizations (NGOs) may also be necessary to acquire support and legitimacy for change.

To attain such legitimacy and strike a balance between internal, top-down led initiatives and bottom-up-consultative processes, a complex organization needs to mix 'loose' with 'tight' coupling. 'Loose' coupling exists in an organizational system where an organization has 'time to react, a chance to make substitutions, [and an opportunity to] delay activities'. It provides space for decentralized authority to exist (Perrow 1986: 149). This is unlike 'tight' coupling which, 'promotes rapid decision-making, centralized decisions with unreflective responses, strict schedules, and ... immediate responses to deviation' (Perrow 1986: 148). The degree of coupling is an important organizational characteristic that determines how an organization responds to threats and other risks in its internal and external environments. Perrow (1986) explains how tight and loose coupling should be examined in conjunction with organizational structure to determine overall organizational behaviour.

Although political science often focuses on decision-making and events to explain change outcomes, organizational routines, rich strategic processes and underlying historical factors of organizations also affect change outcomes. Weaver and Leiteritz (2005) move closer to explanations of organizational change in the Bank, arguing that culture 'constrains the extent to which formal institutional modifications in the structures, rules and espoused agendas of the organization will translate into deep behavioural shifts' (*ibid*: 384). While this may be one explanation of organizational reform outcomes in the Bank, change outcomes and processes at the organizational sub-unit and departmental level may proceed differently. Thus, more thorough analyses of international organizational change processes and outcomes are required. To analyse punctuated change phenomena in the Bank, the consideration of all levels of strategy and policy change are important, to show how processes were decided and outcomes achieved.

Based on these insights, an opportunity exists to continue moving beyond structural and actor-centred studies of Bank behaviour and further into the 'black box' of international organizations. The historical, structural, political and managerial considerations of the Bank's radical change process can offer a greater understanding of how large, complex international organizations change. The empiricism below explains how the creativity of staff, involvement of new actors, support from key leaders and significant analytical work prompted radical change to the Bank's 1991 Forest Strategy and 1993 Forest Operational Policy.[1]

Responding to performance indicators and overcoming inertia

The Bank's 1991 Forest Strategy and 1993 Forest Operational Policy was an initial response to public concerns about increasing deforestation rates in the mid-to-late1980s. At this time, much of the blame for forest degradation lay with the forest industry. In an attempt to address this perceived negative impact on forests, the Bank's 1993 Forest Operational Policy included a ban on all concessional logging activities in Bank projects in tropical moist forests, with the aim of curbing deforestation rates. However, when the 1993 Bank Forest Operational Policy took effect, its 'do no harm' approach to forest management had a 'chilling effect' in the years that followed (Lele *et al.* 2000). The Bank's many forest project failures, such as those in Brazil, had a negative impact on recipient countries' willingness to undertake new Bank forest work. Thus, as new demand for Bank work in the forest sector decreased, the 'chilling effect' emerged.

During 1991–9, Global Environment Facility (GEF) project lending activity in the forest sector amounted to US$370 million, which was used primarily to address the conservation-oriented concerns of NGOs (Campbell and Martin 2000: xi). This success story about GEF funding shifted attention from the real problem about how the 1991 Forest Strategy addressed conflicting priorities in International Bank for Reconstruction and Development loans or International Development Association credits in addressing conservation (see essays in Lele 2002). Clear evidence was suggesting the 1991 strategy and 1993 policy needed to be changed, as reports about the strategy and operational policy's poor performance were being increasingly received by Bank country offices.

Continued internal feedback on the Bank's poor performance in the forest sector helped prompt and ensure change to the 1991 Forest Strategy and 1993 Forest Operational Policy. The Operations Evaluation Department (OED), the Bank's internal evaluation and monitoring office, produced the most comprehensive problem assessment. As early as 1996, OED studies indicated that the success of Bank forest projects were low, and a full report by the OED in 2000 created a bigger drive for changing the direction of the strategy (e.g. Lele *et al.* 2000). These performance indicators included: low levels of interest in Bank projects in developing countries; a decreasing financial return on Bank forest projects; and the inability of the Bank's 1991 Forest Strategy to address the scope of the deforestation problem.

As early as 1997, the ESSD Vice President and Network Head took notice of the Bank's poor performance in the forest sector. That same year, World Bank President Wolfensohn directed his staff to revise the 1991 Forest Strategy and 1993 Operational Policy with, many said, the intention of radically restructuring its contents (interviewee #2, November 2003). Clearly, corporate leadership influenced the strategy and policy revision process.

Additionally, Bank staff working on forests supported this action. Many staff involved with the strategy and policy review process believed that new strategic approaches were needed, since the 1991 strategy process was cursory, reactive to NGO concerns about deforestation and did not discuss important definitions such as the meaning of concessional logging. A number of factors also encouraged the Bank to have a more thorough review process, rather than a 'simple desk review' of the strategy and analysis of the forest lending portfolio. They included: the nature of the Bank's involvement in the contentious forest sector; the changing environment affecting 1993 forest policy; the Bank's move towards programmatic approaches to lending at a country level; and the Bank's desire to direct a greater share of its resources to the local levels and to test innovative approaches to community-based interventions (Sherman 2001: 4).

President Wolfensohn initially appointed a strategy coordinator to lead the Bank's revised strategy and policy process. The new coordinator assembled an informal, five-person team composed of Bank staff, primarily from the ESSD Network, that had all been working on the forest issue for some time. These members met in an initial brainstorming session to discuss how the strategy might be approached, and expected the strategy process to conclude in about six month's time.

However, a number of inertial forces in the Bank had to be overcome before a new strategic approach could be formed. Inertia was built by the assembling of an *ad hoc* forest strategy team, composed mostly of existing technical Bank staff, which relied on routine methods of gathering information. The ESSD Vice President and Network Head also did not have a high-level of trust in the Bank staff taking part in the strategy formulation process, and there was a low level of cooperation between team members (interviewee #1, January 2004).

In addition to questioning the staff's ability to manage the process and satisfy the Bank's organizational requirements, such as liaising with the Operational Policy staff, the staff lacked clear guidance on how to form a policy and strategy document. The initial forest strategy team realized that the 1993 Forest Operational Policy was really a strategy, and was unsure of how to move forward the strategy process. Without adequate leadership support and clear directives, the forest strategy team relied on old routines in their strategic approach to revising the strategy and policy.

One way in which this affected the strategic process was that initial consultations on the strategy included NGO stakeholders and donors only within the Washington beltway. Moreover, the initial resistance to change was also apparent during external consultations with NGOs, which did not want the Bank's focus on conservation to shift. Reasons for this included negative results from Bank projects, such as the Polonoreste project in the Amazon. Although the Polonoreste forest project was designed to construct gas pipelines through forest-rich areas, the project led to wide-scale deforestation and certain elements, notably the construction of the pipelines, were never completed (Wade 1997). Previous negative outcomes of Bank projects, coupled with the conservation-oriented agendas of NGOs inside the beltway, reduced the initial forest strategy team's ability to change the 1991 strategy and 1993 policy's contents.

As a result, the first stage of the strategic review process had a balancing effect on the level of overall strategic change within the Bank. This is because inertia had increased in the central organizational system. Organizational norms concerning forest sector lending within the Bank were strong and the perception that forests were a low priority within the Bank hindered organizational staff's ability to change the strategy process. Additionally, centralization of the revision process reinforced the organization's behaviour of 'tight' coupling, involving highly centralized, rapid decision-making processes. This limited the Bank's ability to conduct extensive outreach to stakeholders even though there was high technical uncertainty about the Bank's approach to conservation and how to address deforestation in forest areas not covered by the 1991 strategy and 1993 operational policy.

Although there were some positive ideas that emerged from the early stages of this process, they were not enough to overcome the organization's low ability to change. The 'big ideas' that emerged from the initial part of the strategy process included the establishment of new partnerships: an alliance with the World Wide Fund for Nature, the CEO Forum on Forests, and a new group, Forest Trends. These ideas would prove influential during the second stage of the strategy, which was marked by a change in the composition of the forest strategy team.

In 1998, the arrival of a new Bank ESSD Vice President and Network Head prompted the appointment of a new strategy coordinator, who was well versed in the Bank's internal administrative process and knew how to consult with a range of Bank offices in designing the new strategy. It was then that the Bank's Board of Directors formally 'requested' the review of the Bank's performance in the forest sector and a Bank-wide investigation on ways to improve it. It became clear to the new coordinator that a broader, two-year timeline was needed to complete the strategy and policy revision process. This challenged the initial assumptions of the previously established forest strategy team, which believed the process could be completed in a few months. However, none of the Bank staff imagined that the entire strategic process would take nearly five years to complete.

The arrival of a new strategy coordinator marked a changed approach to the strategic process. The Bank's newly established forest strategy team was given a great deal of flexibility when creating a new strategic approach. External consultants were also hired to work on the revised strategy. The strategy coordinator agreed to find new approaches to gathering ideas at the regional level using consultants and building trust using the Bank's existing partnerships, especially with the private sector.

The staff's ability to change its strategic approach was also aided by the events of the Bank's organizational restructuring in 1995–6, which provided a window for innovative and precedent-setting activities. Thus, the team's reliance on old organizational norms and routines decreased. The process that emerged focused first on the strategy, which involved an OED analytical review and consultant-led regional workshops; second, on the negotiation of the policy; and third, on the formation of a business plan.

Innovation in the strategic change process

Due to the new forest strategy team's longer-term perspective on the strategy process, the new coordinator was able to put a different strategic approach into action. The new strategy coordinator helped the forest strategy team gain credibility within the organization early in the forest strategy and policy revision process by frequently communicating the team's progress to other Bank staff. In 1998, at the Executive Board's request, the team first proposed a structure for the overall strategy process (interviewee #2, November 2003). The new strategy process and coordinator, new staff, the high levels of technical uncertainty and the institutional mandate, resulted in a broad, regional-level investigation of the Bank's forest activities and a break with old Washington-centred approaches.

However, it was also a costly approach. The Bank's forest strategy team had to find the financial resources needed to conduct the decentralized stakeholder consultations. As one interviewee noted,

> if you wanted support from a region or country you had to pay them, but we didn't have the money. So there initially was no buy-in to the process. Whenever [the team] wanted to integrate someone from the Africa region [the team] had to pay him, [and it] became difficult.
> (interviewee # 2, November 2003)

As a result, the team had to independently raise a large amount of funding for the Bank's new strategic approach before the regional stakeholder consultations could be held.

Yet, the team members involved in fundraising believed in the 'convening power' of the Bank to acquire new funding. The Bank had convening power, some believed, because it had enough influence to get new policies and strategies passed through the Executive Board and enough to do solid on-the-ground work at the country level. Thus, there was a perception from the donor community that, despite the failings of the current Forest Policy, Bank staff were capable of getting things done and successfully implemented. In the end, financial resources not dedicated to lending activities – that is, countries' trust funds located at the Bank – were used to fund the strategy and policy process.

To obtain a more comprehensive view on the failings of the 1991 Strategy and 1993 Policy, as well as to determine whether to retain the ban on concessional logging, the Bank hired two consultants from the World Conservation Union (IUCN) to conduct stakeholder workshops, at least one in each of the six main World Bank regions. Regional Bank staff and IUCN consultants took the lead in establishing and facilitating the external workshops, after it was suggested by the Bank's strategy team that the IUCN consultants might have more success in gathering new ideas at this stage of the process. The IUCN began an NGO 'self-selection' process in each of the countries where the workshops were held. This was generally received well by the NGO community involved with the workshops. Initially, however, these facilitators received negative responses from the workshop attendees, who questioned the consultants' objectivity. Nevertheless, the consultations generated immense amounts of feedback and new ideas for the revised strategy and policy.

While regional consultations were conducted, other workshops and meetings were held on key areas where the Bank sought to improve its engagement in the forest sector. For instance, the CEO Forum on Forests, which was established by President Wolfensohn in 1998 to increase private sector interest in forests, was held a number of times during the forest policy and strategy review process. The forest strategy team also held workshops on the role of plantation forestry, the underlying causes of deforestation, forests and sustainable livelihoods, forest law enforcement and forest market trends. These areas were identified as gaps in the Bank's knowledge of forest sector activities.

While the regional consultations and analytical work was proceeding, it also became apparent to the strategy team that internal buy-in through the OED was required. As a result, two separate processes emerged: the strategy development process, which was largely dominated by consultations and analytical work, and the OED review of the 1991 Forest Strategy and 1993 policy implementation. Although the OED review provided some analytical insight and greater evidence for the necessary change in the forest sector policy and strategy, it was not a primary determinant of the strategic approach taken by the Bank staff. Rather, the OED review and evaluation served as complementary evidence to the information from the regional consultations as to why significant revisions to the content of the 1991 Forest Strategy and 1993 Operational Policy were needed.

The OED review, which was not published until 2000, was a major reason for the delayed completion of the forest strategy process (interviewee #3, January 2004). This delay, however, significantly increased Bank staff's ability to change the content of the Forest Strategy and Operational Policy. While the OED report was being assembled, a significant amount of outreach and consultations were conducted. Additionally, the strategy team assembled the Technical Advisory Group (TAG), consisting of stakeholders from the regional consultations. The TAG was primarily composed of NGOs from external consultations, and was to maintain the Bank's transparency during the latter stages of the strategy process and during the policy process. This may have helped increase the process legitimacy of the new forest strategy and policy in the eyes of NGOs while generating new ideas for it (Sherman 2001).

To gain further internal organizational support for the strategy, OED staff conducted a staff survey on the 1991 strategy and 1993 policy. Staff wanted: a more flexible policy that allowed the commercial logging of tropical moist forests, which took a more multi-sectoral approach to working on forests; acknowledgement of the high-risk, politically difficult project designs that take into account social and environmental issues; a greater appreciation of the problem of corruption; and a clearer strategy to mobilize GEF resources (World Bank 2000: 48–50). This was an important step in generating internal organizational advocates for change to the new strategy and policy. Combined with the major substantive errors of the 1991 strategy and 1993 operational policy, it helped provide the drive for substantial content changes that were eventually contained in the revised strategy and policy documents.

Information from the OED review, stakeholder consultations and other analytical work was then largely controlled by the ESSD Forests Team. The Forests Team took into consideration the bulk of the comments from the consultations. In the early stages of the revision process, the staff clustered information under two themes: poverty alleviation and sustainability, which included a discussion of governance and public goods. From the very beginning, it was clear to Bank staff that a forest strategy would not successfully emerge without considering both of those issues, 'because they were all encompassing' (interviewee #1, January 2004). Bank staff believed, because of the overarching nature of the issues, it would be hard to disagree with either of them.

By the time the Executive Board received an early draft of the strategy in 2000, the Bank staff were basically committed to the contents of the strategy and few major substantive changes to the draft strategy were made. As one interviewee noted:

> we put a few things in [the strategy] that we hadn't thought of. For instance, areas like community forestry, small and medium enterprises, the concept and definition of high-value conservation forests. We had to address all of those detailed questions [related to these issues] and ... there was a lot of input that came from NGOs and others.
>
> (interviewee #1, January 2004)

This suggests that if norms and routines can be broken and new information obtained during the initial stages of strategic processes, greater inclusion of stakeholders and informal governance structures can result.

However, other contents of the draft strategy were not as uncontroversial. One of the more controversial pieces of the draft strategy was that it proposed to lift the logging ban that had been in effect from 1991. Nevertheless, the Bank forest strategy team felt confident that the information they had received from stakeholder consultations, analytical work, and the OED review supported a lifting of the ban. As one interviewee noted,

'in conversations with Wolfensohn, he asked, can you defend the organization if we lift the logging ban? [The strategy team] felt ... it would be wrong
to keep the ban. So then he gave [the strategy team] the go ahead' (interviewee #2, November 2003). Due to support from corporate leadership and
mounting analytical evidence, the new draft strategy did not include the ban
on logging activities and the staff turned to negotiating the contents of the
draft forest policy.

This second phase of the strategy process proved to be fruitful in a
number of ways. It resulted in the generation of new ideas and a change of
strategic process, involved new stakeholders as participants in the process,
and established new ways of problem solving. Emergent networks of stakeholders formed through workshops, and informal meetings allowed for open
exchange of information and led to the convergence around new ideas for
the revised forest strategy. The informal structure of the networks created
enough entropy to allow new ideas to penetrate the Bank's organizational
sub-system and enter its strategic process. Thus, it helped to loosen the
bureaucratic chain of command in the Bank. Such a loose coupling of
organizational structure also provided a space for new managerial processes
to emerge, allowing for broader strategic choices for both the draft strategy
and policy.

The drafting of the forest strategy helped the Bank forest strategy team
rethink the content and process of both the 1991 strategy and 1993 policy.
It also became clear to the team that a new forest strategy alone would not
be enough to create substantial changes to the Bank's forest sector work,
and that an additional, more specific policy document was needed. During
the drafting of the new operational policy on forests, however, strong
organizational norms re-emerged to have a significant influence on the
formation and negotiation of its contents.

Controlling policy formation

After the staff's shift in attention from the draft forest strategy to the policy
occurred, organizational influences and norms began to shape the policy
formation process. The policy took longer to negotiate than the strategy.
This was largely attributed to staff's reliance on bureaucratic management
approaches and the established norms and practices of the Operations
Policy and Country Services Network.

The forest policy formulation did not occur until November 2000, and
the strategy was put aside while policy negotiation was taking place. In
previous policies, the intention to implement was prevalent, but the creation
and adherence to new operational policies presented much stricter, more
binding guidelines for the Bank's work. As one interviewee said, 'an
Operational Policy is what will get you in front of the Inspection Panel,
which of course is the major disincentive in the Bank' (interviewee #1,
January 2004).

Therefore, the new forest policy was to provide concrete guidelines on what Bank staff 'must' do when designing and implementing a project. The new strategy would complement this process, as a reflection of what 'might' be done in any forest-related project. In other words, the contents of a Bank strategy seemed additional and optional to those actions contained in a Bank operational policy. As a result, a close working relationship with the Operations Policy and Country Services Network was maintained throughout the negotiation of the revised Forest Operational Policy. The Operational Policy staff dictated the policy formulation approach and prevented some of the new draft forest strategy content from being infused into the new operational policy on forests.

This created discord among the Bank's internal and external stakeholders. The limited ability of NGOs to participate in the policy formation process and the compromises involved led to discontent among many NGOs. The Bank forest strategy team indicated that NGO groups had an influence on the wording that went into the policy, but many NGOs disagreed over their influence on the policy-making process. Internally, there were also clear limitations in the policy formation process, firstly because not everyone in the Bank was happy about changing the operational policy on forests, and secondly because the Operations Policy and Country Services Network and Executive Board became the primary decision-makers for the new policy's contents.

Nevertheless, the Bank staff working on the policy noted that such an approach was appropriate because the Board had a 'right' to negotiate the document before it was discussed with the outside world, and that Bank staff were meant to exercise this right (interviewee #1, January 2004). There was some *ad hoc* consultation with external stakeholders during policy formation, but a coherent and structured policy was not formally introduced to the outside community at the outset of the policy process. Bank staff knew that a draft policy could not be circulated to the outside community until the Board had discussed a preliminary draft of the new policy.

In the end, the policy tried to balance the demands of internal processes and external stakeholders by attempting to address all stakeholder feedback contained in the strategy. Although the Bank attempted to be inclusive in the latter stages of the policy development, it seemed too late. When the Bank's new draft forest strategy and policy were released for public comment in June 2002, there were immediate reactions to both documents from NGOs such as Environmental Defense, Forest Peoples Programme, Friends of the Earth, Greenpeace and Rainforest Action Network (2003). From June 2002 until October 2002, the Bank received comments from external stakeholders. These included concerns that: structural adjustment policies were not integrated with the forest policy and strategy and did not address the issue of forest governance sufficiently; the definition of 'critical forests' was not enough to protect old-growth forests; and the new strategy had limited applicability to the Bank's Natural Habitats Operational Policy.

Some of the more scathing feedback came from other NGOs who suggested that the Bank's revised Forest Operational Policy was 'seriously flawed' and 'represents a dangerous set-back for the world's forest ecosystems and the people whose livelihoods depend on them' (Horta 2002). Some called the regional consultations held by the Bank a 'sham', noting that forest dependent peoples and biodiversity could seriously be harmed under the new policy. These concerns were publicly voiced by NGOs during the stakeholder consultations, but were not explicitly addressed in the draft Forest Operational Policy.

The Bank responded to NGO criticisms by noting that NGO concerns would be addressed during the revision of a Bank operational policy on adjustment lending (World Bank, undated). It also indicated that it would support an independent monitoring and certification approach for Bank projects. Finally, it agreed that the revised forest policy should be implemented in conjunction with a number of other Bank operational policies, including those on indigenous peoples and natural habitats. It has yet to be seen how such an approach will work in practice.

The Bank policy formation process conformed to the Operations Policy and Country Services Network's approach and criteria, and involved little external stakeholder engagement in the process. This shows that the centralized control of the policy formation reinforced hierarchical and cultural routines of the Bank in making operational policies 'the law' to follow. Innovative and loose governance structures such as those in the strategy's regional consultation process were obviated and bureaucratic routines relied upon.

The policy formation process increased inertia in the Bank's internal environment and delegitimized the policy process and output in the eyes of some NGOs. Despite this, the Bank's forest team pressed ahead with the final components of the strategic process. Before the strategy and policy could be reviewed and considered for approval by the Executive Board, the forest strategy team was required to construct a business plan.

Making the new strategy and policy 'bankable'

The Business Plan was developed in coordination with the Committee on Development Effectiveness, which is usually responsible for the 'formal scanning' of documents before they are sent to the Board. The forest strategy team presented the draft strategy and policy documents to the Committee two or three times, then some direction from the Board was given, and subsequently further feedback on the strategy and policy documents was gathered from external stakeholders. Only then was the Business Plan written to make it consistent with what had been written in the strategy and policy (interviewees #1, April 2003; #3, January 2004).

Initial drafts of the Business Plan were developed in late 2001 by the same Bank staff who had drafted and negotiated the new forest strategy and policy. The point of the Business Plan was to show specific deliverables of the draft strategy and policy. Whereas the draft strategy and policy documents discussed the vision of the Bank's forest work more broadly, the Business Plan provided new, concrete performance indicators to the Board. One interviewee noted:

> when you present a strategy, you have to show how you will implement the deliverables, how they relate to the objective and how they will achieve such objectives. ... You have to explain how this will be done on a year to year basis. ... In other words, the strategy has to be 'Bankable'; you have to show how it's going to be done, how it will be paid for and who will be responsible for it.
>
> (interviewee #1, January 2004)

The strategy team recognized the need for identifying the responsibilities of those in the organization that would implement the document as well as establishing a clear process for verifying its financial success.

Developing a Business Plan that reflected the strategy's contents was essential, as the Business Plan would capture crosscutting elements of the Bank's work and was important to its successful implementation. The final draft forest strategy contained three pillars (mirroring the World Bank's environment strategy to be implemented at the same time), which were meant to be interdependent and all-encompassing of other aspects of forests. The first pillar was 'harnessing the potential of forests to reduce poverty in line with the Millennium Development Goals'; the second pillar was 'integrating forests in sustainable economic development'; and the third pillar was 'protecting vital local and global environmental services and values' (World Bank 2003: 20). The three pillars captured the multi-sectoral approach to forests that had been emphasized early in the strategic process and in multilateral processes such as the Intergovernmental Forum on Forests and the UN Forum on Forests.

The manager of the ESSD Forests Team marketed the strategy to the Executive Board, noting the integrated nature of the strategy captured in the three pillars and its relationship to the Business Plan. The manager noted the importance of the budget to the implementation of the strategy. In the end, the required incremental Bank budget to increase sector work amounted to approximately US$1.5–2 million a year from 2002 to 2007 (interviewee #1, January 2004). As a result, the Business Plan represented a much more quantitative, specific document with a focus on implementing the broader vision expressed in the strategy document.

Upon reviewing the Business Plan, the Executive Board did not base its decision to approve the Plan on the amount of money required for the new strategy's implementation, but instead based its decision on projected increases to economic and sector work. While this may be a future internal, quantitative measure of the new strategy's success, it does not provide similar quantitative or qualitative indicators of forest and environmental sustainability. If the performance indicator of the new strategy is mostly financially based, it will give greater credence to NGO criticisms that the Bank is more concerned with portfolio lending than environmental sustainability. However, Bank staff defended such indicators, arguing that such an increase in sector work is not necessarily an increase in the overall envelope of lending, but rather an increase in the Bank's overall presence in a given area.

Eventually, the Executive Board approved the revised forest strategy and policy and the Business Plan only once, in October 2002. Those involved in the policy-making process indicated that the policy was 'far more important' than the strategy document, because not adhering to the policy documents in the field could have serious implications for the Bank staff implementing project and programme work. As one interviewee noted: 'policy is the law; strategy is the goal; policy is the law and the matter you must follow in the Bank' (interviewee #4, January 2004).

The 2002 revised forest policy emerged as a stand-alone policy, but also one that takes into consideration the Bank's operational policies on environmental assessment, natural habitats, cultural property, involuntary resettlement and indigenous peoples. Bank staff designing Country Assistance Strategies are now required to take the revised forest operational policy into consideration. In all cases, implementation of a forest project involves prior distribution of environmental assessments and results of forest assessments to the public.

Assessing the new outputs and the strategic change process

The overall effect of the 2002 Revised Forest Strategy and Operational Policy resulted in process innovation and significantly new content outputs. The net effect was a punctuated change at the departmental level. This did not lead to transformational or radical changes in the overall Bank system. It was, however, a significant departure from previous behaviours and norms in the Bank's managerial practice and approach to forests in the early 1990s. This was due to high levels of technical uncertainty on forests that existed in the late 1990s, and the consultative planning process that increased the legitimacy and information feedback required for change.

The strategic change process needs to be viewed as a whole, since without the revision of the strategy and policy at the same time, the Executive Board would not have approved either of the documents alone. Thus, the entire strategic change process encompassed the strategy, policy and business plan formation. The utilization of the Business Plan helped build cohesion between the two documents and adhered to a legitimate routine established by the Executive Board.

The strategic change process exhibited a number of positive and negative feedback behaviours. While the policy process represents negative feedback behaviour in the overall process, it was not the determinant of overall strategic change. Policy formation may have increased organizational inertia and decreased the amount of policy choices, but the strategy process and draft contents enabled the policy content to shift radically. Thus, the inertia created by the policy formation process only somewhat decreased the Bank's ability to change.

The dominant feedback effect occurred during the establishment of a new strategy approach, where external stakeholder consultations, new information from Bank staff and other analytical work radically shifted forest strategy content and Bank policy. This not only led to a process innovation in establishing new mechanisms for stakeholder outreach, but also led to significantly new outputs in both the strategy and policy documents. This is because the boundary created for the collection was broad due to loose coupling of the Bank's organizational structure, and resulted in the creation of new informal governance structures.

Such a redesign of governance structures may help with the 2002 Revised Forest Strategy and Operational Policy's implementation. Hult and Walcott (1990: 9) note that 'heightened responsiveness ... may be furthered by redesigning governance structures. This may help bridge "the gap between performance and vision"' (World Bank 2004: 6) as well as the 'governance gap', by promoting more inclusive stakeholder engagement and counteracting incremental adaptation of new ideas (Tussie and Riggirozzi 2001).

In utilizing information from the consultation outputs, the analytical documents and other OED reports, however, the revised strategy took a long time to write and finalize. There was a large amount of lag time taken by Bank staff between the time of the consultation and the actual negotiation of the strategy documents. Nevertheless, such a loose coupling effect may have helped tension to dissipate within and outside the Bank on the content of the forest strategy. Trust and cooperation between the Bank staff, IUCN facilitators and other stakeholders was built up over time and may have facilitated the strategy negotiation process. As one participant noted:

> we had very few serious disagreements from any one really on the final strategy, although there were some groups that would disagree with the strategy. [Despite this, many] groups from private sector and social groups were on board and there were very few disagreements with the priorities of the strategy.
>
> (interviewee #1, January 2004)

However, other Bank donor countries noted that the 'pendulum had swung in the opposite direction' by infusing too many NGO ideas into the strategy (interviewee #5, May 2003). Regardless, the Bank had obtained buy in from the main groups of stakeholders early in the strategic process, because they had taken care to include them in the initial stages of the process.

However, these new capabilities directed at 'listening' were costly, and largely driven by external consultants. In the future, minimization of transaction costs will be key to gathering new information at the regional level. The Bank hopes to reduce transaction costs in future by:

> bringing more countries to a situation where they can absorb more programmatic assistance in this sector. This approach will be implemented under country programs ... after some initial encouragement through corporate funding to cover the higher initial costs of preparing investments in this sector.
>
> (World Bank 2004: 9)

Although the forest strategy team knew the Bank had a significant amount of convening power, the energy of the policy and strategy entrepreneurs may be unique to the Revised Forest Strategy and Operational Policy process. Unless significant threats to the Bank's performance emerge in other sectors in the future and new personnel are assembled who take an active part in raising funds and gaining the support of key constituencies, the same consultative process is probably not replicable.

The transformational change exhibited in the forest strategy and policy process was primarily due to corporate leadership decisions, the creativity of the forest strategy team and significant technical evidence of the Bank's poor performance in the forest sector. If adequate momentum had not been present to carry the five-year process to completion, the strategy process would most likely not have resulted in such a transformative change. If similar strategic exercises were attempted within the Bank at this juncture, they would be costly, lengthy and risky. Future approaches to strategic change will be dependent on: the amount of funding available in the sector undertaking the strategic exercise; the level of technical uncertainty of the problem; fervent support of corporate leadership for the change process; and external stakeholder demands for process legitimacy.

The Bank's Revised Forest Strategy and Operational Policy process represents a timely and important undertaking, which significantly changed its operations at the regional level. It is not clear at this time whether the high transaction costs associated with the revision outweigh the costs of not carrying one out or of approaching it differently. Although the full scale of the Bank's changed policy and strategy will be assessed in 2007, demand for project work has already increased 'from US$20 million in fiscal year (July–June) 2001 to US$104 million in fiscal year 2004. The project financing planned for fiscal year 2005 is estimated to reach US$106 million' (World Bank, undated).

Despite this seemingly positive financial indicator, the environmental, social and cultural benefits of the Bank's changed approach have yet to be known. Additionally, in late 2005, the ESSD Forests Team was being reorganized, which could have a negative effect on the implementation and evaluation of the 2002 revision. While there were clear benefits to using the consultative process during the strategic process, the overall cost effectiveness and value to on-the-ground forest communities will be known when implementation evaluations of the Revised Forest Strategy and Operational Policy are conducted.

Conclusion

The World Bank's Revised Forest Strategy and Operational Policy process gives particular insights into the way the Bank responded to poor performance indicators in its operating environment. These performance indicators included: low levels of interest in Bank projects in developing countries; a decreasing financial return on Bank forest projects; and the inability of the previous strategy to address the scope of the deforestation problem. As a result of the Bank's poor performance in the forest sector, President Wolfensohn and the Bank's Executive Board decided that a review of the 1991 Forest Strategy and 1993 Forest Operational Policy was needed. Bank coordinators were given a great deal of flexibility when planning a new strategic approach to draft the revised forest strategy. It included new approaches to gathering ideas at the regional level using consultants, establishing new partnerships and building trust through the Bank's existing partnerships, especially with the private sector. The staff's ability to change its strategic approach was also aided by the events of the Bank's organizational restructuring in 1995–6.

The new strategic approach helped the Bank gain considerable amounts of new information on forests and forest problems. Additionally, the significant time required for the consultation process and the compilation of the OED evaluation increased the Bank's ability to change the final 2002 Forest Strategy and Operational Policy. Additionally, it helped overcome established organizational norms embedded in previous strategic approaches.

While a new approach was taken to strategy formulation, and a significant amount of new ideas emerged during the strategic process, such flexibility decreased during policy formation. One reason for this was the high level of influence of the Operations Policy and Country Services Network on Bank staff. The perceived threat of breaking operational policy practices and policy formulation approaches decreased the forest strategy team's ability to significantly change the content of 1993 operational policy. Nevertheless, a few key ideas from the final revised strategy were contained in the revised policy, which represented a significant departure from the 1993 policy.

In general, the Revised Forest Strategy and Operational Policy process shifted from a loosely controlled strategy process to a tightly controlled policy process. The strategy process became more institutionalized the more information was retained and processed at the central organizational level.

Such effects are more clearly seen during the 1993 policy revision, especially because specific organizational guidelines prevailed in determining the strategic approach for policy decisions. This was due in large part to Bank staff's accountability to the Executive Board and stringent policy approach of the Operations Policy and Country Services Network, which provided 'the law' for Bank staff to follow.

This punctuated change outcome was dependent largely on the strategy innovation process and shift in content output. While the policy formulation process did not result in new process innovations, the strategy process allowed adequate flexibility, openness to new ideas and accountability to a range of stakeholders. Although the implementation of the 2002 Revised Forest Strategy and Operational Policy has shown evidence of improved financial performance in the Bank's forest sector work, the long-term implications of the revision are yet to be known.

It may well be that high financial costs necessary to operationalize the Bank's new strategic approach may make it a less attractive approach for other areas of the Bank in the future. Additionally, without an internal restructuring in the Bank, a high external threat to the Bank's performance and personnel turnover in a number of Bank offices, the likelihood of a similar level of change to other departmental-level policies and strategies is low. Incremental change is also likely to occur during the next revision of the 2002 Forest Strategy and Operational Policy.

Note

1 Data collection on the Bank's strategy and policy revision process was conducted from October 2002 until March 2004. In total seventeen interviews were undertaken with thirteen people.

References

Barzelay, M. and Campbell, C. (2003) *Planning for the Future: Strategic Planning in the U.S. Air Force*, Washington DC: Brookings Institution Press.

Baumgartner, F. and Jones, B. (eds) (2002) *Policy Dynamics*, London: University of Chicago Press.

Campbell, J. G. and Martin, A. (2000) *Financing the Global Benefits of Forests: The Bank's GEF Portfolio and the 1991 Forest Strategy*, Washington DC: World Bank.

Eldredge, N. and Gould, S. J. (1972) 'Punctuated Equilibria: An Alternative to Phyletic Gradualism', in T. J. M. Schopf (ed.) *Models in Paleobiology*, San Francisco: Freeman, Cooper and Co.

Environmental Defense, Forest Peoples Programme, Friends of the Earth, Greenpeace and Rainforest Action Network (2003) 'Open Letter to Mr James D. Wolfensohn – President of the World Bank', 22 October 2003, available at http://www.foei.org/forests/letter.html

Horta, K. (2002) 'World Bank's Draft New Forest Policy: A License to Trash the World's Forests', *World Rainforest Movement Bulletin* August 2002, Environmental Defense Fund.

Hult, K. M. and Walcott, C. (1990) *Governing Public Organizations: Politics, Structures, and Institutional Design*, Pacific Grove CA: Brooks/Cole Publishing Company.

Kingdon, J. (1995) *Agendas, Alternatives and Public Policies*, 2nd edn, New York: HarperCollins.

Lele, U. (ed.) (2002) *Managing a Global Resource: Challenges in Forest Conservation and Development*, World Bank Series on Environment and Development, vol. 5, London: Transaction Publishers.

Lele, U., Kumar, N., Husain, S. A., Zazueta, A. and Kelly, L. (2000) *The World Bank Forest Strategy: Striking the Right Balance*, Operations Evaluation Department, Washington DC: World Bank.

McNeill, D. (2005) 'Power and Ideas: Economics and Global Development Policy', in D. Stone and S. Maxwell (eds) *Global Knowledge Networks and International Development: Bridges Across Boundaries*, Warwick Studies in Globalisation, London: Routledge, 57–71.

Perrow, C. (1986) *Complex Organizations: A Critical Essay*, 3rd edn, London: McGraw-Hill.

Pettigrew, A., Ferlie, E. and McKee, L. (1992) *Shaping Strategic Change: Making Change in Large Organisations*, London: Sage.

Sastry, M. A. (1997) 'Problems and Paradoxes in a Model of Punctuated Organizational Change', *Administrative Science Quarterly* 42, 244.

Sherman, M. (2001) *Forest Policy Implementation Review and Strategy: Consultation Process*, Internal Document of the NGO and Civil Society Unit of the World Bank's Social Development Department.

Tushman, M. and Anderson, P. (1987) 'Technological Discontinuities and Organization Environments', in A. Pettigrew (ed.) *The Management of Strategic Change*, Oxford: Blackwell, 89–122.

Tushman, M. and Romanelli, E. (1994) 'Organisational Transformation as Punctuated Equilibrium: An Empirical Test', *Academy of Management Journal* 37, 1141–66.

Tussie, D. and Riggirozzi, M. P. (2001) 'Pressing Ahead with New Procedures for Old Machinery: Global Governance and Civil Society', in V. Rittberger (ed.) *Global Governance and the United Nations System*, Tokyo: United Nations University Press, 158–80.

Van de Ven, A. H. (1987) 'Four Requirements for Processual Analysis', in A. Pettigrew (ed.) *The Management of Strategic Change*, Oxford: Blackwell, 330–41.

Van de Ven, A. H., Polley, D. E., Garud, R. and Venkataraman, S. (1999) *The Innovation Journey*, Oxford: Oxford University Press.

Wade, R. (1997) 'Greening the Bank: The Struggle over the Environment, 1970–1995', in D. Kapur, J. P. Lewis and R. Webb (eds) *The World Bank: Its First Half Century*, Washington DC: Brookings Institution Press, 611–734.

Weaver, C. and Leiteritz, R. (2005) '"Our Poverty is a World Full of Dreams": Reforming the World Bank', *Global Governance* 11, 369–88.

World Bank (2000) *A Review of the World Bank's 1991 Forest Strategy and its Implementation: Volume 1 and Volume 2*, Operations Evaluation Department (OED), Washington DC: World Bank.

——(2003) *Sustaining Forests: A World Bank Strategy*, Washington DC: World Bank, October, available at http://www.worldbank.org/forests

——(2004) *Sustaining Forests: A Development Strategy*, Washington DC: International Bank for Reconstruction and Development.
——(undated) 'Implementing the Forest Strategy: Q and A', available at http://lnweb18. worldbank.org/ESSD/ardext.nsf/14ByDocName/QAImplementingtheForestsStrategy/ $FILE/Q&Aforwebsite.pdf

6   The World Bank and pension reforms

M. Ramesh

Debates over pension reforms display a level of intensity and scrutiny that few policies can match. No organization has played a more central role in the debate than the World Bank. This chapter will analyse the World Bank's position in the debate by examining two key documents it has published on the subject: *Averting the Old Age Crisis* (1994) and *Old-Age Income Support in the 21st Century* (Holzmann and Hing 2005). It will show that contrary to widespread assumptions that Bretton Woods institutions are at the forefront of efforts to dismantle the welfare state, the Bank's recent document shows increasing rather than decreasing commitment to expanding and diversifying income support for the aged. There is certainly no evidence of institutional efforts to promote across the board a 'race to the bottom', or a 'race to the top' for that matter. What we have instead is something more like a race to the middle, with weakening and strengthening of pension systems going on at the same time. The explanation for the trend is complex, comprising a range of social, economic, and cognitive factors.

The World Bank is a major player in pension reforms, especially in developing countries. It provided 204 loans with some pension component to sixty-eight countries in the period 1998–2004, accounting for 16 per cent of its total adjustment loans during the period (Holzmann and Hinz 2005: 56). The years 1997 to 1999 were the highest for pension-related lending. However, more important than financial assistance is the intellectual impact it has had on the direction and content of pension reform in member countries. Its reports and publications enjoy tremendous legitimacy in policy circles and find widespread support within national governments of both developed and developing countries, obviating the need for pressure through loans or other means. Adoption of reforms that are consistent with the Bank's position win the member country plaudits from international financial markets and business commentators and therefore members often see it in their interest to adopt them.

Pension policy is a relatively new subject for the World Bank because it has not traditionally been a significant concern in developing countries. It stumbled upon the subject in the course of its work on poverty and safety nets in the context of the economic recession afflicting many of its member countries during the 1980s. The rapid ageing of the population in the industrialized countries combined with prolonged fiscal crises in many others exacerbated the urgency of the problem and drew the Bank into the debates.

The publication of *Averting the Old Age Crisis* instantly catapulted the Bank into the forefront of pension debates. The report was notable not only for the comprehensive analysis and solutions it offered but also the widespread support and intense criticisms it immediately attracted. The principles espoused in the report were so influential that they came to be referred to as 'The New Pension Orthodoxy'. By the end of the 1990s, most countries around the world were engaged in at least some discussion if not effort to reform their pension schemes along the lines proposed by the report.

However, it was soon apparent that not all was going to plan for a variety of social, economic, and political reasons, but also due to the report's flawed assumptions and analyses. Many researchers associated with the World Bank began to consider and ask questions about the 1994 report. After long deliberations and extensive consultation, they came out with the *Old-Age Income Support in the 21st Century* in 2005. The new document retained the essence of its predecessor but made many subtle changes that together suggest a different direction for reform.

1994: weakening the state's role

Averting the Old Age Crisis offers a solid commentary on ageing and its fiscal implications and on the main existing mechanisms for providing income support to the aged. It gives special prominence to the inadequacies of the existing government-managed Pay-As-You-Go (PAYG) arrangements and then uses them to build a case for their replacement with privately managed and fully funded private schemes. The report is, however, best known for its proposal for 'Three Pillars of Old Age Income Security': 1st Mandatory Public pillar, 2nd Mandatory Private pillar, and 3rd Voluntary Private, as outlined in Table 6.1. below. The report recommended that all

Table 6.1 The three pillars of old age income security

Pillar	Objective	Financing	Programme features
1st	Poverty prevention, through redistribution	Tax financed	Mandatory; Publicly managed; Means-tested subsistence benefit
2nd	Income smoothing, through savings	Fully funded, from contributions	Mandatory; Privately managed; Entitlement benefits equal contributions
3rd	Income smoothing, through enhanced savings	Fully funded, from contributions	Voluntary; Privately managed; Entitlement benefits equal contributions

governments must establish all three pillars as a comprehensive solution to the diverse income-related problems faced by the aged.

The first pillar is meant to be a 'basic' pillar designed to prevent poverty within a section of the population with no or little income to save for their retirement. It would be a means-tested public assistance programme providing flat or needs-based benefits to all whose income falls below a certain socially accepted level. The programme would be managed by the government and would be funded from its general revenues. It recognizes that in every society, regardless of income levels and savings rate, there are people who for a variety of reasons – for instance, disability, life-long poverty, intermittent work history – cannot meet even their essential needs for subsistence during old age.

The second pillar is also a mandatory programme but is based on very different principles and works very differently. Its purpose is not to prevent poverty but smooth income over one's lifecycle: save during the working life and draw upon it for consumption during retirement. It is funded from private contributions by employees or employers or both. The rate of contribution is set by the government and is expected to be at a realistic level to be sufficient to finance retirement without unduly curtailing current consumption. However, unlike the first pillar which draws on government's current revenues, the second pillar is a 'fully funded' scheme in that beneficiaries draw only on what is accumulated in their own account. Since members draw on their own savings, they get what they have saved; there is no means test and there is no redistribution. The scheme is to be managed by professional fund managers on a competitive basis with the objective of maximizing return for their customers.

The third pillar is similar to the second pillar except that it is voluntary. Its purpose is to encourage people to save more than mandated under the second pillar arrangement so that they can enjoy higher level of income during retirement. It is also meant to compensate for the rigidities of the other pillars that may prevent people from adequately planning for their old age. To entice people to participate in the scheme, tax concessions are to be allowed which make it particularly attractive to high-income households.

Of the three proposed pillars, it is the second that turned out to be the most salient and also the most controversial. A key reason for the prominence it received in the debates was its stated preference for privately managed savings-based schemes over publicly administered social insurance schemes. By explicitly stating its position, the World Bank became a direct participant in the ongoing acrimonious debate over private versus public pensions.

Another remarkable feature of the report was its call for diversification of pension schemes to serve a different purpose. It pointed out that governments had traditionally relied heavily on only one scheme which not only made it difficult to meet different needs of pensioners but also made it more risky. Thus while the second pillar was to be the norm, there was also to be a basic pillar of those unable to save for whatever reason and a voluntary pillar for those seeking additional income.

The third notable feature of the report was that, unlike earlier (and many subsequent) reform proposals which recommended increased contribution or reduced benefits as a response to impending fiscal hardships in the face of population ageing, *Averting the Old Age Crisis* recommended the establishment of additional schemes.

Fourth, the report explicitly tied the issue of pensions to economic growth, as the subtitle of the book (*Policies to protect the old and promote growth*) made amply clear. It sought to design a scheme that would promote rather than stymie growth, unlike the existing programmes in many countries, which it claimed were a burden on the economy. Its proposals were deliberately designed to remove work disincentives, in addition to promoting savings and capital markets. It especially emphasized the importance of additional savings, which it argued was desirable not only for promoting individual responsibility and reducing the government's fiscal responsibility, but also promoting economic growth. The proposed private management of savings was expected to promote national financial markets and the fund management industry, which were believed to entail their own numerous positive externalities for the national economy.

Finally, the overall thrust of the report was to restrict the government's dominant role in income protection to only poverty prevention. In the area of income smoothing, the government's role was to consist largely of providing a legal framework for savings, investment and market competition. It took a particularly dim view of the political pressures on governments which led them to use pensions for political purposes that undermine the programme's viability and cause economic distortions. This belief led it to be sceptical of social insurance schemes which, in its view, had been undermined by promises of overly generous benefits without imposition of appropriate premiums to adequately finance them. It recommended the replacement of social insurance with savings schemes because the latter contained in-built mechanisms for preventing political interference.

The publication of the report unleashed a global debate on pension reform followed by a flurry of policy activities in a large number of countries. Some of the nuances of the report were lost in the ensuing years as it came to be increasingly associated with the promotions of the savings-based pension schemes (that is, the second pillar). The perception was partially the result of the highly visible role played by the report's lead economist, Estelle James, in defending and promoting the second pillar rather than the entire package of proposals.

The promotion of savings-based schemes was particularly inappropriate in low-income countries where income levels were often too low to allow significant savings and the financial infrastructure was too weak to allow the emergence of an investment management industry. The obsession with the second pillar undermined the viability of the first pillar without providing sufficient protection through the second pillar (Charlton and McKinnon 2001: 55).

The report also showed misguided denigration of social insurance as a means of providing adequate old age income security. Although it was not the first to do so, it rightly pointed out the unsustainability of implicit deficits caused by governments' promise of pension benefits unmatched by adequate contribution by members. Instead of examining alternative ways of addressing the problem, the report recommended their replacement with non-redistributive and privately managed savings schemes. Deficits are not inherent to social insurance and they are no more vulnerable to political interference than savings arrangements, as became apparent during the banking crisis in Chile in the 1980s and in Argentina in the 2000s. It is arguable that savings schemes too carry an implicit state guarantee (Barr 2002: 20), and thus an implicit debt for the state, which is no different from that associated with PAYG schemes which are an object of much criticism. It is also arguable that while the 1994 report claimed to simultaneously pursue both income maintenance and economic development objectives, it in fact privileged the latter. The dominant theme of its recommendations is maintaining the scheme's financial viability and promoting economic development rather than promoting income security for the aged. While the two are no doubt closely related, the latter is a vital objective in its own right and needs an adequate policy response.

Another weakness of the report was that it underestimated the complexity of the task of reforming pensions. It not only seemed to believe that the problems were similar around the world, but also that the solutions were the same. It was soon discovered that not only were the problems somewhat different but that, especially, the conditions under which the reforms could be introduced were yet more different (Orszag and Stiglitz 1999). It also underestimated the financial costs of transforming PAYG schemes into fully funded schemes because the government and the working population will be paying for the pension of the current retirees while saving for their own future retirement.

It also misunderstood the workings and macroeconomic effects of PAYG and savings schemes and as a result arrived at misguided conclusions about the undesirability of the former. In overall macroeconomic terms, there is no difference between PAYG and savings schemes (Barr 2002; Eatwell 2003; Thompson 1998), except that the latter limits the pursuit of redistributive goals and exposes members to potential financial uncertainties.

In its enthusiasm for promoting the second-pillar schemes, the report's authors, Bank officials, did not fully explain the risks involved in relying on privately managed investments. The extent to which members find their income from savings plans sufficient for retirement depends on investment performance, which in turn depends considerably on luck. Such uncertainties do not sit well with the purpose of social security, the main *raison d'être* of which is to promote security among people without income. Most major stock markets have been in a slump for almost five years, and some are yet to recover to the level achieved in the late 1980s. While individuals have some choice regarding when they retire and can continue working until their investments reach the desired level, this may never happen or not happen soon enough. As one commentator sums it up bluntly: 'The stock-market model of pensions, investment and economic growth is unimpressive in terms of providing the economic and social benefits which it promises' (Minns 2001: xii).

In addition, privately managed defined contribution schemes often suffer from high administration and marketing costs that are not sufficiently acknowledged in the report. The idea that competition among fund managers will drive down costs and thus leave more for the investors is not borne out by evidence. As Orszag and Stiglitz (1999: 29) point out, 'Competition, however, only precludes excess rents; it does not ensure low costs.' Chile and the United Kingdom are examples of high competition among managers of private retirement funds co-existing with high administration and marketing costs. It is not uncommon for costs to exceed returns to investors.

2005: rebalancing the state's role

In the years following the 1994 report, the Bank's position on pension reform began to soften, as reflected in a 2000 paper by one of its senior staff members (Holzmann 2000). By 2002, sufficient time had passed for not only empirically testing the assumptions and analysis of the 1994 report, but also assessing how its recommendations had worked out in practice. A group of Bank staff members, led by the Director of the Social Protection unit, Robert Holzmann, initiated the re-examination process. The result was published in 2005 'as a policy note, not as a research paper' nor the Bank's official position on the subject (Holzmann and Hinz 2005: 5). Nevertheless, the seniority and stature of the people involved in its preparation suggest that the document did reflect the Bank's current thinking on pension reform.

The 2005 document is notable for its reflective analysis of the problems faced by the aged and consideration of an expanded range of mechanisms for dealing with them. Instead of recommending specific mechanisms, it proposes key principles, goals and evaluation criteria for designing income schemes for the aged. It proposes that pension benefits should be adequate, affordable and sustainable over the long run and sufficiently robust to adjust to changing circumstances. The document will be best remembered, however, for its conceptualization of the multi-pillar system as consisting of five rather than three complementary components (Table 6.2).

The zero pillar is meant to be an essential pillar in the pension edifice in all countries, rich and poor. It corresponds to the first pillar of the 1994 report but is given a more central role in the new formulation. It is meant to provide a minimal level of protection to all those without sufficient income

Table 6.2 The five pillars of old age income security

Pillar	Objective	Financing	Programme features
0	Poverty alleviation, through redistribution	Government's general revenues	Mandatory; Publicly managed; Means-tested; Minimum benefits
1st	Income replacement, with some redistributive component	Contribution, employer and/or employee on PAYG or partially funded basis	Mandatory; Publicly managed; Defined benefits or notional defined contributions; Earning-related benefit
2nd	Income smoothing, through savings	Tax-preferred private savings or private insurance; fully funded	Mandatory; Privately managed; Defined contributions; Benefits equal contribution plus returns on investment
3rd	Income smoothing, through enhanced savings	Tax-preferred private saving; fully funded	Voluntary; Privately managed; Fully funded defined benefits or defined contribution; Benefits equal contribution plus returns on investment
4th	Continuing protection where possible	Financial and other assets	Voluntary; Privately and informally managed; Informal intra-family or inter-generational financial and non-financial help, e.g. housing, healthcare

during retirement. The benefits may be in the form of universal benefit available to all elderly, or means-tested public assistance available only to the needy. Eligibility conditions are meant to be flexible so as to include all those who need support. The funding for it is to come from the government's general revenues, as a contribution requirement would have the effect of excluding some potential beneficiaries.

The proposed first pillar is a new proposal targeted at the working poor, those who do not or cannot save, and those who face unusually high longevity or market risks (for example, financial market collapse at the time of retirement). As the document sums it up: 'First pillars address, among others, risks of individual myopia, low earnings even within the formal economy, and inappropriate planning horizons due to uncertainties of life expectancies and financial market risks' (Holzmann and Hinz 2005: 37). The structure of the programme may be of Defined Benefits or 'Notional'

Defined Contribution (NDC) types. While the benefits are to be related to income, the relationship is to be loose so as to allow some redistribution to those who need additional support. It is to be financed from contributions by employers and employees on a PAYG basis, though there is scope for some pre-funding. The level of contribution, and consequently benefits, is to be modest so as to not impose a heavy tax burden on members or promote work disincentives.

The second and third pillars, similar to their namesakes in the 1994 document, are designed to promote savings for retirement so that subscribers can enjoy a higher standard of living than the minimum standard made available under the zero and first pillars. However, the second pillar is mandatory while the third pillar is voluntary so that only those who can afford to save more take advantage of the latter in the form of tax concessions. Both pillars may be designed in a way so as to provide longevity insurance in the form of periodic annuities for life.

The fourth pillar is an entirely new proposal and is in response to the recognition that informal mechanisms play a vital role in providing income protection to the aged and others. Family members and home ownership are vital sources of income and other support and need to be considered while designing an overall income protection system for the aged. However, the report recommends no specific government measure to promote their fourth pillar except to consider its role while designing other pillars and ensuring that they are not undermined.

Unlike its predecessor, however, the 2005 document does not recommend that every country must build all the pillars. The choice of pillars and their design would depend on the government's objectives and, more importantly, existing arrangements and the overall fiscal and political conditions. The note (Holzmann and Hinz 2005: 72–3) recommends different reform strategies for low, middle and high-income countries divided by the level of stress experienced by the existing pension system. Each country is to choose its appropriate combination depending on its objectives and circumstances. In high-income countries, governments may choose to have only the first and second pillars, with the zero pillar included under the first. In poorer countries, the zero pillar is likely to be the dominant scheme with a relatively small role for the first and second pillars. However, in many low-income countries with low incomes and large informal sectors, it may not be possible to establish either the first or the second pillar in any meaningful sense. In such a case, they may choose only a minimal zero pillar and the voluntary third pillar (Holzmann and Hinz 2005: 74). Commenting on the recent shift in position, a scholar closely linked to the Bank noted: 'The new view of the Bank emphasizes that pension reform can have a very different shape but a new pension system has to do better on each of the main items the existing pension schemes are criticized for (Rutkowski 2004: 320).

The 2005 document, while retaining its predecessor's multi-pillar theme, is in many respects substantially different. Its tone is less didactic and prescriptive and its recommendations are accompanied by more nuanced qualifications. Its recommendations are, accordingly, more about principles and broad directions of reform rather than detailed programme design. Second, it is more accepting of innovations, evident in its acknowledgement of Notional Defined Contribution, a clearinghouse approach to consolidation and distribution of contributions, and informal fourth pillar arrangements.

Third, the 2005 note is more emphatic in its recognition that income protection and not economic development is a pension system's primary objective. While listing the principles for reform, it clearly states 'adequate, affordable, sustainable, and robust pensions' as the 'primary goals' and 'contribution to economic development as the secondary goals' (Holzmann and Hinz 2005: 48–9). The relative importance of the different objectives is embodied in the central role it ascribes to the zero pillar in its conception of the multi-pillar system. It correctly recognizes that there can be no viable income maintenance system without a basic social safety net that protects those who for a variety of reasons cannot qualify under any scheme based even on partial contribution. As it put it, 'Savings, either individual or through past employment, is really not a feasible source of old age income for the lifetime poor. Moreover, even for those employed in the formal sectors, most jobs do not provide pensions' (Holzmann and Hinz 2005: 27). The problem is likely to be aggravated in the future with the proliferation of part-time and informal employment.

Fourth, the 2005 note displays an appreciation of the differences in political circumstances and administrative capacity across nations. It explicitly recognizes that it may not be possible to replace or change existing schemes as easily as suggested in the 1994 report and builds the limitations into its analysis and recommendations. It also acknowledges the different conditions, needs and political capacities that exist in developed and developing countries, and countries faced with crisis and those that are not.

Finally, the 2005 document is more circumspect than its predecessor on the limitations of savings-based retirement schemes. According to its summary of the key limitations (Holzmann and Hinz 2005: 38),

Pure capitalized individual savings systems expose participants to substantial risks as they seek to translate a stock of savings into a flow of retirement income at the point of withdrawal from the labor market due to (1) interest rate volatility (Alier and Vittas 2001; Burtless 2000) or (2) limited capacity to manage mortality risk through inefficiencies in private annuity markets (James et al. 1999; James *et al.* 2001; Mitchell *et al.* 2000).

This recognition of the limits leads it to treat the zero and first pillars, and not the second, as was the case in the 1994 report, as the lynchpins of the pension system.

However, the 2005 document also leaves some problems insufficiently addressed. It continues its predecessor's support for the voluntary third pillar which may not be entirely justified. There is no compelling reason why society as a whole should subsidize savings by the rich, especially if they have already received tax concessions for savings under the second pillar. The savings to government from not allowing additional tax concessions could help fund other projects, including the zero pillar.

The 2005 document also offers no fresh ideas on how to reduce costs and promote transparency and certainty in benefits under privately managed second- and third-pillar schemes. High administrative costs and severe fluctuations in returns are significant drawbacks of the arrangement and, given the Bank's expertise, more could have been done to think of ways to improve them.

Moreover, the note also continues to subscribe to its predecessor's exaggerated cynicism towards PAYG social insurance-based defined benefits schemes. Insurance is a powerful instrument for protecting against risks and achieving other social and economic objectives. It does not have to be unsustainable as there are relatively straightforward ways of adequately funding it without imposing an additional fiscal burden on government. The crises faced by many existing social insurance schemes are often rooted in the fact that these schemes were designed at a time when actuarial sciences were not fully developed and the enormity of the costs of ageing was not fully understood. It is now possible to design financially sustainable insurance plans that are adequately funded for any given level of benefits. Difficulties in reforming existing PAYG schemes (which trigger political opposition from those likely to lose out) are not necessarily relevant to the design of new PAYG schemes.

Another myth the 2005 note continues to subscribe to is that of a government's capacity to regulate private managers of savings funds. The fact is that most governments, especially in the developing world, simply lack the capacity to regulate the financial industry in a way that safeguards and promotes the investors' interests. Governments that can effectively regulate private schemes can be expected to also manage public schemes, thus undermining the case for private management.

Factors shaping the World Bank's position

Writings on changes in social security policies are for the most part directed at the national level and explain the changes with reference to some combination of domestic and international conditions (see Brooks 2004; Huber and Stephens 2000; Muller 2004; James and Brooks 2001; Melo 2004; Orenstein 1999). While there are significant differences among them in terms of the variables they emphasize, they typically cite influence and pressure from international financial institutions (IFIs), including the World Bank. Explanations also address changes in social and economic conditions (for example, ageing and fiscal crisis) or domestic political circumstances as the key determinants of changes in pensions policy. There is virtually nothing available on how or why IFIs themselves change their policy positions. A plausible explanation must necessarily come from exploring a range of factors.

Traditional structural or agential explanations of policy changes cannot go far towards explaining changes in the World Bank's perspective on pensions. There was nothing in the structure of global capitalism that predisposed the Bank to first favour private savings and, especially, later promote a more measured approach. Nor can the shifts be explained as a result of pressure from powerful pressure groups or clients. Business groups, no matter how powerful, do not have direct access to the Bank to shape its thinking. Similarly, there is little evidence of national governments, who are the Bank's main clientele, pressuring it to change its position on pensions, because the dominant members themselves do not have the sort of programmes the Bank is promoting.

A more plausible explanation lies in the realm of social and economic circumstances and policy learning. Changes in demographics, economic conditions and investment returns form the context within which the World Bank's positions are formed, buttressed by its continual learning from the actual operation of pension systems and their reforms.

Recognition of the challenges involved in looking after an ageing population has formed the backdrop to all pension reform efforts, including the Bank's. While ageing was not a significant problem in most developing countries (the Bank's main clients) in the 1980s, its enhanced involvement in economic restructuring in Latin America and its subsequent involvement in the reconstruction of Eastern European economies changed that. Both regions had mature and under-funded social insurance-based pension plans whose conditions were expected to continue to worsen with population ageing unless they were fundamentally reformed. Thinking about reform of their pension schemes led to the preparation of *Averting the Old Age Crisis*, and the concerns specific to the region are evident throughout this report. Not only did the Eastern European and Latin American experiences shape the content of the report, but also its reception in policy circles, which at the time were grappling with ageing problems and were only too keen to accept what appeared to be a workable solution from a reputable organization.

Declining rates of saving, especially in the developed countries, was another condition shaping the Bank's position on pensions. While in the developing world the savings rate itself was not low, overall low-income levels limited the scope for total savings. Since making pension schemes support economic development objectives was an important consideration for the Bank in the early 1990s, it saw the savings-based aged income scheme as a less painful way of promoting savings and, as a corollary, investment. It did not matter that there was no strong evidence supporting this view, and indeed in the case of Chile the evidence showed that pensions privatization had a negative impact on savings (Mesa-Lago 1998). The emergence of industries associated with fund management was expected to further reinforce economic development.

Deep economic crises also had a striking impact on perceptions of the problems facing pensions and the solutions to them (Madrid 2002; James and Brooks 2001). The economic morass afflicting the Latin American and Eastern European countries encouraged the Bank to recommend radical changes to their pension systems and at the same time prepare people to accept the proposed changes. The subsequent improvement in economic conditions in the two regions in the mid-1990s seemingly vindicated the reforms and further legitimized them. Perceptions began to change once more with the financial crises that struck Asia in 1997 and subsequently Russia, Brazil and Argentina. Many of these same countries had been portrayed earlier as models of sound policy reform, and the meltdown shook confidence in the usefulness of the recommended reforms. The case of the East Asian countries was particularly remarkable because it demonstrated that growth and sound macroeconomic policies were not sufficient for sustained poverty reduction. The changing perception is reflected in the World Bank's (2001: 8) pronouncement: 'Shock-resistant risk management programs, including safety nets, income support systems for the elderly, and well-functioning labor markets with social safeguards are essential to reduce poverty over the long term and to protect gains already made.'

Short-term economic and financial market fluctuations too conditioned the World Bank's views on pension reforms. Economic and especially stock market booms in much of the Americas, Europe and Asia during the early and mid-1990s made for sanguine assessment of returns on private investment by privately managed pension funds, and this optimism was reflected in the 1994 report. The ensuing economic recessions and depressed equity market conditions of various magnitudes in the late 1990s tempered this perception and suddenly the publicly managed PAYG schemes did not look all that bad – the changed assessment was reflected in the 2005 document. Indeed, many began to wonder if pensions, which necessarily are about income security in old age, should be built on something so fickle as returns on risky investments, as proposed for the second- and third-pillar arrangements.

The general intellectual and policy milieu of privatization and deregulation that enveloped policy discussions in the 1980 and early 1990s was also reflected in the 1994 report. By the late 1990s many of the reforms had not delivered all they had promised, and policy commentators were more circumspect.

Changes in social and economic conditions do not, however, by themselves lead to changes in how international organizations view a policy problem and its solution. There was an associated process of cognitive learning going on which led to changes in perspective. All thriving institutions – and the World Bank is one such institution par excellence – are learning organizations. They are constantly in the process of learning, adapting, and problem solving. The 1994 report was a product of the Bank's learning from the experiences of managing reform in Eastern Europe and Latin America between the mid-1980s and mid-1990s (Charlton and McKinnon 2001: 90). The lessons from the stock market crash in Asia in the late 1990s and in Europe and USA after 2000, and the actual performance of privatization-inspired reforms, led to more realism and a tempering of enthusiasm for the stock market as a generator of pensions.

Learning about ageing and the shortcomings of social insurance, as well as about savings-based insurance and the limitations faced by the poor, led to a more measured position on pensions. The greatest effect, however, was that of a large-scale evaluation of pension reforms in Latin America by many researchers associated with the World Bank, which was completed in 2002 (Gill *et al.* 2004). The study found that the newly established second-pillar schemes had low coverage, earned low returns, largely excluded the poor and, remarkably, were not immune to political intervention. This was a devastating critique of the second- and third-pillar arrangements that were at the centre of the 1994 report.

Changes in intellectual orientation of the prominent pension experts also had an impact on the Bank's position on pensions. The late 1980s and early 1990s were characterized by the dominance of 'dry' neoclassical economic thinking both within and without the Bank, and this was evident in the 1994 report. The intellectual tradition is highly sceptical about the state and has immense confidence in the ability of the market to deliver desirable, if not always desired, solutions to public problems. The situation began to change in the mid-1990s with the entry of many new economists into the pensions debate who challenged both the logical and empirical bases of the 1994 report (Barr 2002; Diamond 2002; Orszag and Stiglitz 1999; Thompson 1998). A seminar on pension reforms in 1999 organized by the World Bank in which its Chief Economist, Joseph Stiglitz, played a lead role, crystallized the criticisms of the three-pillar proposals into a coherent critique and marked the beginning of the end for the line of thinking espoused in *Averting the Old Age Crisis*. Stiglitz's criticisms particularly helped legitimize criticisms of the World Bank's orthodoxy and paved the way for fresh thinking (Melo 2004: 327), which was subsequently reflected in the 2005 note. Bank President Wolfensohn's efforts to improve the Bank's image by increasing commitment to addressing social concerns formed a hospitable context for fresh thinking on the subject.

Conclusion

The publication of *Averting the Old Age Crisis* in 1994 marked a turning point in the debate on pension reform. Using its vast expertise in public policy, the Bank proposed a three-pillar pension arrangement that avowedly promoted social protection as well as economic development. Notwithstanding serious reservations about the proposal, it set the benchmark for efforts to reform pension systems around the world. All significant discussions on pension reform in the subsequent years directly or indirectly referred to, though not necessarily agreeing with, the key points raised in the report.

It was soon realized that the report was built on tenuous assumptions and questionable analysis. Its limitations were aggravated by subsequent commentary from some of its key authors which oversold the benefits, underemphasized the risks, and conveyed the impression that promotion of private savings and private fund management had precedence over social protection. Unsurprisingly, not many countries adopted the entire proposed reform package. In the few countries, mainly in Latin America, that did make comprehensive reforms along the lines suggested by the report, subsequent evaluations found the results to fall vastly short of expectations.

The growing unease with the proposals led to serious rethinking within and beyond the Bank. While the Bank remains officially committed to the 1994 report, many researchers and officials associated with the Bank published a clarifying note in 2005 that indicates a significant departure from the official position. The new document emphatically recognizes that social protection and not economic development is the pension plan's key objective, acknowledges the importance of local, social and political conditions in determining the actual content of reforms, and allows for greater variety and innovation in programme design.

Both documents are products of the social, economic and political conditions of the period in which they were written, and of the lessons that the Bank drew from them. The 1994 report was the product of the conditions in the late 1980s and early 1990s when the Bank was deeply involved in economic restructuring in Eastern Europe and Latin America, from which it drew universal conclusions about pensions. The financial unsustainability of the pension programmes in the face of rapid ageing, combined with deep economic problems faced by the two regions at the time, coloured the Bank's perception and led to an overemphasis on economic concerns at the expense of social objectives. Similarly, its sanguine assessment of the desirability of privately managed savings-based schemes was significantly influenced by buoyant stock markets during the 1990s. The collapse of the stock market and outbreak of economic crises in Asia and Latin America in the late 1990s, and adverse findings on the actual performance of the implemented reforms, made the Bank more circumspect about relying heavily on private savings and private management of pension funds.

The study shows that the changes in the Bank's views are not a functionalist response to changes in structural conditions, because there was no structural shift in the global economy or polity in the late 1990s that might have led the Bank to change its position. The forces explaining the change were more contingent, related to specific social and economic developments and the lessons the Bank drew from them. The case also highlights the importance of policy learning. For the Bank to be relevant, it had to respond to the flaws in its proposals as they became apparent, or risk losing its lead position in the debate to other international organizations, notably the International Labour Organization.

The study also shows that there is no evidence of a 'race to the bottom' in terms of the Bank's views on the state's role in pensions. The proposals in the 2005 policy note are a significant advance not only in relation to its own earlier position, but also in terms of what actually exists in much of the world. Adoption of the 2005 recommendations would provide decidedly superior social protection than do the existing programmes in nearly all countries.

References

Alier, M. and Vittas, D. (2001) 'Personal Pension Plans and Stockmarket Volatility', in R. Holzmann and J. Stiglitz (eds) *New Ideas About Old Age Security: Toward Sustainable Pension Systems in the 21st Century*, Washington DC: World Bank.

Barr, N. (2002) 'Reforming Pensions: Myths, Truths, and Policy Choices', *International Social Security Review* 55(2), 3–36.

Brooks, S. M. (2004) 'Interdependent and Domestic Foundations of Policy Change: The Diffusion of Pension Privatization around the World', paper presented at the Annual Convention of the International Studies Association, Montreal, 19 March 2004. http://psweb.sbs.ohio-state.edu/faculty/sbrooks/Brooks_diffusion_2004.pdf

Burtless, G. (2000) 'Social Security Privatization and Financial Market Risk', Center on Social and Economic Dynamics, Working Paper no. 10, Washington DC: Brookings Institution Press.

Charlton, R. and McKinnon, R. (2001) *Pensions in Development*, Aldershot: Ashgate.

Diamond, P. A. (2002) *Social Security Reform*, Oxford: Oxford University Press.

Eatwell, J. (2003) 'The Anatomy of the Pensions "Crisis" and Three Fallacies on Pensions', http:// www.cerf.cam.ac.uk/publications/files/Eatwell-pensions crisis.pdf

Gill, I. S., Packard, T. and Yermo, J. (2004) *Keeping the Promise of Old Age Income Security in Latin America*, http://wbln0018.worldbank.org/LAC/LAC.nsf/ECA-DocbyUnid/146EBBA3371508E785256CBB005C29B4?Opendocument

Holzmann, R. (2000) 'The World Bank Approach to Pension Reform', *International Social Security Review* 53(1), 11–34.

Holzmann, R. and Hinz, R. (2005) *Old-Age Income Support in the 21st Century: An International Perspective on Pension Systems and Reform*, World Bank. http://www1.worldbank.org/sp/incomesupportfiles/OldAgeSupportPrelimWeb.pdf

Holzmann, R. and Stiglitz, J. (eds) (2001) *New Ideas About Old Age Security: Toward Sustainable Pension Systems in the 21st Century*, Washington DC: World Bank.

Huber, E. and Stephens, J. (2000) *The Political Economy of Pension Reform: Latin America in Comparative Perspective*, Occasional Paper 7, Geneva: United Nations Research Institute for Social Development.

James, E. and Brooks, S. (2001) 'The Political Economy of Structural Pension Reform', in Holzmann, R. and Stiglitz, J. (eds) *New Ideas About Old Age Security: Toward Sustainable Pension Systems in the 21st Century*, Washington DC: World Bank, 133–70.

James, E., Ferrier, G., Smallhout, J. and Vittas, D. (1999) 'Mutual Funds and Institutional Investments: What Is the Most Efficient Way to Set Up Individual

Accounts in a Social Security System?', World Bank Policy Research Working Paper no. 2099, Washington DC: World Bank.

James, E., Smallhout, J. and Vittas, D. (2001) 'Administrative Costs and the Organization of Individual Account Systems: A Comparative Perspective', World Bank Policy Research Working Paper no. 2554, Washington DC: World Bank.

Madrid, R. L. (2002) 'The Politics and Economics of Pension Privatization in Latin America', *Latin American Research Review* 37(2), 159–82.

Melo, M. A. (2004) 'Institutional Choice and the Diffusion of Policy Paradigms: Brazil and the Second Wave of Pension Reform', *International Political Science Review* 25(3), 320–41.

Mesa-Lago, C. (1998) 'Comparative Features and Performance of Structural Pension Reforms In Latin America', *Brooklyn Law Review* 64(3), 771–93.

Minns, R. (2001) *The Cold War in Welfare: Stock Markets Versus Pensions*, New York: Verso.

Mitchell, O. S., Myers, R. and Young, H. (2000) *Prospects for Social Security Reform*, Pension Research Council, Philadelphia PA: University of Pennsylvania Press.

Muller, K. (2004) 'Latin American and East European Pension Reforms: Accounting for a Paradigm Shift', in Rein, M. and Schmähl, W. (eds) *Rethinking the Welfare State: The Political Economy of Pension Reform*, Northampton MA: Edward Elgar, 348–71.

Orenstein, M. A. (1999) *How Politics and Institutions Affect Pension Reform in Three Post-Communist Countries*, Policy Research Working Paper, World Bank.

Orszag, P. R. and Stiglitz, J. E. (1999) 'Rethinking Pension Reform: Ten Myths About Social Security Systems', paper presented at 'New Ideas About Old Age Security' conference, Washington DC, 14–15 September 1999.

Rutkowski, Michal (2004) 'Home-Made Pension Reforms in Central and Eastern Europe and the Evolution of the World Bank Approach to Modern Pension Systems', in Rein, M. and Schmähl, W. (eds) *Rethinking the Welfare State: The Political Economy of Pension Reform*, Northampton MA: Edward Elgar, 319–33.

Thompson, Lawrence H. (1998) *Predictability of Individual Pensions*, OECD Working Paper AWP 3.5, Paris: OECD.

World Bank (1994) *Averting the Old Age Crisis: Policies to Protect the Old and Promote Growth*, Oxford: Oxford University Press.

——(2001) *Social Protection Sector Strategy: From Safety Net to Springboard*, Washington DC: World Bank.

7 Change in international organizations: innovation or adaptation?

A comparison of the World Bank and the International Monetary Fund

Antje Vetterlein

Introduction

During the last decade, the World Bank has undergone significant reforms. Often these changes are referred to as a paradigm shift from the Washington Consensus to the post-Washington Consensus (Fine *et al.* 2001; Board and Cavanagh 1999; Williamson 2003). While both focus on markets and economic policy, the latter understands development as a transformational process that also has social, political and cultural dimensions. The question this chapter intends to address is: How can we explain policy change in international organizations (IOs)?

Conventional realist approaches to the study of international relations do not provide a sufficient answer. For these primarily explain the creation, purpose and influence of international organizations in the context of systemic factors of member states' interests and the distribution of power among them (Krasner, 1985; 1983). By doing so, they not only neglect the fact that international organizations are, to a certain extent, autonomous, but they also ignore the internal processes of these organizations as well as the aspect of organizational culture. This chapter will focus on policy innovations *within* international organizations as a notable factor in explaining the World Bank's move towards a much broader understanding of development. It will perceive international organizations as quasi-autonomous actors that do not merely adjust to their outside world but are actively engaging in innovative behaviour and continuously shaping it.

Recently, two alternative theoretical approaches have entered the realm of international relations that address this missing focus on international organization agency, namely principal-agent (P-A) models and organizational sociology. Both approaches understand policy change of international organizations from the level of the organization, ascribing them autonomy, and thus agency, and searching for explanatory variables. Rather than understanding policy change in international organizations as a static cause-effect relationship, however, my analysis will discuss it as a *process*, taking place in two steps. Furthermore, introducing the concept of organizational *personality*, I argue that it makes sense to overcome the rationalist-constructivist divide which both approaches follow. This argumentation is presented by means of the empirical case of policy change in the World Bank, using the International Monetary Fund (the Fund hereafter) as a contrasting case.

The remainder of this chapter is structured as follows. After a brief overview of recent reforms in the World Bank and a summary of the main characteristics of its new development approach, the second section presents my assumptions of how policy change in international organizations might be fruitfully theorized. Drawing on many recent studies that emphasize the World Bank's autonomy and independence (Weaver forthcoming; Weaver and Leiteritz 2005; Nielson *et al.* 2004, 2003a, 2003b; Barnett and Finnemore 1999; Miller-Adams 1999; Naím 1994), I would argue that the organizational autonomy varies among international organizations, and that the Bank enjoys more of it than most others. Thus, it makes sense to consider organizational autonomy in a relative sense, by contrasting international organizations and explaining their differences.

The third and main section of the chapter will be dedicated to arguments and explanations of four conditions of change in international organizations that were retrieved from the empirical analysis. The chapter forms part of a broader research project on the development of social (development) policies in the World Bank and the Fund from the late 1970s until today (Vetterlein, 2006). From this analysis, it was possible to extract four conditions of change in international organizations, whose impacts vary according to the organization's personality. In turn, these are (1) the consistency of the newly introduced policy issues with the organization's original mandate; (2) the degree of autonomy from its principals; (3) the existence of internal advocacy; and (4) the nature of the external event. I will draw on this study selectively for the purpose of my theoretical argument. The final section concludes and presents some generalizations about change in international organizations.

Towards a Post-Washington Consensus

The term 'Washington Consensus', coined by John Williamson in 1989 (1998, 1990), has in the development community come to be associated with the neoliberal economic policy framework promoted by the World Bank and the Fund, and its most powerful shareholder. Roughly, this framework emphasizes the importance of deregulation, privatization and market liberalization to further economic development in developing countries.

In the late 1990s, a host of critics inside the development establishment, led by the World Bank's previous chief economist, Joseph Stiglitz, called for a broader development agenda (Stiglitz 1998a, 1998b). The development perspective of what became known as the 'Post-Washington Consensus' goes beyond economics and defines development in a holistic manner as a transformational process that affects a whole society. Hence, while the advancement of the economy is still a very important element, it is no longer considered *the* precondition to achieve the other goals of poverty reduction, democracy-building, and sustainable development. In fact, social development of a society is perceived to be as much a cause of an increase in GDP as an effect (Stiglitz 1998a, 1998b).

This means the development challenge is reframed from achieving macroeconomic stability and economic growth to sustainable economic growth and poverty reduction. Following this change in how the problem is defined, the underlying objectives, and the means to achieve development policies, have shifted and broadened as well. Accordingly, a multidisciplinary form of aid assistance is called for, which in turn requires the integration of different sources of local and technical knowledge, in such fields as anthropology, sociology and ecology.

Under President Wolfensohn, the World Bank adopted numerous new initiatives and policies. When he arrived in the Bank in 1996, the organization was under pressure from many sides. The NGO critique, manifested in the '50 years is enough' campaign in 1994 (Danaher 1994), continued to question the development impacts of its financing. Its internal incentive structure was scrutinized for promoting a 'culture of loan approval', in which staff was focused on approving loans rather than preparing sound projects and monitoring their impacts (Wapenhans *et al.* 1992). Furthermore, there was increasing competitive pressure because of growing private capital flows, which undermined the Bank's role and influence in some countries.

From his first day in office, Wolfensohn promised wide-ranging internal reforms in order to shift the Bank's culture of loan approval into a culture of 'development effectiveness' and 'accountability' with a focus on economic, social and environmental policies as priority areas in the Bank (World Bank 1995). One of his first moves was the *Strategic Compact* in 1996. While this compact was mainly intended to alter the Bank's organizational structure and make it more accountable, client-oriented and efficient, at the same time, it was aimed at shifting the Bank's basic mission towards a more comprehensive development approach that integrated economic and social development. Other policies followed that tried to operationalize the new spirit in the Bank. The *Comprehensive Development Framework* (CDF) announced in 1996, and the *Partnership Initiative* in 1997, are two prominent examples. The Bank together with the Fund engaged in the *Heavily Indebted Poor Countries* initiative (HIPC) in 1996, which was in 1999 combined with the *Poverty Reduction Strategies* (PRS). All of these developments are a reflection of the organization's involvement into new policy issues such as poverty, participation, environment, transparency, country ownership and accountability.

In sum, these policy innovations suggest a different understanding of the development challenge, which espouses a different set of values than the Washington Consensus. As the above-mentioned policies attempt to operationalize this new perspective, we can observe a new development-political paradigm that emerged in the late 1990s. While some of these innovations have yet to be implemented, they should not be conceived as rhetorical exercises. Therefore, the question then is why and how this paradigm shift came about.

Organizational personality as the determinant for policy change

If we leave conventional international relations theories aside and immediately focus on approaches in international relations that account for internal processes in international organizations, there are two relevant strands of theory: P-A models and more sociological approaches that focus on the internal social life of organizations (for an overview, see Barnett and Finnemore 2004, 1999). The starting point of P-A models is the assumption that member states (principals) delegate authority to the IO (agent) in the belief that the agent will act in the principal's interests. Such models are premised on the assumption that performance gaps appear between the principal and the agent since the agent is assumed to be a rational actor, striving for its own interests. They would then explain change in IO behaviour by the degree of influence the principal, that is, the member countries, exerts over its agent. The principals are able to employ several control mechanisms to prevent the agent's 'shirking' or 'slippage' behaviour (Pollack 1997), such as changing the incentive structure (Cortell and Peterson 2003), monitoring or selecting specific change agents (Nielson *et al.* 2004, 2003a).

This explanation of policy change, as depending on the preferences and capacity of external actors to control agents, only reveals part of the whole story. It neglects the cultural dimension of an organization, which is the main contribution of organizational sociology. Besides formal rules and the organization's interests, its internal culture might function as a powerful resistance against exogenous forces, or rather, as an intervening variable. Internally, an IO perceives and interprets external stimuli according to its own way of thinking and subsequently responds in a way that accommodates the new issue to its norms, routines, patterns of interaction, and language. Many studies, all of them focusing on the World Bank (see Weaver forthcoming; Weaver and Leiteritz 2005; Nielson *et al.* 2004, 2003b; Miller-Adams 1999; Fox 1998; Naím 1994), provide evidence for these adjustment processes as a function of the culture of the respective organization.

The analysis here goes beyond this rationalist-constructivist divide by arguing that the actions of principals, and the response of the agent, as driven by its internal organizational culture, are interrelated. Thus, the more fruitful line of inquiry is investigating under what *conditions* one of these variables might be more decisive than the other. In this context, the concept of organizational personality is introduced as an intervening variable. An organizational personality comprises of formal rules, incentive structures, informal regulations, patterns of interactions, norms and routines, and might function as a lens through which external factors get refracted. It might thus be a decisive factor that influences under what conditions change is taking place in international organizations.

Theoretical framework

Organizational change in international organizations is conceived in the context of a response to a challenge to the organization's procedures and common ways of thinking regarding specific issues. This pressure often stems from the IO's environment, which not only includes its member states, but also other (collective) actors such as NGOs, investment banks and development aid agencies. Such pressure can also be exerted from the inside. Thus, the World Bank is embedded in an institutional structure within international relations. It also has its own organizational structure that consists of individual actors. It is individual actors who take decisions, and thus shape policies. For their definition and possible solutions of the policy problems, they draw on an available stock of knowledge about development policy. In other words, one could argue that *institutions, power* and *cognitions* draw the context in which individual *actors*, who are conceived of being the carrier of social change, are positioned and act (see Wagner 1990; Giddens 1984).

Organizational change can then be conceived to take place in two steps: first, the organization is embedded in and confronted with its environment. It will change its behaviour and policies if external pressures endanger its own existence and power position. From this pressure, a discrepancy might emerge between what the organization thinks it *ought* to do and what it thinks it *is* doing, which in turn might lead to an initiative to change (March and Olsen 1975). However, the organization does not merely adapt to external requirements. In a second step, the organization's *personality* is perceived to function as a filter through which new knowledge enters, is refracted, and thus shapes *how* these new claims and ideas are processed internally.

While the first stage of this proposed two-step model refers to the conditions of the possibility of change, the second stage represents the conditions of change. In relation to the latter, the organization's personality is interpreted as the independent variable that determines the qualitative aspect of change. Such a personality constitutes an organization and defines it internally, and also in its relations with the outside world. That means the same external factor might differently impact and trigger internal responses depending on the organization's personality.

The analysis will compare the differences in personality between the Bank and the Fund, which will shed light on the conditions that might be conducive to organizational learning or stagnation. In this respect, three organizational characteristics are decisive: (1) the original mandate of the organization; (2) its formal structure internally (hierarchy, units, centralization) and externally (financial independence); and (3) the professional composition of its staff, all of which have been themselves subject to change to various extents.

1   The charters of the two organizations suggest that they would respond differently to external criticisms addressing their development approach. While the Fund's main purposes are quite clear, namely to 'promote international monetary cooperation ... facilitate the expansion and balanced growth of international trade ... [and] promote exchange stability',[1] the Bank's *Articles of Agreement* include the assistance 'in the reconstruction and *development* of territories of members'[2] as its major objective. Development is a much fuzzier goal, and thus, more susceptible to reinterpretation and expansion. Hence, in light of these mandates, social development, for instance, will more likely be a topic for the Bank than for the Fund.

2   Two aspects of their organizational design can be differentiated: the degree of financial independence from their member countries and their formal organizational structure. In both aspects, I assume the Bank's structure as more instrumental in organizational change than the Fund's. Regarding the first aspect, the Bank might be more autonomous since its organizational design allows it to invest some of its capital contribution on the capital market, which provides financial independence at least to a certain degree. With respect to the latter aspect, the Bank is less hierarchical than the Fund and more decentralized, with a so-called matrix structure. This characteristic leads to a more competitive atmosphere inside the organization, where different units compete against each other and lobby for their policy agenda at the management as well as the board level. Hence, there might be greater incentives for staff creativity as well as for policy advocacy, which in turn trigger policy change in organizations.

3   The staff structure might be an even more decisive variable that has an impact on different modes of change, or learning, in international organizations. The Bank has always had a greater professional mixture. Over the last decade, it has increasingly hired non-economic social scientists, a development reinforced in 1996 with the *Strategic Compact* that aimed at a change in staff structure as well as in staff interaction and collaboration. While economists at the Bank are increasingly obliged to work together with other social scientists and listen to their advice regarding the social impact of projects and programmes, economists at the Fund are still rarely interacting with professionals from other disciplines, a fact that is assumed to have consequences for policy-making and change.

All three variables that shape the organization's personality internally also impact on the organization's relation to its external environment, and thus influence its ability and path of change. In this sense, the concept of organizational personality goes beyond that of organizational culture, which mainly considers internal processes as determining change in international organizations. It combines external pressure by principals and internal cultural aspects, and thus allows for flows in both directions. Consequently, it is not only possible that pressure from the outside can lead to change inside, but one could also assume that external events are used strategically by insiders to initiate change.

It is thus of interest to consider under what conditions policy change in international organizations takes place. Based on a comparison between the Bank and the Fund, the analysis suggests that an interplay between four factors determines the conditions for policy change. Depending on the personality of the organization, the extent of the variation of these factors and their combination lead to different modes of change on a continuum from mere adaptation to innovation. These four aspects will be explained more in detail below.

The conditions of change: innovation or adaptation?

The organizational mandate established at the foundation of the organization serves the aim to achieve some mutually agreed, identifiable and publicly stated ends. However, the organizational goal is much more important than it might seem at first glance. Such an objective, once agreed upon, will then determine the organization's belief system, namely the values that influence an organization's interpretation of its environment, and subsequent responses to it. In other words, the establishment of a specific goal or the determination to achieve it has implications for the way specific situations will be defined. It provides explanations for the problems that are perceived within this frame, and thus offers specific solutions to the problem in the form of policies. But rather than influencing only the definition capacity provided by the chosen belief system, it also shapes the actual functioning of organizations in terms of skills, knowledge and professional background of staff, including their different approaches to the topic regarding definitions, methodologies, analysis, and decision-making procedures. One can therefore assume that the organizational mandate has an impact on policy change in international organizations.

The comparison between the Bank and the Fund provides evidence that it has been much easier for the Bank to get involved in social (development) policies and issues of poverty reduction. This is not surprising, since the objective of development can be defined in many ways, as evidenced throughout the history of the Bank. Document analysis reveals that development in the Bank was defined as 'human and economic development' during the 1970s (World Bank 1980), which changed to 'economic development' over the course of the 1980s (World Bank 1988; Demerel and Addison 1987) and to 'economic *and* social development' in the early and mid-1990s (Birdsall 1993). Today, 'equitable', 'inclusive' and 'sustainable' development is the objective of the World Bank (Davis 2004; World Bank 2001). These changing definitions of the objective of the Bank's activities came hand-in-hand with different definitions of the policy problem as well as different policy means to solve them (Vetterlein 2006). In other words, the broad goal of development allowed the Bank to easily reframe it, according to the respective gist at the time without colliding with its *Articles of Agreement*. It never needed to change its original goal.

The Fund, on the other hand, is in a different position. It is a financial institution with purely economic goals, which make it difficult for the organization to get engaged with social policies. When there was pressure during the late 1970s to take on a so-called 'basic needs approach' (Gerster 1982), the Fund responded with the acknowledgment that its programmes might have implications for income distribution (Heller *et al.* 1988; IMF 1986), a rather economic translation of the issue. Nevertheless, by the end of the 1980s, the Fund acknowledged the *social* costs of adjustment pro-grammes after a process of several years in which new arguments were incrementally introduced into the debate, the most prominent of which was the 'short-term cost and long-term benefit argument' (IMF 1986). This reasoning was an attempt to legitimize the Fund's macroeconomic policy advice which was assumed, despite some short-term social costs, to benefit in particular the poor since it will lead to economic growth, and hence, to poverty reduction (for more detail, see Vetterlein 2006: ch. 4). It also was an attempt of the organization to remain in the economic realm of develop-ment. It was only after Michel Camdessus, the Fund's Managing Director from 1987 to 2000, redefined its goal of economic growth into high-quality growth in 1990 that the Fund officially introduced social safety nets as a means to mitigate adverse social effects of its programmes (Camdessus 1990; IMF 1993). High-quality growth included sustainable growth accom-panied by investment in human capital as well as poverty reduction and equity in opportunity.

Even today, while the Fund is lending to LICs under the PRSP framework, which clearly states poverty reduction as its first priority, its involvement in social issues and poverty reduction is subject to debate and doubt. For example, it is commonly understood that '[i]n the family of international organizations, the social components of country programs are primarily the responsibility of the World Bank and other organizations, not the Fund' (Gupta *et al.* 2000: 1). Furthermore, a number of Directors on the Fund's Board explicitly refer to the organization's mandate and warn 'that the Fund should not allow its primary mandate to be diluted', but should rather 'contribut[e] to poverty reduction mainly through its support of eco-nomic policies that provide a conducive environment for sustained growth' (Gupta *et al.* 2001: 28). To be sure, there have also been struggles going on over the Bank's involvement in social issues. However, such clear references to the Bank's original mandate and the consistency of the policy issue with its goal could not be found in Bank documents.

In other words, the original mandate of the organizations seems to be decisive for change in two ways. First, it determines how easily a new issue resonates with the organization's goals and working procedures, and thus is taken up and triggers policy change. In other words, the organizations will most seamlessly take on new objectives if doing so does not require additional capacity or new methodologies, skills and knowledge. This touches upon the second observation, that in order for an organization to even 'see' a problem, the issue needs to be made to fit the main objective, the existing value system and its corresponding procedures. This is easier to pursue the fuzzier an organizational objective is formulated in the first place, as the Bank's example showed. In that sense, it was much more difficult for the Fund, since it needed to extend and redefine its objective in order to be able to deal with issues of poverty reduction.

In sum, the mandate determines an openness of an organization that, depending on its degree and the policy area, might more or less facilitate organizational response to external pressure and thus change. Even if the design of the mandate allows for change, the organization must have the operational autonomy to independently change its behaviour.

Organizational autonomy from 'principals'

While the two organizations are to a certain extent accountable to their members, in particular the donor community, they are also independent of them. They are 'living' collectivities with their own dispositions of which they take advantage. They both possess huge amounts of specialized knowledge and expertise, and run their own research departments, which makes it hard for the principals to comprehensively monitor and control all their activities. This is not to say that the member countries are completely powerless. The important question in the context of this chapter is whether autonomy really has an impact on the mechanisms of change.

The Bank seems much more autonomous from its principals than the Fund (see also Naìm 1994). There are two reasons for this. First, the Bank's fiscal independence allows it to bypass the Board in decisions on hiring staff, conducting research or creating new units, all of which are important activities that shape organizational behaviour. It was augmented during McNamara's presidency, when member countries' contributions grew, staff numbers tripled and more importantly, the Bank increased its capital base by raising more money on the private markets by extending its activities to the European capital market (Kapur *et al.* 1997). Second, besides its partial financial independence, the organizational personality of the Bank, arising from some of the characteristics of its organizational structure, provides for the conditions of a strong management and a rather weak Board. As a more complex and decentralized organization than the Fund, it is difficult for member countries to stay abreast of its activities. Its fuzzy organizational objectives and its engagement with so many issues made it easier for the Bank's management and staff to sell policies and new agendas to the Board under the label 'development'. This was perpetuated by the introduction of the matrix structure in 1996, which increases competition among staff and enhances lobbying behaviour for new policies.

The Fund, on the other hand, completely depends on its principals for its finances. Every decision to expand Fund staff or create new departments is subject to a Board decision. Horst Köhler's attempt, for instance, to hire more social scientists for the organization, in order to consult economists in social aspects of their work, was rejected by the Board (interview of 19 March 2004). In fact, the few non-economists who are presently working in the Fund[3] are also not financed by the organization itself, but are funded by the UK's Department for International Development (DfID). Furthermore, as a result of its hierarchical and highly controlled internal structure, there is generally less lobbying taking place in the Fund. The conditions in the Fund are much more controlled and the Board has much more oversight over the organization's activities. Attempts at convincing the Board to take on new agendas are also less likely, as its organizational mandate is more circumscribed.

Ayres (1983) points out that at the World Bank, management decisively determines what is going on, whereas at the IMF, the Board is much stronger and exerts much more influence and control over the organization's course of action.[4] Similarly, the president of the Bank has more leverage in decision-making than the managing director of the Fund. This is not to say that the managing director does not play any role, as we have seen with the example of Camdessus' approach to extend economic growth to high-quality growth.[5] However, the Bank's president is freer to express visions, as in Wolfensohn's CDF, or carry out organizational restructuring, as in the case of the *Strategic Compact*. In a similar way, this is also true for Bank staff. As change in the Bank can take place as a result of top-down as well as bottom-up initiatives, the Fund is much more hierarchically structured, with Board consent preconditioning many changes.

Even if the organization is autonomous and rather open to change, that alone will not necessarily trigger initiatives, in particular when new issues do not (immediately) correspond with the IO's goals, norms and procedures. It requires internal advocacy that actively brings external events and pressure in line with the internal functioning of the organization.

'Champions' and internal advocacy

New policy issues and approaches will not automatically be integrated into the organization's activities, as staff do not simply follow instructions given by management or the Board. Instead, staff activity itself is a decisive factor in triggering change (interviews of 7 and 8 April 2004; also Fox 1998 or Kardam 1993). The analysis of the Bank in particular shows that certain internal advocates employing specific strategies of promoting policies facilitate the process of change as well as influence its path. In organization theory, such actors are referred to as 'adaptors', since they perceive the gap between 'is' and 'ought' and try to change the situation within the organization accordingly. Other terms are 'policy entrepreneurs' (Polsby 1984), 'internal advocates' (Kardam 1993), 'insider reformers', or just 'reformists' (Fox 1998). One of my interviewees called them 'champions' (interview of 8 April 2004; see also Bebbington *et al.* 2004). It broadens the concept to also include other highly influential figures in the organization's environment, such as the president or the managing director or very public persons.

The following points, which intend to illustrate the activities of such policy advocates, stem exclusively from observations in the Bank. Internal advocates are individuals or groups of people who actively identify and initiate new policy issues by mobilizing facts, deploying knowledge and building alliances – internally as well as externally, and thus foster policy change. One reason for such activities might be their professional convictions. Staff members do not act in a vacuum, but according to their specific background, training and value system. They are committed to their 'professional upbringing' that embeds their behaviour within certain norms and values. Different professions come with their mind-sets to the organization and bring different definitions of the situation, data and methodologies to the fore. This might stimulate not only discussions but also advocating behaviour by certain actors who try to promote their agendas. However, the driving force might not only be the (rather political) conviction of staff members, but also their interest in a professional career, as well as the will to secure their own positions within the organization or the status of the units or departments they work in.

This plays a particularly important role in such highly politicized organizations as the Bank and the Fund, and within the former is a source of the discontent between economists and so-called non-economic social scientists (also called NESSies, see Kapur *et al.* 1997: 375). The different perspectives on development held by economists and non-economic social scientists was one of the most striking observations during interviews (see also Davis 2004; Nielson *et al.* 2003b; Kanbur 2001; Wade 2001; Williams and Young 1994). One interviewee referred to these disagreements as part of a 'battle' that is going on (interview of 8 April 2004).

From the interviews at the Bank and subsequent empirical analysis, it was possible to retrieve a variety of strategies pursued by these advocates, such as (1) promoting a new topic within the organization, (2) networking with internal but also external actors such as academics, representatives of NGOs and other policy practitioners and building powerful alliances in order to exert their agendas; (3) lobbying within the organization at the Board or high-level management level; or (4) using external pressure or (re)framing certain events in a way that the organization's attention is drawn to a specific problem as well as extending the organization's goal by reinterpretation. For almost all of these strategies, the case of the Sociology Group in the Bank provides good examples (for more information on the group, see also Davis 2004; Cernea 2004, 2002; Kardam 1993). This group tried to promote more of a social agenda in the Bank's policies by writing research papers and organizing internal seminars to which they invited interested staff members and external guests. When Wolfensohn assumed the presidency, certain staff immediately started lobbying management to strengthen the social agenda in the Bank (two interviews of 8 April 2004) and their demands were viewed favourably. One year after Wolfensohn came to the Bank, the CDF was adopted. Further, the group created an internal network, which through constant lobbying at the management level resulted in the foundation of the *Social Development Department* in the course of the *Strategic Compact*. These advocates have been also forming links with external networks, especially NGOs, whose members they increasingly place inside the organization as consultants or permanent staff.[6] They thus actively and strategically use external pressure or specific events to increase pressure on the organization.[7]

Such activities are less common in the Fund. One explanation refers to its 'intellectual monocropping', which contrasts with the mixture of Bank staff that provides better conditions for the emergence of champions. Another explanation might be the Fund's different understanding regarding how it presents itself to the outside world. The Fund has always sought to create an impression that there is a consensus over its policies inside the organization, and this is reinforced by the loyalty among staff. Thus, open debates would run counter to one of the Fund's informal rules, to mediate one view. While some disputes over certain problems do occur, these are somewhat 'invisible' to external observers. In sum, the strategies of such champions can affect how an organization might either learn faster or just adapt slowly by gradually reducing its resistance to external pressure.

The nature of the external event

Even if the organization is open to change, new issues fit its mandate, and it has enough leverage to act independently, change does not happen without a stimulus. In the beginning of this chapter it was theorized that change takes place when a gap is perceived between intended and actual performance, or when discrepancies are perceived between 'is' and 'ought'. Usually, such (knowledge) gaps arise from two different sources: either external criticism or due to an event that happens in the broader context of the organization that is independent from its specific will or interests. Due to the mismatch between the organization's predictions and the actual event, or the recognition of the organization's inability to appropriately respond to certain problems, such events can shake the organization's self-understanding and the image it has of itself. In other words, in order to induce policy change, the event needs to be disruptive to the organization's daily life.

However, the extent to which an event or critique triggers change partly depends on the type of organization. This is in particular true for the latter case, the criticism. It matters *who* criticizes and if such criticism is perceived as legitimate. It seems that the organizational personality determines the significance of the critique. Comparing the Bank and the Fund demonstrates this aspect in more detail. While the World Bank absorbs criticism from all sides – particularly under Wolfensohn, who tried to accommodate everyone – the Fund is rather selective in choosing to respond to external criticism.

The process leading to the Fund's eventual participation in the PRSP reveals a reversed image of how different things are in the Bank's sister organization. The decision by the Fund to participate in the PRSP process in 1999 can be understood as a combination of two events: First, the external evaluation of the Enhanced Structural Adjustment Facility (ESAF) by Kwesi Botchwey, a well-known and highly recognized economist in the Fund, which revealed in a staggering way the Fund's inability or insufficient knowledge to predict and deal with every kind of financial imbalance (Botchwey *et al.* 1998). Second, the impact of this critique was enforced by the onset of the East Asian crisis in 1997. 'Credible' criticism is crucial in the Fund, and credibility is tied to economics. It is hard for non-economists to approach the organization, and among economists, only the 'good' ones are taken seriously.[8] Thus, even though it raised similar issues, Botchwey's criticisms found more resonance than any NGO protest, since it conformed to the Fund's organizational language. This 'credible' critique, in combination with the experience of the East Asian crisis, affected the organization tremendously in its self-understanding and self-esteem. Following this crisis, Camdessus stressed the need for a social pillar within the international financial system (see Gupta *et al.* 2000). Thus, due to this exogenous shock, causing a situation of uncertainty and perplexity, the ESAF review's effect was much greater and its critique more influential. Following the subsequent participation of the Fund in the PRSP initiative, the organization addressed precisely the three critical points raised by that review.[9]

Due to its more diverse staff and its engagement in a variety of issues, the Bank is more easily approachable. But even in the case of the Bank, criticism alone is not enough to enact change, as the case of the Narmada dam in India has shown. Although NGOs approached the Bank several times, it was not until internal advocates strategically used these external criticisms that an external evaluation was commissioned, which opened up policy space for a significant learning process inside the Bank (Fox 1998).

Apart from the professional composition of staff, another explanation might be the nature of their respective operations. The Fund's lending programme focuses on implementing macroeconomic reforms through indirect fiscal mechanisms, which seems to offer less opportunity for NGO scrutiny than the Bank's development projects, where adverse environmental and social impacts can be more easily detected and ascribed to specific actors, and thus used to mobilize protest.

Table 7.1 compares the organizational characteristics of the World Bank and the IMF.

Table 7.1 Organizational characteristics of the World Bank and IMF

Organizational characteristics	World Bank	IMF
Mandate	Broad and fuzzy mandate which can be easily reinterpreted.	Clearly defined objective which does not leave much leverage for reinterpretation but needs to be redefined.
Organizationally formal structure – internally	Huge, in size, decentralized, matrix structure.	Smaller, centralized, clear hierarchical structure.
Externally	Partly financially independent from its principals.	Fully financially dependent on its principals.
Staff Structure	Mixture of professions (civil engineers, agricultural experts, biologists, economists, sociologists, political scientists, anthropologists).	Only macro economists and financial experts.
Consequences for Change	More autonomy from the Executive Board.	Less autonomy from the Executive Board.
	Amoeba that embraces many different ideas/mandates and players, with high levels of competition and lobbying among units but also a high degree of creativity inside but very slow/inefficient in implementation and organizational change (flexible to the outside and rigid inside).	Closed entity that focuses on a few objectives and rigid/inflexible towards any changes, with high levels of control and loyalty among staff but also a high degree of conformism but if change is decided upon it is very efficient in its implementation (rigid to the outside but flexible inside).

Policy change – an interplay of four factors

The preceding discussion has shown how organizational personality shapes the way in which organizations appear to deal with their environment and the demands for change (see Table 7.1 above). The discussion has focused on two aspects of policy change in international organizations: first, the conditions under which policy change in international organizations occurs, and second, the different processes of change in international organizations identified as either adjustment or learning. In relation to the first line of inquiry, the comparative analysis between the Bank and the Fund identified some factors that help us understand the mechanisms of change in the Bank and the Fund. In doing so, no one factor was singled out as decisive. Yet, policy is not simply a reaction to random events. Rather, influenced by the organization's personality, it is the interplay of four factors that in their degree and timing of appearance, and through their combination, are able to open up policy space in specific situations, which enables the organization to change in a certain way.

It seems that the first two factors – the organization's autonomy and the consistency of new topics with the organization's goals and procedures – provide for the context and are, so to speak, *constants*. The latter two – advocacy and the external pressure – are intervening *variables*. If we conceive of the issue like this, it is possible to consider different cases as models where all of these four aspects appear to different degrees. In other words, it allows us to generalize and analyse different international organizations and policy issues in terms of these four conditions.

The Bank demonstrated a high degree of change which could be generalized as follows: if the policy topic in question fits the organization's original mandate, and if the organization is rather independent in its decisions on the type of policies and research it wants to engage in, as well as possessing an organizational culture that leaves room for internal debate, competition and lobbying, and also creativity, the degree of change in such an organization will be rather high. External stimuli play a less important role, or in other words, do not have to shake the organization's basic pillars for something to change. In that sense, the organization is proactive and quicker in taking up and responding to external stimuli, not necessarily waiting for top-down instructions, and more likely to initiate changes from the bottom-up by staff action.

The case of the Fund's changing definition of social issues serves as an example of a low degree of policy change which could be summarized as follows: if a new issue brought to the organization is not consistent with its original objectives and procedures, if its formal organizational structure makes the organization more dependent on its member countries as well as providing little opportunity to deviate from formal procedures and the status quo, and if its staff composition is less conducive to creativity and debate about the organization's role, the extent of change will be low but will still depend on external events and the activities of some (single) internal advocates. Under these conditions, the organization is rigid against change. Instead, it is more likely to adapt to external stimuli, in particular from its principals, initiated from the top down rather than due to NGO pressure and/or staff activities.

Following the second question, the objective was to get to know how organizational features influence the way international organizations change or, one could also say, learn. Jachtenfuchs (1996) distinguishes between simple and complex learning (see also Haas 1990; Nye 1987). Accordingly, simple learning is based on a stimulus-response concept, and is driven by correcting errors in order to ensure the survival of the organization. Thus, it is rather an efficiency-oriented behaviour concerned with optimizing the adaptation of an organization to its environment. In contrast, the latter relates to the 'belief system' (Sabatier 1987) of the actor or underlying norms, objectives and policies (in Jachtenfuch's language, 'frames') of an organization (Jachtenfuchs 1996). Complex learning then has taken place when the organization's frames have changed.

At first glance, it thus seems that the Fund is a simple learner whereas the Bank is a complex learner. However, this is not necessarily the case. Both of these two organizatîons have changed their frames and both have also changed their objectives and practices. In a sense, the Fund even more so since its clearly and narrowly defined goal required a redefinition in order for it to be able to change its policies. By contrast, the Bank's fuzzy goal allows it to address many issues by reinterpreting but without changing its goals.

Nevertheless, the processes of change in these two organizations were different. Consequently, it is more fruitful to make a distinction between *adaptation* and *innovation* as two modes of learning. Adaptation, on the one hand, is characterized by passivity and resistance to change. In an organization that is adapting, change is more likely to come from top-down instructions and through power or coercion exercised by the Board. Innovation, on the other hand, can be understood as an active process where the organization is flexible and gets voluntarily involved in new issues. In such organizations, while it is still possible for change to be initiated from the top down, bottom-up processes are much more likely. In other words, innovation and adaptation are two (rather extreme) values on a continuum that measures learning. The Bank and the Fund are examples of each type.

Conclusion

This chapter has discussed and compared the determinants of policy change at the World Bank and the International Monetary Fund. It argues that the Bank is more autonomous of its principals than the Fund, which means policy change is more likely to be induced by staff and/or management. When interacting with its external environment, the Bank seems to embody an organization that acts like an amoeba, actively embracing many different ideas, absorbing information, criticism, and people from outside. While it seems very flexible to the outside, it is rather inefficient in implementing new policy agendas internally.

In contrast, the Fund is a closed entity that focuses almost exclusively on a few objectives determined by its original mandate and does not get easily diverted by new ideas. It is at first resistant to any suggestion of change that seems to come from the outside, but as soon as a consensus is decided upon internally and secretly behind closed doors, change will be implemented immediately without deviance. As internal advocacy does not play a major role, the Fund is rigid to the outside but flexible internally.

In sum, the analysis has shown that policy change in international organizations can neither be fully explained by principals' influence nor by the organizational culture. Both factors play a role and are intertwined, a phenomenon which was captured by the concept of the organization's personality. Comparing the Bank and the Fund in terms of their personality revealed that the Bank is much more innovative and active in searching for new issues to take on criticisms to process internally. Therefore it is not surprising that it has been changing tremendously over the last decade and became in many ways the precursor of the Post-Washington Consensus, at least within the Bank–Fund working tandem. Nevertheless, one should be careful of extending conclusions from the Bank's case to other international organizations. The conditions of a high degree of autonomy combined with a highly ambitious president, as well as very active internal advocates who both used external events in broadening a fuzzy goal, do not necessarily hold for other international organizations, as the example of the Fund makes clear.

Notes

1 Article 1 (i–iii), see http://www.imf.org/external/pubs/ft/aa/aa01.htm. Its mandate was extended in 1986 to include economic growth in order to allow the organization to engage in private investment (for more detail, see Riesenhuber 2001).
2 Article 1 (1), see http://web.worldbank.org/WBSITE/EXTERNAL/EXTABOUTUS/ 0,contentMDK:20049563~pagePK:43912~menuPK:58863~piPK:36602,00.html#11 (emphasis added).
3 As a consequence of the developments by the end of the 1990s, most importantly the East Asian crisis in 1997, in 1999 the African Department recruited two social scientists who specialized in social policies, in order to support the department in questions of design and implementation of social safety nets in programmes. There is also one other social policy expert presently working in Food and Drug Administration.
4 See Martin (2003) on the relations between Fund management or staff and its Board. Applying a P-A model on the development of conditionality practices in the Fund, she comes to the conclusion that staff/management has some autonomy but '[a]t the same time, the Board retains the power to retract and restrict staff autonomy, and at times exercises this power' (Martin 2003: 43).
5 Another example is his push regarding capital account liberalization, which is well documented in Leiteritz 2005.
6 Consider for example John Clark, who was hired to head the NGO Unit in 1992 after a couple of years trying to poach him from OXFAM.
7 A very successful example is the case of the Narmada dam in India (for details, see Fox 1998).
8 There are other examples: contrary to Stiglitz, who lost his credibility after attacking the Fund in too personal a manner, Köhler was not esteemed highly by the 'hard-core economists' for reasons of performance: 'He has not published in any well-known economic journal' (interview of 7 April 2004).
9 These aspects were, first, a decisive lack of ownership of ESAF; second, insufficiencies in the protection of the poor, and third, the findings blurred the established division of labour between the international organizations.

References

Ayres, R. L. (1983) *Banking On the Poor: The World Bank and World Poverty*, Cambridge MA and London: MIT Press.
Barnett, M. and Finnemore, M. (1999) 'The Politics, Power and Pathologies of International Organizations', *International Organization* 53(4), 699–732.

——(2004) *Rules for the World: International Organizations in Global Politics*, Ithaca NY: Cornell University Press.

Bebbington, A., Guggenheim, S., Olson, E. and Woolcock, M. (2004) 'Exploring Social Capital Debates at the World Bank', *The Journal of Development Studies* 40(5), 33–64.

Birdsall, N. (1993) *Social Development is Economic Development*, WPS 1123, Washington DC: World Bank.

Board, R. and Cavanagh, J. (1999) 'The Death of the Washington Consensus?', *World Policy Journal*, fall, 79–88.

Botchwey, K., Collier, P., Gunning, J. W. and Hamada, K. (1998) *Report of the Group of Independent Persons Appointed to Conduct an Evaluation of Certain Aspects of the Enhanced Structural Adjustment Facility*, Washington DC: World Bank.

Boughton, J. M. (2001) *Silent Revolution. The International Monetary Fund 1979–1989*, Washington DC: IMF.

Camdessus, M. (1990) 'Aiming For "High Quality Growth"', *Finance and Development* 27(3), 10–11.

Cernea, M. (2002) 'Transcript of Interview with Michael M. Cernea', *The Bank's Oral History Program*, interview conducted by Becker, W. H. and Zenni, M. T., Washington DC: World Bank.

——(2004) 'Culture? ... at the World Bank? Letter to a Friend', unpublished manuscript.

Cortell, A. P. and Peterson, S. (2003) *Altered States. International Relations, Domestic Politics, and Institutional Change*, Lanham MD and Oxford: Lexington Books.

Danaher, K. (ed.) (1994) *50 Years is Enough: The Case Against the World Bank and the International Monetary Fund*, Boston MA: South End Press.

Davis, G. (2004) *A History of the Social Development Network in the World Bank, 1973–2002*, Social Development Paper 56, Washington DC: World Bank.

Demerel, L. and Addison, T. (1987) *The Alleviation of Poverty Under Structural Adjustment*, Washington DC: World Bank.

Fine, B., Lapavitsas, C. and Pincus, J. (eds) (2001) *Development Policy in the Twenty-first Century*, London and New York: Routledge.

Fox, J. A. (1998) 'When Does Reform Policy Influence Practice? Lessons From the Bankwide Resettlement Review', in Fox, J. A. and Brown, L. D. (eds) *The Struggle for Accountability. The World Bank, NGOs, and Grassroots Movements*, Cambridge MA and London: MIT Press, 303–44.

Gerster, R. (1982) 'The IMF and Basic Needs Conditionality', *Journal of World Trade Law* 16, Nov./Dec., 497–517.

Giddens, A. (1984) *Constitution of Society. Outline of the Theory of Structuration*, Cambridge: Polity.

Gupta, S., Dicks-Mireaux, L., Khemani, R., McDonald, C. and Verhoeven, M. (2000) *Social Issues in IMF-Supported Programs*, IMF Occasional Paper 191, Washington DC: IMF.

Haas, E. B. (1990) *When Knowledge is Power. Three Models of Change in International Organizations*, Berkeley: University of California Press.

Heller, P. S., Catsambas, T. and Ke-young, Chu (1988) *The Implications of Fund-Supported Adjustment Programs for Poverty: Experiences in Selected Countries*, IMF Occasional Paper 58, Washington DC: IMF.

IMF (1986) *Fund-Supported Programs, Fiscal Policy, and Income Distribution*, IMF Occasional Paper 46, Washington DC: IMF.

——(1993) *Social Safety Net in Economic Reform*, Internal Document EBS/93/34.

Jachtenfuchs, M. (1996) *International Policy-Making as a Learning Process? The European Union and the Greenhouse Effect*, Aldershot: Avebury.

Kanbur, R. (2001) 'Economic Policy Distribution and Poverty: The Nature of Disagreements', *World Development* 29(6), 1083–94.

Kapur, D., Lewis, J. P. and Webb, R. (1997) *The World Bank. Its First Half Century*, Washington DC: World Bank.

Kardam, N. (1993) 'Development Approaches and the Role of Policy Advocacy: The Case of the World Bank', *World Development* 21(11), 1773–86.

Krasner, St D. (1985) *Structural Conflict: The Third World Against Global Liberalism*, Los Angeles and London: University of California Press.

Krasner, St D. (ed.) (1983) *International Regimes*, Ithaca NY: Cornell University Press.

Leiteritz, R. J. (2005) 'Explaining Organizational Outcomes: The International Monetary Fund and Capital Account Liberalisation', *Journal of International Relations and Development* 8(1), 1–26.

March, J. G. and Olsen, J. P. (1975) 'The Uncertainty of the Past: Organizational Learning Under Ambiguity', *European Journal of Political Research* 3, 147–71.

Martin, L. (2003) 'Distribution, Information, and Delegation to International Organizations: The Case of IMF Conditionality', available at http://www.internationalorganizations.org/martinimf.pdf (accessed 18 April 2005).

Miller-Adams, M. (1999) *The World Bank. New Agendas in a Changing World*, London: Routledge.

Naim, M. (1994) 'The World Bank: Its Role, Governance and Organizational Culture', paper of the Carnegie Endowment for International Peace, available at http://www.carnegieendowment.org/publications/index.cfm?fa = view&id = 759 (accessed 21 January 2005).

Nielson, D., Tierney, M. and Weaver, C. E. (2003a) 'Delegation to International Organizations: Agency Theory and World Bank Reform', *International Organization* 57(2), 241–76.

——(2003b) 'Reforming the World Bank: Beyond the Rationalist-Constructivist Divide in Understanding IO Change', paper presented at the 2003 Annual Meeting of the APSA, 28–31 August 2003.

——(2004) 'The Argument is the Incentive: Agency, Organizational Culture and the World Bank's Strategic Compact', paper presented at the Conference on Theoretical Synthesis in the Study of IO, Washington DC, 7 February 2004.

Nye, J. S. (1987) 'Nuclear Learning', *International Organization* 41(3), 371–402.

Pollack, M. A. (1997) 'Delegation, Agency and Agenda Setting in the EC', *International Organization* 51(1), 99–134.

Polsby, N. W. (1984) *Political Innovation in America: The Politics of Policy Initiation*, New Haven CT and London: Yale University Press.

Riesenhuber, E. (2001) *The International Monetary Fund under Constraint. Legitimacy of its Crisis Management*, Boston MA, The Hague and London: Kluwer Law International.

Sabatier, P. A. (1987) 'Knowledge, Policy-Oriented Learning, and Policy Change. An Advocacy Coalition Framework', *Knowledge: Creation, Diffusion, Utilization* 8, 649–92.

Stiglitz, J. E. (1998a) 'More Instruments and Broader Goals: Moving Toward the Post-Washington Consensus', the 1998 WIDER Annual Lecture in Helsinki.

——(1998b) 'Towards a New Paradigm for Development: Strategies, Policies, and Processes', 1998 Prebisch Lecture at UNCTAD in Geneva, Switzerland, available at http://www.worldbank.org/html/extdr/extme/jssp101998.htm (accessed 7 January 2002).

Vetterlein, A. (2006) 'The Politics of Development Discourse. From the Washington to the Post-Washington Consensus', Ph.D. thesis, European University Institute, Florence.

Wade, R. H. (2001) 'Showdown at the World Bank', *New Left Review* 217, 3–36.

Wagner, P. (1990) *Sozialwissenschaften und Staat. Frankreich, Italien, Deutschland 1870–1980*, Frankfurt am Main and New York: Campus.

Wapenhans, W. A. *et al.* (1992) *The Wapenhans Report*, Portfolio Management Task Force, Washington DC: World Bank (also published under the following title: *Effective Implementation: Key to Development Impact*).

Weaver, C. E. (forthcoming) *The Rhetoric, Reality and Reform of the World Bank*, completed manuscript under review.

Weaver, C. E. and Leiteritz, R. J. (2005) 'Our Poverty is a World Full of Dreams. Reforming the World Bank', *Global Governance, A Review of Multilateralism and International Organizations* 11(3), 369–88.

Williams, D. and Young, T. (1994) 'Governance, the World Bank and Liberal Theory', *Political Studies* XLII, 84–100.

Williamson, J. (1990) 'What Washington Means By Policy Reform', in Williamson, J. (ed.) *Latin America Adjustment: How Much Has Happened?*, Washington DC: IIE.

——(1998) 'Latin American Reform. A View From Washington', in Costin, H. and Vanolli, H. (eds) *Economic Reform in Latin America*, Fort Worth TX and London: Dryden Press, 106–11.

——(2003) 'The Washington Consensus and Beyond', unpublished manuscript of a speech given at the World Bank, 8 May 2003.

World Bank (1980) *World Development Report: Poverty and Human Development*, Washington DC: World Bank.

——(1988) *Adjustment Lending. An Evaluation of Ten Years of Experience*, Policy and Research Series, Washington DC: World Bank.

——(1995) 'Wolfensohn Lays Out Future Direction of World Bank', press release 96/S21, 10 October 1995, Washington DC: World Bank.

——(2001) *World Development Report 2000/1: Attacking Poverty*, Oxford: Oxford University Press.

Part II
Confronting the outside

8 The poverty of amnesia
PRSPs in the legacy of structural adjustment

Celine Tan

The Poverty Reduction Strategy Paper (PRSP) approach was introduced in 1999 by the World Bank and the International Monetary Fund (IMF) to replace structural adjustment programmes (SAPs) as the operational framework through which concessional development financing[1] to low-income countries[2] would be assessed and disbursed by these financial institutions. Conventional analyses of the PRSP project have focused largely on the success or failure of this initiative in addressing, both procedurally and substantively, the deficiencies of structural adjustment lending.

These foregoing discussions have, however, taken place within the confined parameters of a self-referential discourse that fails to challenge the legacy of state re/formation upon which the PRSP framework was built. Structural adjustment pioneered new modes of intervention into developing countries, and new modes of governance at the international level, and a critical impact of the disciplinary force of structural adjustment policies has been the creation of a domestic political space for the imposition of PRSP reforms. Efforts at restructuring the state that were pivotal to structural adjustment policies have resulted in the fragmentation of state autonomy, which has paved the way for successful insertion of the PRSP framework in these countries.

This chapter argues that the PRSP framework, and, by implication, the 'new architecture of aid' – the constellation of financing modalities that emerged in the aftermath of structural adjustment – could only be operationalized as a result of the regulatory precedents set by structural adjustment policies. Moreover, the PRSP approach could only be realized as a result of the impact of structural adjustment programmes on the machinery of the state in recipient countries. Understanding the contribution of this legacy of structural adjustment to the conceptual and operational framework of the PRSP approach enables us to resolve the theoretical contradictions that plague existing analyses of the PRSP framework.

PRSPs in the new architecture of aid

When introduced, the PRSP approach was to be the operational manifestation of the 'new development paradigm' of the 1990s, aimed at achieving greater development objectives, notably poverty reduction and greater account-ability of resource allocation (World Bank 2004a: 1). PRSPs replaced Policy Framework Papers (PFPs) as preconditions for concessional and grant financing from the Bank and the Fund. Consequently, a corollary to the inception of the PRSP framework has been the development of new finan-cing instruments to replace structural adjustment lending, namely the Pov-erty Reduction and Growth Facility (PRGF) replacing the IMF's Enhanced Structural Adjustment Facility (ESAF) and the introduction of Poverty Reduction Strategy Credits (PRSCs) from the Bank's concessional lending arm, the International Development Association (IDA). Access to the PRGF and PRSCs, as well as debt relief under the Enhanced Heavily Indebted Poor Countries Initiative (HIPC II) is contingent upon the country completing a PRSP and having the PRSP assessed by Bank and Fund staff.

The PRSP approach draws its underlying principles from the Compre-hensive Development Framework (CDF), one of James Wolfensohn's operational legacies at the World Bank and the Bank's latest blueprint guiding its financing operations in member countries. But as a mechanism for accessing resources from multilateral debt relief and concessional lending from the Bank and the IMF, the PRSP approach institutes these principles as regulatory requirements.

The World Bank distinguishes the PRSP from the CDF in terms of the 'attachment of resources to the PRSP', where the 'CDF is described as a set of principles, processes, or mechanisms', the PRSP represents 'a programme of action' and 'an instrument of policy implementation [which] must detail priorities, targets, indicators, costings and financing plans, and procedures for monitoring' (World Bank 2003: 13). In this respect, the PRSP approach goes further than the instrumentality of the PFPs by focusing not only on the *outcomes* of policy-making and policy negotiation between the financing institutions and the client state, but also on the *process* of formulating national economic plans.

The reorientation of international development policy *vis-à-vis* low-income countries in the decade preceding the inception of the PRSP framework was clearly a response to a carefully couched problematic, driven by three sets of concerns: that negative impacts of structural adjust-ment reforms were leading to a deterioration in the social and economic condition of communities in countries under SAPs,[3] that there was a need to reform both the system of aid delivery to low-income countries, and to ensure that aid was managed and disbursed domestically to alleviate the pressures on the poor.

The 'Washington Consensus' which provided the conceptual foundation for regulating access to development financing and monetary stabilization programmes in the 1980s and early 1990s was increasingly being perceived, both by critics of structural adjustment policies and by many executors of the policies within the international donor community, as failing to achieve the objectives of development and poverty reduction, even by its own criteria (interviews, 2003–5; see also Christiansen with Hovland 2003; IMF 2004; Rowden and Ocaya-Irama 2004; World Bank 2004a). This economic rationale championed economic growth led by market forces as solutions to resolving the 'crisis of development' in the South (see SAPRIN 2004: 1–4). Structural adjustment programmes (SAPs) provided the disciplinary framework under which Washington Consensus-style reforms, such as liberalization, privatization and fiscal and monetary austerity, could be instituted in developing countries to generate foreign trade, capital and investment.

PRSPs sought to redress the economic relativism of structural adjustment programmes by framing a conceptual approach to development financing that went beyond the fiscal and monetary straitjacket of SAPs, and at the same time, redressing the democratic deficits inherent in the process of accessing development financing by enabling a more inclusive framework to development policy-making.

The PRSP approach institutionalizes the general principles of the CDF. First, each PRSP is required to be *country driven*, meaning the policies outlined in the PRSP are tailored to the country's specific circumstances and are generated by the country itself in a process involving broad-based participation from civil society and other members of the community. Second, PRSPs need to be *results-oriented*, focusing on outcomes, chiefly poverty reduction, in the formulation of public action and ensuring these outcomes are monitored. Third, PRSPs have to be *comprehensive*, acknowledging the multi-dimensional nature of poverty and the need for integral poverty reduction programmes. Fourth, PRSPs are required to be *partnership-oriented*, involving the cooperative efforts of national governments, civil society, bilateral and multilateral donor agencies and other financing institutions in generating a poverty-reduction programme. And finally, PRSPs must be based on a *long-term perspective* of economic planning, prioritizing poverty reduction, at the same time making institutional reforms and improving capacity building in areas such as governance and accountability (IMF and World Bank 1999: box 1).

In this manner, the PRSP framework moves away from the reductionist approach to economic policy-making that characterized SAPs by placing an emphasis on wider developmental priorities. The assumption underlying economic adjustment under SAPs was that the economic growth generated would 'trickle down' to the general population, alleviating poverty as the economy corrected itself. The PRSP approach, on the other hand, prioritizes specific poverty-reduction strategies – albeit underpinned by overall economic growth – in the economic planning, including assessing poverty impacts of economic policies, prioritizing social sector expenditure in national budgets and integrating such concerns into a 'consistent macroeconomic framework over a three-year horizon' (IMF and World Bank 1999: para. 15).

The PRSP process also reinstates, at least nominally, the concept of *agency* in development financing policy and practice by institutionalizing the requirements of participation and partnership in the financing operations of the Bank and Fund. This represents a significant departure from the PFPs, documents establishing 'the policies necessary for the successful stabilization and adjustment' drafted by the Bank and Fund and negotiated with borrowing country governments (Mosley *et al.* 1991: 53).

PRSPs are instead geared towards facilitating '[b]road participation of civil society, other national stakeholder groups, and elected institutions' and involve '[c]onsultations with representatives of the poor' in order to incorporate the concerns of the community into the design and implementation of development programmes in the country (IMF and World Bank 1999: para. 19). Countries are required to detail their participatory processes in their PRSPs, including descriptions of the type and degree of involvement of different stakeholders in the process and the relationship between the PRSP and other national development plans, but they are not evaluated on the participatory process (World Bank and IMF 2005: annex 1, fn. 4). This concept of *ownership* of development programmes represents a key shift in the discourse of development policy and practice brought about by the PRSP and the larger 'new architecture of aid'.

New realities or continuities?

At the heart of the PRSP project lays the fundamental assumption on the part of its architects and proponents that the new framework addresses, both procedurally and substantively, the criticisms that were directed at the previous adjustment financing framework. This is achieved by institutionalizing the aforementioned conceptually divergent mechanisms for regulating the flow of financial resources to low-income developing countries. Critics of the approach have, however, mostly argued that the PRSP process represents nothing more than a hortatory gesture towards addressing the problems associated with structural adjustment, by focusing on redressing the procedural deficits without reforming the substantive content of SAPs (see for example Rowden and Ocaya-Irama 2004; World Vision 2002).

In 2004, the IMF's Independent Evaluation Office (IEO) review of the PRSP–PRGF framework acknowledged this tension between the emphasis on ownership of economic policies and the role of the Bank and the Fund as both financiers and evaluators of the process and the economic outcomes to be achieved by PRSP-linked resources. According to the IEO, this tension manifests itself particularly in the question of 'policy space' – of enabling a country's policy-making autonomy, while at the same time maintaining the Bank and the Fund's ability to 'satisfy themselves on the soundness of country policies and the implicit assumption that they can help improve outcomes by influencing policy choices through (a) policy advice ... and (b) conditionality' (IMF 2004: 40, para. 4).

However, these critiques focus on the processes and policies located *within* the PRSP project, and not on its insertion in a more complex history of structural adjustment and its impact on state construction in developing countries. This analytical approach limits our understanding of the impact of PRSPs on the constitution of the state and on the effect of its universality in the wider construction of global economic governance. Specifically, it fails to offer a resolution to the tension between the processual shifts towards focus on ownership and participation, and the realities of financial conditionality and the dynamics of power that underlie the relationships of parties to the PRSP framework. Ignoring the historical continuities between structural adjustment policies and the PRSP approach to development financing will not only mask these realities but will also validate the new disciplinary force of the PRSP approach.

Both postcolonial and dependency theorists have long argued for the need to locate present-day economic, social and political realities of developing countries in the colonial encounter and the structures of colonial capitalist exploitation that have continued in the postcolonial era. Dependency and post-dependency development theorists, notably Andre Gunder Frank, Paul Baran and Giovanni Arrighi, have situated the economic stagnation and impoverishment of Southern states in 'distorted structure of economy and society' created by the 'penetration of colonial capital' and the continued 'expropriation of economic surplus' to the northern metropolis at the expense of development in the south (Hoogvelt 2001: 38, 40). Without locating the current problems in the historical continuum of colonial exploitation and the means in which postcolonial states were inserted into the international economy, dependency theorists argue that the exploitative economic and political chains between the North and South will not be broken (see Arrighi 2002, 1982; Amin 1977).

Viewing the current international political economy as part of the continuing legacy of imperialism, postcolonial legal scholars argue that these exploitative relationships were 'embodied and perpetuated by a system of international law which continued to operate after the achievement of independence by the Third World' (Anghie 2004: 208). The inherent asymmetry of postcolonial international relations is obscured by the presumption of sovereign equality, shaped as such 'as to preclude scrutiny of its historical engagement in the colonial encounter' which, in turn, masks the continued reliance upon colonial 'relationships of power and inequality' to sustain present 'economic and political superiority' (Anghie 2004: 215).

For Fitzpatrick, this 'formal' equality (the converse of substantive equality) enables the entrenchment of a 'new imperialism' in which 'direct colonial imposition' is replaced by 'contractual modes of domination' whereby postcolonial states 'agree to and enforce the terms of their own subjection', including through conditional loans of the Bank and Fund (Fitzpatrick 2001: 212). Here, Fitzpatrick draws a distinction between the neo-colonial thesis of the dependency theorists and this form of disciplinary power, arguing that this new imperialism is more nuanced and predicated upon the 'consensual' entry of nation states into the international order with all its inequities. The developing nation state is disciplined through the reformation of internal legal and regulatory structures that enable the continued control by ex-colonial nations over the economic resources of the peripheral states exercised in 'dependent compliance' (Fitzpatrick, 2001: 214).

Towards this end, the PRSP project may be viewed as an extension of the SAPs in serving to legitimize and manage this inequity at the global level. Rather than addressing the fundamental flaws within the global economy that create the social and economic upheaval in low-income countries, the objective continues to be one of reinforcing 'the legitimacy of the debt-servicing relationship while maintaining debtor nations in a straightjacket which prevents them from embarking on an independent national economic policy', that is the legacy of Bretton Woods' policy-based lending (Chossudovsky 1997: 51). This is facilitated through the reform of state apparatuses in SAP/ PRSP countries (see below).

The PRSP process, however, represents a significant shift in the management of the unequal relationship between the global North and South from the modalities of SAPs. While power remains exercised by the World Bank and the IMF through conventional macroeconomic and structural conditionalities, the appropriation of discursive space by the episteme of the PRSP approach dramatically changes the operation of power from an overt to a diffused form. This creates what Chossudovsky refers to as a 'counter ideology' to generate a stylized debate about 'poverty' and 'development' and 'participation' which develops alongside the official dogma on liberalization, privatization and deregulation (Chossudovsky 1997: 42).

The prevailing discourse of the PRSP endorses a break with the legacy of structural adjustment so that, once again, the external reality of development financing is focused on the developing state and its shortcomings rather than on the asymmetry of power in the donor/recipient relationship and the injustices of the political and economic order into which this relationship is inserted. The burden for the 'crisis of development' and the need for external financing is pointedly placed, once again, within the domestic sphere, residing in a 'fundamental weakness of governance' on the part of the recipient countries (Pahuja 2000: 798) rather than with the power relationships that underlie the aid relationship. Unsurprisingly then, the solutions propounded by the PRSP approach take the form of what Pahuja has characterized as 'externally imposed institutional reform' which 'bears a remarkable resemblance to the "civilizing mission" of the colonial power ... the establishment of modern government' (Pahuja 2000: 798–9). The story of the PRSP therefore needs to be re-historicized to take into account the role played by structural adjustment in creating the regulatory environment in which a process such as the PRSP approach may be realized.

Adjustment legacies

The introduction of structural adjustment was a critical turning point in the history of globalization, particularly in relation to the regulatory mechanisms that facilitated the processes of economic and financial globalization. The consequence of aid dependency for countries facing resource deficits, as a result of the combination of commodity price collapse and oil shocks in the late 1970s and early 1980s, was acquiescence to the intrusive conditionalities of economic reform programmes that accompanied the ascendancy of the Bretton Woods institutions in the global governance regime in the period that followed.

This centralization of control in the hands of the two institutions that oversaw the restructuring of a raft of postcolonial states in the post-New International Economic Order (NIEO) era has resulted in a near-universalization of a framework of regulatory reform in these disparate states. The paradox of the PRSP framework is that while it was designed to facilitate more democratic reforms to pre-existing frameworks of accessing development financing for low-income countries, the PRSP reforms were themselves introduced within the inherently imbalanced structural relationships between donor/financier and client/recipient. The fact that the PRSP framework has been successfully implemented in over fifty low-income countries to date (World Bank 2004b) is testimony to the leverage the Bank and Fund have over their low-income members.

The PRSP framework is a highly intrusive approach to regulating access to development financing. The norms that form a part of the regulatory structure of the PRSP framework require extensive legal and political interventions into the countries which seek financing under this framework. Aside from assigning a prescribed process to the countries which undertake to produce a document – the PRSP – in support of their application for financing from the international development community, chiefly the World Bank and the IMF, the PRSP framework requires the establishment of institutional structures to facilitate this process and for the monitoring of the outcomes in the proposed strategy post-disbursement.

Contrast this situation with regulatory reform in any other domain and it is clear that the PRSP framework has been inserted into a policy space where consent – of both the governing entities (the state) and the governed (the citizenry) – have been appropriated or negated by previous structural interventions, resulting in a regulatory vacuum. This scale of involvement in a country's legal and political processes could only have been achieved as a result of conceptual and operational precedents set by structural adjustment policies which created an enabling environment for the insertion of PRSP-type reforms in countries seeking concessional assistance from the Bank and the Fund.

Legacy 1: policy-based lending

The PRSP approach to development financing may be regarded as the operational pinnacle of the trend towards 'policy-oriented' aid that began with the inception of structural adjustment in the 1980s. By linking social and economic development to a larger agenda of structural reform policies, SAPs broke away from the piecemeal approach that had characterized previous development financing. While the 'policies' driving the different operational frameworks may have changed, the essence of a policy-driven model of engagement between the donor community and the client countries remains the same. The terms of financing are inherently tied to a policy brief subscribed to by the donor policy-makers, and engagement takes the form of 'policy dialogue', described by Cassen and associates as 'exchanges between aid donors and recipients about the domestic policy framework, influencing the outcome of an aid transfer and the behaviour of the economy as a whole' (Cassen and associates 1986: 69).

Prior to the early 1980s, World Bank financing for member states primarily took the form of 'investment' or 'project' lending. Project support operates within a fixed cycle with clearly defined goals, ring-fenced expenditures and a limited time scale. Conditions attached to project loans were limited to those ensuring financial and fiduciary oversight over the project, such as setting the terms and conditions for repayment and drawing up lists of permitted and prohibited expenditures.

The introduction of 'policy-based lending' – the disbursement of funds based on a programme of reform in recipient countries as opposed to financing an earmarked project – under SAPs created a new type of financing with new forms of conditions. Structural adjustment lending entailed the disbursement of loans to countries facing balance of payments difficulties, to enable governments to undertake a programme of economic reforms agreed upon between the governments and the World Bank. These programmes were also often accompanied by stabilization programmes agreed upon between the countries concerned and the IMF.

Originally, structural adjustment lending was permitted in the Bank only if there was 'an acute balance of payments need (actual or potential)' (Shihata 2000: 83) in the country and where external resources to finance this gap could not be met through other financing means (World Bank 2004c: 12, para. 19). However, this requirement was effectively dispensed with in 1996, allowing the Bank to disburse adjustment lending to countries with fiscal deficits but no apparent balance of payments problems (Shihata 2000: 83). Overall, this increased the volume of adjustment loans provided by the Bank and enabled SAPs to be implemented in countries that did not necessarily require the economic restructuring that accompanied SAPs. Adjustment lending peaked at over half of total Bank lending in 1999, and again in 2002, before petering out to an average of one third of total lending in 2003 (World Bank 2004c: 16).

The shift from project-based development financing to such 'policy-based lending' substantially altered the nature of negotiations between the financiers and the borrowers. As Degnbol-Martinussen and Engberg-Pedersen observe, the change from projects to programmes altered the nature of dialogue from 'being mostly a technical dialogue about capital, technology and organization, to an all-encompassing political dialogue about the structure of society and management of society's development processes' (Degnbol-Martinussen and Engberg-Pedersen 2003: 41).

This legacy can be witnessed clearly in the approach of the 'new archi-tecture of aid' that underpins the PRSP framework. Alongside the switch from PFPs to PRSPs was the reorganization of the Bank's adjustment lending operational policy and the renaming of 'adjustment lending' as 'development policy lending' (DPL). The determinants for the new lending policy for the Bank under the new Operational Policy on Development Policy Lending (OP 8.60) – which replaced the Operational Directive on Adjustment Lending Policy (OD 8.60) – now include considerations of social and political structures in addition to economic factors. The policy document states that '[t]he Bank's decision to extend development policy lending is based on an assessment of the country's policy and institutional framework – including the country's economic situation, governance, envir-onmental/natural resource management, and poverty and social aspects' (World Bank 2004d: para. 2).

The change in nomenclature reflects the all-encompassing nature of financing under this new approach to development financing. As the World Bank itself explains, the change from the term 'adjustment lending' to 'development policy lending' was not only meant to signal 'the fundamental developmental nature of the lending instrument' but it also reflects the 'shift from a short-term macroeconomic focus to a longer-term developmental and institutional focus' (World Bank 2004c: 11, para. 17).

In line with this shift, priority for financing under the PRSP framework is given to programmatic policy-based loans, in particular the PRSCs that have been designed to support country PRSPs through financing resource gaps in the budget and associated structural and social reforms (World Bank 2001: 11–12). These reforms have included a strong focus on reform-ing public institutions, in particular budgetary and financial management, and decentralizing government in PRSP countries.[4] At the same time, the Bank has maintained the economic discipline of SAPs in the new lending policy, insisting that loan funds are only disbursed 'upon maintenance of an adequate macroeconomic policy framework' and the compliance with cri-tical structural conditions in the member state's programme of reform (World Bank 2004d: para. 13).

The PRSP approach thus deepens the 'policy' aspects of development financing pioneered under structural adjustment through: (a) increasing financing to developing countries for 'policy reform', including reforming public expenditure, in order to prioritize social sector expenditure in national budgets; and (b) expanding the types of policy reform financed and deepening existing policy interventions. The consequence of this shift has been to expand the already wide policy mandate of the Bretton Woods institutions in client countries.

Legacy 2: interventionist economics

The linking of financial disbursements to policy reform under structural adjustment lending radically altered the nature of the relationship between the parties to the financing agreements, that is, between the borrower countries and the World Bank and IMF. This facilitated a trend towards what Pincus (2002) refers to as the 'social engineering' of developing societies, whereby the restructuring of societies and economies could be engineered in order to produce targeted outcomes, such as economic growth and/or poverty reduction.

In their analysis of aid policies in the 1980s, Cassen and associates note that to some observers, including economist Ann Krueger (who was later appointed as IMF deputy managing director in 2001), the 'most important function of aid' is not to supplement resource flows to developing countries, but instead 'to induce policy reforms engendering efficient resource allocation and economic growth' (Cassen and associates 1986: 69). In other words, the objective of concessional financing to developing countries was not to supplement their capital flows, but to use it as a guise under which policy reforms can be pursued to produce institutions that can generate domestic resources.

Structural adjustment lending therefore departed not only from the pre-existing modalities of development financing, but also from their objectives. Development financing under SAPs was not just about meeting the resource gaps of countries, but also about restructuring economies and making the availability of resources contingent upon such reforms. The conditions for access to resources for development under structural adjustment became less about capacity to repay than about enabling regulatory reforms consistent with the Washington Consensus.

The legacy of this interventionist policy of the Bretton Woods institutions is evident in the CDF–PRSP approach, underlying which 'is the belief that somehow these largely intangible benefits [of development planning] can be programmed, produced and measured like any other project output' (Pincus 2002: 78). This includes the facilitation of intrinsically political reforms such as the engendering of domestic political consensus for development policy-making under the aegis of 'country ownership', creating harmonizing structures for the coordination of aid delivery under the umbrella of 'partnership' and the technicalizing of redistributive policies and public expenditure management under the guise of 'results focus' (World Bank 2004e).

The CDF–PRSP approach goes beyond the 'good governance' reforms piloted by the World Bank in the 1990s which, while focused on creating the institutional structures (such as the rule of law and public financial management) as a corollary to successful implementation of SAP reforms, were de-linked from the core of policy-making in client countries and functioned mostly as ring-fenced projects. The CDF–PRSP approach instead seeks to reinstate the regulative capacity of the state through the reconfiguration of key domestic processes and institutions and by linking the disbursement of financing to such reforms.

This process of restructuring the state apparatuses takes place on two fronts: (1) through the imposition of a standardized mechanism for policy discussion and formulation – the PRS process – and a universal blueprint for developing national development plans – the PRSP document; and (2) through efforts to centre key policy-making processes on the PRSP and to standardize bureaucratic practice along the principles established by the PRSP approach as discussed above.

This type of intervention has been made possible due to the legacy of structural adjustment, because the design of structural adjustment had enabled the international financial institutions to permeate the internal structures of recipient countries in ways that were not possible before. Where Bank and Fund bureaucrats previously possessed only the autonomy to dispense technical advice on (a) project implementation (in the case of the Bank); and (b) the domestic monetary and fiscal policy insofar as they impact on domestic economic stability and international financial cooperation (in the case of the Fund), SAPs endowed these institutions with the political capital to capture key policy-making spaces within the domestic economy.

The PRSP approach, while seemingly aimed at redressing the problem of 'ownership' (or lack thereof), not only deepens this external intrusion in domestic affairs, but it is in itself also a by-product of this interventionist mode of financing. Tying access to financing to a political process such as the PRSP process could only be achieved in an environment where the state's capacity to negotiate has already been compromised by geopolitical and economic imperatives.

Christiansen and Hovland's study of the historical narrative of the PRSP project and its role in multilateral policy change found that there was little government input into the processes of formulating the norms of the PRSP framework. The PRSP approach was developed from the efforts of a cluster of political actors and policy-makers, including Northern governments, transnational non-governmental organizations (NGOs) and institutional officials of the Bank and the Fund resulting from epistemic and policy shifts in the North (Ahmed 2004; Christiansen with Hovland 2003).

While there has been substantial input from development policy-makers within the Bank and the Fund alongside engagement with civil society groups, notably transnational NGOs and the epistemic community in the North, the absence of any significant contribution from the South, both from Southern policy-makers and civil society, is glaring. The authors conclude that aside from limited discussion at the executive board levels, 'the contribution of Southern governments was largely indirect [through] the demonstration effect of poverty reduction programmes in practice [namely] Mozambique, Tanzania, Bolivia, and especially Uganda' (Christiansen with Hovland 2003: 21).

For many of the Southern governments, participating in the PRSP approach is in effect participation by coercion, an enforced cooperation premised on a real necessity for concessional financing from the multilateral development agencies. According to Koussari, the consequence of this dependence on external resources, secured through the reforms of structural adjustment policies, has been the loss of autonomy to reject subsequent intrusions (Koussari 2005). Most PRSP countries, he observes, have agreed to undergo the PRSP process not because of the process' viability and potential to achieve development objectives, but as another bureaucratic condition for release of funds. In turn, borrowing governments have tended to exercise self-censorship through actively discouraging debate on key economic issues in order to produce a PRSP that would not be rejected by the Bank and IMF (Rowden and Ocaya-Irama 2004: 7–8).

Legacy 3: centralization of control

The requirement for staff assessment and executive board consideration of the PRSP is a further reflection of its structural adjustment heritage. The PRSP framework calls for closer collaboration between the Bank and the Fund, both at the country level and at the policy levels in Washington, in order to ensure that country 'policy actions to raise growth and reduce poverty are integrated into a coherent framework of macroeconomic, structural and social policies', based on 'a common country-specific perspective' (IMF and World Bank 1999: para. 23).

The concern is that, since the PRSP process currently forms such an integral part of the development financing system, it extends the centralization of control at the hands of the Bretton Woods institutions, a precedent that was set by the structural adjustment approach. Although the PRSP process has now been revised to eliminate the requirement for explicit endorsement by the Bank and Fund executive boards of a PRSP's suitability as the basis of concessional lending, the PRSP remains central to these financing operations (IMF 2005: para. 3). With the Joint Staff Assessment (JSA) now replaced by the Joint Staff Advisory Note (JSAN), staff do not have to recommend endorsement by the boards but can instead be more frank in their evaluations of PRSPs and identify 'priority areas' for strengthening PRSP strategies during implementation (IMF 2005: paras 3 and 5). Approval of new financing is contingent upon countries redressing such weaknesses (IMF 2005: para. 11).

The permanency of the structural adjustment reforms had been tightened through greater control at the bureaucratic level of the Bank and Fund, which was necessitated by the increasing overlap in the jurisdictions of the two institutions since the inception of SAPs. When the institutions were first created, both were given clear and separate mandates – the Fund was to focus on monetary and fiscal stability and the Bank on reconstruction and development (see IMF and IBRD Articles of Agreement, Article I) – and until the inception of structural adjustment, both complied largely with the constitutional demarcations.

With the advent of SAPs, the jurisdiction of the Fund and the Bank with regard to their role in development financing began to overlap. As the Bank began lending to finance macroeconomic shortfalls, so did the IMF begin lending to stimulate economic growth and development. The establishment of the Structural Adjustment Facility (SAF) in 1986 cemented the IMF's role in low-income countries and heightened the problem of 'cross-conditionality' – the practice of 'one institution withholding approval for a loan until the conditions of the other institutions were satisfied' (Boughton 2001: 648). The PFP was the result of this conflict. When the SAF was transformed into the Enhanced Structural Adjustment Facility (ESAF), the Bank and Fund introduced the PFP as a coordinating vehicle for the adjustment lending operations of both institutions.

The end result, however, was not greater coordination, but greater constraints over the policy autonomy of borrowing countries. Mosley *et al.*'s extensive study of the World Bank's policy-based lending observed that the introduction of the PFP further curtailed the borrowing country's ability to develop its own economic development agenda. The PFP effectively created 'a managed duopoly of policy advice' whereby the decisions of Bank and Fund are rarely challenged by client countries, particularly 'in the case of the poor, indebted countries where conditionality already bites the hardest' (Mosley *et al.* 1991: 55).

The design of structural adjustment programmes was to facilitate the reform of regulatory regimes within borrowing states that did not conform to the prevalent economic and political ideology of the time. This coincided with the fear among financiers in industrialized countries that Third World states would withdraw from the international economic system on their own terms. Given the hegemony of the USA and its allies within the governance structure of the World Bank and the IMF, it is no surprise that SAPs operationalized the reforms that were pursued by the dominant member states, that is, the G7 members, in other regulatory fora during that period.

The PRSP not only deepens this centralization but is, in itself, a result of this concentration of power. Over the years, the control of the Bretton Woods institutions over developing countries, both in terms of financial and intellectual leverage, has led these institutions to appropriate the leadership in development financing by default over other bilateral and multilateral financiers. The efforts at funnelling all development aid through the PRSP framework are testimony to the power these institutions wield at the global policy level in this area.

While it serves as a mechanism for accessing aid from a variety of international donors and financiers, the PRSP framework remains institutionally tied to the Bretton Woods institutions, as approval rests with the Bank and Fund boards. Other aid agencies do not sit on the JSAN committee and do not have a say, but are encouraged to use the PRSP as a basis for organizing their financial support to PRSP countries. The Bank and the Fund acknowledge that '[t]he Bretton Woods institutions will be expected to play a central role in [the] effort' towards donor harmonization and alignment, as the joint staff assessments of the PRSP and the PRSP country's Annual Performance Review (APR) is being viewed as 'a critical input to the country authorities and donors in evaluating overall [Poverty Reduction Strategy] implementation' (World Bank and IMF 2004: para. 97).

The fear that some practitioners and observers have now is that the PRSP approach is being used as an overarching framework for the international aid system, including the facilities established under the aegis of the United Nations. Koussari contends that there is an urgent need to consider the increasing subordination of the UN agencies to the PRSP framework, and hence of the UN system to the Bretton Woods institutions, if aid is increasingly funnelled through a framework controlled by the Bank and the Fund (Koussari 2005). The PRSP framework is already being aligned alongside the UN's Millennium Development Goals (MDGs), a set of development objectives that have been established as international development targets and serve as indicators of countries' performances in areas such as health, education and access to natural resources, and there is concern that strategies employed to meet these objectives will become dependent on the Bank's and the Fund's interpretation of what constitutes sound economic policy.

The consequences of this are detrimental, not only to governance in PRSP countries, but also to global governance in general, since the control of resource flows to developing countries is placed in the hands of institutions with a less democratic and less transparent governance structure than that of the one-country, one-vote structure of the United Nations.

Legacy 4: withering of the developmental state

By far the most important impact of SAPs upon recipient countries has been their effect on the constitution of the state. Reforms under adjustment programmes were premised on the notion that state intervention in the markets stagnated economic growth and created inefficiencies and distortions in the production and delivery of goods and services. To redress this, recipient countries had to scale back government intervention in and ownership of the domestic economy through the deregulation and liberalization of economic sectors, the privatization of state-owned enterprises, and the removal of government subsidies for domestic productive sectors.

Meanwhile, fiscal and monetary austerity promoted by IMF stabilization programmes involved ceilings on budget deficits and freezes or reductions in government expenditure levels, curbs on monetary supply in the domestic economy, including limits on domestic resource mobilization through taxes, and the devaluation of national currencies (Rowden 2004: 11; SAPRIN 2004: 176). At the same time, non-negotiable conditions of external debt

servicing in most stabilization loans resulted in many highly indebted recipient countries spending a disproportionate amount of their budget on debt
servicing[5] while adhering to low-inflation targets that limited the amount of
resources that could be generated and spent by the government.[6]

The imposition of such policies on developing countries has led to a
steady erosion of the function of government in these countries. Removing
the state from economic activity and curtailing government regulation of
domestic economic sectors have served to circumscribe the role of government, leaving little left for governments – including those democratically
elected to serve the interests of the electorate – to do except to enforce
policies set for them by external parties and create an enabling environment
in which foreign capital is free to operate. At the same time, the stringent
public expenditure controls, limits on domestic resource mobilization and
debt-servicing requirements under SAPs, have curbed the amount of
resources available to governments to undertake basic government tasks,
such as the provision of healthcare, education and public utilities for the
poor.

SAP policies to cut government expenditure have meant that many low-
income countries are now dependent on aid to plug not only the fiscal gap
in national budgets, but also to fund personnel in the civil service. For
example, fiscal austerity in sub-Saharan Africa has not only cut the number
of civil service personnel but also precipitated a brain-drain of highly qualified civil servants as a result of declining real wages (Sender 2002: 194).
Consequently, it is not uncommon in many of these countries to have government personnel directly funded by bilateral aid agencies, either through
financing the salary of a government official or worse, through the second-
ment of government personnel from the donor country into the recipient
country's civil service. Additionally, bilateral and multilateral aid is often
channelled through technical assistance projects – delivered by expatriate
consultants – to build or supplement domestic government capacity.

The reliance on development financing as a means of sustaining elemen-
tary governmental functions has serious implications for the autonomy and
sovereignty of the state in question. Coupled with the 'process of weakening
or dismantling prior public regulations and controls' (SAPRIN 2004: 75)
through the liberalization and deregulation policies, this has severely curtailed
not only the autonomy, but also the *authority* of the state. For example, the
SAPRIN study found that deregulation of financial sectors has weakened
state institutions while strengthening private interests and that '[a]fter two
decades of structural adjustment, governments do not have enough authority
and legitimacy to even pursue complementary and corrective reforms'
(SAPRIN 2004: 76).

Abugre contends that the neoliberal policies of SAPs have precipitated 'a
new crisis of the state' in countries affected by these policies, particularly
those in sub-Saharan Africa, whereby the functions of government have
been gradually eroded to the extent that there is no effective state left: 'As a

result of the policies of structural adjustment, you have a situation in Africa now where there are good, active *governments*, but hardly any space for *governance*' (Abugre 2005).

This undermining of state capacity in countries under structural adjustment is worsened by the policies of decentralization and privatization of the public service delivery pursued by the Bank and the Fund in recent years through SAPs and other lending instruments, such as Community-Driven Development (CDD) projects and Output-Based Aid (OBA). Policies of decentralization bypass central government by shifting the decision-making and financing for development projects to sub-national governments or local communities, eroding the fiscal autonomy of the state and weakening the administration of national government as a whole. As they undermine national budgetary and other administrative processes, these policies not only result in inconsistent spending allocations and uneven coverage of public services and other state functions, but also weaken political accountability and create opportunities for intervention by other parties into the political affairs of the state.

The replacement of government with private entities, such as non-governmental organizations (NGOs) and corporations, weakens the compact between the state and its citizens, and creates the opportunity for the proliferating private, profit and non-profit sector to capture key policy-making spaces. The abstraction of the state from the provision of essential services, such as healthcare and education, 'removes an important impetus for democratic participation' as '[t]he retreat of the tentacles of government diminishes both the direct experience of citizens of their government's efficiency and also their level of vested interest in the performance of the state' (Whaites 2002).

Many non-governmental, non-corporate entities working in the delivery of basic services in low-income countries are branches of large, Northern transnational NGOs. These organizations have, on the basis of the scale of their operations at the grassroots as substitute providers of goods and services not supplied by cash-strapped governments, demanded a larger influence in the formulation of aid policy within donor agencies, as well as in national and local policy-making processes in recipient countries. The advocacy role of these organizations, in particular their demands to be heard in policy circles, has played an important part in contributing to this shift from structural adjustment programmes to the 'new architecture of aid' (Ahmed 2004; interviews, 2003–5).

The PRSP approach has therefore taken root in a political and economic vacuum in which the apparatuses of governance and the functions of government have been weakened by successive onslaughts of structural adjustment reforms, and where this vacuum has been partially filled by private entities and agencies that are by and large linked operationally to organizations external to the countries in which they operate. As observed by Gould and Ojanen: 'A novel feature of the PRS is the extent to which a certain category of private, non-state actors have succeeded in legitimizing demands for inclusion in the direct exercise of decision-making power' (Gould and Ojanen 2003: 49). While increased participation in policy-making is laudable, it is questionable when this is achieved through a corresponding erosion of state capacity and authority.

Conclusion

The above discussion has demonstrated that 'successful' implementation of the PRSP framework is therefore a corollary to the 'successful' implementation of SAP policies. The deeper and more intrusive the policies of structural adjustment, the weaker and more aid-reliant the state, resulting in a severely diminished capacity to resist the institutional reforms that condition access to development financing. The paradox of this heritage is rarely represented in the 'post-Washington Consensus' discourse that accompanies the PRSP approach to development financing and the accompanying 'new architecture of aid'.

Far from reflecting a break with the relationships of power and control that underpinned the SAPs, the PRSP framework represents instead continuity with the dynamics of power that characterized the policies of structural adjustment. SAPs have curtailed state authority, state autonomy and state activity in domestic socio-economic and political spheres. The need to reconstruct the state through the imposition of a participatory process of policy-making that engages the government in discussion with the citizenry, and the reassertion of state autonomy through the representational practice of 'ownership' of development policy, can only be evidence of this dynamic.

Furthermore, the drive to recreate the institutional structures of post-structural adjustment states through rehabilitating, albeit marginally, the state's capacity to govern and make policy under the guise of 'country ownership' reflects the interventionist mode of governance that was the hallmark of structural adjustment. The rationale behind the PRSP framework is therefore an extension of the paternalistic attitude that permeated the structural adjustment project – that developing states needed to be assisted to create institutions that were necessary for development and that developing states were incapable of doing so without external assistance. For the countries implementing structural adjustment policies, and now the PRSP reforms, the driving force is less about the efficacy of these measures in bringing about the desired economic and social outcomes than about fulfilling the conditions for economic survival.

To ignore the legacy of structural adjustment is also to validate the discursive power of the PRSP framework that is seeking to monopolize representations of the relationships between the patron and the client. As Sender contends, the assumption of a 'deficiency of capacity' on the part of the state targeted for reform under the new financing and development policy framework 'provide[s] support for another set of politically convenient arguments [where] the blame lies with the incapacity of the unfortunate countries concerned rather than with the quality of aid policy design and implementation in Washington' (Sender 2002: 192–3).

The decoupling of the PRSP approach from its legacy in structural adjustment therefore masks the continuities between these two modalities of governing access to resources for development, and this artificial de-linking decontextualizes the PRSP framework from its place in the evolution of development financing as a mechanism of globalization and a mechanism of control. PRSPs therefore represent not only continuity with the perniciousness of structural adjustment policies, but also with the technologies of colonial management. The re-historicizing of PRSPs within the narrative of structural adjustment may therefore assist in situating the PRSP framework back in the political and economic inequities of international political economy and the historical conditions for such inequities.

Notes

1 The term 'development financing' is generally used to refer to all forms of financing for economic development purposes, commercial or otherwise, and undertaken both by the private and the public sectors. I use the term 'development financing' to refer to what is commonly known as 'development aid' or 'official development assistance' (ODA), official financial or technical transfers from donor countries to recipient countries or multilateral institutions provided on a concessional basis (see OECD DAC 1987: para. 2).

2 These countries are those eligible for concessional financing from the World Bank's soft loan arm, the International Development Association (IDA) and from the IMF's PRGF. To qualify, countries must have a per capita income of US$965 (based on figures for financial year 2005) (see World Bank 2005a).

3 In spite of the promises of economic growth and prospects for a raised standard of living under SAPs, poverty, by the World Bank and IMF's own accounts, rose in most countries that underwent structural adjustment. According to World Bank and IMF figures, the number of people living below the poverty line (delineated at US$1 a day) in most parts of the world rose between 1990 and 2000, many in countries where SAPs were introduced in the 1980s (World Bank and IMF 2004 and World Bank 2003 in World Bank 2004a: 2, fig. 1.1). In sub-Saharan Africa, this 'headcount' rose from 47 per cent to 49 per cent with a corresponding zero rate of economic growth in the same period (World Bank 2004a: 1–2).

4 The Bank estimates that more than 45 per cent of all PRSC conditions involve public sector reforms, of which more than 64 per cent 'specifically address weaknesses in public financial management' (World Bank 2005b: para. 66).

5 The SAPRIN study found that the largest single item of expenditure on the national budget was interest payments on public sector debt. In Ecuador, debt servicing reached 52 per cent of government expenditure in 2000, reducing to 43 per cent in 2001 after debt rescheduling. These conditions, coupled with the requirement for currency devaluation against the US dollar – which reduces government capacity to purchase goods and services from abroad – have led to significant cuts in public spending, particularly in social sectors such as health and education (SAPRIN 2004: 182).

6 For a detailed critique of the IMF's low-inflation targets and their impact on social sector spending, see Rowden 2004.

References

Abugre, C. (2005) Presentation at the Global Civil Society Strategy Meeting on International Financial Institutions in Accra, 23–6 February 2005.

Ahmed, M. (2004) 'Bridging Research and Policy', paper presented at the Development Studies Association Annual Conference 2004: 'Bridging Research and Policy', London, 6 November 2004.

Amin, S. (1977) *Imperialism and Unequal Development*, Hassocks: Harvester Press.

Anghie, A. (2004) *Imperialism, Sovereignty and the Making of International Law*, Cambridge: Cambridge University Press.

Arrighi, G. (2002) 'The African Crisis: World Systemic and Regional Aspects', *New Left Review* 15, May–June.

——(1982) 'A Crisis of Hegemony', in Amin, S., Arrighi, G., Frank, A. G. and Wallenstein, I. (eds) *Dynamics of Global Crisis*, New York: Monthly Review Press.

Boughton, J. M. (2001) *Silent Revolution: The International Monetary Fund 1979–1989*, Washington DC: IMF.

Cassen, R. and associates (1986) *Does Aid Work? Report to an Intergovernmental Task Force*, Oxford: Clarendon Press.

Christiansen, K. with Hovland, I. (2003) 'The PRSP Initiative: Multilateral Policy Change and the Role of Research', Overseas Development Institute (ODI) Working Paper 216, August 2003, London: ODI.

Chossudovsky, M. (1997) *The Globalization of Poverty: Impacts of IMF and World Bank Reforms*, Penang: Third World Network.

Degnbol-Martinussen, J. and Engberg-Pedersen, P. (2003) *Aid: Understanding International Development Cooperation*, London, New York and Copenhagen: Zed Books and the Danish Association for International Cooperation.

Fitzpatrick, P. (2001) *Modernism and the Grounds of Law*, Cambridge: Cambridge University Press.

Gould, J. and Ojanen, J. (2003) 'Merging in the Circle: The Politics of Tanzania's Poverty Reduction Strategy', Policy Paper 2/2003, Helsinki: Institute of Development Studies, University of Helsinki.

Hoogvelt, A. (2001) *Globalization and the Postcolonial World. The New Political Economy of Development*, 2nd edn, London: Palgrave.

IMF (2005) 'Guidance Note for Fund Staff on the Modified Poverty Reduction Strategy Framework and the Implications for PRGF and HIPC Operations', 30 June 2005, Washington DC: IMF.

——(2004) *Report on the Evaluation of Poverty Reduction Strategy Papers (PRSPs) and the Poverty Reduction and Growth Facility (PRGF)*, Washington DC: IMF.

IMF and World Bank (1999) 'Poverty Reduction Strategy Papers – Operational Issues', 10 December 1999, Available at http://imf.org/external/np/pdr/prsp/poverty1.htm (assessed 9 September 2005).

Interviews with World Bank and IMF staff and civil society (2003–5).

Koussari, K. (2005) presentation by UNCTAD Special Coordinator for Africa at the plenary session on Poverty Reduction Strategy Papers, Global Civil Society Strategy meeting on International Financial Institutions, Accra, Ghana, 23–6 February 2005.

Mosley, P., Toye, J. and Harrigan, J. (1991) *Aid and Power: The World Bank and Policy-Based Lending*, vol. 2, London: Routledge.

OECD (1987) *DAC Guiding Principles for Associated Financing and Tied and Partially Untied Official Development Assistance*, Development Assistance Committee of the Organisation for Economic Cooperation and Development (OECD DAC), adopted by the OECD DAC on 24 April 1987.

Pahuja, S. (2000) 'Technologies of Empire: IMF Conditionality and the Reinscription of the North/South Divide', *Leiden Journal of International Law* 13(4), 749–813.

Pincus, J. R. (2002) 'State Simplification and Institution Building in a World Bank-Financed Development Project', in Pincus, J. R. and Winters, J. A. (eds) *Reinventing the World Bank*, Ithaca NY: Cornell University Press.

Rowden, R. (2004) 'Blocking Progress: How the Fight Against HIV/AIDS is Being Undermined by the World Bank and the International Monetary Fund (IMF)', a policy briefing by ActionAid USA *et al.* September 2004, Washington DC: ActionAid USA.

Rowden, R. and Ocaya-Irama, J. (2004) 'Rethinking Participation: Questions for Civil Society About the Limits of Participation in PRSPs', an ActionAid USA/ActionAid Uganda discussion paper, April 2004, Washington DC: ActionAid USA and Uganda.

SAPRIN (Structural Adjustment Participatory Review International Network) (2004) *Structural Adjustment: The SAPRIN Report – The Policy Roots of Economic Crisis, Poverty and Inequality*, London and New York, Penang, Manila and Bangalore: Zed Books, Third World Network, Ibon Foundation and Books for Change.

Sender, J. (2002) 'Reassessing the Role of the World Bank in Sub-Saharan Africa', in Pincus, J. R. and Winters, J. A. (eds) *Reinventing the World Bank*, Ithaca NY: Cornell University Press.

Shihata, I. (2000) *The World Bank in aChanging World*, vol. III, The Hague: Kluwer Law International.

Whaites, A. (2001) 'Introduction', in Whaites, Alan (ed.) *Precious States: Debt and Government Service Provision to the Poor*, Monrovia CA: World Vision International.

Whaites, A. (ed.) (2002) *Masters of Their Own Development? PRSPs and the Prospects for the Poor*, Monrovia CA: World Vision International.

World Bank (2005a) 'IDA Borrowers', June 2005. Available at http://web.worldbank.org/WBSITE/EXTERNAL/EXTABOUTUS/IDA/0,contentMDK:20054572~menuPK:115748~pagePK:51236175~piPK:437394~theSitePK:73154,00.html (9 September 2005).

——(2005b) 'Poverty Reduction Strategy Credits: A Stocktaking', 24 June 2005. Washington DC: World Bank.

——(2004a) *The Poverty Reduction Strategy Initiative: An Independent Evaluation of the World Bank's Support through 2003*, Washington DC: World Bank.

——(2004b) 'Board Presentations of PRSP Documents, as of December 23 2004', Washington DC: World Bank.

——(2004c) 'From Adjustment Lending to Development Policy Lending: An Update of World Bank Policy', Policy Paper, August 2004, Washington DC: World Bank.

——(2004d) 'Operational Policy 8.60: Development Policy Lending', August 2004, Washington DC: World Bank.

——(2004e) 'Supporting Development Programs Effectively: Applying the Comprehensive Development Framework Principles: A Staff Guide', Washington DC: World Bank.

——(2003) *Toward Country-led Development: A Multi-Partner Evaluation of the Comprehensive Development Framework Synthesis Report*, Washington DC: World Bank.

——(2001) 'Adjustment Lending Retrospective: Final Report', 15 June 2001, Washington DC: World Bank.

World Bank and IMF (2005) 'Guidelines for World Bank and IMF Staffs for Joint Advisory Notes (JSAN) for Poverty Reduction Strategy Papers', Washington DC: World Bank and IMF.

——(2004) 'Poverty Reduction Strategy Papers – Progress in Implementation', 20 September 2004, Washington DC: World Bank.

World Vision (2002) *Masters of their Own Developmen? PRSPs and the Prospects for the Poor*, ed. Alan Whaites, Monrovia CA: World Vision International.

9   Becoming green

Diffusing sustainable development norms throughout the World Bank Group

Susan Park

Introduction

This chapter compares the identities of two of the World Bank Group's (WBG)[1] lesser-known affiliates: the International Finance Corporation (IFC) and the Multilateral Investment Guarantee Agency (MIGA). Both became increasingly active during Wolfensohn's tenure, but remain relatively unexamined. Moreover, throughout the Wolfensohn decade, both institutions were challenged by environmental organizations – which are described here as transnational advocacy networks – to adopt norms of sustainability. These processes are reminiscent of previous environmental advocacy against the Bank, and demonstrate how the affiliates faced similar normative pressure yet responded in different ways (Rich 1994). Their responses, it is argued, derive from their distinct identities. This makes generalizable claims about Wolfensohn's WBG limited, although the degree that the affiliates followed the Bank, and Wolfensohn's contribution to affiliate actions, become apparent throughout.

This chapter argues that transnational advocacy networks socialized both IFC and MIGA through direct (network–affiliate) and indirect (network–state–affiliate) influence, beginning with the organizations' projects and policies. These interactions involved micro-processes of socialization: persuasion, social influence and coercive pressure (Park 2005a). Arguably, the process of contesting and creating sustainable development between the affiliates, states and the advocacy networks led to a reconstitution of IFC's identity, but not MIGA's. Instead, MIGA continued to contest rather than help create a shared understanding of sustainable development. This chapter propounds that non-state actors influence the identities of the affiliates through politicizing issues such as the environment (Price 1998). Yet socialization remained uneven across the WBG at the end of Wolfensohn's tenure.

Socialization, the World Bank Group and sustainable development

Within international relations, rationalist theories, including neoliberalism and neorealism, point to the instrumental interests of states informing international organizations' actions (Nielson and Tierney 2003). While states determine international organization mandates, scope and functions, how they interpret and operationalize these in certain ways and not others remains a key concern (Ruggie 1998: 859). As such, constructivists have documented how ideas influence actors' identities, including how international organizations spread norms (Barnett and Finnemore 2004). Where the norms international organizations diffuse originate from is a central concern for constructivists. Relevant here, is what influences the WBG affiliates' understanding of their mandates and where new norms originate (Park 2005a).

This chapter goes beyond simple rationalist accounts of member states pushing for affiliate change through foisting environmental and social policies onto organizations (Nielson and Tierney 2003). It provides a comprehensive account of how transnational advocacy networks worked independently, and with states such as the United States, to engage the affiliates to (re)create sustainable development. While rationalism may explain why an international organization changed its behaviour (as a result of material rewards or punishments) it does not examine the degree to which actors are altered, or their identities reconstituted, as a result of normative change (Gutner 2005). Constructivism provides a framework for understanding how changes in the social structure alter international organization practices (actions and beliefs) through constant interaction.

The WBG affiliates operate in a social structure of international norms that inform their behaviour. Norms have structural characteristics and are defined as 'shared expectations about behavior held by a community of actors' (Finnemore 1996: 23). An organization's identity includes its mandate and bureaucratic culture based on its dominant profession, and is both subjective and intersubjective. Organizations act according to their identity, yet internal ideas of self are mediated by external norms and vice-versa, shaping actors' interests (Wendt 1999: 224). Thus, an international organization's identity is informed by how it perceives itself and is perceived by others.

Shared understandings of international organization behaviour are initially created by states establishing the organization. This is reinforced through internal practices as well as interactions with state and non-state actors. Yet international organization identities are not fixed; they often diffuse different norms from those they began with (Wendt 1999: 22). For example, the Organization of Security and Cooperation in Europe recreated norms of security; while the World Bank shifted towards poverty alleviation (Adler 1998: 149; Finnemore 1996: 89–128). How international organizations shift to diffuse new norms is central to the argument that international organizations embody norms from interaction with state *and non-state actors*.

There has been substantial analysis of the Bank's environmental shift (Rich 1994; Le Prestre 1989; Wade 1997). While environmental organizations have been prominent in pushing for improved environmental procedures within the Bank, early work on Bank interactions with environmental organizations was 'methodologically weak' and 'backed by selective evidence' (Gutner 2002: 27). Recent scholarship has attempted to overcome this by systematically explaining the World Bank's incorporation of environmental activities through a rationalist Principal-Agent model (P-A model) (Gutner 2005; Nielson and Tierney 2003). The P-A model analyses the relationship between member states (principals) and autonomous international organizations (agents). For example, member states such as the US coerced the Bank to implement environmental components into its operations by threatening to withhold funds (Nielson and Tierney 2003: 265).

Although the model includes non-state actor contributions, they are assumed to be part of the state: principals are collectives made up of various delegations including different government agencies and lobby groups (Nielson and Tierney 2003: 248). Therefore, the model does not adequately recognize non-state actors' transboundary nature. Transnational advocacy networks are non-state actors that organize collectively around issue-based campaigns across state boundaries. They include research and advocacy non-governmental organizations (NGOs); activists; local social movements; foundations; the media; churches; trade unions; consumer organizations; intellectuals; parts of international organizations and states (Keck and Sikkink 1998: 9). Networks blur the distinction between collective and multiple principals, because the P-A model views non-state interactions with international organizations through the prism of state-centrism. This marginalizes how advocacy networks influence bodies such as the WBG. How networks contest and (re)create norms appropriate for international organization behaviour is important in determining how their actions are perceived.

Regarding IFC and MIGA, transnational advocacy networks politicized an area of WBG operations not previously politicized before: the environmental impact of their investments and guarantees (Price 1998: 621). Groups within the transnational advocacy network influencing IFC (especially on Pangue) included: the American Anthropological Association Bank Information Center (BIC); Center for International Environmental Law (CIEL), Friends of the Earth (FoE); International Rivers Network (IRN); Natural Resources Defense Fund (NRDC); Red Bancos (a regional NGO network); Grupo de Accion por el Bibio (GABB); and 400 Chilean citizens including indigenous Peheunche people and Chilean Congress members (Park 2005b). The network opposing MIGA was mainly constituted by: BIC, the Berne Declaration, Campagna per la Riforma della Banca Mondiale, the CIEL, Down to Earth, FoE, ProjectUnderground, and Urgewald; although numerous project-specific groups were also active.

The networks contested IFC's and MIGA's promotion of development norms that overlook environmental factors. Until the mass campaigns of the 1980s, shared assumptions about how to achieve development through economic modernization dominated the development discourse. Throughout the 1980s and 1990s, environmental organizations have been at the forefront of challenging the Bank's purely economic prescriptions.

Sustainable development aims 'to ensure that it meets the needs of the present without compromising the ability of future generations to meet their own needs' (World Commission on Environment and Development 1987: 8). Yet how the Bank interprets and reproduces sustainable development norms depends upon what operations are considered sustainable by international organizations, states and non-state actors. The World Bank now routinely undertakes environmental impact assessments and monitoring, upheld by safeguard policies (SPs) and accountability mechanisms. This, it is argued elsewhere, resulted from contesting and recreating development norms with states and advocacy networks (Park 2005a). Intrinsic to the argument that the World Bank is more 'green' is that its environmental and information disclosure policies are now recognized as the norm both within the Bank and internationally, although debates continue over the Bank's ability to comply (Gutner 2005).

The socializing effect of transnational advocacy networks

Socialization is defined as a process whereby agents endogenize ideas that are constitutive of the social structure in which they exist (Schimmelfennig 2000: 110–12). The social structure informs how agents behave, but not necessarily what they will do. Networks are affected by the practices of international organizations, and as norm entrepreneurs, they respond to international organizations by attempting to reconstitute their identities (Finnemore and Sikkink 2001: 400–1). Changes in international organiza-tion practices (actions and ideas) as a result of this interaction represent a change in socially shared understandings of an organization's identity. Socialization is therefore interactive: reconstructing norms through con-testing the appropriate role of international organizations in areas such as development. In turn, actors' identities and interests reconstitute norms, such that '[A]ny given international system does not exist because of immutable structures, but rather the very structures are dependent for their reproduction on the practices of the actors' (Koslowski and Kratochwil 1994: 216). Thus, processes of socialization create new organizational identities *and* new social structures.

Two avenues of socialization, direct and indirect, demonstrate how net-works contest and recreate international organization identities by way of three 'micro-processes': persuasion, social influence and coercive lobbying (Checkel 1999). First, *persuasion* involves 'changing minds, opinions and attitudes about causality and affect (identity) in the absence of overtly material or mental coercion' and can succeed when the actor is exposed to counter-attitudinal information repeatedly over time (Johnston 2001: 496, 499). Second, transnational advocacy networks also engage *social influence*, involving the distribution of social rewards and punishments including 'shaming, shunning, excluding, and demeaning.' Alternatively, rewards 'might include psychological well-being, status, a sense of belonging, and a sense of well-being derived from conformity with role expectations' (Johnston 2001: 499). Third, *coercive pressure* stems from transnational advocacy networks persuading states to use material pressure on international organizations as elaborated below.

'Direct socialization' is where transnational advocacy networks interact with the affiliates. The networks attempt to persuade international organizations of the relevance of particular norms through ongoing campaigns. This includes meetings, letters, emails and phone calls. *Social influence* includes the use of demonstrations, protests and petitions at international organization project sites, offices or headquarters, or praise through press releases and web posts. Yet international organizations do not just conform to social structures, but also mediate and recreate them through their responses.

'Indirect socialization' is where advocacy networks *persuade* member states to engage the organization and press for new norms to be adopted (*coercive pressure*). Advocacy networks can thus shape how state power is used because states have the ability to establish international organization policies. This is part of the socialization process because the very act of changing an international organization's actions (establishing environmental policies) influences its interests (how it designs projects) and ultimately its identity (what it believes its role to be).

In the case of the affiliates below, determining specific actions as unacceptable for international organizations with development mandates via social influence, persuasion and coercive pressure, led to a rethink by the IFC (but not MIGA) about how to remain an industry leader. Leadership includes identifying with and then promoting previously imposed sustainable development ideas. Both direct and indirect socialization are necessary in the socialization process because they demonstrate a convergence of ideas around increasingly accepted norms of international organization behaviour shared by the organization, states and non-state actors.

Norm contestation and diffusion: comparing IFC and MIGA

Advocacy networks interacted repeatedly with IFC, MIGA and states over their 'problem projects' and policies, with varying outcomes. In each instance, advocacy networks attempted to socialize the affiliates through direct and indirect processes providing opportunities for norm contestation and creation between advocacy networks, states and international organizations.

The International Finance Corporation (IFC)

Created in 1956, IFC shares its board of governors, directors and president with the Bank, but has its own mandate, operations, articles of agreement and funding. Currently, IFC has 177 members, and the voting and influence is determined by the amount of share capital 'paid in' (the US dominates with 23.65 per cent). IFC raises additional funds through international capital markets.

Its mandate is to partially finance and facilitate financing for private enterprise in developing countries where capital is not readily available (Mason and Asher 1973: 351). IFC is 'the largest multilateral source of loan and equity financing for private sector projects in the developing world' (IFC 2002a: attachment II). By 2004, IFC's committed portfolio had reached $17.9 billion: 74 per cent loans, 20 per cent equity investments, and 6 per cent finance and risk management products (IFC 2004a).

IFC furthers development through providing venture capital for private projects in developing countries; through attracting international investors; and by providing technical assistance to companies and developing country governments. As demonstrated below, IFC's mandate shifted in 1998 as a result of network influence to play 'a leading role in the development of a sustainable private sector' (IFC 1998: 8). Prior to this, sustainable development was not integral to IFC's mission (Park 2005b: 103). As a financial institution, IFC is predominantly staffed with investment bankers. However, there has been a dramatic increase of environmental specialists from one in 1989 to ninety-nine in 2004 (of approximately 2,200 staff). Over 60 per cent of environmental and social specialists are now located in investment departments and regional offices and are also involved at an earlier stage of IFC's project cycle. IFC now evaluates all projects for their environmental impact, thus mainstreaming environmental ideas through all project sectors. Moreover, IFC has increased environmental and social development spending from $2 million in 1994 to $12.5 million in 2004 (IFC 2004b: 40, 53). Significantly, IFC is recognized by advocacy networks for being concerned with environmental improvement, and IFC now diffuses sustainable development norms through the establishment and promotion of the Equator Principles (interview with BIC, September 2001; Wright, this volume).

The Multilateral Investment Guarantee Agency (MIGA)

In comparison to the IFC, MIGA was established in 1988 with its own board of governors, directors, convention (constitution), budget, and chairman. The President of the World Bank was nominated as Chairman of MIGA's Board of Directors, who nominates the Executive Vice-President, the Agency's head. MIGA currently has 165 members, divided into 'capital-exporting' states seeking political risk insurance and 'capital-importing' states requesting technical assistance. Members have equal votes and subscribe to MIGA's capital stock, giving the Agency its underwriting capacity (Shihata 1991: 284). MIGA provides political risk insurance covering non-commercial risk to investors in developing countries and technical assistance to developing states to attract private investment (World Bank 2001). By the mid-1990s MIGA had already grown to one of the largest investment risk insurers in the world, with over $1.6 billion in outstanding liabilities, and could boast the facilitation of $19 billion in direct foreign investment (FDI) between 1988 and 1997 (MIGA 2001).

MIGA's mission statement does not specifically incorporate environmental aspects of development: MIGA aims 'to promote foreign direct investment into developing countries, in order to support economic growth, reduce poverty and improve people's lives' (MIGA 2004). As a political risk guarantor agency, it is primarily staffed by risk analysts. It plays a central role in the insurance industry as an affiliate of the WBG, attracting the attention of the networks. In 1997, MIGA created the Environment Unit, which currently houses two environmental and one social specialist (of 130 MIGA staff). In 2002 the agency adopted environmental and social safeguard policies while engaging in heated debates with advocacy networks contesting sustainable development. As a result, the networks have considered MIGA a 'dinosaur' regarding its views on sustainable development (interview with CIEL, September 2001). MIGA plays a central role in the insurance industry as an affiliate of WBG, attracting the attention of the networks, detailed below.

Problem projects

Transnational advocacy networks first began promoting sustainable development norms for IFC and MIGA by contesting 'problem projects' (Wirth 1998). This took place through direct socialization: opposing affiliate actions through protest (social influence) at the project level and through dialogue (persuasion) at the policy level. This occurred simultaneously with indirect socialization, where advocacy networks influenced state perceptions of affiliate behaviour (coercive pressure). Interestingly, because of the affiliates' indirect development roles as intermediaries between shareholders and projects, it was never assured that opposing IFC- or MIGA- backed projects would halt environmental degradation. Yet, as demonstrated below, advocacy networks undertook similar campaigns to oppose the affiliates' support for problem projects. The first advocacy network campaign against IFC, the Pangue dam, compares to similar (although less successful) campaigns against MIGA.

Contesting IFC: the case of the Pangue dam

The Chilean Pangue dam was the most controversial project in IFC history and one that would affect future IFC operations (IFC 2005: 1; Park 2005b). IFC classified Pangue as a World Bank Category A project because of its high environmental and social impacts, although IFC had no environmental and social safeguards at the time (IFC 1992). Category A projects have high-risk environmental impacts, while category B projects have serious but mitigatory impacts, and category C projects have negligible impacts.

The network opposed the project through direct socialization as early as 1990. Petitions were sent by the consolidating network to IFC prior to the loan's approval in 1992 (GABB letter to President Preston, February 1992; NRDC letter to President Preston, April 1992). Indirect socialization began in 1991 when the network questioned the US Executive Director's (US-ED) position on IFC's investment in Pangue (IRN letter to the US Executive Director, April 1991). In January 1992, the US Treasury met with IFC regarding the environmental and social impacts of the dam. The company, Pangue S.A., sent a copy of the Environmental Assessment to the US-ED, and in May the US-ED was one of a number of directors involved in meetings with the network (GABB 1995: attachment 1). The US-ED then abstained from voting on the Pangue project. The Alternate US-ED argued that the dam demonstrated 'what we see as a general failure of recent World Bank hydroelectric projects to assess adequately, and in a timely manner, the likely impacts of proposed projects to fisheries and aquatic biodiversity' (Alternate US-ED statement to IFC Board, December 1992).

Significantly, the Alternate US-ED requested information from Pangue S.A. (a subsidiary of Endesa) including specific reports for the network (Alternate US-ED letter to Pangue S.A., April 1992). The US, by way of the Treasury and through its representatives in IFC, advocated on behalf of the network, revealing the extent to which its role had been socialized by the networks. While indirect socialization in this project campaign was success-ful in influencing the Alternate US-ED's position on Pangue, it was not able to mitigate the project's environmental effects. However, indirect and direct socialization would continue to influence IFC.

In 1997, IFC threatened to declare Endesa in default for its failure to meet the loan's environmental and social conditions. The situation triggered the involvement of Wolfensohn, who urged the Chilean government to mediate. In doing so, Wolfensohn referred to two independent critical reviews of IFC's 'handling of the environmental appraisal and supervision of the Pangue project and the compliance of . . . Endesa with their obligations under the IFC agreement' (Wolfensohn letter to Chile's Finance Minister, February 1997). The reports were prepared at the urging of 'green lobbies'.[2] The first report documented an independent investigation contracted by IFC in 1995 by American anthropologist Theodore Downing. It listed Pangue's impacts: unchecked in-migration to a previously isolated area, land speculation and deforestation, as well as severe limitation of Pehuenche land rights and the general failure of the Pehuen Foundation to protect the indigenous community (Downing 1996: 5).

In 1995, the network filed a complaint with the World Bank Inspection Panel, that IFC had violated eight IFC/Bank environmental and social safeguards (GABB 1995: 6–7). The Inspection Panel is a mechanism that allows recourse to peoples affected by Bank projects. The claim was rejected because the Inspection Panel does not have the power to inspect IFC projects, although IFC must meet World Bank policies and has the same directors, governors, and president (GABB 1995: 4–5). In response, Wolfensohn commissioned an autonomous internal review of Pangue in 1996, which was undertaken by Jay Hair, a former president of both the National Wildlife Federation and the International Union for the Conservation of Nature.

The Hair report stated that 'IFC did not follow fundamental World Bank Group requirements in any consistent or comprehensible manner throughout the development and implementation of the Pangue Project', and that '[T]here was no evidence in the record that comprehensive and systematic monitoring of requirements to determine compliance with relevant World Bank Group requirements were either (a) identified within IFC or to the project sponsor or (b) subsequently monitored' (Hair 1997: 35, 38). The Hair report demonstrated IFC's difficulties in implementing sustainable development. Indeed, the dam's environmental impacts were not systematically addressed and have since been accepted as a major problem by IFC (Park 2005b).

The project was a 'wake-up call' to IFC over its use of Bank safeguard policies. It revealed fundamental weaknesses in adopting but not endogenizing sustainable development norms, which were highlighted when Endesa did not fulfil its requirements. Following Pangue, the network aimed to influence IFC to improve its environmental safeguard policies.

Contesting MIGA

Advocacy networks also questioned MIGA's role as part of the WBG, undertaking both direct and indirect processes of socialization of MIGA, beginning with its 'problem projects'. The networks claimed that MIGA had guaranteed investments in numerous problem projects after the Freeport McMoran gold mine in West Papua (1995). These included: the Omai gold mine in Guyana (1995); the Kumtor gold mine in the Kyrgyz Republic (1995) with the World Bank; the Lihir Gold mine in Papua New Guinea (1997); the Antamina mine in Peru (1999); the Brazil–Bolivia gas pipeline (1999); and the Julietta mine in Russia (2000); a soft drink plant in Bosnia-Herzegovina (2000); the Bujagali hydroelectric power project in Uganda with the Bank (2001); and the Buljanhulu mine in Tanzania (2002) (Friends of the Earth *et al.* 2001). These campaigns made MIGA aware that environmental and social problems may affect business as usual, although the extent to which projects were halted or ameliorated was limited. However, the following section demonstrates that MIGA incorporated environmental and social safeguard policies soon after the explosion of campaigns targeting MIGA.

These campaigns have had limited success on the project sponsors in terms of halting the project's environmental degradation. In the first case, the West Papuan mine, the mining company Freeport McMoran instituted environmental and social plans to limited effect (Leith 2003). While MIGA was not the focus of the campaign in West Papua, as was IFC with Pangue or the World Bank with Polonoroeste and Narmada, advocacy networks attempted direct socialization of MIGA through social influence and persuasion. Direct socialization of MIGA was a small component of the campaign, but it was effective. Not because MIGA cancelled Freeport's coverage, but because MIGA was roused to investigate the network's claims.

However, MIGA's coverage was cancelled by the company prior to its investigation – an act which drew media attention to MIGA and Freeport. Freeport may have been concerned about having to meet the environmental and social standards of MIGA and Freeport's main insurer OPIC (which had threatened to cancel Freeport's insurance over environmental concerns). Had Freeport remained a client, it is conceivable that the insurers would have strengthened their monitoring efforts on environmental and social safeguards as a result of direct socialization. In 1998 OPIC strengthened its existing policies (OPIC 1999). Also in 1998, MIGA began drafting its own safeguard policies as other problem project campaigns emerged. Direct socialization thus played a role, as did indirect socialization: the networks pressured the US government-sponsored (though privately run) OPIC, the project's main guarantor. The knock-on effect of ensuring environmental and social standards may have influenced MIGA's decision to establish safeguards in 1998.

These project campaigns therefore emphasize the role that political risk insurers can play in diffusing sustainable development norms via socialization. This politicizes yet another aspect of the development process. Such problem projects are more than incidental on an analytical level, because it was at the height of numerous campaigns that MIGA introduced environmental and social safeguard policies.

Safeguard policies and environmental monitoring

As outlined below, processes of direct and indirect socialization influenced IFC and MIGA to both establish and then strengthen environmental and social safeguard policies. Advocacy networks attempted direct socialization of IFC and MIGA through normative pressure at the policy level. Indirect socialization occurred by influencing the US to pressure IFC and MIGA to implement policies and environmental monitoring. The responses of the two affiliates are illuminating.

IFC policy reform

In 1989 IFC created an Environment Division and appointed its first, and at the time only, environmental advisor. IFC emulated the Bank by introducing environmental categories (A to C) for its projects according to their potential impact on the environment. Yet in 1990, only seven of 160 projects reviewed were deemed to have potentially significant environmental impacts; the volume of projects for review was beyond the capacity of one permanent staff member (IFC 2002c: 30). In 1993, during the direct socialization of the Pangue project campaign, IFC began to revise its use of World Bank safeguard policies (SPs).

Beforehand, there had been the assumption that IFC would adhere to Bank standards. Through indirect socialization, the networks influenced key parts of the US, who in turn supported a sustainable IFC. The networks assisted the US Congress by drafting a law requiring IFC (and other MDBs including MIGA) to improve information disclosure necessary to ensure sustainable development (the Pelosi Amendment) (Keck and Sikkink 1998: 149). The US adherence to sustainable development norms is evident in its advocacy and leadership on environmental issues within MDBs, especially IFC (United States Treasury 2001: 2).

IFC's 1993 adoption of policies signified the establishment of safeguards as being part of IFC rather than the ill-defined use of Bank policies that had tentatively been in place since 1988, with *ad hoc* amendments in 1990 and 1992. Concurrent with the mass campaign against the Pangue dam, IFC reviewed the Environment Department and drafted a 'best practice manual' (IFC 1996: 77–8). Yet, it was the Pangue Inspection Panel claim in 1995 that had convinced IFC to completely review its approach to environmental and social issues. It was not until direct and indirect socialization by transnational advocacy networks relating to the Pangue project culminated in the Inspection Panel claim in 1995, that IFC began to realize the importance of environmental and social aspects of development. One IFC staff member states that the Pangue campaign really affected IFC's outlook (interview with NGO Officer IFC, September 2001). The network supports this view, arguing that IFC became much more responsive after the Pangue claim, by adopting, and then endogenizing, SPs (interview with BIC, September 2001). Indeed, recommendations from the 1997 Hair report led to a full review and the comprehensive establishment of IFC's own environmental and social safeguard policies in 1998 (IFC 2002c: 31).

Transnational advocacy networks therefore helped reconstitute IFC by pressing for the affiliate to have its own safeguard policies. The establishment of comprehensive safeguards in 1998 was the result of continued socialization in the form of calls, meetings and consultations with the network. While there are remaining concerns about SP implementation in individual projects, IFC has become a leader among multilateral financial institutions in integrating environmental and social considerations into its operations and lending requirements (interview with CAO, September 2001). From 1998, IFC became committed to incorporating social and environmental concerns into its operations.

Since then, IFC has established the independent Operations Evaluation Group (OEG), as well as other internal monitoring mechanisms. In 2001 OEG presented findings for its recently matured operations by evaluating

171 randomly selected investments approved between 1993 and 1995, and evaluated between 1998 and 2000. Two thirds of projects were deemed satisfactory or excellent for their environmental, social, and health and safety requirements. The OEG concluded that only 4 per cent of projects were unsatisfactory because they were 'concentrated in high risk countries' where 'ineffective legal and regulatory regimes ... undermine projects' compliance' (OEG 2002: 2–4). From 2004, the OEG will continue to monitor unsatisfactory projects and from 2005, IFC aims to link environmental evaluations back into the project cycle (IFC 2004b: 41–2). Other review mechanisms were also established: the Environment and Social Risk Rating (ESRR) system which identifies projects with a high risk of non-compliance (in 2001); and a Quality Portfolio Management (QPR) system (in 2000) to assist environment and social specialists (CAO 2002: 19).

In 1999 Wolfensohn established the CAO Office with assistance from transnational advocacy networks and IFC appointed its first liaison to the NGO community (Park 2005b). IFC senior management then asked the Compliance Advisor/Ombudsman (CAO) to review its 1998 SPs. The CAO report outlined IFC's main weaknesses: 'the weak system supporting the SPs, including lack of specific objectives, weak project monitoring and supervision, and poor integration ... into IFC's core business' (CAO 2003: 7). Yet, the review stated that there was no drastic shift after adopting the 1998 SPs, but a 'steady progression and evolution of practice', and that SPs are having an overall positive effect, contributing to beneficial environmental and social impacts (CAO 2002: 23–42). Finally, it stated that the safeguards often go beyond the 'do no harm' approach (CAO 2003: 6). IFC is currently in the process of implementing new Policy and Performance Standards to replace its safeguard policies in 2006 after the 2003 CAO report and after protracted but fitful consultation with transnational advocacy networks.

Throughout the 1990s and early 2000s, IFC implemented substantial organizational changes, including: incorporating sustainable development concerns into its mission statement; dramatically increasing environmental and social staff; and providing leadership in introducing SPs into the finance industry. These changes are significant in demonstrating not only a change in IFC interests and practices, but a shift in its identity: from having no social and environmental conscience, to a position of 'do no harm', to the present 'do good' (IFC 2002c: 2). Further 'beyond compliance' changes demonstrate IFC's commitment to sustainable development norms: IFC now reports on its own greenhouse gas emissions and its environmental footprint (IFC 2001: 57). It instituted a Sustainability Initiative in 2001 to centre its approach to sustainable development lending and investment (IFC 2001: 51). The Initiative embodies a triple bottom line approach, which equals a commitment to 'people, the planet and profits' (IFC 2002c). Its success will be determined by IFC's marketing of sustainable development to project sponsors (see Wright, this volume, Chapter 4).

This is already being addressed by the recent introduction of the Equator Principles by investment banks. On 4 June 2003, ten large investment banks adopted the Equator Principles, ten voluntary environmental and social guidelines that will influence an estimated $10 billion in global investment over the next ten years.[3] These principles were initiated by IFC and demonstrate how IFC has begun to diffuse sustainable development throughout the project finance industry.

Crucially, the network supports the view that IFC has changed. They argue that IFC's environment department is both useful and growing, and that IFC seems genuinely concerned with environmental improvement and global issues (interview with BIC, September 2001). Indeed, advocacy networks perceive IFC to be 'better than the Bank' in terms of responding to interactions with the networks. Furthermore, IFC is seen to be less bureaucratic in responding to environmental problems and incorporating environmental issues into IFC work (interview with Conservation International, October 2001). IFC's identity therefore informs how it reproduces and transforms sustainable development through its operations (interview with FoE, September 2001). The project and policy changes outlined throughout, along with the recent 'beyond compliance' measures detailed, demonstrate IFC's identity shift. This compares with MIGA's limited shift towards sustainable development.

MIGA policy resistance

Transnational advocacy networks attempted to influence MIGA's environmental and social safeguard policies through the same interactive processes. This section demonstrates the Agency's foot-dragging in establishing its own policies, by outlining network processes of direct and indirect socialization. Advocacy network concerns are that MIGA's identity as an international political risk insurer is at odds with its developmental objectives, and that MIGA shows no sign of becoming accountable and transparent (Friends of the Earth *et al.* 2001).

In 1999, MIGA formally adopted IFC's environmental safeguards. Prior to this, there was the same assumption that MIGA would adhere to IFC standards just as IFC had previously adhered to the Bank's. The Agency began implicitly using Bank and IFC safeguard policies for its appraisals in 1991 (OEU 2003: 7). In 1996, advocacy networks began arguing that there was 'a series of double standards between the World Bank's public and private sector lending operations' (Bosshard 1996a). The network argued that environmental assessment guidelines were less strict and comprehensive for MIGA projects and they were occurring too late in the project cycle, while the guarantee process allowed little time for a proper appraisal. The Berne Declaration argued that MIGA did not have its own environmental department, subcontracting its environmental project analysis to IFC. At that time IFC had a small department with seven staff and three consultants, reviewing between 200 and 250 new projects a year while supervising approximately 1,000 ongoing projects. The network claimed that up to 1993, only ten of MIGA's 185 projects were classified as Category A, even though MIGA underwrites projects known for their high environmental impacts such as mining and infrastructure (Bosshard 1996b).

In response, the Agency created an in-house environmental unit in late 1997. The unit currently has two environmental specialists, and employs consultants to undertake project appraisals. MIGA began drafting its own specific environmental policy in 1998, and in May 1999 MIGA's board adopted interim SPs from IFC's environmental and social policies (Van Veldhuizen 2000: 54). In early 1999, MIGA initiated a fifty-day comment period open to all stakeholders, including investors, insurers, businesses, MDBs and civil society, on MIGA's draft environment policies. MIGA's interim SPs were permanently adopted in 2002 (MIGA 2003). According to MIGA's lead environmental specialist, '[T]he environmental assessment policy formalizes an approach to environmental review that has been taken by MIGA for many years' (Van Veldhuizen 2000: 54).

The formal adoption of environmental and social safeguard policies demonstrates how MIGA responded to the pressure of advocacy networks, although it does not signify that an identity shift has occurred. MIGA's introduction of safeguard policies provides little indication of their impact on the organization. This contrasts with the extensive discussions and reviews that have taken place within IFC since 1998, and by the CAO over IFC policies from 2001 to the present.

Significantly, MIGA noted that the process of adopting specific IFC environmental safeguard policies applicable to MIGA-insured investments had been 'less than satisfactory'. MIGA stated that this was partly the result of IFC having only officially adopted four of the Bank's eight safeguard policies and that progress had been limited while awaiting IFC's safeguard policy review (2001–3). MIGA intends to adopt specific environmental and social safeguard policies from IFC's new Policy and Performance Standards that will replace its SPs in 2006. MIGA awaits IFC's conversion because its private sector needs are more akin to IFC than to the World Bank, and the Agency has limited capacity to undertake these conversions itself. MIGA therefore relies on IFC policies, even when these may not suit a political risk insurer. It also uses Bank policies when there are no IFC policies to cover specific environmental issues – although these are less likely to suit MIGA. Yet MIGA is a small affiliate of the WBG and it is natural that it should rely on IFC, although IFC and MIGA are separate institutions with distinct operations and MIGA is not legally bound to the policies of IFC. The CAO review emphasizes that IFC and MIGA need to come to a formal arrangement in order for MIGA's operations to be policy-compliant.

The networks also argue that MIGA has done little to monitor the impacts of the investment projects it underwrites. In 1998, after network pressure on MIGA's problem projects and its lack of environmental policies, the Agency released its first Development Impact Review, evaluating twenty-five projects covered by MIGA guarantees. In 2001, a more extensive Development Impact Review was undertaken evaluating 52 projects from 27 states and representing 75 per cent of all active projects backed by MIGA between 1990 and 1996 (West and Tarazona 2001: 25). While environmental impacts of MIGA-backed projects are mentioned within the reviews, only ten projects (17 per cent) were visited by environmental specialists.

Considering that manufacturing, mining, infrastructure and tourism sectors account for 60 per cent of sectors evaluated (West and Tarazona 2001: 26–7), and generally have significant environmental and social impacts, this demonstrates the need to analyse how to assess sustainable development. Environmental specialists involved in the evaluation process identified 10 of the 52 projects as requiring environmental monitoring (West and Tarazona 2001: 29). No projects failed on environmental grounds. Of the 52 projects analysed, 22 were not measured, none failed, and none were deemed 'untraceable' (or impossible to measure). However, little explanation is given as to why some projects were not measured. MIGA continues to underwrite projects in high environmental impact sectors such as oil, gas and mining, yet there is no response to advocacy network campaigns within these reports. Established in 2003, MIGA's Operations Evaluation Unit (OEU) argued that 73 per cent of its extractive industry projects reviewed by the recent WBG Extractive Industries Review were consistent with current MIGA safeguard policies, but it suggested that more needs to be done on information disclosure, due diligence, monitoring compliance and reviewing social safeguard outcomes (OEU 2003: 9–13).

The networks also state that MIGA lacked 'environmental and social accountability for the projects it guarantees' (Friends of the Earth *et al.* 2001). They claim that MIGA's monitoring capacity remains weak because the organization is 'not equipped properly to continue monitoring ... [so that] the project[s] it insures adhere to MIGA's standards and policies, especially in environmental and social areas' because of limited staff and no ongoing monitoring system (Down to Earth 2001). The network further argued that MIGA's clients are not screened for their past social, environmental, labour and human rights records. MIGA replied that it

> has turned down and cancelled projects that have not complied with our environmental and social requirements. Companies know that they have to be environmentally and socially responsible if they come to any of the institutions of the World Bank Group for support.
>
> (MIGA letter to FoE, July 2001)

In September 2001 MIGA's response had become strident, highlighting increasing network–MIGA tension:

MIGA's activities do not promote or subsidize poor corporate behaviour at the expense of people and the environment. The broad statements made in the report that MIGA's activities are anti-environmental ... are untrue. And there is no evidence to support the claims that MIGA's clients have poor environmental and human rights records.

(MIGA letter to FoE, September 2001)

In April 2002, the networks replied that MIGA had an outdated and overly constrained understanding of development. They further note the discrepancy of listing (but not making public) the environmental impact assessments for Category A projects, while exempting Category B and C projects. This is, they argue, 'clearly unsatisfactory for a publicly-financed development institution'. Unlike IFC, MIGA has not been socialized by advocacy networks as evidenced by these network admonishments:

We find the tone of your response disappointing and unproductive. ... Mischaracterizing the nature of our critiques only shows that MIGA has little interest in recognizing its weaknesses as a development institution. We have found MIGA to be duly resistant to reform and find MIGA's progress in reform efforts to be wholly inadequate. This has led many organizations to conclude that MIGA has little interest in conforming its policies and practices to the World Bank's ... and has led many to conclude that MIGA should no longer function as part of the World Bank Group.[4]

This exchange demonstrates how MIGA moved from explicitly ignoring, then rejecting advocacy network claims, to engaging and responding to issues with more comprehensive measures such as the OEU, an institution comparable to the World Bank's Operations Evaluation Unit and the IFC's Operations Evaluation Group. While the OEU is a positive step in establishing a more permanent evaluation process, it remains to be seen what the long-term impact on MIGA operations will be. MIGA is engaging with the networks, although this does not necessarily mean that MIGA has endogenized sustainable development. Advocacy network attempts at direct socialization continued with a 2003 publication which outlined MIGA's 'secretive stance' and its weak SPs compared with the other affiliates (Environmental Defense *et al.* 2003: 4). While MIGA argues that it is among the most transparent political risk insurance agencies and that it encourages export credit agencies to improve their environmental standards, it has not endogenized norms of sustainable development (MIGA 2004).[5]

Regarding indirect socialization, there is little evidence to suggest that the network is informally engaged with key US government agencies on strengthening MIGA's policies, as has been the case with IFC. However, the network was active in politicizing the need for the CAO to overlook IFC and MIGA operations with the support of the US-ED (Park 2005b). In addition, the network has engaged in indirect socialization of MIGA by persuading the US Congress to increase pressure on MIGA to reform its projects and policies. Friends of the Earth claimed victory in 2001 when the US gave partial lending of $5 million to MIGA rather than the $10 million requested for MIGA's capital increase, although this has not had a demonstrable impact on MIGA.[6] MIGA has slowly instituted policies, rather than viewing these policies and monitoring procedures as important goals in themselves.

The relatively limited changes of adopting safeguard policies do not provide evidence that socialization has occurred. Importantly, the Agency does not highlight its role as a sustainable development underwriter. Only recently has there been information publicized on its environmental activities (via its website), although sustainability remains absent from its mission statement. In addition, MIGA has limited professional staff to undertake environmental and social monitoring. As such, transnational advocacy networks argue that MIGA's identity has not changed, as witnessed by the interactions between the network and MIGA detailed above. The networks argue that MIGA acts like an 'ostrich' rather than engage with them (although this is changing in the post-Wolfensohn era). As a result, the networks still consider MIGA outmoded in its views of sustainable development (interview with FoE, October 2001). This contrasts with the recognition that various networks have given to IFC.

Perhaps most revealing however, is the view of the CAO regarding MIGA's attitude to sustainable development. CAO sees MIGA as a 'closed book' and that MIGA is 'harder to fathom' in terms of its commitment to sustainable development compared with IFC. In short, IFC is considered to be 'way ahead' on sustainable development issues (even compared with the Bank) because of the type of organization MIGA is (interview with CAO Office, September 2001). This reinforces the network's view that MIGA is not interested in endogenizing sustainable development. MIGA is considered to be a 'dinosaur' based on its political risk insurance identity where its project cycle and services make it impossible for it to meet WBG safeguards (interview with CIEL, September 2001). Some activists state that the environment is 'not on their [MIGA's] radar screen' and that socializing efforts have not had much success, leaving NGOs like Friends of the Earth convinced that MIGA should be shut down (interview with BIC, September 2001).

The confrontational nature of the network–MIGA interaction may be the very beginning of the socialization process, where opposition and contestation is the basis of initial interaction. A conflictual stance allows the organization's norms to be questioned, and for dialogue to begin – even if it is combative. This is reminiscent of the initial process of socializing the World Bank in the early 1980s and differs sharply from the style of engagement between advocacy networks and both the Bank and IFC in the late 1990s. MIGA vehemently rejects the claims that it does not promote sustainable development, remaining in the norm contestation phase. However, it does accept that there are 'challenges' in reconciling its insurer identity with sustainable development. Transnational advocacy networks attempted direct and indirect socialization processes through IFC and MIGA's projects and policies. The effect has been the initial creation of a form of sustainable development within the affiliate, but its reactive and reluctant stance has meant that MIGA has a long way to go towards endogenizing sustainable development compared with IFC.

Conclusion: norm contestation and diffusion

This chapter posited that examining WBG affiliates during Wolfensohn's reign would enable generalizations about the WBG's identity. However, the comparison of direct and indirect socialization by transnational advocacy networks of two of the WBG affiliates, revealed stark differences. This is a similar finding to that in Riggirozzi's chapter (this volume, Chapter 11). IFC and MIGA responded in different ways to persuasion, social influence and coercion through lobbying from transnational advocacy networks on their projects and policies, demonstrating their distinct identities. IFC has embraced sustainable development norms as a result of socialization, endogenizing sustainable development through its operations and beginning to diffuse these norms through the project finance industry (interview with FoE, September 2001). Contra IFC, MIGA continues to contest sustainable development with the networks, demonstrating the Agency's opposition to the norm diffusion process. MIGA's political risk insurance identity remains at odds with its development identity. While Wolfensohn did play a role in promoting greater facilitation of WBG–network interactions, as evidenced in the Pangue project, and by establishing the CAO to cover both IFC and MIGA, this has not led to an overarching WBG sustainable development identity. Changes in the post-Wolfensohn era, however, beg continued attention.

Notes

1 The World Bank Group includes: the International Finance Corporation (IFC); the International Centre for Settlement of Investment Disputes (ICSID); and the Multilateral Investment Guarantee Agency (MIGA). The 'World Bank' or 'Bank' includes the International Bank for Reconstruction and Development (IBRD) and International Development Association (IDA).
2 *Financial Times*, 'World Bank Arm Warns Endesa', 21 February 1997, p. 3.
3 Statement by Peter Woike, IFC Executive Vice President, Equator Principles Press Conference, 4 July 2003.
4 Letter from FoE, Urgewald and Reform the World Bank Campaign to MIGA's Corporate Relations Group, 3 April 2002.
5 MIGA, response to NGO stakeholder comments, note 64, public discussion ending 5 February 1999. http://www.miga.org (accessed 2 December 2003).
6 Friends of the Earth, 'Multilateral Investment Guarantee Agency Fact Sheet'. http://www.foe.org (accessed 2 December 2003).

References

Adler, E. (1998) 'Seeds of Peaceful Change: The OSCE's Community Building Model', in Adler, E. and Barnett, M. (eds) *Security Communities*, Cambridge: Cambridge University Press, 119–60.

Barnett, M. and Finnemore, M. (2004) *Rules for the World: International Organizations in World Politics*, Ithaca NY: Cornell University Press.

Bosshard, P. (1996a) 'The Private Sector Lending of the World Bank Group: Issues and Challenges', January 1996, the Berne Declaration, Switzerland. http://www.2.access.ch/evb/bd/privlend.htm (accessed 20 January 2003).

——(1996b) 'A Case Study about MIGA's Lihir Island Goldmine Project in Papua New Guinea', February 1996, the Berne Declaration, Switzerland. http://www.2.access.ch/evb/bd/privlend.htm (accessed 20 January 2003).

Checkel, J. T. (1999) 'Norms, Institutions, and National Identity in Contemporary Europe', *International Studies Quarterly* 43(1), 83–114.

CAO (Compliance Advisor/Ombudsman) (2003) 'Assessment by the Officer of the Compliance Advisor/Ombudsman in relation to a Complaint Filed against IFC's Investment in Endesa Pangue S.A.', CAO Assessment Report May 2003, Washington DC: IFC and MIGA.

——(2002) 'Review of IFC's Safeguard Policies: Draft for Comment', CAO Office Report, Washington DC: IFC and MIGA. http://www.cao-ombudsman.org/env (accessed September 2002).

Downing, T. (1996) 'A Participatory Interim Evaluation of the Pehuen Foundation', IFC 2067, AGRA Earth and Environment: Downing and Associates.

Down to Earth (2001) 'The Multilateral Investment Guarantee Agency (MIGA): Whose Interests are Served and at What Cost?', *Down to Earth Fact Sheet Series* 16, http://www.dte.gn.apc.org/ (accessed 21 January 2003).

Environmental Defense, Friends of the Earth and International Rivers Network (2003) 'Gambling with People's Lives: What the World Bank's New "High Risk/High Reward Strategy" Means for the Poor and the Environment', http://www.environmentaldefense.org (accessed 2 December 2003).

Finnemore, M. (1996) *National Interests in International Society*, Ithaca NY and London: Cornell University Press.

Finnemore, M. and Sikkink, K. (2001) 'Taking Stock: The Constructivist Research Program in International Relations and Comparative Politics', *Annual Review of Political Science* 4, 391–416.

Friends of the Earth (2000) *Dubious Development: How the World Bank's Private Arm is Failing the Poor and the Environment*, Washington DC: Friends of the Earth.

Friends of the Earth, Urgewald, and Campagna per la Riforma della Banca Mondiale (2001) *Risky Business: How the World Bank's Insurance Arm Fails the Poor and Harms the Environment*, Washington DC: Friends of the Earth.

GABB (Grupo de Action por el BioBio) (1995) 'The BioBio Dams in Chile: Violations of World Bank Policies and Lack of Accountability at the International Finance Corporation', claim before the Inspection Panel and petition before the IFC Board of Executive Directors, Chile, GABB.

Gutner, T. (2005) 'World Bank Environmental Reform: Revisiting Lessons from Agency Theory', *International Organization* 59, 773–83.

——(2002) *Banking of the Environment: Multilateral Development Banks and Their Environmental Performance in Central and Eastern Europe*, Cambridge MA: MIT Press.

Hair, J. (1997) 'Pangue Hydroelectric Project (Chile): An Independent Review of the International Finance Corporation's Compliance with Applicable World Bank Group Environment and Social Requirements', IFC Internal Review, Washington DC: IFC.

IFC (International Finance Corporation) (2005) *Lessons Learned: Pangue Hydroelectric Summary*, Environment and Social Development Department, Washington DC: International Finance Corporation.

——(2004a) *IFC Annual Report 2004*, Washington DC: International Finance Corporation.

——(2004b) *Sustainability Report 2004*, Washington DC: International Finance Corporation.

——(2002a) 'Strategic Directions', Confidential Report to the Board of Directors, International Finance Corporation, 8 March 2002.

——(2002b) 'Basic Facts About IFC', cited: http://www.ifc.org/about/ (accessed 3 December 2002).

——(2002c) *The Environmental and Social Challenges of Private Sector Projects: IFC's Experience*, Lessons of Experience Series 8, Washington DC: International Finance Corporation.

——(2001) 'Building a Sustainable Development Roadmap: IFC's Strategy to Ensure Environmental and Social Responsibility', *Environment Matters*, IFC Annual Newsletter: 48–51.

——(2000) 'Environment and Social Safeguard Policies', http://www.ifc.org/about/ (accessed 2 November 2000).

——(1998) *IFC Annual Report 1998*, Washington DC: S&S Graphics, International Finance Corporation.

——(1996) 'Financing Private Infrastructure', Lessons of Experience series no. 4, Washington DC: World Bank.

——(1992) 'IFC Board Approves Pangue Dam', IFC press release no. 92/32.

Johnston, A. I. (2001) 'Treating International Institutions as Social Environments', *International Studies Quarterly* 45(4), 487–515.

Keck, M. and Sikkink, K. (1998) *Activists Beyond Borders: Advocacy Networks in International Politics*, Ithaca NY and London: Cornell University Press.

Koslowski, R. and Kratochwil, F. (1994) 'Understanding Change in International Politics: The Soviet Empire's Demise and the International System', *International Organization* 48(2), 215–47.

Leith, D. (2003) *The Politics of Power: Freeport in Suharto's Indonesia*, Honolulu: University of Hawaii Press.

Le Prestre, P. (1989) *The World Bank and the Environmental Challenge*, Selinsgrove PA: Susquehanna University Press.

Mason, E. S. and Asher, R. E. (1973) *The World Bank Since Bretton Woods*, Washington DC: Brookings Institution Press.

MIGA (Multilateral Investment Guarantee Agency) (2004) *Annual Report 2004*, Washington DC: MIGA.

——(2003) *Annual Report 2003*, Washington DC: MIGA.

——(2002) 'MIGA's Interim Issue Specific Safeguard Policies', *MIGA Policies*, http://www.miga.org/ (accessed 25 November 2002).

——(2001) 'MIGA: The First Ten Years', http://www.miga.org/ (accessed 12 June 2001).

Nielson, D. and Tierney, M. (2003) 'Delegation to International Organizations: Agency Theory and World Bank Environmental Reforms', *International Organization* 57(2), 241–76.

OEG (Operations Evaluation Group) (2002) 'Annual Review of IFC's Evaluation Findings: FY 2001', *OEG Findings*, Washington DC: The World Bank Group.

OEU (Operations Evaluation Unit) (2003) 'Extractive Industries and Sustainable Development – MIGA's Experience', http://www.miga.org/ (accessed 2 December 2003).

OPIC (Overseas Private Investment Corporation) (1999) 'OPIC Environmental Handbook – April 1999', http://www.opic.gov/ (accessed 28 January 2003).

Park, S. (2005a) 'Norm Diffusion within International Organizations: A Case Study of the World Bank', *Journal of International Relations and Development* 8(2), 114–41.

——(2005b) 'How Transnational Advocacy Networks Socialize IFIs: A Case Study of the International Finance Corporation', *Global Environmental Politics* 5(4), 95–115.

Price, R. (1998) 'Reversing the Gun Cites: Transnational Civil Society Targets Land Mines', *International Organization* 52(3), 613–32.

Rich, B. (2002) 'The World Bank under James Wolfensohn', in Pincus, J. R. and Winters, J. A. (eds) *Reinventing the World Bank*, Ithaca NY: Cornell University Press.

——(1994) *Mortgaging the Earth: The World Bank, Environmental Impoverishment and the Crisis of Development*, Boston MA: Beacon Press.

Ruggie, J. G. (1998) 'What Makes the World Hang Together? Neoutilitarianism and the Social Constructivist Challenge', *International Organization* 52(4), 855–85.

Schimmelfennig, F. (2000) 'International Socialization in the New Europe: Rational Action in an Institutional Environment', *European Journal of International Relations* 6(1), 109–39.

Shihata, I. (1991) *The World Bank in a Changing World: Selected Essays*, Dordrecht: Martinus Nijhoff.

United States Treasury (2001) 'Annual Report to Congress on the Environment and the Multilateral Development Banks, FY 2001', US Treasury Press Release Report 3051, US Treasury Office of Public Affairs. http://www.ustreas.gov/press/release/report3051.pdf (accessed 2 December 2002).

Van Veldhuizen, H. (2000) 'Multilateral Investment Guarantee Agency', *Environment Matters*, IFC annual newsletter, Washington DC: World Bank.

Wade, R. (1997) 'Greening the Bank: The Struggle over the Environment, 1970–1995', in Kapur, D., Lewis, J. and Webb, R. (eds) *The World Bank: Its First Half Century*, vol. 2, Washington DC: Brookings Institution Press, 611–734.

Wendt, A. (1999) *Social Theory of International Politics*, Cambridge: Cambridge University Press.

West, G. and Tarazona, E. (2001) *Investment Insurance and Developmental Impact: Evaluating MIGA's Experience*, Washington DC: The World Bank Group.

Wirth, D. (1998) 'Partnership Advocacy in World Bank Environmental Reform', in Fox, J. and Brown, D. (eds) *The Struggle for Accountability: The World Bank, NGOs and Grassroots Movements*, Cambridge MA: MIT Press, 51–79.

World Bank (2001) 'MIGA Corporate Overview', *World Bank Development News: Issue Briefs*. http://www.worldbank.org/html/extdr/pb/miga.htm (accessed 5 June 2001).

World Commission on Environment and Development (1987) *Our Common Future*, Oxford: Oxford University Press.

10 Partnership and the reform of international aid

Challenging citizenship and political representation?

Pascale Hatcher

Introduction

The turn of the century has witnessed a shift in the practice of development assistance. The trauma of the Asian financial crisis, the structural adjustment programme's (SAP) questionable score card, and, to some extent, the rise of anti-globalization movements, have led to a series of declarations announcing a wind of change in development organizations' practices. Indeed, the new millennium marked the beginning of a wave of introspection in the development community, leading to a range of so-called 'new' policies and practices, such as the OECD's Development Aid Committee (DAC) call for a 'New Partnership', the unanimously embraced Millennium Development Goals, and the World Bank's quest for a development paradigmatic shift under its former president, James Wolfensohn.

The World Bank has been at the forefront of the development reform with the introduction, in 1998, of the first element of what has led to the Integrated Development Model (IDM). Recognizing the pivotal role that should be played by the state and civil society, this model would, according to Wolfensohn, put developing countries' governments back 'in the driver's seat':

> What is new is an attempt to view our efforts within a long-term, holistic and strategic approach. ... Such development should, in our judgment, be a participatory process, as transparent and as accountable as possible within the political climate prevailing in each country. ... It is a holistic and strategic approach to development based on country ownership and partnership. ... It is also a commitment to expanded partnerships, transparency, and accountability under the leadership of the government.
>
> What is new is that the international financial architecture must reflect the interdependence of macroeconomic and financial with structural, social and human concerns.
>
> I personally believe that unless we adopt this approach on a comprehensive, transparent, and accountable basis, we will fail in the global challenge of equitable sustainable development and poverty

alleviation. We will fail to build a sustainable international architecture for the coming millennium.

(Wolfensohn 1999: 30)

These shifts within the Bank's rhetoric bring us to a critical juncture where the institution is openly addressing the very nature and functions of the state and civil society. However, these reflections appear to lead us to a paradox: it seems that, on the one hand, we are witnessing the birth of a social shift which calls for a greater role for civil society but, on the other hand, the same reform brings forth a set of institutional shifts that could bypass the political debates arising from a more involved civil society.

This chapter addresses this apparent paradox at the heart of the IDM. It explores how the World Bank has come to influence the political balance between civil society and the state, and the political implications this poses to the very notion of citizenship in borrowing countries. It argues that the IDM champions a technocratic form of governance which, combined with its functionalist view of civil society, is depoliticizing the notion of citizenship in countries undergoing political and economic reform.

The chapter is divided into three sections. The first section sets the birth of the World Bank's IDM in a historical context. The second section analyses the institutional reforms at the heart of the IDM and their political implications for borrowing states. The last section addresses the 'social' dimension of the IDM. It explores how the World Bank's renewed interest in civil society, combined with the institutional shifts towards a greater technocratic mode of governance, as demonstrated in the second section, are challenging the very notion of citizenship in countries under reform.

Context

As a result of the Asian financial crisis' political aftermath, the foundation of Washington Consensus policies (Williamson 2000) has been severely shaken, especially the deep belief in the perfection of the free market. The most famous attack was launched by the former chief economist of the World Bank, Joseph Stiglitz. In 1998, this 'rebel within' proclaimed the emergence of a post-Washington Consensus. Denouncing the narrow pursuit of economic growth through market deregulation, Stiglitz argues that it is imperative to recognize that a certain amount of state intervention in the economy could have positive effects (Stiglitz 1998, 1999).

The World Bank gradually embraced the shift through the adoption of new aid allocation criteria and mechanisms. These will be referred to in this chapter, as forming the Integrated Development Model (IDM).

The World Bank attributes paternity of the IDM to former president Wolfensohn, who in 1998 gave a speech on the urgent need to adopt a new development paradigm that would be more 'comprehensive' than the structural adjustment paradigm that it was meant to replace (Wolfensohn 1999).

As described in Table 10.1 below, the Bank historically has divided its past development efforts into two main paradigms: the 'planning paradigm' that prevailed until the late 1970s, and the 'structural adjustment paradigm' which arose in response to the debt crisis (World Bank 1999: 4).

However, the Bank's acknowledgment of the structural adjustment programmes inefficiencies – as enumerated in Table 10.1 – led Wolfensohn to state that if fifty years of aid efforts had indeed led to better living conditions, great efforts remained to be done in order to fight poverty (World Bank 1999). This admission of failure revealed an urgent need, at the dawn of a new century, for aid to become more efficient (World Bank 1999: 2). It led to the birth of the Comprehensive Development Framework (CDF), a third and 'new paradigm' that was expected to reconcile the macroeconomic imperatives with structural, social and human needs (World Bank 2000a). The CDF was introduced as a management tool theorizing the emerging consensus among the major donors on the need for a new stakeholder partnership that would make aid efforts more efficient. Thus, drawing on the call of OECD-DAC in 1996 for a 'New Partnership' and from the

Table 10.1 Three development paradigms according to the World Bank

Planning	Adjustment	CDF
• Pervasive market failures; Government-led development	• Pervasive government failures; Market-led development	• Situation-dependent failures; Country-led development through partnerships
• Centrally driven; detailed blueprints	• Short-term adjustments	• Long-term vision, social transformation, adaptive learning process
• Investment-led development; Resource allocation by administrative fiat	• Incentive-led development; Investments and institutions follow it	• Investment, incentives, and institutions; considered jointly
• Planners and engineers dominant	• Economists and financial experts dominant	• Multidisciplinary approach
• Industrialization with import substitution	• Liberalization and privatization	• Liberalization, regulation, and industrial policy to match state capability
• Donors fill resource gap	• Donors determine resource envelope	• Country drives aid coordination based on comparative advantages
• Donors place foreign experts	• Donors impose policies	• Donors provide advisory assistance to empower stakeholders with options
• Marginal role for monitoring and evaluation	• Donor-driven monitoring of policy implementation	• Participatory monitoring and evaluation to enhance learning and adaptation

Source: adapted from World Bank 1999: 4.

convergence of views between the United Nations, some non-governmental organizations (NGOs), and other members of the international development community (Wolfensohn 1999; World Bank 2001), the CDF's stated originality was to muster emerging ideas from development actors and to set them all in one single framework.

The CDF was to be reinforced by specific policies and aid allocation mechanisms, that in turn would not only create a greater coherence in aid allocation and build a stronger partnership between governments and donors, but also enhance civil society participation (Wolfensohn 1999). Fostering local ownership and social capital, civil society's participation would, according to the World Bank, increase the reforms' efficiency (World Bank 2001). Civil society organizations are said to be closer to the poor, better able to promote transparency, and are deemed to be less bureaucratic or corrupt than governmental organizations (World Bank 2000b, 2000c). These organizations would therefore facilitate the decentralization process and would be, overall, a monitor of state activities. As the World Bank proclaimed in its 1999 CDF proposal: 'In all its forms, civil society is probably the largest single factor in development' (Wolfensohn 1999).

Less than a year after instigating the CDF, the Bank launched the Poverty Reduction Strategy Papers (PRSPs) in March 2000, which are now championed by the World Bank as the embodiment of the IDM's philosophy:

> The CDF is the foundation for the new partnership between developed and developing countries to achieve improvements in sustainable growth and poverty reduction that will help countries achieve the MDGs [Millennium Development Goals]. ... The CDF approach, operationalized through PRSPs in low-income countries, provides the common foundation for implementing this new partnership at the country level.
>
> (World Bank 2006)

Today, the Poverty Reduction Strategies (PRS) embody the most concrete materialization of the IDM. The central stated objective of these strategies is to reduce poverty. According to the World Bank and the International Monetary Fund (IMF), poverty is a 'plague', which can no longer be ignored. Swamped with the burden of debt and weak economic growth, the governments of the Heavily Indebted Poor Countries (HIPCs) face a blatant incapacity to reach the international development goals. Rooting itself in the annual World Bank and IMF's joint meeting of September 1999, the PRS are a new form of aid conditionality. HIPCs are required to present a Poverty Reduction Strategy in order to gain access to any debt relief or concessional loans. This strategy must be summarized in a Poverty Reduction Strategy Paper (PRSP), which covers a three-year period. The 1999 initiative's objectives are to allocate the funds freed from debt release to poverty reduction.

PRSPs are now a precondition for most of the concessional loans to the world's seventy poorest countries. According to the World Development Movement, they would affect the fate of a billion and a half people (Marshall *et al.* 2001).

Individual PRSPs must be written by the government with the participation of its 'civil society'. According to the Bank, the concept refers to 'the wide array of non-governmental and not-for-profit organizations that have a presence in public life, expressing the interests and values of their members or others, based on ethical, cultural, political, scientific, religious or philanthropic considerations'. These include community groups, non-governmental organizations (NGOs), labour unions, indigenous groups, charitable organizations, faith-based organizations, professional associations, and foundations.

In theory, participation in the PRSP process increases the strategy's efficiency and induces local ownership. Thus, civil society is invited to elaborate a diagnosis of the causes of poverty. Such a diagnostic is the pillar of the poverty-reduction strategies in the country's various sectors. Once the participation and writing process is over, the final document is presented for approval to the Bank and Fund's joint committee.

Beyond the Bank's discursive emphasis on poverty reduction, the birth of the IDM originated in the double failure of the structural adjustment era: its inefficiency and its lack of legitimacy (Powell 2004). Indeed, the next section addresses the Bank's quest for greater efficiency in its portfolio; while the third section analyses the Bank's pursuit of legitimacy, embracing civil society's participation.

The politics of partnership

In order to achieve a greater efficiency in poverty reduction, it had become imperative to rethink the relationship between, on the one hand, the major donors themselves, and on the other, between the donors and the local governments. Thus, the new partnership implies that donors should strive for aid coherence and rethink conditionality in order to promote reform ownership.

The conditionality model, which has been said to be at the root of the SAPs, has produced mixed results. As the 1990s unfolded, SAPs gradually exposed a highly complex process that necessitated the multiplication of conditionalities in order to achieve economic growth to such a point that a single loan could be subjected to more than a hundred conditionalities (Harrigan *et al.* 1995: 43). As the 1999 *Annual Review of Effectiveness* bluntly stated:

> The fact of growth and poverty in the 28 countries [studied] between 1991 and 1997 are sobering. ... These findings confirm the view underlying the CDF: that the battle against poverty is being lost and that business as usual will not accomplish the objectives of the development community.
>
> (World Bank 1999: 17)

The report also stated that less than half the Bank's projects in the fiscal year of 1998–9 had the potential to achieve sustainable results, a performance that would inscribe itself in the statistical trend of the entire decade (World Bank 1999: 7). At the heart of the problem resides the knowledge that only 53 per cent of conditionalities were respected (World Bank 1998: 52).

The failure of conditionality has generated lengthy debates on aid effectiveness (World Bank 1998; Dollar and Levin 2004; EURODAD 2002; Wood 2004). Amidst this literature, it has been suggested that aid should reflect a new partnership between donors and indebted countries, in order to trade 'conditionality' for 'selectivity' (Development Assistance Committee 1996). The Bank-authored report *Assessing Aid* gave way to the 'selectivity' argument, suggesting that development assistance is more about supporting good institutions and policies than providing capital (World Bank 1998: 13). It argues that there is no relation between financial development assistance and economic growth, unless a differentiation is made between countries exercising good governance and those who do not (World Bank 1998: 37). Thus, when two countries have the same poverty rate, financial aid should be assigned with 'strategic selectivity'. That is, given to the country exercising good governance (Dollar and Levin 2004). As for the other countries, they would benefit from the Bank's 'ideological assistance' (World Bank 1998: 84), rather than its capital. As it makes clear, 'the role of aid in difficult environments is to educate the next generation of leaders, disseminate information about policy, and stimulate public debate where possible' (World Bank 1998: 48).

Such conclusions have not only been reiterated by the Bank's more recent report on 'Low Income Countries Under Stress' (World Bank 2002) but also by bilateral donors and, more noticeably, by the Bush adminstration through the Millennium Challenge Account (Gore 2004).

If until now, the 'aid culture'[1] has hampered donors' enthusiasm for the selectivity argument (Harrigan *et al.* 1995; Thomas 2004), the Bank's *2003 Annual Review of Development Effectiveness* states that in the absence of a 'relatively good policy environment',[2] donors should limit or postpone lending until there are 'clear signals that reform is under way' (World Bank 2004: x). The Bank's own scorecard between 1999 and 2003, however prudent, does suggest a higher concentration of aid to countries with a good or improving policy environment (World Bank 2004: 13). During this period, World Bank lending was concentrated in countries that had 'relatively good' policy environments, with 89.4 per cent of Bank lending going to countries with a Country Policy and Institutional Assessments (CPIA) ranking of 3.0 or better in 1999, and 96.6 per cent going to such countries in 2003.

The rationale behind this turn to greater selectivity is undermined by two main findings. First, a recent study has suggested that aid would indeed be effective not only in terms of poverty reduction but also in terms of growth, irrespective of the policy environment (EURODAD 2002: 7). Second, there is no existing consensus among the aid community on how 'good policies' will bring forth poverty reduction, if at all. As stated by a critic in a brief on CPIA, if 'there is consensus that the *mechanism* is broken', the 'debate over the *content* of the conditions continues' (Powell 2004). Indeed, if there is a consensus on the necessity to implement reforms 'conductive of pro-poor growth and widespread poverty reduction' (World Bank 2004: viii), the theoretical roots of such reforms certainly remain highly contentious, as is the case with the increasing interest in institutional reforms. As stated by the Bank itself: 'meaningful policy change' is a change 'that alters incentives and affects the distribution of income and power' (World Bank 2004: 9).

In promoting policy reform, the Bank focuses on policies that: (a) improve the climate for investment and growth; (b) promote social inclusion in growth and development; (c) promote environmental sustainability; and (d) improve governance (World Bank 2004: 1). The path chosen by the World Bank brings forth an extremely constricted definition of governance. The concept answers to many definitions, and may be associated with issues such as democracy, human rights, and participation. Indeed, as explained by Campbell, 'governance' has sometimes been situated – by the UNDP amongst others – within the broader framework of sustainable development:

> in turn [this framework] reflects concerns with regard to the basic needs of local populations, as well as the diversity of their experiences and cultures. This framework is seen as a point of entry in the struggle against poverty and to reduce inequalities between countries and within them.
>
> (Campbell 2000: 4)

In contrast, the Bank's institutional take on the concept carries a neutral and apolitical connotation, suggesting that governance addresses essentially technical issues. However, it is highly political, since in the name of governance, the World Bank directly tackles what the state function should be and what relationship it should have with the market and society (Wilks and Lefrançois 2002).

The Bank's enthusiasm for institutions is situated in a functionalist and minimalist framework that promotes a specific set of institutional and legal reforms. In the Bank's view, the state, whose primary mission is to put in place the institutional foundation for a market economy, must institute a legal framework and apply policies that do not create any distortions. This emphasis on a specific set of institutional reforms should be viewed, not as a retreat of the state from the economy, but rather as a re-conversion of the state to its former role. As stated by Campbell: 'it is the strategies not aimed at exportation and those that favour social reforms that are put aside in the adjustment and the denationalization process' (our translation, Campbell 1996: 19). Consequently, the current enthusiasm for institutions should not be read as the end of the last development model but rather as the opposite. This position is underlined by Jayasuriya:

> The PWC [Post-Washington Consensus] is best seen not as a departure from the policies of structural reform but should be understood as an attempt to develop a political institutional framework to embed the structural adjustment policies of the Washington consensus.
>
> (Jayasuriya 2003: 2)

The IDM's technical turn seeks to 'protect' the state from social pressures so that the technocrats may be free to take 'neutral' decisions. This 'technocratic' approach to governance depoliticizes social issues while reintroducing new norms that are restrictively redefining social and economical rights. This increasing isolation of the state from the public space is quite alarming, especially at a time when the World Bank is reflecting on ways to modify the state's architecture itself. That is, to redefine the executive, legislative and judiciary spaces. In her analysis of the Bank's *Tool Kit: Commitment to Reform Diagnostics*, Campbell demonstrates how the institution, under its role as a 'knowledge center', enters the political arena as it offers advice to assess: 'the political desirability of proposed reforms, the political feasibility (including opposition to this project or to broader reforms inside or outside of the government), and the sustainability of reform, including potential changes in key stakeholders'.[3]

There is no doubt that donors have to address the questionable score card of aid efficiency. From local corruption to predatory states, donors are indeed faced with a significant governance predicament. However, as argued by Campbell, the new aid allocation mechanisms are increasingly 'locking-in' borrowing governments to a specific path of institutional reforms that brings forth an extremely constricted definition of governance. She argues that in Africa, the concept of conditionality could be replaced by the notion of 'verrouillage', which translates as 'locking in'. The new aid mechanisms that make all aid conditional to a prior introduction of institutional reforms, means that borrowing governments are less able to embrace alternative paths of reform (Campbell 2002: 2). More generally, this 'locking in' can be construed as a political turn that is in violation of the World Bank's own article of agreement. This technocratic turn entails serious legitimacy issues regarding the very notion of citizenship, as discussed in the following section.

The politics of civil society

While the analysis of aid reform points towards an attempt to ignore the political dimensions of the institutional framework it promotes, the introduction of a set of 'social' concepts in the IDM matrix might appear to be in direct contradiction to the technocratic agenda. Indeed, the IDM calls for mechanisms, such as the PRS, that promote the 'participation' of 'civil society'. However, by closely defining the theoretical basis of these concepts, one might observe that, far from being contradictory, these two processes are quite complementary. This section addresses these processes in two steps. First, it will explore the concept of participation embedded in the IDM. This will bring forth the political dimensions linked to the concept. The second step will observe how, under the IDM, the renewed emphasis on 'civil society' is jeopardizing the concept of citizenship.

Civil society participation and the IDM

The debate at the Bank surrounding poverty reduction and the social agenda is not new. At the beginning of the 1980s, the turn to strict application of economic reforms relegated social measures to the period following economic recovery. However, the complexity of the adjustment process would soon force the Bank to address the long-term process of the reforms that were theoretically only supposed to last two or three years.[4] The poverty-reduction agenda thus became more prominent at the turn of the 1990s, when the Bank acknowledged that the absolute priority given to economic reform would have to be tempered by a poverty reduction agenda (Hayami 2003). 'Poverty reduction is the Bank's overarching objective' (Culpeper 1997: 83) declared Lewis T. Preston, the Bank's president prior to Wolfensohn. Amidst the Post-Washington Consensus, Wolfensohn would give the Bank its new mantra: 'Our dream is a world free of poverty.'

Through the IDM and its renewed poverty-reduction agenda, civil society was invited to play a fundamental part in the development process. This growing enthusiasm for CSO is reflected in the Bank's financial support for projects in which civil society organizations take part, which has increased from 21 per cent in 1990, to 72 per cent in 2003 (World Bank at http://www.worldbank.org/civilsociety).

However, after four years of the PRSP process, there is a growing body of literature asserting that the PRSP civil society 'participation' dimension could actually be nothing but an attempt by the Bank to give legitimacy to the reforms (Grusky 2000; McGee and Norton 2000; Oxfam International 2001). Indeed, some analyses of the PRSP process and final papers have suggested that the Bank's IDM is but a change in discourse (Whaites 2000; Oxfam International 2001). This has led some critics to conclude that the Bank's reform is a rhetorical exercise that will lead to no real departure from the path of the structural adjustment programmes with regard to policy design (McGee and Norton 2000; Oxfam International 2001; Wood 2004; Jones and Hardstaff 2005).

Beyond the PRSP inconsistencies, the mechanisms of melding a 'top down' agenda with a 'grass root participation process' is bound to raise concerns. As acknowledged by the Bank, there is a 'need to lessen the tension between the PRSP role as a process for building domestic consensus and ownership and the roles that it plays with regard to debt relief and access to aid resources' (World Bank 2004: 22). However, one must wonder to what extent the Bank and the Fund would be inclined to accept a PRSP deviating from orthodox prescription. Moreover, considering the importance of international aid allocation for the HIPC, it is highly unlikely that indebted governments would actually risk presenting a document that did so (Grusky 2000: 1).

Defining civil society: a political exercise

Civil society in itself is an elusive concept (Van Rooy 1997; Biekart 1999; Edwards 2004). It has many definitions and serves the purposes of plural interests (Fowler, in Van Rooy 1997). It has been the 'private' side of civil society, perceived as more efficient than the state, which has attracted the neo-liberal development thinkers to the concept. Civil society organizations (CSOs) are indeed defined as having a comparative advantage over the state and the private sector. Similar to the manner in which it defines governance, the World Bank's approach to civil society is functionalist and bypasses the political issues inherent in the complexity of the concept. Indeed, under the new aid framework civil society organizations have a triple role to play: (1) to provide 'accountability'; (2) to provide services to the poor as sub-contractors of the state; and (3) to provide legitimacy to the reforms.

Under the IDM, civil society is perceived as an 'accountability' provider. Its comparative advantages over the state make civil society representative of the plural interests of the poor and to consequently be seen as more accountable to the poor than the state. The latter is defined as a grouping of rent-seeking individuals, as a result of which, donors are turning to civil society to counter the governance predicament. As such, CSOs are contracted as external monitors by foreign donors or as agents to stimulate demand among poor people for effective service (Lister and Nyamugasira 2003: 95).

The second role given to CSOs under the IDM is one of service provider, as sub-contractors of the state. The collapse of the Keynesian model and twenty years of SAPs have transformed the developing state's role as service provider. Indeed, CSOs are viewed as the 'new patrons of the public interest' (Kamat 2004: 158) and, as such, they are sub-contracted to deliver the social programmes that were formerly under the state's jurisdiction. The trend towards 'ex-ante' reforms, rather than the conditionality model, has favoured a switch from project-oriented aid to programme aid (Lister and Nyamugasira 2003).

The third role given to civil society under the IDM is undeniably to provide legitimacy to the reforms. CSOs are perceived as grassroots organizations whose members participate directly in the projects and thus benefit from direct support. As such, CSOs are seen as accountable to the poor, whom they represent through this 'bottom-up' approach. Kamat underlines that there has been a curious shift in who bears the legitimate responsibility in promoting the public good:

In a curious flip-flop of what served as a universal conceptual frame for development planning, the state, today, is represented as fragmented by private interests (otherwise referred to as corruption), and hence inept at representing the will of the people, whereas civil society is seen as the honest broker of 'the people's interests'.

(Kamat 2004: 160)

For Biekart, there are two main questions linked to the confusion created by the use of the concept of civil society: (1) who belongs to it? and (2) what are its properties? (Biekart 1999: 32).

Lafortune's analysis of the Bank's enthusiasm for the concept addresses Biekart's questions by arguing that the institution's take on civil society brings us back to the contemporary actor's triangle – state, civil society, private sector. It modifies civil society's legitimate sphere of intervention by reducing, on the one hand, its legitimate composition – only the poor are legitimate interlocutors, non-poor voices are disregarded – and on the other hand by confirming civil society's participation in very specific areas of debate (Lafortune 2003). This trend raises questions related to the IDM's conceptual absentee: citizenship.

Redefining political society

Under the neo-liberal model, the concept of citizenship is reduced to the technicalities of participating in the electoral process. Stripped of their political implications, the mechanisms of participation are the market and, through an identity of producer/consumer, citizens seek to maximize their individual interests. The ultimate citizen right is that of the individual who, as such, must be granted the greatest freedom possible. That is, the state's jurisdiction should be 'restricted to a bare minimum as any positive role impinges on the rights of the individual' (Taylor 1998: 24). This new type of 'market citizenship' clashes with the values and norms of the former post-war 'social democracy' model. In this new model, civil society has an over-arching importance, as it is the realm in which participation takes place, while the political arena is shrinking:

This [civil society] is now the primary site of citizens' associations and is the terrain upon which the citizens interact with other individuals and grouping, and upon which citizens compete with one another. Civil society becomes the key site of socio-economic struggle, replacing political society as the key site of political struggle.

(Taylor 1998: 26)

Citizenship is closely linked to the notion of rights: political, civil and socio-economic. However, addressing the question of rights raises political issues closely related to power relations and resource allocation. In focusing on civil society, rather than citizenship, the IDM is able to bypass the realm of 'political society', which Biekart defines as: 'an intermediate realm of actors (political parties) and institutions (election, legislature), mediating, articulating and institutionalizing the relations between the State and civil society' (1999: 58). It could thus be argued that the IDM aid mechanisms specifically bypass the realm of political society in indebted countries, in order to complement the technocratic approaches linked to the institutional reforms that it also promotes. As observed by UNRISD, there is a need to tackle the political implications that might arise from an increasing technocratic mode of governance:

> Pressure to standardize macroeconomic objectives encourages governments to restrict policy making to experts and insulate key economic institutions from democratic scrutiny. This may affect democratization in two ways. First, it may distort the structure of accountability by encouraging national authorities to be more responsive to financial markets and multilateral institutions than to fledgling parliaments and citizens. Second, social policies, which were crucial in consolidating Western democracies, may be treated as residuals of macroeconomic policy, and democratization that does not conform to neoliberal economic orthodoxy dismissed as populism.
> (United Nations Research Institute for Social Development 2000: 1)

The Bank's new enthusiasm for the concept of social capital reinforces this thesis. From Coleman to Fukuyama (and sometimes the ideas of Bourdieu), the concept of social capital has many definitions. However, it is Robert Putnam's work on the concept that has generated the most echoes at the Bank. Through this theoretical choice the concept is divorced from its political roots, ignoring power relations. Social capital is indeed increasingly used by the Bank in community-driven development and project ownership schemes, in a direct link to the IDM main pillars. However, as argued by Harriss, the Bank's take on social capital

> systematically evades issues of context and power. ... This mystification serves the political purpose of depoliticizing the problems of poverty and social justice and, in elevating the importance of 'voluntary association' in civic engagement, of painting out the need for political action.
> (Harriss 2002: 12)

Deprived of its political dimensions, the concept of social capital may serve as a technical response to social issues that are highly political by bypassing questions that are linked to notions of rights and social justice (Harriss 2002; Ponthieux 2003; Bebbington *et al.* 2004).

Jayasuriya illustrates this in the context of the necessity to manage the rise of unemployment following the Asian economic crisis:

Political management of unemployment was as much an ideological experience as a policy venture mainly because the intent of many of these social programs was to shift the burden of unemployment on to communities or individuals. ... Therefore, building on notions such as social capital or community empowerment, social programs have had the effect of turning unemployment from a social issue or a social problem to one of social conduct.

(Jayasuriya 2003: 2)

Absent in such conceptions are references to the notion of 'rights'. In redirecting the state's traditional function as provider of rights (civil, political and socio-economic), civil society is entrusted with the responsibility for promoting the common good. However, as civil society is becoming increasingly instrumental in the current technical management of social demands, the question of its actual representativeness demands further attention.

Hearn's study is pertinent in this regard. Her analysis reveals how bilateral and multilateral donors have contributed, throughout the 1990s, to building a very specific kind of 'civil society'. This donor support would come to reinforce civil society organizations:

foreign support to civil society in all three countries [Ghana, South Africa and Uganda] is not about the breadth and depth of actually existing, largely rural based civil society. Donors are not funding the popular sector of society, but are strengthening a new African elite committed to the promotion of a limited form of procedural democracy and structural-adjustment-type economic policies in partnership with the West. The sixty or so organizations that I identified as donor-funded form the core of the kind of liberal civil society that is being 'socially engineered' in Africa.

(Hearn 1999: 4)

This hijacking of civil society dislocates the concept from its normative definition as representative of 'grassroots' organizations and the voice of popular demands. Indeed, Hearn highlights the issue of the representativeness of NGOs and the conflicting interests they might be defending:

'local associations' and NGOs ... are not necessary democratically representative organizations, nor democratically accountable, and might be attractive because they appear to offer the possibility of a kind of democracy through 'popular participation', but without the inconveniences of contestational politics and the conflicts of values and ideas which are a necessary part of democratic politics.

(Hearn 1999: 8)

Thus, while the new development model is presented under the umbrella of inclusiveness, it seems that, in practice, it might actually do the exact opposite. In fact, while a small proportion of society is given a voice on apolitical matters, the concepts of rights and democracy are being forgotten, as are, at the same time, parliaments and political parties.

Conclusion

The World Bank's discursive shift towards a more social vocabulary is an undeniable legacy of the Wolfensohn presidency (Jones and Hardstaff 2005; Action Aid and coll. 2005). Never before had the Bank pushed an agenda recognizing civil society's participation, country ownership and a multi-actor partnership as a prerequisite for poverty reduction and economic growth in countries under reform. Through the CDF, but more importantly the PRSPs, the institution's new model has been challenged by critics who have suggested that this discursive shift within the Bank is but a public relations exercise. This chapter has challenged this analysis of the Bank's IDM by suggesting that the political impacts of the IDM are more than discursive. Indeed, building on two decades of structural adjustment programmes, the IDM champions a technocratic form of governance which, combined with its functionalist view of civil society, is depoliticizing the notion of citizenship in countries under reform.

This mutation from 'citizenship' to 'civil society' brings us to a slippery road where 'rights' are replaced by mechanisms that 'target' the poor. This process is depoliticizing redistributional issues. At the heart of this transformation resides the highly political question of who owns the legitimate right to make demands on the state.

On a long-term basis, this type of social management will indeed be cost-effective for governments under reform who already have difficulties addressing their debt servicing. However, this trend also marks an end to the ideal of universal provision, and simultaneously narrows the population's legitimate opportunities to make political demands. While African parliaments' track records have been far less than perfect, they remain nonetheless the main institutional vehicle for democratic representation.

However, one must question the residual political role that has been allocated to the people's representatives in the IDM (Jones and Hardstaff 2005; Action Aid and coll. 2005). The World Bank has recently acknowledged the importance of greater participation for members of parliaments within the PRSP process and, as such, the research initiatives on the subject have been multiplying (World Bank at http://www.worldbank.org/wbi/; Jones and Hardstaff 2005). However, the technocratic basis of the IDM suggests little future possibilities for members of parliament to not only challenge PRSP content but, on a larger scale, to support alternative models to the main economic orthodoxy supported by the Bank.

Notes

1 While bilateral and multilateral donors argue in favour of an aid system that allocates funds towards the poorest countries with a relatively good institutional environment, the reality of the political and economic interests of bilateral donors is still influencing the aid flow. For an illustration of the Canadian case see Campbell and Hatcher 2004.

2 A 'relatively good policy environment' is to be defined as having

> 'relatively good' policies for productive use of development assistance for poverty reduction, the World Bank requires an overall score of at least 3.0 on the Bank's Country Policy and Institutional Assessment (CPIA) index. Of 136 countries rated in 2003, 112 had CPIAs of 3.0 or greater. A rating of 3.0 on the CPIA scale in a policy area indicates that there are deficiencies in one or more of the criteria being rated in that area, while a rating of 4.0 indicates that a country is dealing quite effectively with most issues in the policy area.
>
> (World Bank 2004: 14)

3 The World Bank's 'Tool Kit: Commitment to Reform Diagnostics, Institutional Analysis and Assessment' is available at: http://www1.worldbank.org/public-sector/toolkitscommitment.htm?OpenDocument

4 From the mid-1980s on, the conditionalities imposed on borrowing states not only multiplied, but also gradually reached beyond the sphere of macroeconomics and finance, engaging with social, human, institutional and environmental issues. Harrigan *et al.*'s (1995) extensive historical analysis of conditionalities is quite revealing on the subject.

References

Action Aid and coll. (2005) 'Kept in the dark: A briefing on parliamentary scrutiny of the IMF and World Bank', Briefing by Action Aid, Bretton Woods Project, the Development Gap, Christian Aid, One World Trust, Afrodad and World Development, April.

Bebbington, A., Guggenheim, S., Olson, E. and Woolcock, M. (2004) 'Exploring the Social Capital Debates at the World Bank', *Journal of Development Studies* 40(5), 33–64.

Biekart, K. (1999) *The Politics of Civil Society Building: European Private Aid Agencies and Democratic Transition in Central America*, Amsterdam: International Books and the Transnational Institute.

Campbell, B. (1996) 'Débats actuels sur la reconceptualisation de l'Etat par les organismes de financement multilatéraux et l'USAID', *Politique Africaine* 61,18–28.

——(2000) *An Overview of Governance*, commissioned paper prepared for the International Development Research Centre (IDRC), Montreal: University of Quebec at Montreal.

——(2002) 'Stratégies de lutte contre la pauvreté en Afrique: Enjeux de développement et de sécurité', presentation to the *Forum sur l'Afrique Centre Canadien pour le Développement de la Politique Etrangère*, Department of Political Science, Faculty of Political Science and Law, University of Quebec at Montreal, 8 February.

Campbell, B. and Hatcher, P. (2004) 'Existe-t-il encore une place pour la coopération bilatérale? Réflexions à partir de l'expérience canadienne', *Revue Tiers Monde* XLV, 179, 666–87.

Culpeper, R. (1997) *The Multilateral Development Banks: Titans or Behemoths?*, vol. 5, Ottawa: Institut Nord-Sud.

Development Assistance Committee (1996) *Shaping the 21st Century: The Contribution of Development Co-operation*, Paris: OECD.

Dollar, D. and Levin, V. (2004) *The Increasing Selectivity of Foreign Aid, 1984–2002*, World Bank Policy Research Working Paper no. 3299, Washington DC: World Bank.

Edwards, M. (2004) *Civil Society*, Cambridge: Polity.

EURODAD (2002) *Moving Beyond Good and Bad Performance*, Brussels, June. Available at http://www.eurodad.org

Gore, C. (2004) 'MDGs and PRSPs: Are Poor Countries Enmeshed in a Global–Local Double Bind?', *Global Social Policy* 4(3), 277–83.

Grusky, S. (comp.) (2000) *The IMF and World Bank Backed 'Poverty Reduction Strategy Papers'*, Comments from Southern Civil Society. Globalization Challenge Initiative. Available at http://www.challengeglobalization.org/html/prsp_may2000.shtml

Harrigan, J., Mosley, P. and Toye, J. (1995) *Aid and Power*, vol. 1, New York: Routledge.

Harrison, G. (2004) 'Understanding the Persistence of Neoliberalism in Africa: From Boundaries to Frontiers', paper presented to the conference 'Neoliberalism Neo-liberalism: A Stock-take after Three Decades', Institute of Social Studies, The Hague, Netherlands, 9–11 September.

Harriss, J. (2002) *Depoliticizing Development: The World Bank and Social Capital*, London: Anthem Press.

Hayami, Y. (2003) *From the Washington Consensus to the Post-Washington Consensus: Recent Changes in the Paradigm of International Development Assistance*, in collaboration with Suzanne Akiyama, Foundation for Advanced Studies on International Development, no. 2003-001. Available at http://www.fasid.or.jp/chosa/kenkyu/ senryaku/kaihatsu/pdf/software/e2003-001.pdf

Hearn, J. (1999) 'Foreign Aid, Democratisation and Civil Society in Africa', Discussion Paper 368, Institute of Development Studies, Sussex.

Jayasuriya, K. (2003) 'Civil Society, Regulatory State and the New Anti Politics', Asia Research Center, unpublished paper.

Jones, T. and Hardstaff, P. (2005) 'Denying Democracy: How the IMF and World Bank Take Power From People', World Development Movement, London, May, available at http://www.wdm.org.uk

Kamat, S. (2004) 'The Privatization of Public Interest: Theorizing NGO Discourse in a Neoliberal Era', *Review of International Political Economy* 11(1), 155–76.

Lafortune, A. (2003) 'La résurgence du concept de société civile dans le discours politique contemporain', political science dissertation, University of Quebec at Montreal.

Lister, S. and Nyamugasira, W. (2003) 'Design Contradictions in the "New Architecture of Aid"? Reflections on Uganda and the Roles of Civil Society Organisations', *Development Policy Review* 21(10), 93–106.

Marshall, A., Woodroffe, J. and Skell, P. (2001) *Policies to Roll-Back the State and Privatise? Poverty Reduction Strategy Papers Investigated*, London: World Development Movement.

McGee, R. and Norton, A. (2000) 'Participation in Poverty Reduction Strategies: a Synthesis of Experiences with Participatory Approaches to Policy Design, Implementation and Monitoring', Institute of Development Studies, Working Paper 109.

Oxfam International (2001) *Making PRSPs Work: The Role of Poverty Assessments*, Washington DC: Oxfam International.

Ponthieux, S. (2003) 'Que faire du "social capital"?', Institut National de la Statistique et des Etudes Economiques, Paris. Série des Documents de Travail de la Direction des statistiques démographiques et sociales, Département des prix à la consommation, des ressources et des conditions de vie des ménages, N°F0306, Division 'Conditions de vie des ménages', Septembre.

Powell, J. (2004) 'The World Bank Policy Scorecard: The New Conditionality?', *At Issue*, Bretton Woods Project, November, available at http://www.brettonwoodsproject.org/atissuecpia

Stiglitz, J. (1998) 'More Instruments and Broader Goals: Moving Toward the Post Washington Consensus', the 1998 WIDER Annual Lecture, 7 January, Helsinki, available at http://www.wider.unu.edu/stiglitz.htm

——(1999) 'Whither Reform? Ten Years of the Transition', World Bank Annual Bank Conference on Development Economics, 28–30 April.

Taylor, L. (1998) *Citizenship, Participation and Democracy: Changing Dynamics in Chile and Argentina*, London: Macmillan Press.

Thomas, M. (2004) 'Can the World Bank Enforce its own Conditions?', *Development and Change* 35(3), 485–97.

United Nations Research Institute for Social Development (2000) 'What Choice Do Democracies Have in Globalizing Economies? Technocratic Policy Making and Democratization', report of the UNRISD International Conference, Geneva, 27–8 April.

Van Rooy, A. (1997) 'The Civil Society Agenda: Switching Gears in the Post Cold War World', presented to the International Studies Association Panel on 'Foreign Aid in the Post Cold War Era', Toronto, March.

Whaites, A. (2000) *PRSP's: Good News for the Poor? Social Conditionality Participation and Poverty Reduction*, produced by the Policy and Advocacy Department, World Vision UK Partnership Offices, Milton Keynes.

Wilks, Alex and Fabien Lefrançois (2002) *Blinding with Science or Encouraging Debate? How World Bank Analysis Determines PRSP Policies*, World Vision International and Bretton Woods Project. Available at http://www.brettonwoodsproject.org/topic/adjustment/a30blinding.html

Williamson, J. (2000) 'What Should the World Bank Think About the Washington Consensus?', *The World Bank Research Observer* 15(2), 251–64.

Wolfensohn, J. D. (1999) 'A Proposal for a Comprehensive Development Framework: a Discussion Draft', 21 January, Washington DC: World Bank.

Wood, A. (2004) *One Step Forward, Two Steps Back: Ownership, PRSPs and IFI Conditionality*, Department of International Policy and Advocacy, World Vision International, Milton Keynes. Available at http://www.globalempowerment.org

World Bank (1998) *Assessing Aid: What Works, What Doesn't, and Why*, New York: Oxford University Press.

——(1999) *Annual Review of Development Effectiveness*, Hanna Nagy and coll., Operations Evaluation Department, Washington DC: World Bank.

——(2000a) *Comprehensive Development Framework: Country Experience Report (March 1999–July 2000)*, World Bank, September.

——(2000b) 'Learning to Partner: Engaging Civil Society', NGO and Civil Society Unit, Washington DC: World Bank.

——(2000c) 'Working Together: The World Bank's Partnership with Civil Society', NGO and Civil Society Unit, Washington DC: World Bank.

——(2001) *World Development Report 2000/2001: Attacking Poverty*, New York: Oxford University Press for the World Bank.

——(2002) *Low-Income Countries Under Stress*, Washington DC: World Bank, April.

——(2004) *2003 Annual Review of Development Effectiveness: The Effectiveness of Bank Support for Policy Reform*, Operations Evaluation Department, World Bank, Washington DC. Available at http://www.worldbank.org/oed

——(2006) 'Africa – Comprehensive Development Framework (CDF)', available at http://web.worldbank.org/WBSITE/EXTERNAL/COUNTRIES/AFRICAEXT/ 0,contentMDK:20236245~menuPK:488501~pagePK:146736~piPK:226340~theSite PK:258644,00.html (accessed 23 May 2006).

11 The World Bank as conveyor and broker of knowledge and funds in Argentina's governance reforms

Maria Pía Riggirozzi

Introduction

This study explores the role of the World Bank in two governance reforms that have been carried out in Argentina since the mid-1990s: judicial reform and anti-corruption policies. In exploring this role, the research seeks to analyse whether the World Bank acted either as simply a 'conveyor' in the transfer of funds and knowledge or as a 'broker' articulating funding strategies with global and local knowledge for the implementation of politically sensitive reforms on the ground.

By implication, the study focuses on two main aspects of James Wolfensohn's presidency, namely, governance and knowledge management. Since the early 1990s, the World Bank's ideological and financial leverage has been enhanced by the development of a knowledge management system for the creation, dissemination and implementation of knowledge related to what constitutes good economic policy. During the last ten years, both the governance and knowledge management agendas attracted the interest of policy-oriented researchers and advocacy campaigners who focused largely on three broad areas of analysis: (i) changes in the institutional and organisational culture of the Bank; (ii) contradictions between technical and political approaches to development; and (iii) new practices in World Bank operations.

Little empirical work has been done on exploring the implications of governance and knowledge management for policy processes in developing countries. Likewise, as studies of the World Bank tend to describe it as a uniform institution, less attention has been paid to how different units *within* the Bank engage with local actors in the promotion of development goals via financial and non-financial means. By overlooking the different patterns of involvement in governance reforms by different World Bank units, existing literature on the World Bank has also subsumed the approach to knowledge, power and policy change either to an almost linear dynamic of knowledge diffusion and lesson drawing (see Finnemore 1996; Park 2005), or to considering it as a result of authoritative knowledge imparted by the Bank (Gilbert *et al.* 2000; Pincus and Winters 2002). Even scholars writing from a critical perspective, albeit from different analytical angles, have reproduced some of these limitations, overemphasising the World Bank's ideological power in facilitating the global expansion of neo-liberal ideas (see Wade 2002; Cammack 2004).

This chapter argues that despite the leverage of the World Bank as a financial institution and a 'knowledge bank', implementation of reform programmes in developing countries is embedded in complex policy processes in which the dominance of a particular actor or paradigm *vis-à-vis* others is not simply sustained by coercive, disciplinary power of the lender. That is, policy change does not entail a one-way exercise of power and imposition of paradigms, but rather, its capacity to amalgamate and find compromise between the World Bank and local knowledge(s). This capacity defines its role as a 'norm-broker'.

This chapter is divided into four parts. The first part analyses the nature and task of promoting new governance reforms for development. The second part discusses knowledge management within the Bank and the implications of knowledge transfer for the institutionalisation of ideas and policy change. The third part defines the World Bank as a 'norm-broker' and its relevance for reform implementation. The fourth part explores empirical patterns of the role of the Bank in Argentina's judicial reform and anti-corruption processes.

The (a)political task of promoting governance for development

Governance has been promoted by the World Bank since the early 1990s, and subsequently by other international institutions, heralding a new normative agenda that promotes pro-market institutional and public administration reforms (World Bank 1994, 2000a). Three main trends pushed forward this agenda within the Bank. First, the negative consequences on sustainable development and growth of economic reform programmes strongly advocated by international financial institutions in developing countries during the 1980s and early 1990s (Edwards 1995; Birdsall and Graham 2000). Second, critical internal portfolio and performance assessments, in particular the Morse Report and the Wapenhans Report, had highlighted deficiencies in World Bank compliance with internal procedures and low levels of return in project management as the main issues affecting the Bank's development impact (Caufield 1996: 259–60; Rich 2002: 27–8). Third, the arrival of James Wolfensohn as president in 1995, which introduced a more 'holistic' development agenda aimed at combining conventional neo-liberal principles with new normative prescriptions for participation, transparency and accountability (see World Bank 2000a).

Although governance as a new approach to development was already in vogue before the arrival of Wolfensohn, his presentation of the Comprehensive Development Framework (CDF) in his first speech to the Bank's Annual Meeting placed it at the centre of its organisational agenda. The

CDF sought to reconcile the Bank's neo-liberal paradigm of downsizing of the state, promoted by the Washington Consensus, with new and politically sensitive goals relating to the state and its institutional capacity to effective investment for development and economic growth (Stiglitz 1999).

Some scholars saw the approach framed within the CDF as a green light for the promotion of new political tasks and new intrusive conditionality (Kapur and Webb 2000; Santiso 2002). Yet, to avoid legal issues or ambiguities in relation to its constitutive mandate (see World Bank 1992: art. IV, section 10), World Bank programmes have sought to advance a liberal economic agenda that does not focus on the political aspects of such reforms, leaving aside considerations of 'democratic' governance (Kiely 1998; Fine 2002).

In 1997, a new institutional infrastructure was set up by Wolfensohn to adjust its institutional and operational practices. It amounted to the most radical reorganisation of the institution since its inception. This reorganisation was based on a proposal that was later known as the Strategic Compact, a corporate strategy that provided new operational guidelines for staff involvement in new areas of assistance, and new financial and non-financial instruments to enhance the influence and performance of World Bank programmes (World Bank 1999, 2003). In short, while the CDF reframed a normative agenda for sustainable development, the Strategic Compact provided the justification and the tools for its involvement in new areas of reform via financial and non-financial activities. The following section concentrates on knowledge as the new centrepiece for the promotion of policy change in developing countries.

Knowledge management and the World Bank

The emphasis on governance and knowledge management paralleled discussions within and outside the World Bank on the negative effects of Washington Consensus policies on growth and poverty reduction in developing countries, and on the effectiveness of conditionality as an instrument to ensure compliance with reforms promoted by international financial institutions (Caufield 1996; Killick *et al.* 1998; Collier 2000).

Traditionally, conditionality was an effective mechanism for enforcing externally promoted policy change in areas of macroeconomic reform such as trade liberalisation, structural adjustment and privatisation. Particularly during the 1980s, the leverage of conditionality was enhanced by the circumstances of debt crisis, which had resulted in highly restricted international financial markets that prevented developing countries from gaining access to private capital (Stallings 1992: 43–4). However, the easing of the international market during the 1990s changed the position of international financial agencies *vis-à-vis* the 'free-of-condition' private market. In this context, it was argued that the imposition of loan conditionality by donors failed to bring about policy change because borrower countries lacked 'ownership of reform policies' (Collier 1997, 2000; Killick 1998).

Knowledge management was sought as a critical resource that had the potential to affect incentives and policy choices within and outside the Bank. Even though the World Bank has always been recognised as a major source of development ideas and economic development research, Wolfensohn's administration envisioned knowledge as a powerful asset within the Bank's operational strategies (Denning 2000). Wolfensohn stated:

> We have been in the business of researching and disseminating the lessons of development for a long time. But the revolution in information technology increased the potential value of these efforts by vastly extending their reach. To capture this potential, we need to invest in the necessary systems, in Washington and worldwide, that will enhance our ability to gather development information and experience, and share it with our clients. We need to become, in effect, the Knowledge Bank.
>
> (1996: 7)

Efforts to integrate money and knowledge within its work included: reorganising the administrative structure to reflect the new mission; articulating in-house and outside knowledge into codified knowledge, creating standards and best practices; and developing networks that cut across units and regional divisions to provide support for Bank staff in issues related to the development paradigm and aid assistance. These networks have been defined thematically; for instance, Environment and Socially Sustainable Development (ESSD), Human Development (HD), Finance and Private Sector Infrastructure (FPSI) and Poverty Reduction and Economic Management (PREM) (World Bank 2002, 2003).

In 1999 staff training activities traditionally carried out by the Economic Development Institute were merged with new capacity building courses for staff and new policy actors in developing countries in the World Bank Institute (WBI). These activities complemented the normative and conceptual guidance provided by the Development Economics Research Group (DECRG), 'the engine of knowledge generation *par excellence*' (Reinikka 2004, interview, 20 May).

The capacity to generate empirical data and to capitalise on an institutional memory identified as the 'knowledge bank' has been a powerful mechanism to justify and legitimise specific policy ideas. Yet, as knowledge is context-dependent, a key explanatory challenge is to assess the significance of the Bank's knowledge in the interplay between actors, incentives and contextual factors. In other words, the challenge is to explain knowledge as a powerful resource without reducing it to a stand-alone or abstract explanatory factor. With this in mind, the following section engages in a critical debate of knowledge and power and outlines a framework to analyse the promotion of governance reforms in Argentina.

Knowledge, money and the World Bank

Mobilisation of knowledge is a key resource for broadening consensus and legitimacy around certain issues for the implementation of politically sensitive reforms. Through the creation and support of certain policy ideas, the World Bank 'frames' the ways in which major topics in development and development economics are conceptualised and packaged for policy implementation (Bøås and McNeill 2004). According to Sending, the capacity to frame or conceptualise knowledge into facts, concepts or theories reinforces the ideological power of convincing others '*that* a certain phenomenon is a problem', and 'that this problem is best resolved in a certain way' (Sending 2004: 68, italics in the original). From this perspective, the World Bank's financial weight and authority as a multilateral development institution confers on the Bank a unique capacity to combine its knowledge-based predicaments with financial strategies to pursue policy reform in developing countries.

Yet, as this chapter suggests, the materialisation of knowledge into policies is a process that is embedded in political, institutional and economic contexts in which actors' incentives can favour or inhibit policy change. Policy ideas, such as those framed within the World Bank's development paradigm, do not evolve in a political (and ideological) vacuum. Actors transmit, contest, or modify certain paradigmatic models and, therefore, facilitate or inhibit the percolation and materialisation of ideas into public policies and institutional forms. Thus, in order to analyse the role of the World Bank in governance reforms in Argentina, it is important to understand how different actors and 'knowledge(s)' shape policy-making processes and policy outputs (Stone 2002: 139). In addressing these issues, this chapter puts forward three arguments:

- The capacity of the World Bank to produce and diffuse knowledge on what constitutes good economic policy (good governance) is a powerful ontological instrument affecting the way people perceive and think of economic development. Thus, production and diffusion of knowledge has become a critical factor within the structure of power and global scope of the World Bank, since it enhances the capacity of the Bank to frame issues and outline solutions.
- Knowledge is an important resource within the World Bank's power structure, in that it is mutually reinforcing with financial capabilities. Yet 'knowledge transferred' is not necessarily 'knowledge taken'. The implementation of politically sensitive reforms in developing countries is intimately associated with the capacity of the World Bank to mobilise financial and knowledge resources via pro-reform networks with local actors.
- The ontological power of the World Bank's knowledge and its instrumentalisation into policy practices defines a new role for the World Bank

as a 'norm-broker'. Therefore, the ability of the Bank to translate knowledge into instruments of policy reform depends on its capacity to act as a 'norm-broker', engaging with local actors for the implementation of policies on the ground.

The cases of judicial reform and anti-corruption analysed in this chapter show that, in the combination of funding and knowledge, Bank staff face a dilemma: either they promote governance-related programmes on the basis of pre-conceived ideas of what constitutes good policies and good reforms, or Bank staff engage with local experts to compromise and amalgamate positions, and utilising joint expertise in the framing of policy reforms and their implementation. Policy change emerges out of the relations between certain actors and World Bank staff, integrating contesting impulses into a broader consensus.

The arguments put forward here thus depart from models of social change that rely upon one-resource determinism studies of world politics, in which relations between developing countries' governments and international financial institutions are assumed to be solely determined by the financial leverage of the latter (for instance, Payer 1982; Wade 2002; Cammack 2004). To avoid narrow interpretations of the role of the World Bank in governance reforms in developing countries, it is important not to simply designate an actor or resource as the most powerful. It is simply analytically misguided to assume that local actors simply agree or consent, or are coerced or co-opted by external development or financial agencies. The argument advanced in this chapter suggests that the power of an international financial institution, such as the World Bank, to implement reforms is not linked to the leverage of conditional loans, but rather to its capacity to engage with key local actors to gain their consent to advance politically sensitive reforms. It emphasises the implications of the configuration of social relations, funds and knowledge for effective materialisation of political projects (also Cox 1986, 1993).

These arguments also depart from more recent constructivist approaches in international relations which associate the relationship between knowledge and policy to the prestige and reputation of international organisations that strongly influence what is considered good, desirable or appropriate behaviour (see Finnemore 1996; Barnett and Finnemore 1999: 711; also March and Olsen 2004). This approach has also been taken by new literature on 'knowledge-based development institutions', which mainly focuses on knowledge transfer as the main factor in inducing policy reform (King and McGrath 2004).

Despite contributing to new forms of conceptualising the role of international organisations, accounts of the World Bank as a 'knowledge-institution', 'intellectual actor', or 'knowledge bank' have two pivotal shortcomings with regards to the role and scope of the Bank. The first one concerns the lack of country-specific analysis that enables a comprehensive understanding of the process by which World Bank knowledge affects the implementation of reform programmes in developing countries. For instance, despite reference to partnership, capacity building, policy dialogues, and other knowledge-sharing activities between knowledge-based institutions and developing countries, research remains weak on the interplay between knowledge producers, knowledge users and policy-makers, as well as distinctive patterns of knowledge/policy and policy outcomes in the negotiation and implementation of policies. Furthermore, the emphasis on knowledge diffusion focuses on a one-way transfer of knowledge, as an a-contextual, uniform process by which ideas are transferred and implemented.

The second aspect refers to an a-critical understanding of the World Bank as a monolithic actor, failing to disaggregate the different involvement of certain agencies within the Bank in the task of knowledge management and the creation of methodological tools to approach development issues.

What follows is that the influence of knowledge on policy change is contextual and contingent, and that the power of the World Bank to influence policy change in developing countries is a process that entails not only the *transfer* of ideas, but rather their *institutionalisation*. In other words, policy change involves a dynamic process whereby societal arrangements between knowledge producers and knowledge users affect the path and thrust of reform implementation. These aspects are particularly relevant in the current context of international political economy, in which policy-making processes have become more decentralised as a consequence of the increasing number and capacity of actors who produce and contest knowledge on a global scale (Stone 2002: 125–31).

Rethinking the role of the World Bank

Most of the existing critical analysis of the World Bank as a financial and knowledge institution has emphasised the powerful role of the Bank in *framing* normative frameworks that circumscribe and justify course of action (Sending 2004; Bøås and McNeill 2004). From this perspective, some scholars emphasised the 'ideological' role of the World Bank in articulating neo-liberal ideas that are hierarchically reproduced as dogmatic paradigms (George and Sabelli 1994; Williams and Young 1994; Mehta 2001; Wade 2002). Knowledge, in short, supports and facilitates the Bank's role in the global expansion of capitalism by framing 'common-sense' and collective ideas (Cox 1993). With both funds to disburse and technical advice to give, the Bank can advance knowledge and enrich the data of certain actors, encouraging recipients to develop certain ideas around a problem and facilitate resources for putting them into practice. World Bank knowledge-related activities can, in fact, affect key actors' perceptions and policy-makers' decisions in the implementation of certain policies at the domestic level. However, it would be analytically misleading to assume that local actors are passive receptors of knowledge conveyed by the Bank.

In an attempt to enhance support for policy change, World Bank staff endorse power relations that in some cases reinforce and in other cases limit the implementation of policy reform. This is specially the case in sensitive policy areas such as governance-related reforms, in which the leverage of the World Bank to advance reform rests not only on its financial power, but also on its capacity to articulate broader bases of consensus with local actors. Sources and channels of knowledge articulation, the mechanisms through which knowledge is disseminated and the combination of financial and knowledge strategies crucially affect policy. Networking activities with local experts, NGO representatives, government officials and other key actors can be effective instruments for the Bank to gain access to policy-makers and key actors who directly affect policy processes.

The policy areas of judicial reform and anti-corruption in Argentina gather distinctive groups of experts that share knowledge about their particular policy area, as well as principles and beliefs which frame policy proposals. In this context, engaging with established networks and local actors, or creating new ones, can help the World Bank staff reproduce policy ideas that can percolate into the policy stream for the creation of institutions needed to enable a well-functioning market economy. Furthermore, the articulation of 'pro-reform networks' may neutralise opposition, thus strengthening the capacity of the World Bank to further promote governance-related norms.

In the literature on public policy, the notion of a network describes the interplay between different actors aiming to arrive at common grounds for policy proposals (Evans 2001). Rather than assuming policy networks act as mere transmission belts in the transfer of purposive agendas and normative principles, policy networks are defined as a configuration of different actors (nationally or internationally based) with recognised expertise in certain issue areas bound either by common goals, views and standpoints, or by their capacity to join resources to achieve certain goals. As argued by Stone, the status and prestige of the members of a network and their higher professional training and expertise regarding a particular problem 'is politically empowering and provides access to the political system' (Stone 1996: 88). In this study, it is suggested that the strength of relationships among actors involved in a network is not necessarily because they share common values, but rather because they endorse or promote particular policies or practices.

The capacity of the World Bank to engage in networks with local actors is inherently associated with its role as a 'norm-broker'. For the purposes of this study, a 'norm-broker' is defined as an *agent that generates, disseminates and institutes norms regarding a political-economic model*. The term 'norm' includes standardised knowledge and ideas, principles and practices that are usually framed into paradigms or policy proposals. This definition suggests that the brokerage role features three activities that are developed independently from each other, but are complementary to the work of the 'norm-broker'.

- As an agent in the *generation of norms*, the norm-broker creates and articulates policy paradigms combining pre-existing and new knowledge around which practices are oriented.
- As a *disseminator*, the norm-broker propagates policy ideas through different channels, such as capacity building; journals, reports, press releases; media websites and cyber forums; and direct contact with local actors and funded projects.
- As an *implementer*, the norm-broker not only utilises knowledge resources creating financial and non-financial instruments for policy change but also engages with local actors through knowledge-related activities for the implementation of programmes on the ground.

While articulation and dissemination of knowledge *per se* imply a unidirectional relation between knowledge producers and knowledge users, the implementation of knowledge implies a more direct impact aimed at changing existing policies and institutions at the local level. The ability to broker deals with key local actors that integrate World Bank best practices and 'global' knowledge with local, context-based knowledge and policy ideas significantly raises the likelihood that local actors implement politically sensitive reforms that are designed jointly between the World Bank and local experts (see also Mintrom 1997; Samoff and Stromquist 2001). From this point of view, the role of the Bank as a 'broker' does not imply a 'neutral' intervention in which its power is used for 'norm-building' (Payne 2001: 39; also Finnemore and Sikkink 1998). In this particular understanding of the concept of 'broker', there is an implicit assumption that the Bank does not act as an impartial facilitator of knowledge, but rather engages with local experts in order to drive through effective implementation of changes in politically sensitive areas of reform.

These arguments are particularly relevant for a country like Argentina, since a strong base of local experts that had worked on policy reform in the areas of the judiciary and anti-corruption existed prior to the arrival of the Bank's mission in the country. Furthermore, contesting ideas that are supported by local experts can be highly political, which explains why task managers may be inclined to act without local experts in the design and implementation of programmes, as this may endanger the transfer of resources, and thus negatively impact their staff performance evaluation. In this case, due to the lack of operational directions that require project managers to work with local experts, task managers either consider reform as a process of *transferring* blueprints and 'best practices', bypassing local experts by negotiating funded projects directly with the government, or engage with local expertise for the framing of the problem and the implementation of the solution.

The brokerage role articulating global and local expertise can make the difference between achieving consensual long-term reforms, or failure from the lack of support and legitimacy for the reform of institutions. It thus provides new grounds for further analysis of the role of the World Bank in policy processes in developing countries (see also Harrison 2005). From the point of view of The World Bank staff, reform either is considered to be the result of a process of amalgamation and compromises between actors' interests and ideas, or it is expected to result from a (rational) decision-making process based on an efficient, cost-benefit choice. In other words, while the role of the Bank as a mere 'conveyor' of funds and knowledge or paradigms underestimates the importance (and power) of local knowledge, the norm-brokerage gives prominence to local experts, and their expertise, considering it functional for effective implementation of changes in politically sensitive areas of reform.

The role of the World Bank in Argentina's governance reforms

The Bank units that have developed governance-related programmes within the judicial system and anti-corruption policy area for Latin America have been the Legal Department, the PREM network and the WBI. Although these units promote governance programmes, mainly via financial activities in the cases of the Legal Department and the PREM, and via knowledge activities in the case of the WBI, they vary in the ways and extent to which funding and knowledge are combined to advance reforms with local actors. Specifically, they differed in how World Bank's managers combined global/ World Bank knowledge and local actors' and experts' knowledge for the definition of priorities and courses of action for reform implementation.

To analyse the role of the World Bank in advancing governance reforms in Argentina, and to understand the ways and extent to which funding and knowledge were combined for that purpose, four points should be considered. First, the analysis of World Bank-supported governance reforms cannot be separated from competing interests and ideas, material capabilities, and contrasting agendas conveyed by local experts and World Bank managers. These are all important factors that affect the role of the Bank in advancing policy reform. Second, anti-corruption and judicial reforms cannot be detached from the context within which they unfolded. In the case of Argentina, it was characterised by a system of highly centralised governance in which presidential powers were systematically used to interfere with norms and procedures regarding the judiciary, particularly during the administration of Carlos Menem (1989–99). Third, the incursion of the executive branch of government in judicial matters made the judiciary its political arm that legitimised controversial procedures for implementing unpopular political and economic market-oriented reforms (Tedesco 2002; Helmke 2003). As a consequence, judicial independence, legitimacy and the rule of law were significantly undermined. Fourth, attempts to reform the system have been affected by a lack of political will among key decision-makers in the executive and the judiciary to modify the *status quo*, and a lack of support for initiatives presented by local experts.

At the national level, several public opinion polls confirmed the alarming deterioration of confidence in the judiciary and the rule of law in Argentina. According to Gallup, at the time of the democratic restoration, confidence in the judicial system was rated at 57 per cent, and by 1991 the percentage had fallen to 26, and by 1993 to only 17 per cent (quoted in Blair and Hansen 1994: 29). Another Gallup poll in 1994 showed that 72 per cent of respondents considered the judges 'too influenced by the government', and 69 per cent believed that the decisions of the Supreme Court were either 'extremely politicised' or 'very politicised' (Larkins 1998: 429, emphasis in original). These concerns were consistent with other surveys and analysis provided by bilateral organisations and international NGOs, such as Transparency International (TI), the Canadian Foundation for the Americas (FOCAL), and the United States Agency for International Development (USAID) (Moreno Ocampo 1993: 199; Manzetti 2000: 18). In 1998, TI's Corruption Perception Index positioned Argentina as one of the most corrupt countries in the world. The increasing appreciation of the costs of inefficient judiciaries for economic development was also reinforced by international financial institutions, such as the World Bank, the International Monetary Fund (IMF) and the Inter-American Development Bank (Miller-Adams 1999; Buscaglia and Dakolias 1996; World Bank 2001b; IMF 2004: 30).

In this context, President Carlos Menem's strategic response to increasing demands for transparency and accountability was pragmatic. A constitutional amendment pursued in 1994 ensured that, although policy and institutional changes were undertaken, the system of governance did not challenge the tight control of the executive over state institutions (Garcia Delgado 1997). For instance, notwithstanding efforts at reform by creating a National Judiciary Council, a Jury of Impeachment and a National Office of Ethics (ONEP), transparency and accountability did not reach further than the setting-up of an 'oversight' infrastructure. In any case, it failed to materialise given the lack of parliamentary agreement on membership, regulatory policies, norms and procedures. The control of the Congress by Menem's Peronist party from 1989 until 1997 enabled Menem to delay rule sanctioning that might have endangered its political manoeuvres and the executive's authority over the removal, as well as the appointment of judges to the Supreme Court (Bill Chavez 2004: 477). It was not until the victory of the opposition party, the Alianza, in the legislative elections of 1997, that a window of opportunity opened and the political context eased. Yet, representatives of the new institutions were not sworn in until the end of 1998, and in the case of the Judicial Council, it only began operating in early 1999, nearly five years after the promulgation of Argentina's new constitution (Finkel 2004: 72).

The structure of incentives was largely divergent and conflicting during Menem's administration (Hammergren 1998). Local actors that were working on proposals for reforming the sector found no interlocutors among the decision-makers and thus only technical, apolitical aspects related to certain regulations and the institutional façade were likely to percolate the policy stream. In other words, when reform proposals were pro-*status quo* and did not alter the internal balance of power that was grounded on a highly dependent judiciary, they were more likely to be supported by Menem's government. Proposals concerning politically sensitive goals related to the functioning of the system, access to justice, provincial governance and the decision-making process in the judiciary were missing from the executive's agenda. In the case of the judiciary, the judges of the Supreme Court were reluctant to undertake reforms that would modify the *status quo*, and the executive did not seek to discomfort an institutional branch so vital for the advancement of its political purposes (Bohmer 2003). Notwithstanding the work of local actors and the increasing demands from different sectors, opportunities for local experts and practitioners to influence policy formulation were often limited (Chayer 2003, interview, 1 December).

This affected the fate of the 'National Plan of Judicial Reform' that was drafted by local experts in 1998 with the support of the Minister of Justice, Ricardo Gil Lavedra, and presented (unsuccessfully) to the executive. The National Plan was the first local initiative based on earlier research conducted by local legal and business think-tanks and the Ministry of Justice (Garavano 2003, interview, 20 November; Lynch 2003, interview, 25 November). Specific attention was given to redesigning the administrative and human resources areas, introducing computerised systems, revamping the Judicial Office and redesigning the division of labour and flow of work, as well as the training of personnel (Plan Nacional de Reforma Judicial 1998). It targeted some politically sensitive issues such as access to justice, and also proposed the creation of a Centre of Judicial Policy and Management Supervision (www.reformajudicial.jus.gov.ar/materiales/plannac.htm. 8 December 2004). Yet, although the Ministry of Justice has the power to present bills and policy initiatives to parliament and to the executive, it has no powers of implementation and enforcement. This situation created disincentives and competing objectives regarding the ideas that informed reforms, the scope of reforms and the pace of reforms, discouraging further linkages between research and policy to work on common ground. However, this did not discourage the involvement and influence of the World Bank in judicial reform, as it was able to combine its financial instruments with its policy paradigm.

From the start, the involvement of the World Bank was shaped by the reluctance of the main domestic actors at the centre of the decision-making process. The judges of the Supreme Court were hesitant to undertake reforms that would change governance aspects of the judiciary, and the executive did not wish to discomfort an institutional branch deemed critical to advancing its political agenda. Therefore, in advancing judicial reform, World Bank staff faced two main dilemmas. The first related to bridging the gap between World Bank codified policies and ideas as best practices and the proposals put forward by local actors and experts in the country. The second concerned how to engage in politically divisive governance reform without contradicting the apolitical mandate of the Bank. In this context, the staff from the Bank's Legal Department faced the dilemma of either securing the adoption of loans by the government and overlooking local-based knowledge, or implementing policies by capitalising on local expertise and strengthening the capacity of local actors to implement those policies.

The political stance implicit in a reform programme supported by local actors made World Bank support difficult, since these conflicted with government incentives in the sector. In this case, the highly political nature of local knowledge conflicted with the Bank's apolitical, technical understanding of reforms, and therefore with its definition and priorities in relation to governance. However, the political incentives of the government, the judiciary and the policy paradigm of the World Bank's Legal Department, did not conflict. In effect, the Bank's Legal unit promoted a reform that targeted issues of court management rather than the politically sensitive goals of access and decision-making processes.

In 1998, the World Bank approved its first lending programme in the sector, the Model Court Development Project/PROJUM (PID 50713). PROJUM included a US$5 million loan aimed at identifying, establishing and evaluating conditions to support a judicial administrative reform. PROJUM was part of an overall legal reform programme to be replicated in other courts (World Bank 1998). So despite the highly political issues raised by the assessment reports and the public discussions with local experts, the Bank's Legal Department designed a programme of reform that narrowly focused on technical managerial aspects of the system related to court administration, and ignored the significant role of court officers.

The Bank's 'depoliticised approach' to judicial reform, to borrow Bøås and McNeill's (2004) concept, made its way onto the government's agenda. It also affected the context in which actors interacted. This is mainly because the Bank's interest in legal and judicial reform was not related to political aspects of the system, but rather to technical ones linked to the conditions that enable a sound investment climate and reduce the costs of commercial transactions (World Bank 2000b). From the point of view of the government, it found a less controversial ally in the World Bank's apolitical stance than in the local proposals (Abramovich 2003, interview, 10 December; Saba 2003, interview, 18 December). In addition, the approval of apolitical, technical loans gave useful signals in response to the uncertainties of private investors without changing the *status quo*. In this case, 'the capacity of funding its policy paradigms and ideas has sterilised local efforts' (Lynch 2003, interview, 25 November).

Nonetheless, the role of conveyor of funds and knowledge was not sufficient to enhance the capacity of the Bank to create an institutional basis for further policy formulation. Its legitimacy was limited and its intervention paradigm questioned by local experts who perceived that the World Bank's

Legal Unit sought to transfer funding and knowledge following a 'donor-driven agenda'. The experience of judicial reform thus shows that, despite the approval of the Bank-sponsored Model Court/PROJUM project, reforming an established institution like the judiciary with restricted participation is difficult to achieve. PROJUM failed because the Bank was not able to broker deals with local actors for the effective implementation of the reform, in particular with local experts within the Ministry of Justice, and lawyers and judges from the selected courts that would implement the policies. Not only have efforts under the Model Court failed to produce concrete results, but also a related project, 'Reform of Justice', under preparation and awaiting an approval date by the Board of the Bank, was cancelled in light of the difficulties experienced with PROJUM (unnamed World Bank task manager 2004, personal interview, 18 May).

In summary, in the case of judicial reform, the Bank acted as 'conveyor' of funds and paradigms, thus focusing on negotiation with the government and overlooking the role of local knowledge. This meant the fate of reform implementation was limited by contending knowledge and policy understanding. In contrast, the process of norm-brokerage in the case of anti-corruption was significant in integrating global/World Bank and local knowledge, and in establishing an effective pro-reform network, thus articulating a productive exchange between local experts, decision-makers and implementers. In this case, the PREM network and the WBI brought in local knowledge for both the framing of policies and their course of action, creating common grounds for the implementation of effective policy change.

Anti-corruption programmes supported by the World Bank were introduced in Argentina in late 1999, on the eve of a change in presidential administrations. In 2000, the Public Sector Group, in collaboration with research done by WBI and the Bank's Evaluation Department, released the 'Anti-corruption Diagnostic for Argentina'. The Bank presented an overview and recommendations to Fernando de la Rúa, who succeeded Menem after the general elections in October 1999. De la Rúa made combating corruption a major priority of the government, and during his first year in office he undertook new initiatives with the support of the PREM network and WBI.

Having experienced the crisis of rampant corruption, de la Rúa was forced to give a rapid and satisfactory response not only to his constituency, but also to donors and external investors. The change in government and the wide perception of 'bad governance' not only provided new opportunities for local experts and NGOs to influence policy-making and anti-corruption programmes, but also gave new opportunities for some World Bank staff to 'fill out' the normative vacuum. Again, Bank task managers involved in the promotion of good governance faced the dilemma of promoting governance programmes on the basis of pre-conceived ideas of what constitutes good policies and good reforms, or engaging with knowledge and local expertise for the framing of both the problem and the solution.

The experience of judicial reform had demonstrated that the lack of compromise with local experts for the design and implementation of policy reform was a formula that led to truncated results (Messick and Hammergren 2004, interviews, 17 December). Development assistance, in that case, was reduced to a process in which codified best practices were considered a commodity to be 'transferred' from the donor agency to a country. Moreover, although the Bank mission obtained government approval and secured loan disbursement, lack of consensus and support from local experts de-legitimised the bases for the implementation of the Bank-supported judicial reform. Evidence showed that the transfer of knowledge, and even the commitment on the part of government agencies to take that knowledge, was insufficient to assure success in the implementation of policies on the ground. Putting local knowledge 'in the driver's seat' was a critical lesson for Bank staff in terms of converting policy ideas into new institutions. This recognition led to a different mode of involvement by PREM and WBI in the field, and to a different dynamic between knowledge and compliance in the implementation of anti-corruption policies. Rather than conveying funds and policy paradigms, the Bank's managers from PREM and WBI fostered common ground 'by supplying not *motivation* but perhaps resources to enable the doers to do what they were already self-motivated to do' (Ellerman 2001: 38).

The change in incentives towards cooperation and exchange was recognised not only among the World Bank staff, but also among local actors. Local experts concerned with anti-corruption reappraised the role of the Bank in governance and acknowledged that particular units in the Bank and their managers were more inclined to combine knowledge and funds in pursuing reforms. They also acknowledged that engaging in networking activities with World Bank managers could, at the same time, be a vehicle to maximise their opportunities of visibility and influence in public policy. Ultimately, synergies for mutual learning between World Bank staff and local actors were based on a mutual need to improve anti-corruption policies at the local level.

Thus, in the case of judicial reform, linkages between local actors and World Bank staff were erratic and inconsistent. By contrast, in the case of anti-corruption engagement with civil society was a fundamental element in furthering reform. In this case, together with local experts and NGOs, in particular Poder Ciudadano, PREM and WBI designed operational tools and analytical work to put anti-corruption projects into practice (Colombo 2003, interview, 3 December; De Michele 2003, interview, 26 December). The WBI and PREM benefited from contributions and exchanges with national experts. They included Luis Moreno Ocampo and Roberto de Michele, founder and president of Poder Ciudadano, respectively, and consultants of WBI; Manuel Garrido, former member of Poder Ciudadano; Marcelo Colombo, head of the Department of Investigation of the Argentine Anti-corruption Office.

In Argentina, two projects were supported by PREM and WBI: a US$410,000 IDF grant approved in June 1999 to support the establishment of the Anti-corruption Office, and the Crystal Government Initiative, a component within a US$30,000,000 Modernisation of the State programme, aimed at enhancing transparency in public administration by disclosure of information. The main elements of the grants included: (i) enhancing the Anti-Corruption Office in areas such as conflicts of interests and standards of ethical conduct; profiling of corruption crimes that are reported to the law enforcement authorities; multiple employment in the Civil Service; unlawful enrichment; the witness protection act; and (ii) measures to stimulate the implementation of the provisions of the Inter-American Convention against Corruption in Argentina (Ministerio de Justicia y Derechos Humanos 2001). The Crystal Project complemented the efforts of the Anti-Corruption Office, as it enforced section 8 of the Fiscal Responsibility Law that establishes the disclosure of public information in relation to public funds (Razzotti 2003). While not explicitly targeting political aspects of preventing corruption but improving transparency in the public administration and modernisation of the state, the support of PREM and WBI helped to develop a system to monitor civil servants, policy-makers, politicians and party candidates. At the same time it opened new institutional channels through which to denounce illegal actions and bureaucratic discretion. Capitalising on local knowledge also helped the Bank to broaden its bases of legitimacy not only to implement programmes in the national arena, but also in other countries.

Networking with local experts and practitioners also reduced the likelihood of local resistance to the implementation of reform programmes. This aspect of consensus building reaffirms that policy change is inherently linked to the way actors articulate divergent ideas, funds and knowledge. The capacity of Bank staff to engage with local experts was not only critical to secure consensus, but also meant the difference between brokering knowledge and funds to mobilise critical support and a failed initiative that alienated crucial consensus.

Conclusion

A multi-year research programme on aid effectiveness, published by the World Bank, stated that while money has a big impact in reform, the knowledge-creation side of aid is the 'generator of reforms' (Dollar and Pritchett 1998: 47). Yet, this chapter has claimed that, despite its financial and knowledge leverage, the World Bank cannot implement its programmes on its own. In a country like Argentina, characterised by high levels of expertise that traditionally interacted and informed policy-making in different areas, the relation of knowledge, power and policy change varied as the Bank acted with or without local experts and their expertise. For instance, in the case of judicial reform, the World Bank Legal Unit was unable to ensure that reforms were implemented because the process was approached simply as a top-down dynamic of persuading the government to approve a pre-conceived reform agenda. This generated resistance and opposition from local experts and implementers of policies. In contrast, the case of anti-corruption illustrated that the staff from PREM and the WBI acknowledged reform as a process of amalgamation and compromise between a variety of actors' interests and knowledge-based proposals for reform.

These contrasting experiences also validate the argument that the World Bank is not a monolithic, uniform institution. The policy process of reform varied depending on the way and extent to which Bank staff sought either to 'transfer' or to 'broker' financial resources, best practices and local expertise to foster the implementation of such policies. Ultimately, the evidence relating to the implementation of governance-related reforms in Argentina provides new grounds for a more profound discussion about the political implications of World Bank involvement in policy-making in developing countries, and the way its promotion of governance reforms affects the institutional and political context in which local actors define political interests and resolve political disputes.

References

Barnett, M. and Finnemore, M. (1999) 'The Politics, Power and Pathologies of International Organizations', *International Organization* 53(4), 699–732.

Bill Chavez, R. (2004) 'The Evolution of Judicial Autonomy in Argentina: Establishing the Rule of Law in an Ultrapresidential System', *Journal of Latin American Studies* 36(3), 451–78.

Birdsall, N. and Graham, C. (2000) *New Markets, New Opportunities? Economic and Social Mobility in a Changing World*, Washington DC: Brookings Institution Press.

Blair, H. and Hansen, G. (1994) *Weighing in on the Scales of Justice. Strategic Approaches for Donor-Supported Rule of Law Programs*. Available at http://www.usaid.gov/our_work/democracy_and_governance/publications/pdfs/pnaax2-80.pdf (accessed 12 August 2003).

Bøås, M. and McNeill, D. (2004) 'Ideas and Institutions: Who is Framing What?', in Bøås, M. and McNeill, D. (eds) *Global Institutions and Development: Framing the World?*, London and New York: Routledge, 206–24.

Bohmer, M. (2003) *Igualadores Retóricos: Las Profesiones del Derecho y la Reforma de la Justicia en la Argentina*, Cuadernos de Análisis Jurídicos, Serie Publicaciones Especiales no. 15, Facultad de Derecho, Universidad Diego Portales, Santiago, Chile. File with author.

Buscaglia, E. and Dakolias, M. (1996) 'A Quantitative Analysis of the Judicial Sector: The Cases of Argentina and Ecuador', World Bank Technical Paper no. 353, Washington DC: World Bank.

Cammack, P. (2004) 'What the World Bank Means by Poverty Reduction and Why it Matters', *New Political Economy* 9(2), 189–211.

Caufield, C. (1996) *Masters of Illusion: The World Bank and the Poverty of Nations*, New York: Henry Holt.

Collier, P. (1997) 'The Failure of Conditionality', in Gwin, C. and Nelson, J. (eds) *Perspectives on Aid and Development*, Washington DC: Overseas Development Council, 51–74.

——(2000) *Consensus Building, Knowledge and Conditionality*. Online. Available at http://www.worldbank.org/research/abcde/washington_12/pdf_files/collier.pdf (accessed 3 June 2005).

Cox, R. (1986) 'Social Forces, States and World Order: Beyond International Relations Theory', in Keohane, R. (ed.) *Neorealism and Its Critics*, New York: Columbia University Press, 204–54.

——(1993) 'Gramsci, Hegemony and International Relations: An Essay in Methods', in Gill, S. (ed.) *Gramsci, Historical Materialism and International Relations*, Cambridge: Cambridge University Press, 49–66.

Denning, S. (2000) *The Springboard: How Storytelling Ignites Action in Knowledge-Era Organizations*, Boston MA: Butterworth Heinemann.

Dollar, D. and Pritchett, L. (1998) *Assessing Aid: What Works, What Doesn't, and Why*, World Bank Research Report. Available at http://www.worldbank.org/research/aid/presentation/sld003.htm (accessed 17 February 2005).

Edwards, S. (1995) *Crises and Reform in Latin America: From Despair to Hope*, New York: Oxford University Press.

Ellerman, D. (2001) 'Helping People Help Themselves: Toward a Theory of Autonomy-Compatible Help', Policy Research Working Paper Series 2693, Washington DC: World Bank.

Evans, M. (2001) 'Understanding Dialectics in Policy Network Analysis', *Political Studies* 49(1), 542–50.

Fine, B. (2002) 'The World Bank's Speculation on Social Capital', in Pincus, J. and Winters, J. (eds) *Reinventing the World Bank*, Ithaca NY and London: Cornell University Press, 203–21.

Finkel, J. (2004) 'Judicial Reform in Argentina in the 1990s: How Electoral Incentives Shape Institutional Change', *Latin American Research Review* 39(3), 56–80.

Finnemore, M. (1996) *National Interests in International Society*, Ithaca NY and London: Cornell University Press.

Finnemore, M. and Sikkink, K. (1998) 'International Norm Dynamics and Political Change', *International Organization* 52(4), 887–917.

Garcia Delgado, D. (1997) 'La Reforma del Estado en la Argentina: de la Hiperinflación al Desempleo Estructural', *Revista CLAD* 8. Available at http://www.clad.org.ve (accessed 15 July 2003).

George, S. and Sabelli, F. (1994) *Faith and Credit: The World Bank's Secular Empire*, Boulder CO: Westview Press.

Gilbert, C., Powell, A. and Vines, D. (2000) 'Positioning the World Bank', in Gilbert, C. and Vines, D. (eds) *The World Bank: Structure and Policies*, Cambridge: Cambridge University Press, 39–86.

Hammergren, L. (1998) *Political Will, Constituency Building and Public Support in Rule of Law Programs*, Centre for Democracy and Governance, Washington DC: USAID.

Harrison, G. (2005) 'The World Bank, Governance and Theories of Political Action in Africa', *The British Journal of Politics and International Relations* 7(2), 240–60.

Helmke, G. (2003) 'Checks and Balances by other Means Strategic: Defection and Argentina's Supreme Court in the 1990s', *Comparative Politics* 35(2), 213–30.

IMF (International Monetary Fund) (2004) *Report on the Evaluation of the Role of the IMF in Argentina, 1991–2001*, Independent Evaluation Office, Washington DC: IMF.

Kapur, D. and Webb, R. (2000) 'Governance-related Conditionalities of the International Financial Institutions', G-24 Discussion Paper Series 6, New York and Geneva: UNCTAD.

Kiely, R. (1998) 'Neo Liberalism Revised? Critical Account of the World Bank Concepts of Good Governance and Market Friendly Intervention', *Capital and Class* 64, 63–88.

Killick, T. with Gunatilaka, R. and Marr, A. (1998) *Aid and the Political Economy of Policy Change*, London: Routledge.

——(2004) 'Politics, Evidence and the New Aid Agenda', *Development Policy Review* 22(1), 5–29.

King, K. and McGrath, S. (2004) *Knowledge for Development?: Comparing British, Japanese, Swedish and World Bank Aid*, London: Zed Books.

Larkins, C. (1998) 'The Judiciary and Delegative Democracy in Argentina', *Comparative Politics* 30, 423–42.

Manzetti, L. (2000) 'Keeping Accounts: A Case Study of Civic Initiatives and Campaign Finance Oversight in Argentina', Working Paper 248, Baltimore: IRIS Center, University of Maryland.

March, J. and Olsen, J. P (2004) 'The Logic of Appropriateness', ARENA Working Papers, WP 04/09, Centre for European Studies, University of Oslo.

Mehta, L. (2001) 'The World Bank and its Growing Knowledge Empire', *Human Organization* 60(2), 189–97.

Miller-Adams, M. (1999) *The World Bank: New Agendas in a Changing World*, New York: Routledge.

Ministerio de Justicia y Derechos Humanos (2001) *Oficina Anti-corrupcion, Informe de Gestion 2001*, Diciembre, Buenos Aires: Ministerio de Justicia y Derechos Humanos.

Mintrom, M. (1997) 'Policy Entrepreneurs and the Diffusion of Innovation', *American Journal of Political Science* 41(3), 738–70.

Moreno Ocampo, L. (1993) *En Defensa Propia: ¿Cómo Salir de la Corrupción?*, Buenos Aires: Editorial Sudamericana.

Park, S. (2005) 'Norm Diffusion within International Organizations: A Case Study of the World Bank', *Journal of International Relations and Development* 8(2), 111–41.

Payer, C. (1982) *The World Bank. A Critical Analysis*, New York: Monthly Review Press.

Payne, R. (2001) 'Persuasion, Frames and Norm Construction', *European Journal of International Relations* 7(1), 37–61.

Pincus, J. and Winters, J. (2002) 'Reinventing the World Bank', in Pincus, J. and Winters, J. (eds) *Reinventing the World Bank*, Ithaca NY and London: Cornell University Press, 1–25.

Plan Nacional de Reforma Judicial (1998) Available at http://www.reformajudicial.jus.gov.ar/materiales/plannac.htm (accessed 17 November 2004).

Razzotti, A. (2003) *Case study: The Crystal Project (Argentina)*, file with author. Available at http://www1.worldbank.org/publicsector/egov/AntiCorEgovSeminar/OID%20Argentina%20presentation%20(Razzotti).ppt

Rich, B. (2002) 'The World Bank under James Wolfensohn', in Pincus, J. and Winters, J. (eds) *Reinventing the World Bank*, Ithaca NY and London: Cornell University Press, 26–53.

Samoff, J. and Stromquist, N. (2001) 'Managing Knowledge and Storing Wisdom? New Forms of Foreign Aid', *Development and Change* 32(4), 617–42.

Santiso, C. (2002) 'Governance Conditionality and the Reform of Multilateral Development Finance: The Role of the Group of Eight'. Available at http://www.g7.utoronto.ca/g7/governance/santiso2002-gov7.pdf (accessed 5 December 2005).

Sending, O. J. (2004) 'Policy Stories and Knowledge-based Regimes: The Case of International Population Policy', in Bøås, M. and McNeill, D. (eds) *Global Institutions and Development: Framing the World?*, London and New York: Routledge, 56–71.

Stallings, B. (1992) 'International Influence on Economic Policy: Debt, Stabilization, and Structural Reform', in Haggard, S. and Kauffman, R. (eds) *The Politics of Economic Adjustment*, Princeton NJ: Princeton University Press, 41–88.

Stiglitz, J. (1999) *Participation and Development Perspectives from the Comprehensive Development Paradigm*, remarks at the International Conference on Democracy, Market Economy and Development, Seoul, Korea, 27 February.

Stone, D. (1996) *Capturing the Political Imagination: Think Tanks and the Policy Process*, London: Frank Cass.

——(2002) 'Knowledge Networks and Policy Expertise in the Global Polity', in Higgott, R. and Morten, B. (eds) *Towards A Global Polity*, London and New York: Routledge, 124–44.

Tedesco, L. (2002) 'Argentina's Turmoil: The Politics of Informality and the Roots of Economic Meltdown', *Cambridge Review of International Affairs* 15(3), 469–81.

Tuozzo, M. F. (2004) 'World Bank, Governance Reforms and Democracy in Argentina', *Bulletin of Latin American Research* 23(1), 100–18.

Wade, R. (2002) 'US Hegemony and the World Bank: The Fight over People and Ideas', *Review of International Political Economy* 9(2), 215–43.

Williams, D. and Young, T. (1994) 'Governance, the World Bank and Liberal Theory', *Political Studies* XLII, 84–100.

Wolfensohn, J. (1996) *People and Development*, Annual Meeting Address, Washington DC: World Bank, October 1.

World Bank (1992) *Governance and Development: Issues and Constraints*, Washington DC: World Bank.

——(1994) *Governance: The World Bank's Experience*, Washington DC: World Bank.

——(1998) 'Project Appraisal Document: Model Court Development Project', Report no. 17459-AR, PREM and Argentina, Chile, Uruguay Country Managing Unit, Washington DC: World Bank.

——(1999) *World Development Report 1998/1999: Knowledge for Development*, New York: Oxford University Press.

——(2000a) *Reforming Public Institutions and Strengthening Governance: A World Bank Strategy*, Public Sector Group and PREM, Washington DC: World Bank.

——(2000b) *Country Assistance Strategy*, Country Management Unit Argentina, Chile and Uruguay PREM Network Latin America and Caribbean Regional Office, Washington DC: World Bank.

——(2001a) *World Development Report 2002: Building Institutions for Markets*, Washington DC: World Bank.

——(2001b) *Argentina Legal and Judicial Sector Assessment*, Legal Vice Presidency, Washington DC: World Bank.

——(2002) *Reforming Public Institutions and Strengthening Governance: A World Bank Strategy. Implementation Update Part 2*, Regional, DECRG and WBI Updates, Washington DC: World Bank.

——(2003) *Sharing Knowledge: Innovations and Remaining Challenges*, Washington DC: World Bank.

Interviews

Abramovich, Victor (2003) Interview with author. 10 December. Buenos Aires.
Chayer, Hector (2003) Interview with author. 1 December. Buenos Aires.
Colombo, Marcelo (2003) Interview with author. 3 December. Buenos Aires.
De Michele, Roberto (2003) Interview with author. 26 December. Buenos Aires.
Garavano, German (2003) Interview with author. 20 November. Buenos Aires.
Hammergren, Linn (2004) Interview with author. 17 December. Washington DC.
Lynch, Horacio (2003) Interview with author. 25 November. Buenos Aires.
Messick, Rick (2004) Interview with author. 17 December. Washington DC.
Reinikka, Ritva (2004) Interview with author. 20 May. Washington DC.
Saba, Roberto (2003) Interview with author. 18 December. Buenos Aires.

12 The missing link in development cooperation integrative frameworks

Revelations from Lebanon's post-war experience in donor-assisted administrative reform

Nisrine El Ghaziri

Introduction

Since the late 1990s, a development cooperation trend has emerged among donors calling for partnership between donors and facilitating programmatic leadership and ownership by the countries receiving aid. This trend came as a response to the failure of development aid to reduce poverty. The new paradigm has two main assumptions. The first assumption is that aid has a better chance to succeed when approaches among donors and between donors and recipients are integrated. The second assumption is that recipient leadership and ownership is necessary to implement changes on the ground. To put this paradigm into practice, development agencies developed integrative frameworks such as the World Bank's Comprehensive Development Framework (CDF) and the United Nations Development Assistance Framework (UNDAF).

The CDF, for instance, proposes a set of interrelated principles that promise to ensure the effectiveness of development cooperation (World Bank 2004). These principles are:

(i)   *long-term holistic vision*: it is postulated that successful development is more likely to be achieved when countries are consistently pursuing integrated and coherent policies and programs;

(ii) *country ownership*: it is assumed that development assistance is most effective when it is driven by demand from the country, rather than internal incentives among development agencies to supply certain types of assistance;

(iii) *country-led partnership*: effectiveness of development efforts is likely to increase when activities of stakeholders from the recipient country and the donor community are better coordinated and unified;

(iv) *results focus*: donors would need to move away from an almost exclusive focus on inputs and outputs (pressure to disburse), to outcomes (achieving sustainable development).

Though attractive, those principles may not succeed in all situations. One context that defies the notions of donor partnership and country leadership and ownership is one where domestic policy-making capacity is weak. Lebanon's post-war experience in administrative rehabilitation and reform is a case in point. Several international donor agencies rushed to assist in the government of Lebanon (GOL) rebuild its public service with little coordination between them. Lebanon's institutional infrastructure was weakened by a protracted civil conflict (1975 to 1989) and suffered structural deficiencies that predate this conflict. Policy-making capacity was particularly atrophied at the time when donors pledged assistance. As a consequence, national leadership of both administrative reform policies and multi-donor assistance was impossible, ownership was weak and donors disputed policy-making for an extended period of time.

This chapter examines how the World Bank in conjunction with other donors, such as the United Nations Development Programme (UNDP) and the European Union (EU), dictated and disputed Lebanon's post-war administrative reform over a ten-year period between 1992 and 2002. It argues that, in the absence of domestic policy-making capacity, the integrative principles of country leadership and ownership were not fulfilled. It also reveals that in the absence of such a capacity, donor competition for policy leadership fragmented the reform program and used it as an arena to claim the merits of their respective approaches to administrative reform. Ironically, this happened in an era characterized by consensus within the international donor community about managerialism – a public management approach that borrows private (business) values and tools – as a best practice to remedy public sector weaknesses.

The following section defines administrative reform and identifies related models. In separate sub-sections, it dissects the administrative reform approaches of the World Bank, EU and UNDP, who influenced the administrative reform policy of post-war Lebanon during the 1990s. This section also compares the policies of those donors. The third section describes Lebanon's policy and public service contexts. The fourth section discusses the inter-donor contest over policy-making. It draws attention to three simultaneous processes where donors filled the national policy vacuum, disputed policy-making in administrative reform and fragmented the reform program along donor-assisted packages. Based on Lebanon's post-war experience in administrative reform, the last section concludes by highlighting the importance of local policy-making capacity for partnership among donors and leadership, and ownership by the recipient country.

Models of administrative reform in the 1990s

Administrative reform is the induced systemic improvement of public sector operational performance. Policy can be explicit or implicit, but it underlies all programs of administrative reform. It implies the general orientations of administrative reform and lays down the framework of guidelines and the boundaries of policy space within which operational and detailed changes are to be made (Dror 1976: 127). Clear policy is necessary for a successful administrative reform program. Practice, however, indicates the commonness of multiplicity, shifts and displacement in goals, which are most likely to occur in contexts where administrative reform involves multiple actors over an extended period of time (Caiden 1991: 164).

Administrative reform has promoted different models of public administration across times and places. *Civil service reforms* prevailed during the 1960s, and centred on curbing patrimonial, amateur and spoils system administration. Typical interventions included structural overhauls based on models of Weberian ideal-type bureaucracies, budget reforms to prevent misappropriation and illegal expenditure, and the establishment of watchdog agencies for central control.

In the 1970s, civil service reforms were complemented by *automation*, which contributed to expediting services to citizens and transforming administrative philosophy and structure towards a greater entrenchment of the norms of efficiency, productivity, rationality, impartiality and other values associated with private or business management (Caiden 1969: 110, 116–17).

Under the pressure of the first wave of neo-liberal economic restructuring, *managerialism* – a predominant international approach to administrative reform premised on private business management – acquired the status of a best practice. Starting in the 1980s, managerialism gained momentum in the 1990s when its influence on the design of administrative reform programs became increasingly noticeable (Heredia and Ross Schneider 2003: 2–4). Managerial reforms came as a reaction to the inefficiency and rigidity caused by the over-regulation and over-centralization of civil service reforms. The administrative cures of managerialism prescribed that a *rules-bound administration*, where senior bureaucrats spend their time advising on making and revising of rules and junior staff rigidly implementing them, be replaced by a *performance-bound administration*. Here, the focus was on delegation and decentralization, performance, and the use of the latest technology (Ukeles 1982). When administrative reforms have a managerialist ethos, the reform menu includes such activities as decentralizing personnel management, eliminating civil service tenure, introducing management by results (including management contracts and performance-based pay), cutting red tape and excessive regulation, increasing the efficiency and customer orientation of bureaucracy, and privatization. International organizations often promoted managerial reforms as part of liberalization-related policy reforms (Heredia and Ross Schneider 2003: 19).

A brief historical overview of World Bank administrative reform models

The World Bank is the world's largest source of official development assistance. In 2002, it provided more than US$19.5 billion in loans worldwide and worked with over 100 developing countries. Its approach to development assistance combines a mix of finances and ideas in the same package (Gilbert *et al.* 2000: 51). On the level of ideas, it is reported to have taken upon itself the role of defining and propagating a model of best development practice, spread through research and publications aimed not only at the World Bank's operational departments, but also at the development community at large. For example, its World Development Report is recognized as a 'highly leveraged intervention in the policy market' (Wilks 1998:1).

Prior to the 1990s, World Bank attention to issues of public administration occurred on a limited scale. It focused on the public institutions responsible for managing and implementing sector-specific assistance (Nunberg and Nellis 1995: 4). Its vision on administrative reform crystallized in two stages during the 1990s. During the first stage until 1997, it recommended governments to roll back the state, rely on market mechanisms and indicators in economic and public administration, and reduce the cost and size of their bureaucracies. This orientation was tied to the overall policy agenda associated with Structural Adjustment Loans (SALs). The second stage started after 1997, when the World Bank aimed to correct imbalances caused by what appeared to be an exaggerated limitation of the role of the state. The focus moved to strengthening institutions and governance, in addition to reducing the cost of and containing the size of the public sector. Those two models are further explored below. They are referred to as *first* and *second generation* models.

First generation administrative reforms rest on an instrumental vision of the state that reflects the principles of the New Political Economy (NPE). This school of thought is rooted in public choice theory, a discipline of economics where people are assumed to engage in political and collective action principally in the pursuit of material self-interest. Therefore, state action is justified in terms of the benefits to human welfare it can bring about, rather than through transcendental arguments about the inherent value of the state as guardian and embodiment of a people, culture or tradition. The state's failure to meet the welfare of people justifies rolling it back (Moore 1998: 39).

First generation administrative reforms started with a focus on cost containment and served mainly the purposes of SALs. This shaped priorities and the choice of instruments to a considerable extent. Wage bill containment was dominant because of its link to fiscal reform and macroeconomic stabilization (Berg 2000: 299). Priorities focused on central government employment, pay and incentives systems, and targeted excessive wage bills, surplus numbers of civil servants, wage compression, and overall salary erosion (Nunberg 1990: ii).

First generation reforms spread quickly. This spread was not based on any solid knowledge regarding the validity and effectiveness of interventions, however; instead, it emerged from a generalization of World Bank structural adjustment initiatives in some African countries (Nunberg and

Nellis 1990: 5–6). Knowledge about both problem definition and oper-ationalization was limited, and many reforms were conducted on a trial-and-error basis. Moreover, impact assessments of the first generation administrative reforms were far from positive. Many reforms were reversed after a successful start (Berg 2000: 295). Their packaging within SALs implied too tight, unrealistic schedules and deadlines constraining activity execution (Shirley 1991: 293–4; Berg 2000: 294–5). Finally, issues of insti-tutional strengthening remained extraneous to the mainstream trend of administrative reform (Nunberg and Nellis 1990: 6, 14, 16).

By the mid-1990s, the World Bank realized that first generation reforms could only scratch the surface of what was required to (re-)construct a well managed and well performing civil service. They left untouched a wide area of long-term structural issues whose resolution was essential to sustainable improvements in administrative capacity. These were to be addressed by second generation administrative reforms where the governance ethos was more pronounced. Change materialized with the publication of the World Bank's 1997 *World Development Report* (WDR) which devoted two chapters on administrative reform (Moore 1998: 43–4). Reforms would still include issues of wage compression, staff reduction, incentives and performance in public personnel management. They incorporated, in addition, institutional strengthening emphases and clearly encouraged deregulation, privatization and liberalization (Cornia 1998: 36). The tone of this report weakened the prevailing World Bank assumption premised on the minimalist state as a requirement for development. Instead, it recommended a balance between state role and capacity (Evans and Moore 1998: 3). The policy shift is premised on New Institutional Economics (NIE). This approach calls for the serious analysis and consideration of institutions, as opposed to NPE, the theoretical inspiration of the first generation reforms (Cornia 1998: 34).

The theoretical and methodological justifications for the revised World Bank approach remained weak, however. While the World Bank seemed to be increasingly engaged in administrative reform activities, the problems which those activities were meant to resolve were hardly elaborated or explained. Instead, structural adjustment continued to be the only justifica-tion. Minimalist tendencies continued to prevail (Hildyard and Wilks 1998: 51) and administrative reform assistance increasingly focused on expendi-ture control (Berg 2000: 292). Evans and Moore (1998: 12) blamed those tendencies on the technical focus of World Bank staff, which showed little sensitivity to the institutional, political and cultural aspects of development. Hence, the World Bank promoted managerialism as a modern and high-technology model meant to enable borrower countries to leapfrog the basic stage of civil service reforms and land directly in the twenty-first century, yet with more emphasis on internal efficiency and less attention to per-formance and responsiveness to citizens (Heredia and Ross Schneider 2003: 19).

UNDP and EU models during the 1990s

As mentioned in the introduction, UNDP and EU were equally active donors to administrative reform in post-war Lebanon. Their policy input was no less determining than that of the World Bank. During the 1990s, the EU's aid program had become one of the largest on the global scale (Robinson and Tarp 2000: 4). EU assistance is generally driven by regional integration as an instrument to alleviate poverty when individual nations are too weak to counter the forces of globalization. An integrated region acting as a free trade area, as a customs union or as a single market, could better withstand international competition, attract foreign investments, and access new technology (Santos 2001: 30–2). Economic reforms premised on neo-liberalism constitute the cornerstone to solving economic and social problems. EU-sponsored economic reforms aimed at improved competitiveness within the regional blocs. They entailed reducing private sector transaction costs, assisting firms to exploit economies of scale, encouraging foreign investment and facilitating macroeconomic policy coordination within a specific region (Cox and Chapman 1999: 13, 83). Managerial reforms complemented economic reforms and focused on the legislative and regulatory framework necessary for the sustainability of neo-liberal policies.

UNDP is the development arm of the UN, and its assistance money comes from contributions of UN member countries, and is dispatched in the form of grants (Moore 1998: 45). Its development cooperation agenda is driven by a focus on human development, with the *Human Development Report* (HDR) as its main intellectual vehicle (UNDP 1995a: xiv). During the 1990s, UNDP defined sustainable human development as 'expanding the choices for all people in society' (UNDP 1997a: 1). In many ways, this concept came as a reaction to the unfavorable impact of neo-liberal economic reforms on people, and suggested an approach that combined market efficiency with social compassion, where people were at the center of development (Hilderbrand and Grindle 1996: iii; UNDP 1995a: xii).

With the adoption of people-centered development, the conviction emerged that governments had failed to identify appropriate roles for the state in development, because of ill-conceived public sector management practices. It was argued that they had been unable to organize and manage systems for identifying problems requiring public action, formulating policies to respond to them, implementing activities in pursuit of policy goals, and sustaining those activities over time (Hilderbrand and Grindle 1996: iv). A remedy to this situation was found in the notion of governance. Governance was seen as a complex array of mechanisms, processes, relationships and institutions through which citizens and groups articulated their interests, exercised rights and obligations, and mediated differences. Besides the state, those included the private sector and civil society (UNDP 1997b: 9).

Concluding remark

Although they emphasized different aspects of administrative reform, the World Bank, EU and UNDP did not differ on a core assumption, namely that effective public service should borrow principles and techniques from private business management. They all supported programs aimed at reducing excessive and costly government, enhancing public service performance, giving more voice and role to non-state actors in public service provision, strengthening the regulatory and legal framework for such arrangements, and enhancing accountability within and by the public sector. As such, they had complementary emphases. These are outlined in summary form in Table 12.1.

Lebanon's policy and public service contexts

> Lebanon is a small Levantine state located on the eastern side of the Mediterranean. Because communalism antedates the establishment of the Lebanese state in 1943, the identity of the Lebanese is an amalgam of a primordial and hereditary attachment to religion, sect, family and region. Traditional loyalties are legitimized and institutionalized by the formal institutions of government that constitute complex microcosms of the families, clans, regions, sects and economic interests that claim to represent the people of Lebanon.
>
> (Khalaf 1987: xi,118).

State, society and public administration

Lebanon acquired features of the modern bureaucracy under the French mandate (1917–43). Its public administration was centralized both organizationally and geographically, bureaucratic decisions were hierarchical, and a great deal of attention was paid to statutes and regulations (Kisirwani and Parle 1987: 19). Appointment to public office was exclusively based on (legal) academic credentials, with the higher bureaucratic positions typically filled by men coming from aristocratic families and holding degrees in law from Université Saint Joseph, the French-language university in Beirut (Hudson 1968: 103).

Social characteristics shaped the Lebanese version of the modern French bureaucracy. Because of traditionalism, sectarianism, patronage, formalism and ritualism, senior bureaucrats behaved like political bosses possessing an office with employees serving as an entourage and depending on their good graces. Political leaders acted as intermediaries between their communities and the central bureaucracy, secured jobs for their constituencies and intervened in the bureaucratic process on their behalf. Because of this *modus operandi*, the public service was more adept at the routine functions commensurate with its predominantly traditional character, such as preserving

Table 12.1 World Bank, EU and UNDP public administration reform policy

Criterion	World Bank	European Union	UNDP
Development doctrine	Reforms should restructure and re-stabilize economies as a prerequisite of growth.	Economic reforms should reduce transaction costs for EU countries, promote competitiveness and encourage regional integration.	Sustainable development occurs when human and social needs are met.
Premises on administrative reform	Public sector cost and size containment; institutional strengthening premised on new public management; liberalization and deregulation of the public service under the banner of governance.	Eclectic menu of reform measures depending on the requirements and implications of economic reform and regional integration; reform measures have, as a bottom line, practices of public management in EU member states.	Administrative reform should be people-centered and focus on human resource development; it can be done regardless of cost and size issues.
Motivation	Intellectual, with an elaborated vision of priorities and instruments.	A combination of geo-political interest and an idealization of European institutional models.	Intellectual, inspired from sustainable human development.
Clarity of the meaning of governance	Gradual elaboration of the concept, focus on privatization, deregulation, transparency and accountability.	Focus on the rule of law, participation, empowerment, equity.	Tentative and gradual definitions, focus on partnership between the state, public sector and civil society.
Institutional facility	Public Sector Development and Private Sector Development Unit.	None.	Management Development and Governance Division.
Intra-organizational debate	Yes; indicated by the consecutive generations of administrative reforms-related publications.	Not transparent.	Yes; several discussion papers and policy documents published by UNDP.
Sensitivity to institutional contexts	Allegedly weak point of the World Bank, blamed for exclusive focus on economic and technical concerns.	Yes; stems from European tradition where the state and institutions have inherent value.	Yes; long history of dealing with governments on administrative reform and capacity building.

order, accommodating pluralistic interests and managing the public service of a small polity, rather than at providing services to citizens (Salem 1973: 80–1, 105).

From 1975 to 1989, fourteen years of civil strife devastated political, economic and social life in Lebanon. The destruction of buildings, facilities and equipment in the public service was considerable. Offices were robbed, destroyed or displaced along war-inflicted geographical divisions. Equipment was stolen, destroyed or not properly maintained. Human capital was depleted by the lethal war and by natural attrition. Capacity with respect to infrastructure, human resources and material means was marginalized (UNDP 1992: 19). The breakdown of government authority, the relocation and dislocation of government offices, forced absenteeism, sub-optimal coordination among organizations and the increase of political and personal influences undermined the quantitative and qualitative capacity to process state functions and deliver services (Kisirwani and Parle 1987: 21–3).

While the war left a visible imprint on the public service, a non-negligible portion of post-war maladministration had its seeds in the socio-political profile of the public administration, which found in the war environment a fertile ground in which to grow. A low sense of civic responsibility meant outright disrespect for the law. Laxity was translated into a weakening of professionalism and career attachment. Absenteeism became increasingly deliberate. Pronounced sectarian segmentation facilitated a reversion to personal and community allegiances, caused uneasy relationships among colleagues and implied a biased treatment of citizens (Antoun 1989: 209).

Obstacles to domestic policy-making

After independence in 1943, modern political institutions (including a parliament, a council of ministers and a presidency of the republic) were established to govern a society with predominantly traditional (religious) loyalties. The political system was sanctioned by a sectarian balance that allocates political positions to sects on the basis of the size of the community. Those institutions were primarily focused on harmonizing the complexities of a national political system with multiple (religious) identities. Consequently, the political landscape featured a weak state apparatus open for political fragmentation and disintegration. The government's policy-making capacity was weak. Sensitive national issues were difficult to settle internally and it was not uncommon for foreign intervention to mediate and resolve internal differences. Lebanon's public service mirrored the country's social and political complexities. In order to survive, any institution had to respect, preserve and promote everybody's interests. Inside public sector institutions, personal dealings, opportunistic negotiation, and pragmatic compromise prevailed over commitment to a given policy or program. Institutional capacity at policy analysis and programming was weak, partially due to the administration's focus on accommodating plural interests (Khalaf 1987; Hudson 1968; Salem 1973).

The post-war climate exacerbated the complexity of policy-making. A residual uncertainty left over from the war predisposed people to focus on survival rather than on long-term planning (Plumpture and McQuillan 1993: 2). In pre-war Lebanon, the President of the Republic was a central and relatively powerful policy and decision actor. Post-war constitutional amendments allocated executive authority to the Council of Ministers, a plural body where Lebanese sects and political affiliations were largely represented. Consequently, policy-making became more difficult (Iskandar 1993). The integration of warlords in government institutions imported the climate of distrust to the national political scene and transformed the strata of higher political officials into a loose collection of individuals focused on factional interests (van der Kloet 2002). Similar policy-making inadequacies existed at the institutional level. The qualitative and quantitative shortage of human resources inflicted by the civil war was a serious blow to the already weak analytical and programming capacity of Lebanon's public administration. Moreover, many of the appointments to senior positions during and immediately after the civil war were politically motivated and involved persons with inadequate professional qualifications (Knox 1992: 10–13).

Donors in action: policy disputes and program fragmentation

In view of the depleted state finances, the government of Lebanon (GOL) requested international assistance in post-war reconstruction. Among other sectors, donors extended assistance to public administration rehabilitation. The National Administrative Rehabilitation Programme (NARP), developed with lead support by UNDP, was the core tool for re-establishing the physical, human and management capacities of the public sector. NARP constituted 145 projects at a cost of US$100 million, covering the supply of office equipment, training, automation and management consultancy services. The World Bank, EU and UNDP, as well as a number of multilateral and bilateral donors, pledged funds to support NARP. Those donors also assisted in creating the Office of the Minister of State for Administrative Reform (OMSAR), a reform mechanism aimed at implementing administrative rehabilitation and reform. Optimistic forecasts for establishing a new public administration prevailed. In 1995, the Minister of Administrative Reform expressed his ambition to restore the basic functionality of the public administration as the executive arm of government and to promote its development along the managerialist paradigm prescribed by the international community as a best practice (El Khalil 1995: 6).

Policy formulation by UNDP (1992–4)

Dividing responsibilities for Lebanon's reconstruction between them, the World Bank and UNDP agreed to allocate issues of economic recovery and

infrastructure to the former and entrust social and institutional development and public administration reform to the latter (van der Kloet 2002).
UNDP's initiative had been carefully planned. Aware of the absence of
advocates of the institutional aspects of reconstruction among both
national and international players, it had formulated a proposal for an
administrative reform program in January 1992, which provided a basis for
establishing contact with other donors and the GOL. When the GOL's anti-
corruption campaign failed in 1993, it welcomed UNDP's proposal as timely.
In 1994, the Council of Ministers designated a Minister of Administrative
Reform who acted as UNDP's government counterpart (UNDP 1995b).

UNDP called for taking post-war reconstruction as an opportunity to
comprehensively *transform* the Lebanese public administration along the
lines of international experience in public sector management. Transformation would take place according to a phased program premised on four
principles. The first and most central principle concerned the *role of the
state*, which would have to play a more active part in guiding the economy,
in enforcing, monitoring and controlling economic policies and in addressing social and equity issues towards the redistribution of income. Another
program value concerned the *simplification and modernization* of organization and management, including monitoring and control mechanisms,
information management systems, the formulation and implementation of
personnel policies, training and bureaucratic procedures. A third program
value rested on *cost efficiency*, which implied siphoning off surplus staff,
reducing the wage bill and improving working conditions through the
decompression of salaries. A fourth value called for *partnership with the
private sector*. This program would serve as an investment program and a
tool for mobilizing technical assistance. Its execution would occur in two
stages where rehabilitation, centered on the reactivation of the administration's basic functions, would precede the complex reforms that require
careful design and political decisions (de Clercq 1992: 7–15).

UNDP invited consultants to materialize its program proposal. However,
contrary to the initial plan, short-term rehabilitation and long-term reform
were launched at the same time, due to a sense among international and
national policy actors that Lebanon had to make up for time lost due to the
civil war. This justified, in their view, speeding up reform to take place
simultaneously with rehabilitation.

In March 1993, a team of national and international consultants was
recruited to survey the rehabilitation needs of public administration. International consultants were recruited on the basis of their experience with a
UNDP programming concept known as the National Technical Cooperation and Assistance Programme (NaTCAP), which claims to align multi-
donor public investment programs with technical assistance components
according to country needs. Under guidance from UNDP, the consultants
completed their mission and consolidated their findings in the NARP (van
der Kloet 2002).

UNDP's involvement in Lebanon's post-war administrative reform coincided with the emergence of the Good Governance path within its policy circles. In 1993, it invited experts from the Institute of Governance in Ottawa, Canada, to materialize good governance practices in Lebanon's public administration context as a way to engage the country in an administrative reform that complied with international standards (van der Kloet 2002). The experts presented the GOL with four reform options. *Strategic reforms* would be tied to socio-economic policy goals and affect the role of government and relations with the private sector. *Structural reforms* would have a less obvious link to socio-economic policy objectives, but they would also address the (re)configuration of power and decision-making processes in the public service. *Enhancement* would constitute a less ambitious reform that only affects the internal efficiency of the bureaucracy. Reforms aimed at *institution building* would establish the foundations of public service in an environment where formal organization is still under-developed. Contrary to UNDP's predisposition to administrative transformation, the consultants recommended that post-war Lebanon start with institution building and enhancement as preludes to larger-scale structural change (Plumpture and McQuillan 1993: 134–5). Their recommendation was declined, however. Instead, the policy choice was made by key decision-makers, including the Prime Minister and the Minister of Administrative Reform, to opt for a strategic approach on grounds of its better conforming to the country's reconstruction policy premised on neo-liberalism and highly influenced by the World Bank and other international organizations (Marshall 2002).

Policy fragmentation (1995–2001) and the role of the World Bank

UNDP's policy leadership was soon challenged by the World Bank as a key financier of the NARP. The Bank's contribution to the NARP signaled the start of a gradual disintegration of the administrative reform program. Much of the program's dissipation was caused by the entanglement of the roles of UNDP, World Bank and the Minister of Administrative Reform prior to the formulation of NARP. To the Minister, the World Bank was a much solicited partner whose engagement was facilitated by the initial role of UNDP (El Khalil 2002). During the period 1992–4, the World Bank and UNDP maintained a conciliatory attitude. UNDP's proposal for an administrative reform program was initially developed to constitute part of a comprehensive World Bank report, *Lebanon's Post-war Stabilization and Reconstruction* (1993), and therefore sought to combine in one document UNDP's preference for a stronger government and the World Bank's emphasis on cost and size containment, employment and compensation systems reform, downsizing, and privatization.

In 1994, the World Bank asserted its role in administrative reform by committing a US$450,000 grant for an institutional development fund. This fund was provided as a prelude to the US$20 million that the World Bank allocated in support of the NARP in 1995. In World Bank practice, such a fund finances technical assistance for institutional development work associated with policy reform, country management of development cooperation, and special operational emphases, particularly for poverty reduction, public sector management, private sector development, and environmental management. In post-war Lebanon, the institutional development fund was used to recruit experts to advise on the prospective World Bank loan and support a number of ongoing reform activities (World Bank 1994; Farah 2002).

The World Bank loan brought not only US$20 million to support NARP, but also emphases that transcended financial assistance and involved '*the design of administrative reform*' (World Bank 1995a: 6–11). NARP itself became an area of disagreement between the UNDP and the World Bank. While UNDP considered NARP to be a tool to rationalize development cooperation for administrative reform under a program umbrella, World Bank officials considered it to be a mere shopping list and called for a more pronounced emphasis on the content of administrative reform.

The UNDP–World Bank conflict over NARP brought their deeper disagreement on the administrative reform policy to the surface. The World Bank argued that public administration reforms should start with a reconsideration of the role of the state, a function that a loose collection of assistance projects like the NARP failed to fulfill. The loan supporting the NARP was hence used by World Bank to remedy what it considered to be a flaw in its program design. In line with its thinking of the early 1990s, administrative reform was to assume the economic-fiscal focus of structural adjustment policies in which the state had to be rolled back and made more cost-efficient. To serve those policy objectives better (from a World Bank perspective), the World Bank loan to administrative reform was initially intended as part of the Fiscal Adjustment Loan for the Ministry of Finance. Lack of consensus among Lebanese policy actors caused this arrangement to be dropped, however (Ramadan 2002).

The Minister of Administrative Reform welcomed the World Bank's intervention as a reformer, which he credited for making the reform 'tangible' (El Khalil 2002). On 27 June 1995, the broad outline of the revised role of the state was described in a Government Statement on Administrative Reform, which claimed that 'Lebanon's ... private sector-centered economic recovery ... cannot be sustained without administrative and civil service rehabilitation and reform', and that 'the Government's ultimate objective is to achieve overtime a smaller, efficient ... public administration, consistent with basic requirements of the State in a free economy' (World Bank 1995b: 9). The statement outlined a number of activities to support rolling back the state that were typical of the structural adjustment policies promoted by the World Bank in the early 1990s. The conduct of a civil service census was a central activity. Other activities included a functional review aimed at reducing the number of public sector positions, a program to reallocate, retrain or retrench temporary workers, the reduction of the civilian wage bill, the simplification of job classification and grading systems, the decompression of compensation and salary scales, the introduction of performance appraisal and the revision of central management and inspection procedures towards an increased delegation to ministries and agencies in exchange for accountability (World Bank 1995b: 9). While released by the GOL, interviews revealed that this statement was in fact drafted by World Bank officials (Moussa 2002).

In 1995, the EU further challenged the NARP by imposing a parallel program. It referred to this program as the 'Assistance for the Re-establishment of the Lebanese Administration' (ARLA) program. EU officials did not explicitly refer to the role of ARLA in re-designing the reform program. Instead, they foresaw an exclusive focus on the institutional development of specific institutions in the public service through the provision of advisory services. Institutional development, in turn, offered the EU a window of opportunity to provide administrative reform input when its assistance package was activated in 2000. Like the World Bank and UNDP, the EU targeted reforms that promoted its development cooperation agenda. In 2000, this agenda focused on economic, fiscal and supportive managerialist reforms. Unlike the World Bank's focus where emphasis was on cost and size containment, the EU focus was on enhancing public sector performance, and preparing the legal and regulatory frameworks for privatization (de Graaf 2003).

Failed re-integration attempts (1996–2001)

Under the banner of formulating an administrative reform strategy that re-integrated the fragmented reform program, the UNDP, World Bank and EU were engaged in another round of policy disputes between 1996 and 2000. The international consultants hired by OMSAR to assist in strategy formulation were pressured by donors to adopt specific policy preferences. The first consultant (1996–7) used new public management – a variant of managerialism – as the conceptual cornerstone of his work. His approach drew on work in progress at the World Bank, diagnosed the core problem of public administration in Lebanon as excessive central controls, and recommended a reform premised on light-touch central regulation in exchange for accountability (Manning 1996: 2–4). This recommendation was rejected by OMSAR as too radical. Lacking internal capacity at policy analysis, OMSAR recruited a second international consultant (1997–9), and clearly instructed him to formulate context-sensitive strategy proposals. However, his proposals were challenged by UNDP policy experts for not complying with its governance agenda. The EU also interfered in strategy formulation. Consultants hired in the framework of ARLA revised and finalized the strategy draft in 2000 with a focus on ensuring a policy direction for ARLA, the EU's assistance package. During the work of those consultants, the World Bank and UNDP regularly requested updates on strategy formulation and their officials made comments and suggestions for change depending on their latest literature.

The strategy document was endorsed by the Council of Ministers in September 2001 (Merhi 2002). This document emerged as the total sum of the input of its various contributors. It prescribed objectives of the reform such as rolling back the state to core functions and downsizing the public service, typical of the World Bank's first generation reforms. It also pre- scribed the enhancement of policy-making and post-audit capacities and the delegation of routine functions and controls to public administrations, typical of the World Bank's second generation reforms premised on new public management. It provided for UNDP's good governance ideals where partnership between the state and non-state actors is encouraged. Finally, it supported the strengthening of legal and regulatory frameworks and the enhancement of performance among civil servants and public organizations, typical of the EU focus.

A few months after the strategy was completed, the UNDP wanted to revisit the integrative framework of Lebanon's development cooperation agenda, including administrative reform. It had then finalized the develop- ment of a new integrative tool known as the United Nations Development Assistance Framework (UNDAF). Like the World Bank's CDF, UNDAF aimed to streamline development operations at the country level. Govern- ance issues were central in Lebanon's UNDAF for the years 2002–5, with civil service reform featuring prominently. OMSAR responded positively to UNDP's request to cooperate in its UNDAF initiative by formulating a national requirement matrix that linked its reform activities to development operations in the area of governance. As it was formulated while donor assistance packages were being implemented, the National Requirements Matrix turned out to be a replica of ongoing projects under fragmented and dissipated policies and programs.

Conclusion

The development cooperation paradigm that emerged in the late 1990s called for inter-donor partnership and for leadership and ownership by the recipient country. International organizations developed integrative frame- works (such as the United Nations Development Assistance Framework and the Comprehensive Development Framework of the World Bank) as platforms for inter-donor partnership and country leadership and ownership. This chapter has found favor with the claims for integrative frameworks, but it has argued that, beyond rhetoric, institutional capabilities in the recipient country are necessary if those claims are to be met. Among those institutional capabilities, it has singled out and discussed policy-making capacity with reference to Lebanon's experience in post-war reconstruction (in the field of public administration). This conclusion will discuss some of the basic tenants of integrative frameworks with reference to Lebanon's weak policy-making capacity.

A central claim of integrative frameworks is that successful development is more likely to be achieved when countries are consistently pursuing integrated, coherent and long-term policies and programs. Lebanon lacked the capacity to formulate its own policies or critically analyze the policies suggested by international organizations due to both structural reasons rooted in governance set-up, as well as to weaknesses inflicted on its institutions by the civil war. Instead of building domestic policy analysis capacity, the donors assisting in country reconstruction filled the policy vacuum by advancing their own assumptions as best ways to rehabilitate and reform the public service, and competed among themselves to impose their policies not only on the recipient country, but also on one another. Because managerialism prevailed in the 1990s as an international best practice in administrative reform, donors traded variants of the same policy. The outcome of their competition, the administrative reform strategy, was a *cut and paste* of their respective inputs. It lacked integration and coherence, and most importantly, relevance to the local context. It claimed a managerialist reform when, by all standards, the requirements of such a reform, such as the full development of Weberian standards of public administration, were lacking in Lebanon.

Another claim of integrative frameworks is that development assistance is most effective when it is driven by demand from the country, rather than by internal incentives among development agencies to supply certain types of assistance. Lebanon's experience revealed that the practice of country ownership defies the idealistic claims of integrative frameworks. Financial need creates a situation of dependence and openness to conditionality. Such a situation is likely to occur in post-war contexts, but it may also emerge in cases of financial need created by other circumstances such as public debt, for example. The failure of local policies may also motivate governments to request policy guidance from donors. In Lebanon, donor assistance was initially sought to alleviate budget difficulties but it was later used to counter criticism of the failure of a local anti-corruption campaign. In this case, the internal incentive to adopt externally defined policies renders the notion and practice of ownership highly intricate.

A third claim of integrative frameworks is that the effectiveness of development efforts is likely to increase when the activities of stakeholders from the recipient country and the donor community are better coordinated and unified. In Lebanon's experience, as discussed in this chapter, those ideals of coordination and unification were not met. Donor cooperation was circumstantial and short-lived. Behind the apparent coordination, donors were planning the next step where they could take over the leadership of administrative reform policy-making. Noticeable in particular was the World Bank's unexpected intervention as a policy actor. This intervention complemented its role as financier and reversed an agreement with UNDP according to which the latter led on matters of institutional development. UNDP's submission to the World Bank's financial and policy clout was temporary. A few years later, it attempted a come-back as an integrator of the fragmented administrative reform program under the banner of UNDAF.

Any other integrative framework has little chance to succeed in Lebanon, however, as long as domestic policy-making capacity remains marginal and dependent on international organizations. Donors, including the World Bank, are challenged to assist countries in creating professional and autonomous policy-making capacity instead of bombarding them with ready-made solutions based on their experience, research and development doctrines, which they ironically acknowledge to be incomplete and sometimes mistaken. Once a professional and autonomous policy-making capacity is created, meeting the claims of integrative frameworks would be less difficult. Such a capacity would critically ponder the policy proposals generated by either national or international actors and formulate policy frameworks that are context-sensitive and hence, not only ensure policy coherence at the abstract level, but also policy coherence with local development needs. Policies that are generated by professional and autonomous policy analysts and nationally owned would possess the authority to coordinate donor assistance and determine the character of partnerships.

References

Antoun, R. (1989) 'The Impact of the War on the Lebanese Administration: A Study in Administrative Disruption', Ph.D. Dissertation, University of York.

Berg, E. (2000) 'Aid and Failed Reforms: The Case of Public Sector Management', in Tarp, F. (ed.) *Foreign Aid and Development: Lessons Learnt and Directions for the Future*, London: Routledge, 290–311.

Caiden, G. (1969) *Administrative Reform*, Chicago: Aldine.

——(1991) *Administrative Reform Comes of Age*, Berlin: Walter de Gruyter.

de Clercq, C. (1992, May) *Public Administration Chapter: Draft for Review* (Internal UNDP document).

Cornia, G. A. (1998) 'Congruence on Governance Issues, Dissent on Economic Policies', *IDS Bulletin* 29(2), 32–8.

Cox, A. and Chapman, J. (1999) *The European Community External Cooperation Programmes: Policies, Management and Distribution*, London: Overseas Development Institute.

Dror, Y. (1976) 'Strategies for Administrative Reform', in Leemans, A. (ed.) *The Management of Change in Government*, The Hague: Nijhoff, 126–41.

Evans, A. and Moore, M. (1998) 'Editorial Introduction', *IDS Bulletin* 29(2), 3–13.

Farah, S. (2002) Previous Director, Institutional Development Unit, Beirut. Interview by author, 27 May.

Gilbert, L., Powell, A. and Vines, D. (2000) 'Positioning the World Bank', in Gilbert, L. and Vines, D. (eds) *The World Bank: Structure and Policies*, Cambridge: Cambridge University Press, 39–59.

de Graaf, M. (2003) Principal Public Administration Expert, Arcadis BMB, Performance Improvement Expert ARLA. Office of the Minister of State for Administrative Reform, Beirut. Interview by author, 4 March.

Heredia, B. and Ross Schneider, B. (2003) 'The Political Economy of Administrative Reform in Developing Countries', in Ross Schneider, B. and Heredia, B. (eds) *Reinventing Leviathan*, Boulder CO: North-South Center Press, 1–29.

Hilderbrand, M. E. and Grindle, M. S. (1996) *Building Sustainable Capacity: Challenges for the Public Sector*, OESP Lessons Learned series, New York: UNDP.

Hildyard, N. and Wilks, A. (1998) 'An Effective State? But Effective for Whom?', *IDS Bulletin* 29(2), 49–55.

Hudson, M. (1968) *The Precarious Republic: Political Modernization in Lebanon*, New York: Random House.

Iskandar, A. (1993) 'Administrative Reform in Lebanon: Issues and Priorities', American University of Beirut/John F. Kennedy School of Government Collaborative Research Programme.

Khalaf, S. (1987) *Lebanon's Predicament*, New York: Columbia University Press.

El Khalil, A. (1995) 'Institutional Renewal and Development', transcript of a presentation at the National Workshop on UN System Cooperation with the Government of Lebanon, Chtaura, 2–5 May.

——(2002) Member of Parliament (former Minister of State for Administrative Reform) May 1995–November 1996. Interview by author, 16 April, Beirut-Ryadh Bank, Beirut.

Kisirwani, M. and Parle, W. M. (1987) 'Assessing the Impact of the Post Civil War Period on the Lebanese Bureaucracy: A View from Inside', *Journal of Asian and African Studies* 22(1–2), 17–32.

van der Kloet, H. (2002) Consultant, Development Cooperation (previous UNDP Resident Representative in Lebanon). Interview by author, 13 March, Breda, the Netherlands.

Knox, D. (1992) *Human and Institutional Development in the Lebanon*, report prepared under auspices of the United Nations Development Programme.

Manning, N. (1996) 'What Does a Good Public Sector Look Like? Resisting Supply-Driven Technical Assistance', paper distributed by author at OMSAR in 1996.

Marshall, C. (2002) Director of the Institute on Governance in Ottawa, Canada, previous consultant commissioned by UNDP to advise on the administrative reform program in 1993. The Hague. Telephone interview by author, 22 November.

Merhi, A. (2002) Director of the Institutional Development Unit. Interview by author, 18 May, Office of the Minister of State for Administrative Reform, Beirut.

Moore, M. (1998) 'Towards a Useful Consensus?', *IDS Bulletin* 29(2), 39–48.

Moussa, T. (2002) Former Senior Informatics Specialist at the World Bank, Beirut. Interview by author, 6 June, Beirut.

Nunberg, B. (1990) *Public Sector Management Issues in Structural Adjustment Lending*, Washington DC: World Bank.

Nunberg, B. and Nellis, J. (1990) *Civil Service Reform and the World Bank*, Working Papers Series (422), Washington DC: World Bank.

——(1995) *Civil Service Reform and the World Bank*, World Bank Discussion Papers (161), Washington DC: World Bank.

Plumpture, T. and McQuillan, C. (1993) *In Service of Lebanon: Institutional Development for the Civil Service of Lebanon*, report prepared under the auspices of the United Nations Development Programme.

Ramadan, B. (2002) Senior Economist at the World Bank's Lebanon Country Office (former Director of the Technical Cooperation Unit within OMSAR). Interview by author, 11 June, the World Bank Lebanon Country Office, United Nations House, Beirut.

Robinson, S. and Tarp, F. (2000) 'Foreign Aid and Development: Summary and Synthesis', in Robinson, S. and Tarp, F. (eds) *Foreign Aid and Development: Lessons Learnt and Directions for the Future*, London: Routledge, 1–14.

Salem, E. A. (1973) *Modernization without Revolution: Lebanon's Experience*, Bloomington IN: Indiana University Press.

Santos, C. (2001) 'European Union Support for Regional Integration Initiatives in Developing Countries', in Cosgrove-Sacks, C. (ed.) *Europe, Diplomacy and Development: New Issues in EU Relations with Developing Countries*, New York: Palgrave, 29–51.

Shirley, M. (1991) 'Public Sector Management Activity at the World Bank', *Public Administration and Development* 11, 293–4.

Ukeles, J. (1982) *Doing More with Less: Turning Public Management Around*, New York: AMACOM.

UNDP (1992) *Development Cooperation Report, Lebanon 1991*, Beirut: UNDP.

——(1995a) *Development Cooperation Report, Lebanon 1994*, Beirut: UNDP.

——(1995b) 'Public Sector Management, Governance, and Sustainable Human Development', a Discussion Paper, New York: UNDP.

——(1997a) 'Governance for Sustainable Human Development', A UNDP Policy Document, New York: UNDP.

——(1997b) 'Re-conceptualizing Governance', Discussion Paper 2, New York: UNDP.

Wilks, A. (1998) 'The Process of Preparing World Development Reports', *IDS Bulletin* 29(2), 1–2.

World Bank (1993) 'Lebanon Stabilisation and Reconstitution', MENA Department, Report No. 11406-LE, March, unpublished.

——(1994) Institutional Development Fund. OMSAR internal document.

——(1995a) Lebanon Administrative Rehabilitation Project.

——(1995b) Administrative Rehabilitation Project: government statement on administrative reform.

——(2004) 'Supporting Development Programs Effectively – Applying the Comprehensive Development Framework Principles: A Staff Guide', Washington DC: World Bank.

13 Fiscal decentralisation in transition economies

The World Bank in a learning process

Krisztina Tóth

a greater degree of humility is called for, acknowledgement of the fact that we do not have all of the answers.

(Joseph Stiglitz)

Introduction

The past ten years of research on the intergovernmental fiscal relations in transition economies have shown that decentralisation is a never-ending, dynamic process and that there are no universal recipes on how to manage it for success. Fiscal institutions need to be refined and adapted to a continuously changing environment. The diversity of historical experiences, social norms, values and political institutions calls both national governments and external donors to find tailor-made answers to country-specific challenges. As the traditional theory of fiscal federalism is too general, it cannot be expected to provide such answers.

This chapter deals with the evolution of the policy agenda of the World Bank with regard to fiscal decentralisation in Central and Eastern Europe. It shows how the failure of the Washington Consensus and the academic discussion on 'fiscal federalism in theory and practice' contributed to a better understanding of intergovernmental fiscal relations. The chapter is divided into three parts. The first part provides a summary of the mainstream neo-classical theory of fiscal federalism and its limited applicability for the analysis of practical problems in intergovernmental finance. The second part deals with the evolution of the development thinking from the crisis of the Washington Consensus until the emergence of the first criticisms of the Post-Washington Consensus, with particular attention to the implications of these different stages on the issues of governance and the public sector. The evolution of the World Bank's decentralisation agenda under the influence of the academic debates in both fiscal federalism and development economics is discussed in the third part of the chapter.

The new orthodoxy and its limits

Intergovernmental fiscal relations exert a substantial influence on the performance of the public sector. The number of hospital beds in a given geographic region, the quality of teaching in primary schools, the extent of unemployment benefits, the timeliness of disaster recovery interventions, the efficiency of public transport and waste collection, and several other characteristics of the public sector of a particular country, may be explained in part by the constitution of the government and the formal and informal interactions between its various levels. Similarly, more general aspects of the public economy such as the volume of national debt, various phenomena of interjurisdictional disparities, regional growth data and competitiveness, as well as the internal macroeconomic stability, may find their explanation partly in the actual pattern of intergovernmental fiscal relations.

Academic interest in this subject emerged as early as the 1950s and relied on the theoretical fundaments of public finance laid down by Charles Tiebout (1956) and Richard A. Musgrave (1959). In later years, Musgrave and Musgrave (1973) as well as Wallace E. Oates (1972) and David King (1984) did considerable pioneer work applying Musgrave's initial theory of fiscal functions (stabilisation, distribution and allocation) conceived for a unitary form of government, to the more realistic situation of a multi-level system. Their inquiry was mainly oriented at finding the proper way of decentralisation, what functions should be assigned to which level of government and how the available resources should be allocated within the public sector. Stipulating that '*in economic terms* most if not all systems are federal' Oates (1972: 18) opened the way to a worldwide academic discussion on the application of Musgrave's theory in a huge variety of political, social and economic contexts represented by a multitude of countries. Primary interest was directed to the optimal pattern of coordination among government tiers that would allow the execution of Musgrave's three functions in the interest of the welfare of the nation. This coordination is assured by a set of intergovernmental fiscal institutions constituted by the territorial structure of subnational governments, the assignment of expenditure functions and revenue sources, intergovernmental transfers, as well as budgeting and borrowing rules.

While the normative framework for most of the literature in fiscal federalism and decentralisation relied on the traditional principles of orthodox (neo-classical) welfare economics, scholars from the 1970s – first in Europe and later throughout the world – started to recognise that they must go well beyond the scope of normative analysis in order to make valid statements on how fiscal federalism works in practice (Oates 1999). A more descriptive approach has emerged, signalling the recognition that there is a genuine value in learning from the experiences of other countries (Blindenbacher and Watts 2003: 16 ff.).

On the basis of the so-called 'European fiscal federalism' launched in the late 1970s, four types of deviation from the standard neo-classical normative framework were discussed in the public finance literature throughout the 1990s, as will be presented.

Variation in time

The vertical structure of government is not static in character (Oates 1990). Whether a country has a long-standing tradition in fiscal federalism or has only recently embarked upon decentralisation, intergovernmental fiscal relations must be constantly adapted to the changing political and socio-economic environment. Ronald L. Watts speaks in this context about the *dynamics* of decentralisation (Watts 2001: 15). Exogenous factors such as developments in national and international markets induce fluctuations in public revenue flows, which may necessitate the revision of the existing revenue assignment scheme in order to reduce vertical and horizontal fiscal imbalances. Technological innovation may raise demand for additional public expenditures, forcing governments to consider the option of out-sourcing certain public services to the private sector or better organise the competence assignment and the financing of the service. External rules such as the deficit and debt limits on the member states of the Euro zone are placing central governments under mounting pressure to coordinate bor-rowing by subnational levels, thus controlling the accumulation of debt. Subtle changes in the common value system of the society (particularly with regard to the weights attached to equity and efficiency) exert an endogenous influence on intergovernmental fiscal relations and possibly call for adjust-ments in the interregional redistribution policy or the funding of public institutions. The relatively fluid and sensitive character of the political bal-ance may add to the uncertainty, as is observed particularly in transition countries where models of public administration reform vary from one government period to another (Horváth 2000: 25).

Geographical diversity

Real world intergovernmental fiscal arrangements rarely follow the classical theoretical model as they are determined by historical, political and socio-economic developments. The diversity of the existing backgrounds leads to important divergences across countries in the pattern of their intergovern-mental fiscal system. The degree of expenditure and revenue decentralisa-tion varies from one country to another, leading to differences in the importance of intergovernmental grants (particularly fiscal equalisation). Tax competition is important in some countries (Switzerland, Canada, the USA) and irrelevant in others (The Netherlands), depending on the fiscal autonomy of subnational governments and the taxpayers' mobility. Or, while orthodox fiscal federalism stipulates that progressive income taxes should be assigned to the central government, municipalities both in Sweden and Switzerland rely on income tax as their major revenue source.

The recognition that widely different systems of intergovernmental fiscal relations may be equally appropriate in their specific context, has contributed to a more intense dialogue among country experts.

Conflicting economic objectives

Based on the analysis of the US economy from the 1950s (capital and labour mobility, overlapping tax jurisdictions, interregional disparities, lack of correspondence between national and local economic cycles, etc.), the early neo-classical literature argued that the fulfilment of stabilisation and equity objectives (through macroeconomic policy and income distribution) should rest with the central government. The allocation function (public service provision) is best assigned to the lower levels. As several authors point out (Scott 1964; Dafflon 1978; Wiseman 1987; Ter-Minassian 1997; Bird *et al.* 2003), this theory does not take into account the autonomy of subnational units which is an essential characteristic of any decentralised system. Autonomous governments have their own views about redistribution and stabilisation that may be different from what the central government proposes. From this perspective, devolution of both the redistribution and stabilisation functions may be justified. This argument receives further support from two insights. As for the redistribution function, experience tells us that labour in Europe is only 'imperfectly mobile' (Scott 1964: 264), which means that redistribution policies by lower-level governments do not necessarily induce distortional migration, and additional benefit may be reaped from the proximity of decision-makers to beneficiaries. As for the stabilisation function, full centralisation imposes an inequitable burden on those constituent units that are not responsible for the macroeconomic imbalance. A joined participation of states in the central government's stabilisation efforts may help solve this problem and avoid adverse cyclical behaviour of subnational units.

Trade-off with non-economic objectives

Efforts to incorporate non-economic objectives in the analysis of intergovernmental fiscal relations were first made by Wiseman (1987), Peacock (1972), Dafflon (1977, 1978), as well as by Breton and Scott (1978) for federal systems. These authors remind us that policies founded upon the sole criterion of efficiency are likely to hurt several non-economic objectives of decentralisation, such as autonomy, political stability, or the protection of ethnic minorities. In order to make federalism (decentralisation) politically acceptable for all constituent units, some degree of economic efficiency must be sacrificed. Decision-makers are often forced into trade-off situations, and the decision will mainly depend on value judgments instead of pure economic rationality. But whose value judgment will prevail in a government system where subnational tiers are vested with particular powers? A common position can only be achieved through negotiations.

Another insight is related to the political dynamics of federalism. Since the optimal assignment of expenditure and revenue responsibilities tends to change over time, the territorial-administrative division of the country should, in principle, undergo more or less frequent revision. The recently emerged concept of functional, overlapping and competing jurisdictions (FOCJ) is an important step in this direction (Frey and Eichenberger 1999). However, as large-scale institutional reforms are often blocked by historic traditions and vested political interests, real-life examples of FOCJ are rather sporadic.

Another important strand of research emerging from the 1950s, Public Choice, criticised the New Orthodoxy mainly on its presumption of a benevolent state. It considers public decision-makers as being utility maximisers with individual objective functions which may differ from that of the community. The theory of 'taming the Leviathan' (restricting the size of the public sector) through interjurisdictional competition (Brennan and Buchanan 1980), as well as the analysis of the bureaucracy's budget maximising efforts (Niskanen 1971), are the principal achievements of this research field.

Since the end of the 1990s, a so-called 'second-generation theory' of fiscal federalism has been emerging. It draws essentially (i) on the Public Choice literature on the political process of federalism and the incentives of voters, bureaucrats and politicians; and (ii) on a new strand of literature treating intergovernmental finance in a setting of imperfect or asymmetric information. What emerges from these sources is:

> a new literature on fiscal federalism that examines the workings of different political and fiscal institutions in a setting of imperfect information and control with a basic focus on the incentives that these institutions embody and the resulting behavior they induce from utility-maximizing participants.
>
> (Oates 2005: 356)

Its primary interest lies in the interpretation of the principal-agent problem in a decentralised setting (central versus subnational governments), the examination of soft and hard budget constraints, the analysis of fiscal federalism as a risk-sharing system, as well as the identification of self-enforcing and self-destructive elements in federal systems.

The early 1990s, when the World Bank and other donor organisations started to advise Central and East European countries on fiscal decentralisation, were thus a fairly colourful period of public finance research. The period was marked by the rivalry of orthodox neo-classical theory and its early challengers: the (originally) 'European' fiscal federalism and the Public Choice approach to intergovernmental finance. Until the present day, the most recent challenger of New Orthodoxy, the second-generation theory of fiscal federalism, has not pervaded the World Bank consultancy on intergovernmental finance in transition economies. However, there seems to be no particular dynamic in play that could block the gradual infiltration of these ideas into the Bank's paradigm, so that the apparition of the first World Bank analyses on information problems and the behaviour of actors in a decentralised setting is merely a question of time.

The limits of the Washington Consensus and its consequences for fiscal decentralisation in Central and Eastern Europe

Simultaneously with the dynamic progress in public finance research, the academic discussion on development economics was undergoing a similarly vibrant period during the 1990s. The evolution of development thinking was the second major factor determining the World Bank's policy agenda on fiscal decentralisation in transition economies from the mid-1990s.

Following the painful experience with dysfunctional states in most Third World countries, the two Bretton Woods institutions – the World Bank and the International Monetary Fund – decided to follow the so-called Washington Consensus (Williamson 1990). This agenda required the state to withdraw from the management of economic activities and to restrict itself to the role of a 'watchman' providing a stable macroeconomic framework so that free market might grow and ensure welfare and stability for the whole nation.

Originally elaborated for a small group of countries in Latin America, the Washington Consensus was recommended to, or imposed on, several developing countries and transition economies from the 1980s and particularly in the 1990s, with only minor modifications to the content. The agenda was not very expansive on the role of the public sector, yet it had four imperatives on the issue:

(i)   zero fiscal deficit,
(ii)   redirecting public expenditure priorities towards primary public services and infrastructure,
(iii) tax reform (broaden the tax base, keep marginal tax rates moderate), and
(iv)   privatisation of state property.

As one fundamental tenet of the Washington Consensus was to restrict the role of the public sector, the modernisation of intergovernmental fiscal relations could not be considered for discussion during the 1980s. The first studies of the World Bank mentioning a possible redefinition of the role of the state in transition economies appeared in the early 1990s (Gelb and Gray 1991; Rice 1991). However, these early studies considered the increasing pressure for decentralisation as a disturbance factor that would complicate the implementation of political and economic reforms.

From the late 1980s and even more in the early 1990s, it became clear that the macroeconomic policy precepts elaborated for Latin America are not entirely adaptable to CEE. Particularly from the late 1990s several studies appeared showing the limits of the Washington Consensus (see Stiglitz 1998a, 1998b; Burki and Perry 1998; Naim 2000; Kolodko 2000; Ahrens 2000, 2002). This sudden wave of criticism did not concern the decentralisation issues that the World Bank proposed to transition economies during the second half of the 1990s, as these were relatively new at that time and their impact could not yet be foreseen. The policy advice on intergovernmental fiscal relations has had to undergo another 'maturation process'. Yet a number of the heavily criticised elements were (at least indirectly) related to the precepts on public sector development and good governance:

1 *Focus on the size of government.* In its endeavour to restrict the role of the state to a minimum, the Washington Consensus generally ignored the need for government intervention in the presence of externalities, potential scale economies, incomplete markets and imperfect information, although these are problems that typically emerge in such dynamic processes as transition.
2 *Treating institutions as a black box.* The Washington Consensus tended to disregard the role of institutions in political and economic development. Institutional reform was basically acknowledged as far as it concerned the rule of law and the institutional framework of a market-friendly environment. However, it failed to recognise that both formal and informal institutions are integral parts of the economy inasmuch as they create incentives for the economic actors. These incentives do effectively influence the economic performance of a nation (Olson 1996; Ahrens 2002).
3 *'Ahistorical' approach.* The Washington Consensus has also been criticised for neglecting the unique historical, anthropological and cultural background of the recipients of policy advice (Kolodko 2000; Ahrens 2000). Countries that have experienced centralisation and dictatorship for several decades cannot engage in rapid liberalisation and deregulation. Attempts to initiate a 'big bang' reform ignore the sensitive issue of sequencing (Stiglitz 1998a: 14) and risk inducing unsustainable development. It must be noted here that the World Bank has been very prudent on the timing and sequencing of reforms since the very beginning of CEE transition (e.g. Gelb and Gray 1991), warning against hurried decentralisation rather than pressing for a 'big bang' approach.
4 *Neglecting alternative objectives and trade-offs.* The Washington Consensus ignored, particularly in its early years, the fact that the health of the economy depends not only on the performance of the markets but also on the quality of the natural environment, access to education and culture, participation of citizens in the policy-making process, and other non-economic factors. Related to this, Stiglitz (1998a) warned that policies designed to address one objective are likely to undermine the

realisation of another objective (e.g. inflation versus unemployment) and in such cases policy-makers must take a stance on priorities.
5 *Zero fiscal deficit.* As critics of the Washington Consensus point out, a certain level of current account deficit may be sustainable, depending on the cyclical behaviour of the economy, the growth perspectives, the means of financing the deficit, the uses of government spending, and other circumstances.

From the late 1990s, a so-called Post-Washington Consensus emerged on the basis of these insights (Stiglitz 1998a, 1998b; Ahrens 2000). Its adherents agreed that increases in living standards, as well as a sustainable, democratic and equitable development, must replace the narrow economic goals in development thinking. They also recognised that institutions matter for economic growth. Recently, however, the Post-Washington Consensus has also been subject to severe criticism for its intellectual narrowness and reductionism, as it tends to overemphasise market failures and generalise the theory of informational imperfections and asymmetries. Moreover, it presumes these imperfections to be pervasive across developing and transition economies.

The evolution of World Bank policy advice on fiscal decentralisation in Central and Eastern Europe

The policy precepts of the World Bank on fiscal decentralisation in CEE evolved against the background of the developments in public finance research, on the one hand, and the discussions around development economics, on the other. The impact of these two domains and the accumulation of field experience are reflected in the writings of senior specialists inside the World Bank (including the World Bank Institute) and independent consultants to Bank projects, from the early 1990s. Obviously, and as is usually clearly stated in the first footnote in several publications, the findings, interpretations and conclusions are entirely those of the authors and do not necessarily represent the view of the World Bank. Nevertheless, considering the great deal of similarities between these papers in terms of guiding principles, hypotheses and findings (external and internal specialists often working together on the same research project), it is perhaps not entirely erroneous to deduce the World Bank's decentralisation paradigm by analysing and synthesising the views of the internal and external experts who advise this institution.

The first wave of systematic reviews on the subject appeared around 1994 (Bird and Wallich 1992 as forerunners; Shah 1994; Wallich 1994; Bird *et al.* 1995). These publications emerged from a genuine interest in fiscal decentralisation in transition economies following the publication of the famous Dillinger report in 1994 (see Ebel and Serdar 2003). The new studies also emerged in response to the recognition that 'intergovernmental fiscal problems in transition economies are both *very different from those of market economies* and *very similar to each other*' (Bird *et al.* 1995: ix) and that they have not yet received sufficient attention. While focusing on the 'big' macroeconomic policy issues of stabilisation, liberalisation, deregulation, trade reform, privatisation and getting prices right, the early literature on transition failed to realise that a well-designed intergovernmental fiscal system is crucial to the achievement of economic reform goals.

Understandably, providing clear guidance on decentralisation was difficult in the early 1990s. First, as Bird and Wallich (1994: 124) recognised, intergovernmental fiscal reforms were taking place 'in context of overall changing and shrinking role of government and strained macroeconomic circumstances'. Stabilisation concerns were dominating the developing agenda of central governments in CEE, slowing down the second wave of reforms of intergovernmental fiscal relations. This was largely a result of earlier policy precepts of the Bretton Woods institutions that emphasised the importance of central government plans and a state-led strategy of economic transition. Second, there was little country-specific information and experience available about CEE, so that transposing the general (albeit very colourful) textbook theories of fiscal federalism was more or less the only possible working method for the World Bank and other donors.

As soon as transitional societies 'survived' the first and probably strongest wave of macroeconomic squeeze and central governments loosened their grip on public expenditures around the mid-1990s, the further development of intergovernmental fiscal institutions came back to the policy agenda in CEE. At the same time, knowledge about these institutions was being accumulated at the World Bank as a result of several bilateral programmes providing financial, technical and professional assistance to transition economies. Thanks to these circumstances, since its beginnings in the early 1990s the advisory work of the World Bank on fiscal decentralisation in CEE was marked by the consensus that a sound intergovernmental fiscal system will contribute to economic growth. As Johannes F. Linn puts it in his foreword to Shah's (1994: v) seminal paper:

> In its policy advice to developing countries, the World Bank has, in recent years, recognized the fundamental need to restructure the public sector to make it more responsive to efficient and equitable provision of public services and the needs of private sector development, thereby enhancing its contribution to economic growth.

Or, as Bird *et al.* (1995: xi) noted in the preface of their volume one year later:

> The research presented in this volume suggests that the design of a well-functioning intergovernmental system may often be the key to successfully achieving such major reform goals of the transition

economies as macroeconomic stability, privatization, and maintenance of a social safety net that is robust enough to make reform palatable to the population.

Both senior researchers inside the World Bank and independent consultants to Bank programmes have increasingly recognised that the impact of decentralisation on welfare is much broader than previously assumed. Rather than being simply a catalyst of economic growth, it affects virtually all aspects of development such as the efficiency and equity of service provision, the 'thickness' of the social safety net, the poverty alleviation programmes, the development of the financial sector and the risk of corruption. However, Litvack and Seddon (1999: v) admit that the totality of these implications is rarely considered:

> Unfortunately, the far-reaching implications of decentralization are often overlooked, as the literature and specialists tend to focus on specific dimensions. Top policymakers in decentralizing countries are often the only ones who address the full range of issues.

In effect, the evolution of the World Bank literature on Central and Eastern European fiscal decentralisation between 1992 and 2005 shows a rapid expansion of knowledge on the subject. It also shows that the orthodox fiscal federalism and its challengers, on the one hand, as well as the orthodox development economics and its challengers, on the other, exerted a more or less important influence on this 'maturation process'.

For most of the period from 1992 until today, the decentralisation agenda of the World Bank has been predominantly inspired by the insights of the Post-Washington Consensus and the so-called European fiscal federalism. The first and most important impact of these domains is the new emphasis on institutions in the discussion of decentralisation; a development factor that used to be largely neglected in the assistance for macroeconomic reforms in CEE through the 1980s.

As Bird (2000) notes, the reform of fiscal institutions is an accretionary process, and the identification of ways to cope with the problems of decentralisation may take several decades. This is particularly true for the informal institutions such as social norms, conventions, moral values or implicit contracts. Examples include the attitude of local governments towards the centre, which is still more of a dependency than a partnership relation, or the passivity of several municipalities (particularly smaller ones) in the management of the local budget. Another typical feature is the strong attachment to political autonomy and property rights. While this attitude is more or less understandable (local governments were deprived of these rights for decades), it is becoming a serious obstacle to interjurisdictional cooperation and market-based solutions of local public service delivery such as contracting and public-private partnerships. Further evidence of the importance of institutions is supplied by Melo (2002). He observes a greater 'inverse flypaper effect' in those countries where subnational governments are largely dependent on intergovernmental transfers. This means that, in case of a sudden drop in the volume of central government grants, local public spending normally does not fall as local authorities fill the gap with own-source revenues in order to continue to provide essential public services to the local population.

Second, beyond the recognition that intergovernmental fiscal institutions matter for economic development, the World Bank's decentralisation agenda is undergoing a continuous adaptation. In essence, this occurs along the four arguments explained in the first part of this chapter.

Variation in time

World Bank authors increasingly recognise that decentralisation is a dynamic process: as circumstances change over time, the design of inter-governmental fiscal institutions must change as well. This presupposes some kind of an error-correction mechanism built into the system that permits an adaptive development in response to changes in needs and capacities (Bird 2000: 27). As for the optimum assignment of expenditures and revenues, both early and later works acknowledge that these are likely to change over time with changes in financial and technological constraints, as well as changes in citizens' preferences (World Bank 1994: 84; McLure and Martinez-Vazquez 2000). Nevertheless, the early writings still tend to rely on the neo-classical theory of fiscal federalism. Proposing, for instance, the centralisation of progressive income taxes and wealth taxes, while excise taxes, sales taxes and income tax surcharges would ideally be assigned to the intermediate level and property taxes and user charges to the municipal level (Boadway *et al.* 1994). The first country reports (e.g. Bird and Wallich 1992) still believed in property tax as a primary instrument of financing local public services, in spite of its apparent deficiencies (it is a highly visible tax; it is difficult to administer in an inflationary context; and the tax base is inelastic). However, the validity of this argument has weakened in recent years, following the recognition that property taxes in practice seldom yield enough revenue to finance local expenditures (Bird 2000). This is all the more true as property assessment in transition economies is still done on the basis of area instead of market value, owing to a lack of adequate valuation techniques and reliable databases. On the other hand, surcharges on the national income tax, which used to be recommended for the regional level, are now increasingly advocated by several World Bank authors as a potential source of revenue for local governments. Croatia already makes use of this instrument, while in Latvia and Hungary its potential impact is currently being analysed (Dunn and Wetzel 2001; Bird 2000).

Another example of changing attitudes towards normative fiscal federalism concerns the 'optimal' share of own-source revenues in the subnational budgets.

In 1994, Bird and Wallich were seriously concerned about the high degree of transfer dependence and the consequent restrictions on the local autonomy and accountability of decentralised governments in transition economies (1994: 116). Even though they recognised that transfers will and must play a role in the future in view of the enhanced expenditure needs of subnational governments in terms of infrastructure development (Bird and Wallich 1992: 26 f.). The following years witnessed a slight departure from the normative proposition on reducing the share of transfers. For Bird (2000), there is no analytical rationale for the argument that accountability requires a given proportion of local expenditures to be financed from own sources. Transfers are always necessary and neither inherently good nor bad. What matters is their design and their effect on policy outcomes. Nevertheless, the debate on the role of intergovernmental transfers is far from being concluded: for Dunn and Wetzel (2001: 2), developing truly autonomous revenues (*a sine qua non* of local autonomy and accountability) remains a principal challenge in most transition economies.

Geographical diversity

Departure from the US model

One of the fundamental insights in this field is that, contrary to the US economy, mobility in CEE economies is far from perfect. The reasons include historical conflicts between urban and rural regions, strong local identities and the fact that housing markets are less developed (McLure and Martinez-Vazquez 2000). Similarly, the Public Choice theory of competing jurisdictions is less compelling in CEE where horizontal relations (whether competitive or cooperative) among subnational jurisdictions of the same level are not yet strong enough to spur growth and innovation in the overall economy. Provinces and municipalities have stronger ties to the centre than to each other, which is partly explained by the relatively high degree of their transfer dependence.

Developed versus transition economies

At the same time, World Bank authors also recognise that not only the US system of intergovernmental finance, but developed systems in general, show a great deal of divergence from those in CEE. As Boadway *et al.* (1994) point out, transition economies tend to be more centralised than industrialised countries and the scope of public sector activities is substantially different. While developed countries spend a much larger proportion of their budget on health, welfare and intergovernmental transfers than do developing and emerging economies, the latter spend a considerable share of their budget on general public services, transport and communications and, in some cases, on defence. This is presumably due to the divergence of expenditure needs and preferences between these two groups of countries. Similarly, revenue assignment tends to be more centralised in transition economies than in industrialised countries, with the central government controlling the major resources and several (if not all) parameters of subnational taxation. Another difference concerns the exposure of subnational governments to vertical fiscal imbalances (De Mello 2000). Since in transition economies decentralisation of service delivery proceeds more rapidly than revenue decentralisation, subnational tiers are dependent on intergovernmental transfers for a large part of their budget and thus fairly vulnerable to fluctuations in the revenue flow. As has been shown above, the judgment of this situation is changing over time.

Differences among transition economies

Even historically closely related countries like those of CEE demonstrate a great variety of intergovernmental fiscal relations depending on their geographic and demographic characteristics, historical, political and institutional context, as well as their progress in decentralisation. As the process of intergovernmental fiscal reform is generally long and complex, the pace of decentralisation in the various fields of intergovernmental finance varies from one country to another. Consequently, at any point in time during the decentralisation process, each building block of intergovernmental fiscal relations presents a multitude of national variations (Dunn and Wetzel 2001: 2; Bird and Smart 2001: 8 ff.). Moreover, it is not possible to start from a *tabula rasa*: every country has its own history, and the actual state of intergovernmental fiscal institutions reflects to a large extent the results of previous policy changes. 'Learning from each other' is possible and even desirable, but in the end each country is likely to follow its own path (Bird 2000). Tables 13.1 and 13.2 illustrate the lack of uniform solutions through the examples of expenditure and revenue decentralisation.

Concerning the assignment of expenditures, the World Bank was remarkably quick in recognising that there is no single best way for deciding which government tier should be responsible for the provision of a particular public service. Rather, the adequacy of any assignment must be judged in terms of how well it achieves the objectives set up by the central government in its decentralization strategy (World Bank 1994: 83; McLure and Martinez-Vazquez 2000). This recognition marks a fundamental departure not only from the neo-classical theory of fiscal federalism but from all sorts of normative standards. Shah adds that different observers and societies may have different views about the ideal balance between centralisation and decentralisation in one expenditure type, and the ways the trade-offs can be overcome (Shah 2000: 7).

In line with these recognitions, the first 'general' precepts for CEE have been continuously replaced by tailor-made recommendations. However, as certain aspects of intergovernmental finance appear to be quite similar

Table 13.1 Expenditure assignments for a sample of CEE countries

Public service	Albania	Bulgaria	Estonia	Hungary*	Latvia	Lithuania	Poland
Police	N	N, I, L	N	L	L, N	N, L	N
Social housing		I	L	*L*	L	L	N
Water and sewerage	N, L	N, I	L	L	L	L	
Waste collection		I, L	L	L	I, L	L	L
Primary and preschool	N	I, L	L	L	L	L	L
Secondary education	N	I	L	L	L	I, L	N
Universities	N	N	N		N	N	
Public health	N		N, L	L	L		
Hospitals		N, I	N, L		N, I	L	
Interurban highways	N	N	N		N	N	
Urban highways	L	N, I, L	L	L	L	I, L	
Electric power supply	N	N	N		N, L	N	
Oil and gas pipelines	N		N		N	N	
Ports and waterways	N					N	
Airports	N	N	N			N	
Railroads	N	N				N	
Urban transportation		I	L		N, I, L	L	
Heating		I	L	L	L	N, L	
Fire protection		N	N	L	N	L	

Source: Dunn and Wetzel 2001.
Notes:
N = national, I = intermediate, L = local level.
* Government levels in italics indicate an optional responsibility.

Table 13.2 Revenue decentralisation in a sample of CEE countries

Revenue parameters	Albania	Czech Republic	Hungary	Poland	Moldova	Serbia
Rate and base setting for local revenues.	Rate only	No	Some	No	No	Rate only
Majority of transfers are formula-based and unconditional.	Yes	Yes	No	Yes	No	Yes
Revenues more or less match responsibility.	No?	No?	No?	Yes	No?	No
Own revenues finance majority of expenditures.	No	No	No	Yes	No	No

Source: Shah and Thompson 2004.

across most CEE countries, World Bank consultants on intergovernmental fiscal reform can still rely on some 'universal principles' (Bird 2000: 1).

Conflicting economic objectives

As has been indicated above, the (US-based) mobility argument does not hold in CEE. Thus, the decision of which government tier should be responsible for which state function (stabilisation, distribution and allocation) must not necessarily be decided upon this basis. Under these circumstances, there is a relatively large potential for an (at least partial) decentralisation of the redistribution and stabilisation functions. As for income redistribution, there are potential efficiency gains attached to the devolution of the social service function to the lower levels of government, unless this is being done with the intention of a downward shifting of public deficit. Macroeconomic stabilisation via vertical cooperation, on the other hand, is not only feasible but also desirable, as the central government may achieve greater commitment at the lower levels if the hard budget constraint emerges as the result of negotiations.

Moreover, the scope of expenditure autonomy of democratically elected subnational governments in transition economies is unprecedented, so that the participation of these units in the redistribution and stabilisation function is almost self-evident. In several countries, including Bulgaria, Hungary, Latvia, Lithuania, Estonia and Ukraine, part of the responsibility for social services is delegated to the local level. In terms of macroeconomic management, the prospective integration of several transition economies into the Economic and Monetary Union requires the cooperation of all government tiers in reducing public deficit and debt levels. Although multinational donors in the early 1990s warned against the excessive indebtedness of subnational governments in these countries as a consequence of unrestricted borrowing, this fear has not been realised so far (though partly due to the relatively underdeveloped state of financial markets).

Beyond macroeconomic balance (stabilisation), interpersonal equity (distribution) and economic efficiency (allocation), there may be several other economic objectives on the agenda of the central government, such as economic growth or the reduction of interregional disparities. Policy-makers must be able to handle the conflicts that arise between these objectives, as well as the differences between local and national perceptions of the weights to be attached to them (Bird 2000: 1).

Broadening objectives and recognition of trade-offs

Applied research on public policies in CEE has revealed that economic goals alone cannot guide the process of decentralisation. Additional objectives such as national integrity, political stability, local autonomy, improved accountability of local politicians towards their voters, minority protection or enhanced citizen participation, must be taken into account in the reform of intergovernmental fiscal relations. When, for example, the performance of the decentralised public sector is to be evaluated, efficiency is no longer the sole criterion. Even though some institutional arrangements are obviously more reasonable from an economic point of view than others, this does not mean that policy-makers give systematic preference to the 'more reasonable' option. This is best illustrated by the ongoing discussion about the future of small village schools in Hungary. Although local councils could make substantial economies in primary education and simultaneously improve the service quality by creating special-purpose districts, they insist on maintaining their own schools for reasons of equity (equal access to education) and economic growth (education as a factor of regional development), and because they consider the local school as being 'the essence of local autonomy' (Balázs and Hermann 2002: 73).

Bringing local user charges to cost recovery level is another recommendation of the World Bank. However, this is difficult to realise in the short term. Here, efficiency and accountability considerations are in opposition to the arguments of equity and political stability, as the introduction of appropriate user charges would substantially increase the cost of living and induce unpopular shifts in income distribution (Bird and Wallich 1994: 114).

In various government strategy papers and academic studies of public sector reform in Central and Eastern Europe, Horváth (2000) and Davey (2002) identified the main objectives (motives) of decentralisation in practice. A classification follows in Table 13.3.

During the past ten years, World Bank consultants had to experience on several occasions that some of their recommendations remained largely unused by Central and Eastern European partner countries. In spite of repeated suggestions to increase local revenue autonomy, reconsider the assignment of expenditure responsibilities among government levels, or consolidate the fragmented territorial structure of local governments, progress in these and several other fields has been remarkably slow in transition economies.

In some cases, conflicting objectives hinder the implementation of external policy recommendations, so that the actual *status quo* cannot realistically be expected to change in the foreseeable future. This is the case with local user charges which are still below cost recovery level, but where an increase would imply a serious trade-off between efficiency and equity. In other cases, the capacity of the government is smaller than what would be necessary for implementing the proposals of external donors, or certain conditions must be met beforehand. Property tax is an example: in order to become a solid revenue source, it should be based on the market value; this, however, necessitates the regular updating of cadastral maps and substantial improvement in the assessment techniques. The introduction of local surcharges on the national income tax is another example, since such a reform is not feasible unless central government tax rates are proportionally reduced.

Table 13.3 Fiscal decentralisation in CEE: a matrix of objectives

Economic objectives	*Political objectives*
• Economic efficiency of public service provision • Administrative rationality • Improved public management techniques • Accountability of local decision-makers • Encouragement of private ownership in the public sector • Compliance with eligibility criteria for the European Funds • Interpersonal and interregional equity	• Democratisation • Pluralism • Local autonomy • Citizens' participation • Protection of minorities • Accountability of local decision-makers • Transparency of the public sector operations • Fight against corruption • Interpersonal and interregional equity
Constitutional objectives	*Social and cultural objectives*
• Recognition of individual and collective rights • Right to self-government (local autonomy) • Horizontal and vertical separation of powers • Universal right to a minimum standard in public services • Impartial application of national laws to the circumstances of individual citizens • Protection of minorities	• Preservation of historical and ethnic identities • Protection of minorities • Developing new rules for modern administrative ethics

Source: author's summary based on Horváth (2000) and Davey (2002).

Such implementation difficulties suggest that policy recommendations that do not find any adherents for several years are not necessarily doomed to failure. What does not work today may work well tomorrow, once the circumstances have become more favourable. Instead, the challenge for policy advisors is to find the optimal sequencing of reforms for each decentralised government system. The emerging literature at the World Bank on the *process* of decentralisation and the issue of the right sequencing (e.g. Guess *et al.* 1997; Bahl and Martinez-Vazquez 2005) suggests that research is likely to continue in this direction.

Conclusion

The aim of this chapter was to examine how the decentralisation agenda of the World Bank in Central and Eastern Europe evolved during the past decade and what intellectual forces were shaping it. Our survey of the Bank's documents and reports on intergovernmental fiscal relations in transition economies from 1992 until today suggests that, beside the normative framework of fiscal federalism, essentially two waves of theoretical discussions constitute the basis of the decentralisation precepts. The first one is related to the crisis of the Washington Consensus in the late 1990s and the resulting Post-Washington Consensus which contributed to a wider recognition of the importance of institutions (including intergovernmental finance) for economic development. The second intellectual foundation is the so-called 'European fiscal federalism'. The adherents of this school have successfully identified the various divergences between US-type fiscal federalism and its European counterpart, thus contributing to a better understanding of how decentralised fiscal systems work in real world practice and how differences can be used for the purpose of 'learning from each other'.

Under the influence of these intellectual sources, policy experts at the World Bank increasingly realised that intergovernmental fiscal regimes tend to change over time with changes in preferences, costs or technical constraints. They have also widely different national characteristics depending on the historical, political and socio-economic background of the countries under review. Hence policy advice is ideally tailored to the specific context of each country and demonstrates a great deal of flexibility to adapt the institutional setting to the changing circumstances. Moreover, World Bank authors have recognised that economic objectives like efficiency, stability, equity and growth are a potential source of conflicts, and the resolution of these conflicts in a decentralised system is fairly difficult as each government level seeks to impose its own interpretation of the objectives on the others. Finally, economic objectives alone cannot guide the design of intergovernmental fiscal institutions: the constitutional, political, social or cultural motives of decentralisation may be equally important in a society.

Such a radical departure from the neo-classical normative context of fiscal federalism may reduce but not eliminate the risk of failure for external donor organisations and consultants. In spite of their increased effort to provide tailor-made solutions to country-specific problems, the World Bank and its partners in development are seeing some of their proposed solutions end up in the drawer of government bureaus, as the time for implementation has not yet come. This reminds us that the right sequencing of policy reforms is key to successful decentralisation, and is thus likely to become the major issue on the World Bank's agenda in the near future.

References

Ahrens, J. (2000) 'Toward a Post-Washington Consensus: The Importance of Governance Structures in Less Developed Countries and Economies in Transition', *Journal of Institutional Innovation, Development and Transition* 4.

——(2002) *Governance and Economic Development: A Comparative Institutional Approach*, Northampton MA and Cheltenham: Edward Elgar.

Bahl, R. and Martinez-Vazquez, J. (2005) 'Sequencing Fiscal Decentralization', background paper prepared for the PREM Week Seminar, Washington, April 2005.

Balázs, É. and Hermann, Z. (2002) 'Education Management and Finance in Hungary: Efficiency, Equity and Quality Problems in the Transition Period', in Davey, K. (ed.) *Balancing National and Local Responsibilities: Education Management and Finance in Four Central European Countries*, Budapest: OSI/LGI.

Bird, R. M. (2000) *Intergovernmental Fiscal Relations: Universal Principles, Local Applications*, Georgia State University, Andrew Young School of Policy Studies, International Studies Program, Working Paper #00–2.

Bird, R. M., Dafflon, B., Jeanrenaud, C. and Kirchgässner, G. (2003) 'Assignment of Responsibilities and Fiscal Federalism', in Blindenbacher, R. and Koller, A. (eds) *Federalism in a Changing World: Learning from Each Other – Scientific Background, Proceedings and Plenary Speeches of the International Conference on Federalism, St Gallen, 27–30 August 2002*, Montreal: McGill-Queen's University Press.

Bird, R. M., Ebel, R. D. and Wallich, Ch. I. (eds) (1995) *Decentralization of the Socialist State: Intergovernmental Finance in Transition Economies*, Washington DC: World Bank.

Bird, R. M. and Smart, N. (2001) 'Intergovernmental Fiscal Transfers: Some Lessons from International Experience', paper prepared for the International Tax Program, Rotman School of Management, University of Toronto, January 2001, revised March 2001.

Bird, R. M. and Wallich, Ch. (1992) *Financing Local Government in Hungary*, Policy Research Working Paper no. 0869, Washington DC: World Bank.

——(1994) 'Local Government Finance in Transition Economies: Policy and Institutional Issues', in Schiavo-Campo, S. (ed.) *Institutional Change and the Public Sector in Transitional Economies*, Discussion Paper no. 241, Washington DC: World Bank.

Blindenbacher, R. and Watts, R. L. (2003) 'Federalism in a Changing World – A Conceptual Framework for the Conference', in Blindenbacher, R. and Koller, A. (eds) *Federalism in a Changing World: Learning from Each Other – Scientific Background, Proceedings and Plenary Speeches of the International Conference on Federalism, St Gallen, 27–30 August 2002*, Montreal: McGill-Queen's University Press.

Boadway, R., Roberts, S. and Shah, A. (1994) *The Reform of Fiscal Systems in Developing and Emerging Market Economies: A Federalism Perspective*, Policy Research Working Paper no. 1259, Washington DC: World Bank.

Brennan, G. and Buchanan, J. M. (1980) *The Power to Tax: Analytical Foundations of aFiscal Constitution*, Cambridge: Cambridge University Press.

Breton, A. and Scott, A. (1978) *The Economic Constitution of Federal States*, Toronto: University of Toronto Press.

Burki, Sh. J. and Perry, G. E. (1998) 'Beyond the Washington Consensus: Institutions Matter', mimeo, Washington DC: World Bank.

Dafflon, B. (1977) *Federal Finance in Theory and Practice – with Reference to Switzerland*, Schriftenreihe Finanzwirtschaft und Finanzrecht, Band 21, Berne/Stuttgart: Paul Haupt Verlag.

——(1978) 'Constitutional Implications of Federal Economic Policy: Who Should Decide What in a Federal System?', in Caroni, P., Dafflon, B. and Enderle, G.

(eds) *Nur Ökonomie ist keine Ökonomie: Festgabe zum 70. Geburtstag von B. M. Biucchi*, Berne/Stuttgart: Paul Haupt Verlag.

Davey, K. (2002) 'Decentralization in CEE Countries: Obstacles and Opportunities', in Péteri, G. (ed.) *Mastering Decentralization and Public Administration Reforms in Central and Eastern Europe*, Budapest: OSI/LGI.

De Mello, L. R. (2000) 'Fiscal Decentralization and Intergovernmental Fiscal Relations: A Cross-country Analysis', *World Development* 28(2), 365–80.

Dunn, J. and Wetzel, D. (2001) 'Fiscal Decentralization in Former Socialist Economies: Progress and Prospects', mimeo, Washington DC: World Bank.

Ebel, R. and Serdar, Y. (2003) 'Fiscal Decentralization in Developing Countries: Is It Happening? How Do We Know?', in *Public Finance in Developing and Transition Countries: Essays in Honor of Richard M. Bird*, eds James Alm and Jorge Martinez-Vazquez, Cheltenham: Edward Elgar.

Fine, B., Lapavitsas, C. and Pincus, J. (eds) (2001) *Development Policy in the Twenty-first Century: Beyond the Post-Washington Consensus*, London: Routledge.

Frey, B. S. and Eichenberger, R. (1999) *The New Democratic Federalism for Europe: Functional, Overlapping and Competing Jurisdictions*, Northampton MA and Cheltenham: Edward Elgar.

Gelb, A. H. and Gray, Ch. W. (1991) *The Transformation of Economies in Central and Eastern Europe: Issues, Progress and Prospects*, Policy and Research series no. 17, Washington DC: World Bank.

Guess, G., Loehr, W. and Martinez-Vazquez, J. (1997) 'Fiscal Decentralization: A Methodology of Case Studies', mimeo, Bethesda MD: Development Alternatives Inc.

Horváth, M. T. (2000) 'Directions and Differences of Local Changes', in Horváth, M. T. (ed.) *Decentralization: Experiments and Reforms*, Budapest: OSI/LGI.

King, D. (1984) *Fiscal Tiers: The Economics of Multi-Level Government*, London: George Allen and Unwin.

Kolodko, G. W. (2000) 'Towards a New (Washington) Consensus', *Journal of Institutional Innovation, Development and Transition* 4.

Litvack, J. and Seddon, J. (eds) (1999) *Decentralization Briefing Notes*, WBI Working Paper no. 19683, Washington DC: World Bank.

McLure, Ch. and Martinez-Vazquez, J. (2000) 'The Assignment of Revenues and Expenditures in Intergovernmental Fiscal Relations', mimeo, Washington DC: World Bank.

Melo, L. (2002) 'The Flypaper Effect Under Different Institutional Contexts: The Colombian Case', *Public Choice* 111 (3–4), 317–45.

Musgrave, R. A. (1959) *The Theory of Public Finance*, New York: McGraw-Hill.

Musgrave, R. A. and Musgrave, P. B. (1973) *Public Finance in Theory and Practice*, New York: McGraw-Hill.

Naim, M. (2000) 'Fads and Fashions in Economic Reforms: Washington Consensus or Washington Confusion?', *Third World Quarterly* 21(3), 505–28.

Niskanen, W. A. (1971) *Bureaucracy and Representative Government*, Chicago: Aldine/Atherton.

Oates, W. E. (1972) *Fiscal Federalism*, New York: Harcourt Brace Jovanovich.

——(1990) 'Decentralization of the Public Sector: An Overview', in Bennett, R. J. (ed.) *Decentralization, Local Governments and Markets: Towards a Post-Welfare Agenda*, Oxford: Clarendon Press.

——(1999) 'An Essay on Fiscal Federalism', *Journal of Economic Literature* 37(9), 1120–49.

——(2005) 'Toward a Second-generation Theory of Fiscal Federalism', *International Tax and Public Finance* 12(4), 349–73.

Olson, M. (1996) 'Big Bills Left on the Sidewalk: Why Some Nations are Rich, and Others Poor', *Journal of Economic Perspectives* 10(2), 3–24.

Peacock, A. T. (1972) 'Fiscal Means and Political Ends', in Peston, M. and Corry, B. (eds) *Essays in Honour of Lionel Robbins*, London: Weidenfeld and Nicolson.

Rice, E. (1991) *Managing the Transition: Enhancing the Efficiency of Eastern European Governments*, Policy Research Working Paper no. 0757, Washington DC: World Bank.

Scott, A. (1964) 'The Economic Goals of Federal Finance', *Public Finance* 19(3), 241–88.

Shah, A. (1994) *The Reform of Intergovernmental Fiscal Relations in Developing and Emerging Market Economies*, Policy and Research Series no. 23, Washington DC: World Bank.

——(2000) *Governing for Results in aGlobalized and Localized World*, paper presented at the International Conference on Federalism, Mexico, March 2000.

Shah, A. and Thompson, T. (2004) *Implementing Decentralized Local Governance: A Treacherous Road with Potholes, Detours and Road Closures*, Policy Research Working Paper no. 3353, Washington DC: World Bank.

Stiglitz, J. (1998a) *More Instruments and Broader Goals: Moving Toward the Post-Washington Consensus*, the 1998 WIDER Annual Lecture, Helsinki, January 1998.

——(1998b) 'Redefining the Role of the State: What Should It Do? How Should It Do It? And How Should These Decisions Be Made?', paper presented on the 10th anniversary of the MITI Research Institute, Tokyo, March 1998.

Ter-Minassian, T. (ed.) (1997) *Fiscal Federalism in Theory and Practice*, Washington DC: International Monetary Fund.

Tiebout, Ch. (1956) 'A Pure Theory of Local Expenditures', *Journal of Political Economy* 64(10), 416–24.

Wallich, Ch. I. (ed.) (1994) *Russia and the Challenge of Fiscal Federalism*, Washington DC: World Bank.

Watts, R. L. (2001) 'The Dynamics of Decentralization', in Bird, R. M. and Stauffer, T. (eds) *Intergovernmental Fiscal Relations in Fragmented Societies*, Fribourg: Institute of Federalism, Basel/Geneva/Munich: Helbing and Lichtenhahn.

Williamson, J. (1990) 'What Washington Means by Policy Reform', in Williamson, J. (ed.) *Latin American Adjustment: How Much Has Happened?*, Washington DC: Institute for International Economics.

Wiseman, J. (1987) 'The Political Economy of Federalism: A Critical Appraisal', paper prepared for the Canadian Royal Commission on Taxation in 1965, *Environment and Planning C: Government and Policy* 5(4), 383–410.

World Bank (1993) 'Lebanon Stabilisation and Reconstruction', by Laurens Hoppenbrouwer, Willem van Eeghan and Yuzuri Ozeki (MENA Dept. II), Report no. 11406 – LE, March 1993, unpublished.

World Bank (1994) *Bulgaria: Public Finance Reforms in the Transition*, Report no. 12273-BUL, Washington DC: World Bank.

Index

Note: page numbers in italics refer to a table

Lightning Source UK Ltd.
Milton Keynes UK
UKOW04f1428020914

237925UK00004B/78/P